APPLIED FINANCIAL ECONOMETRICS
IN E-COMMERCE

CONTRIBUTIONS TO ECONOMIC ANALYSIS

258

Honorary Editors:
D.W. JORGENSON
J. TINBERGEN†

Editors:
R. BLUNDELL
J.-J. LAFFONT
T. PERSSON

ELSEVIER
Amsterdam – Boston – Heidelberg – London – New York – Oxford
Paris – San Diego – San Francisco – Singapore – Sydney – Tokyo

APPLIED FINANCIAL ECONOMETRICS IN E-COMMERCE

Sardar M.N. Islam
Centre for Strategic Economic Studies
Victoria University
Melbourne, Australia

and

K.B. Oh
Graduate School of Management
La Trobe University
Victoria, Australia

2003

ELSEVIER
Amsterdam – Boston – Heidelberg – London – New York – Oxford
Paris – San Diego – San Francisco – Singapore – Sydney – Tokyo

ELSEVIER SCIENCE B.V.
Sara Burgerhartstraat 25
P.O. Box 211, 1000 AE Amsterdam, The Netherlands

First edition 2003

British Library Cataloguing in Publication Data
Islam, Sardar M.N., 1950-
  Applied financial econometrics in e-commerce. -
  Contributions to economic analysis ; 258
  1.Finance - Econometric models 2.Electronic commerce -
  Econometric models
  I.Title II.Oh, K. B.
  332'.015195
  ISBN 0444513086

Library of Congress Cataloging in Publication Data
A catalog record from the Library of Congress has been applied for.

ISBN: 0-444-51308-6
ISSN: 0573-8555 (Series)

⊗ The paper used in this publication meets the requirements of ANSI/NISO Z39.48-1992 (Permanence of Paper).
Printed in Hungary.

INTRODUCTION TO THE SERIES

This series consists of a number of hitherto unpublished studies, which are introduced by the editors in the belief that they represent fresh contributions to economic science.

The term 'economic analysis' as used in the title of the series has been adopted because it covers both the activities of the theoretical economist and the research worker.

Although the analytical methods used by the various contributors are not the same, the are nevertheless conditioned by the common origin of their studies, namely theoretical problems encountered in practical research. Since for this reason, business cycle research and national accounting, research work on behalf of economic policy, and problems of planning are the main sources of the subjects dealt with, they necessarily determine the manner of approach adopted by the authors. Their methods tend to be 'practical' in the sense of not being too far remote from application to actual economic conditions. In addition they are quantitative.

It is the hope of the editors that the publication of these studies will help to stimulate the exchange of scientific information and to reinforce international cooperation in the field of economics.

The Editors

FOREWORD

The dramatic growth in electronic communication and commerce in the last decade has seen the death of the telegram and associated telegraphic transactions and has opened an incredible range of financial activities, products and markets. Traditional theory and analysis is obviously inadequate for the analysis of these developments and traditional economic theory needs to be extended to cover them.

This book is designed to investigate contemporary financial and economic issues in this emerging market. New models are developed, quantitative methods are revisited and new economic issues are discussed. The authors have considerable experience in research in applied analysis and in financial econometrics and are well suited to exploring the new avenues opened up by these recent developments in the finance industry.

There are few books currently available which address these issues. This monograph fills that gap. The theoretical issues are nicely balanced by the application of the author's own AEMM model, which provides a methodology to value e-commerce stock and to incorporate appropriate valuation factors and risk. Thus, this book will appeal to researchers and practitioner alike. I commend this valuable contribution to the literature.

G C O'Brien
Dean
Faculty of Law and Management
La Trobe University
Bundoora Victoria
Australia

PREFACE

Electronic commerce or e-commerce is a new phenomenon in the financial markets. The rapid advances made in the information and communications technology sector have facilitated the advent of e-commerce and has resulted in global market euphoria over technology stocks in financial markets. This book is based on the premise that an initial characterisation of the e-commerce sector is necessary as a precursor to a more profound understanding of the market mechanism and asset pricing process. The development of e-commerce as a consumer market is reviewed in this book. The issues and factors contributing to this development are identified, analysed and the implications for equity valuation of e-commerce related stocks are discussed and explained. Various economic variables that influenced Australian e-commerce stock returns from July 1999 to June 2000 are examined. A critical review of existing theories of stock valuation and their empirical relevance to e-commerce is presented.

Investors use valuation models in determining and evaluating stock values. Due to the limitations of existing valuation models, this book develops a new approach for the valuation of e-commerce stocks. This approach consists of firstly, identifying the pervasive economic factors, both local and international, that influence the Australian financial market; and secondly, conducting tests on the statistical significance of these factors on e-commerce stock valuation. The factor identification process in this study seeks to ensure that equity investments in the e-commerce sector will maximise financial return when these variables are included in the risk analysis. This book adopts an important and recent approach to econometric specification, estimation and testing in relation to e-commerce stock valuation. Econometric analyses including stationarity tests, cointegration modelling, volatility and predictability analyses and efficient market hypothesis checks are performed. Empirical tests are conducted using existent asset pricing models on the e-commerce data, within the context of behavioural study. Three types of risk are analysed in the volatility study as measured by beta – company risk, sector risk and portfolio risk. Portfolio selection analyses are performed on the e-commerce stocks and other assets to highlight their risk-return characteristics in a portfolio context. This allows conclusions to be drawn concerning the investment strategy adopted by portfolio managers in relation to e-commerce stocks. The results show that the AEMM model developed in this book is applicable to other financial markets for determining the factors for valuation and analysis of e-commerce stocks. Using the model, forecasts can be made with the appropriate variable values. Public policy implications of the empirical findings are stated.

As there is relatively less research done on the role of financial intermediation at the macroeconomic level in the knowledge economy, this book makes contribution to the literature in this area by providing a systematic integration and investigation of the financial issues in the emerging knowledge economy through an empirical investigation of the e-commerce sector.

x

This book provides an example of rigorous research studies in finance and it can be used as a reference book by researchers, academics, practitioners, policy makers, and postgraduate students in the areas of finance, financial econometrics, financial economics, monetary economics, and development economics. It can be used as a reference or as an additional text for a finance subject at the Masters or Doctoral level.

The material in this book is based on the doctoral thesis submitted by K. B. Oh to the Victoria Graduate School of Business, Victoria University, Melbourne, for the Doctor of Business Administration degree. This book is the result of cooperation between the authors, in particular to S. M. N. Islam for his invaluable input in Chapter 7, and the order of the names has nothing more than alphabetic significance. The authors thank S. Bose, M. Kumnick, M. Clarke and S. Guo for providing research and editorial assistance in preparing this book. This book has benefited from the generosity of R. Harbridge, P. Sheehan and N. Billington for making the necessary resources available and sharing their knowledge, experience and encouragement in bringing it to completion. We also convey our gratitude to L. Muscolino, P. Riebeek and J. Happee at Elsevier Science/North Holland for their patience and support in making this book a reality.

Sardar M. N. Islam
Centre for Strategic Economic Studies
Victoria University
Melbourne, Australia

K. B. Oh
Graduate School of Management
La Trobe University
Melbourne, Australia

October 2002

CONTENTS

List of Tables

List of Figures

List of Appendices

xx

CHAPTER 1

Introduction

1.1 Background

The valuation of financial assets and pricing has been an important area in the study of economics and management. Although valuation of common stocks is a relatively developed area, the empirical characterisation and valuation of e-commerce stocks is a fairly new area of scientific research. The levels of information and the information processing mechanisms available to the average investor on the e-commerce sector are lagging compared to more traditional sectors in the market. *Literature on the characteristics of the Australian e-commerce sector in terms of statistical evidence is not widely researched and a valuation model for e-commerce stocks has yet to be developed for Australia.* The interest in the financial aspects of e-commerce, whose pervasive role spans across all sectors in the economy, is in order to understand the workings of financial markets pertaining to the e-commerce sector and recent research work conducted in this area include Oh (2001), Oh and Islam (2001), Bontis and Mills (2000), Demer and Lev (2000), Hand (1999) and Amir and Lev (1996). The objectives of this book are: firstly to develop a new theoretical framework for explaining characteristics of e-commerce stocks, from the point of view of returns, and determinants of valuation for e-commerce stocks; and secondly to test this model by using e-commerce financial data for Australia. *The contribution of this book is an empirical characterisation of the Australian e-commerce sector and the development of an improved financial econometric modelling approach for the financial market issues of the e-commerce sector.* This is posssibly the first comprehensive book that conducts an empirical analysis of the e-commerce sector using econometric modelling and provides an insight into some of the important issues in the e-commerce financial market such as market efficiency, valuation, volatility, predictability, optimal portfolio choice and policy development.

1.1.1 Emergence of the New Economy

The commercialisation of the Internet since the mid-1990s caused firms to undergo a fundamental change more profound than any since the Industrial Revolution. As in the United States, Australia has registered remarkable economic performance in recent years experiencing an above average rise in trend growth (GDP per capita) (OECD 2000). Such economic performance is indicated by strong non-inflationary growth, high stock-market valuations, low unemployment and a rapidly changing economy in which information and communications technology (ICT) plays an increasingly important role in restructuring economic activities. The pervasive role of ICT applications spans across a wide range of sectors in the economy and is anticipated to herald the era of the New Economy[1] that entails higher non-inflationary growth. In many industries, the pervasiveness of this change is just starting to become clear and firms are only beginning to exploit the opportunities and address the threats. The present world, a virtual world, is one where information plays an important role in both our lifestyle and, by implication, in commerce as a complement of that lifestyle. The Worldwide Web (WWW) is inextricably entangled in the webs of law, custom and commerce – the tissues of our daily life (Cohen, Delong and Zysman 2000). It is very different from the physical world we have come to know in the past. The virtual world is one where knowledge reigns supreme and this knowledge, as a virtual good, is capable of being traded.

E-commerce, an application of the Internet, has grown exponentially over the past five years and is generally expected to continue this trend in the medium-term (Coppel 2000). The Internet is increasingly used to cater for the sales, production and distribution activities of firms and is becoming the preferred medium for gathering and distributing information. Estimates for electronic transactions anticipate a minimum five-fold growth over the next three to four years, as shown in the Table 1.1.

Table 1.1 Consultant Estimates of Worldwide E-Commerce ($ billion)

Consultants	1999	2003	Average Annual Growth %
e-Marketer	98.4	1,244	89
IDC	111.4	1,317	85
ActivMedia	95	1,324	93
Forrester Low*	70	1,800	125
Forrester High*	170	3,200	108
Boston Consulting Group	1000	4,600	46

*includes Internet-based EDI.
Source: Coppel (2000).

The recent global market euphoria and volatility of technology stocks in the US and to a lesser extent in the Asia-Pacific Region, including Australia, has raised questions regarding the underlying value of market capitalisations that appear to defy all conventional financial evaluations and economic fundamentals (Greenspan 2000). The present market scenario for e-commerce stock valuation is unclear and at best is an inconsistent measurement of e-commerce equity investment (Bontis and Mills 2000).

The Australian e-commerce industry structure generally consists of three major groups of e-commerce firms:[2]

---

[1] The "New Economy" refers to a world in which people work with their brains and the primary resource of the firm is intellectual property. In the new economy, communications technology provides the platform for competition and innovation is more important than mass production.
[2] 'Surfing for Fundamentals in the Internet Sector', *Shares*, September 1999.

(i)   the incumbents: firms that possess the necessary skills and expertise for organic growth;

(ii)   the migrators: firms with few embryonic net businesses that they hope to consolidate and expand into new areas; and

(iii)   the acquirors: usually ex-mining firms investing in e-commerce businesses either through direct investment or reverse takeover.

1.1.2 Relationship Between Financial Markets and Real Economic Activity

The movements in the Australian stock prices since World War II were closely connected to the rate of economic growth and economists had no trouble in explaining the resulting stock returns by standard valuation models where stock prices are determined by market fundamentals. But the recent growth and volatility of the technology stock prices are more troublesome and the question has been asked whether these stock prices can still be explained by fundamentals, or whether speculative bubbles and fads govern these prices. Studies conducted on speculative bubbles have proven unsuccessful in testing directly for them (Ahmed, Ehsan, Koppl, Rosser and White 1997; Hamilton and Whiteman 1985).

An argument for the current valuation of technology-related stocks is that information technology, which provides the impetus for the current market boom on a global scale, is a fundamental factor transforming the economy (De Long 1996). The high growth rates observed in the US (and Australia) are the beginning of this transformation and profit growth is expected to continue. The stock market reflects this future growth of the economy because investors, optimistic about the new economy, factor this into their investment decisions. Economic growth in the post-industrial era is expected to occur at a faster rate and earnings growth would also be faster than before and this fundamentally justifies the current stock prices. It follows that the value of e-commerce stocks is currently based on the potential outcomes and economic impacts of e-commerce – the forces underlying its development. Therefore, the market efficiency pertaining to e-commerce stocks is crucial from both the corporate finance and public policy perspectives as it impacts on the continued growth of the Australian economy. In finance, the word efficiency is taken to mean that a capital market is said to be (informationally) efficient if it uses all of the available information in setting the prices of assets (Fama 1970; Ross 1980). The basic intuition of efficient markets is that investors process the information that is available to them and would then take investment positions in the market in response to their information as well as in relation to their personal situations. This would eliminate concerns the investor may have about the pricing mechanism and enable a full appreciation of the financial conditions of the capital markets to take positions in assets. The implication of the efficient market hypothesis (EMH) in corporate finance is that if the market is efficient then firms can embark on e-commerce investments without doubts over the financial conditions (the same applies to individual stock investors).

From a public policy perspective and considering the economic impetus from developments in e-commerce or the ICT sector generally, an inefficient market would arguably require some form of government intervention. The degree of government intervention will depend on the level of market efficiency vis-à-vis the behaviour of the e-commerce firms/investors and equity market. Chief financial officers (CFO) surveyed (EIU 2000) doubt the effectiveness of traditional metrics to evaluate key elements of operating in the new e-commerce economy. The CFOs' concerns include the accuracy of forecasting e-commerce operating parameters (approximately 45% of respondents) and the inability to forecast future activity based on historical performance. There is a need to review the traditional valuation models and offer alternative approaches to value e-commerce investments incorporating new e-commerce parameters or factors.

1.2 E-Commerce and Finance

This research will benefit investors by providing knowledge and expertise to make better informed, more rational and universal investment decisions. The new economy poses a major challenge to the CFO of a firm in terms of making investment evaluations while maintaining fiscal prudence based on the relevant information set.

Since early 1999, the Australian e-commerce sector continues to dominate stock market news as they increasingly account for a larger slice of the market capitalisation and affect market volatility. The valuation of e-commerce companies on the Australian Stock Exchange is growing in importance with more start-up firms seeking public listing for fund-raising and more established firms merging for synergy to exploit e-commerce opportunities.[3] This situation has also been fuelled by the pro-active involvement of many government agencies in the promotion of e-commerce.

There is a need to clarify the investment process into steps and choices that help to overcome investor ignorance and identify the most appropriate valuation process for estimating the absolute investment value of an e-commerce firm and its common stock. The significance of this research lies in the exploration, identification and analysis of the key variables and practices that impact on e-commerce equity valuation. In this context this book will make significant contributions to the body of knowledge as follows:

- Promote and foster academic research to develop a systematic quantitative model incorporating factors that can address the deficiency in the traditional valuation models vis-a-vis equity valuation of e-commerce.
- Broaden knowledge of what are the critical success factors that e-commerce managers need to focus on to increase the value of firms and maximise the wealth of its shareholders.
- Further the development of a decision analysis tool for e-commerce equity investment in a portfolio context.

---

[3] Such as the recent strategic alliance between Telstra with Cyber Pacific Century of Hong Kong and the equity positions taken by Telstra in Solution 6 and Sausage in Australia.

1.3 Research Objectives

De Long (1996) suggests that information technology is the new impetus for the economic condition. He also suggests that the economy is on the threshold of post-industrial transformation, with accelerating economic growth, earnings growth, dividend growth and stock-price growth; and that while past valuation methods based on earnings and dividends assume that economic and profit growth will continue at roughly the same pace as in the past, the pace of growth in the new economy will be faster than in the past.

In a world of certainty, the value of an asset is simply the present discounted value of expected stream of returns. If this were not so, the possibility for riskless arbitrage would exist. To ensure that an investor does not pay more than the worth of the asset, the intrinsic value, reflecting the cash flows from the asset has to be substantiated by economic reality. The idea of the rational investor and the efficient markets hypothesis (discussed below) underpin stock prices. They reflect the true value of economic fundamentals and market efficiencies and prevent attempts by investors to make excess profits.

The use of Discounted Cash Flow Models (DCFM) in valuation analysis has been widely accepted by both practitioners and academics as a sound approach to investment decisions (Chew 1997; Wilner, Koch and Klammer 1992; Cheung 1993). The DCFM method applied to equity valuation and based on earnings characterised by profits, dividends or free cash flows has traditionally been used to estimate the value of common stocks. Today, most electronic commerce (e-commerce) firms do not have a history of earnings that enables the application of such models to their stocks. While the DCFM approach is applicable in certain circumstances pertaining to the valuation of e-commerce firms at the micro-level, i.e. where there are positive earnings. Is the current value of publicly traded e-commerce stocks too high where, in most cases, the firm has not even registered a profit? Should these stocks be measured by their fundamental values? Fundamental values refer to the prices stocks ought to sell for based on real business economic value, apart from speculation. The traditional valuation method of weighing a stock's share price against the company's earnings does not work in the current situation of e-commerce firms (Wooley 1999; Taylor 1999). While the financial performance of most e-commerce firms does not justify their market value (Bontis and Mills 2000), there is a need for a more profound understanding of the issues and a comprehensive valuation method to address the situation.

There has been enormous growth in e-commerce on a global scale as reflected by e-commerce stock prices and not all this growth can be explained by the firm's financial fundamentals. The current market valuation techniques and practices adopted by investors and analysts are disjointed and largely unintegrated, subject to individual techniques. The objective of this research is to develop a structured method of e-commerce investment appraisal using broad economic factors.

1.4 Aims

This book studies the e-commerce sector in Australia. The research aims to provide an empirical characterisation of the Australian e-commerce sector and to investigate whether economic activity in Australia can explain e-commerce stock returns by using statistical tests on data drawn from the period 1999-2000. This data series characterises market behaviour of the Australian e-commerce sector across a period in which market changes (see Section 4.2.1 for details) have taken place in the economics of e-commerce investment.

1.4.1 General Aim

The current proliferation of Internet usage has drastically altered lifestyles and new Internet based business opportunities[4] are created with the advent of more powerful, interactive and user-friendly hardware and software that will continue to change the way firms deliver their products and services to consumers. Likewise, consumer behaviour will evolve to take into consideration features of this new delivery channel.

The need for a more definitive and pro-active universal approach to the valuation process is the motivation behind this research and it aims to provide an empirical and quantitative contribution to the understanding of how e-commerce issues are addressed in the valuation of security prices. This research will provide knowledge, insights and recommendations for a working valuation model to investors and practitioners in the context of e-commerce equity investment.

1.4.2 Specific Aims

The specific aims of the book are the following:
1) Using financial econometrics modelling techniques to evaluate and document the characteristics of the e-commerce sector, vis-à-vis pervasive economic variables that permeate e-commerce equity valuation, volatility, predictability and market efficiency.
2) Enunciate the short, medium and long-term implications and ramifications of specific Internet innovations and activities, as they pertain to e-commerce, investment policy and the value of the firm or its share price.[5]
3) Identify the industry practices and related adaptations (from traditional valuation models) as they pertain to investment policies and guidelines affecting e-commerce equity analysis.

---

[4] Total purchases over the web, 1997 – US$10b; total purchases over the web, 2001 (projected) – US$220b; of which 80% will be business to business. Source: International Data Corp posted on www.computerworld.com on 29 December 1997. Actual business to consumer spending was estimated to be US$8.2 billion in 2nd quarter 2000 (24/7/00, www.retailindustry.about.com). The Boston Consulting Group predicted that U.S. online B2B would generate US$2.8 trillion in transactions by 2003 (27/1/00, www.ecommercetimes.com).
[5] Percentage of worldwide Web sites that are profitable 1997 is 30%, Source: ActivMedia, Inc. as posted on www.computerworld.com on 29 December 1997.

4) Determine the pervasiveness, extent and long-term relationship of economic variables that affect e-commerce stock prices (returns).
5) Ascertain where more profound financial engineering may be needed to respond to modify or replace existing models or practices adopted by the investment industry in the valuation of the e-commerce stocks.
6) Develop and numerically estimate and implement a valuation model for electronic commerce stocks.
7) Ascertain the return-generating characteristics of e-commerce stocks and their implications for portfolio investment managers and public authorities.
8) Highlight the emerging issues pertaining to the development of e-commerce as a market and the public policy implications thereof.

1.5 Contributions of this Book

This research predominantly considers non-standard balance sheet or income statement information as inputs to develop a valuation model that overcomes the limitations of traditional valuation methods (Keenan 1970). A reasonably good understanding of the factors that influence e-commerce stock prices should remedy some of the irrational exuberance of this market sector by identifying the 'rational' from the 'irrational' elements of e-commerce stock prices. The contribution this book is as follows:

- *a definition and conceptual analysis of e-commerce equity valuation* since valuation is central to the other financial issues such as market efficiency, predictability and volatility;
- *a quantitative estimate of key variables* that affect the value of e-commerce firms;
- *development of a valuation model*, the Australian E-Commerce Multifactor Model (AEMM), to address equity investment decisions and to analyse the relationships between equity investment decisions and valuation of e-commerce equity;
- a comprehensive econometric investigation of the financial characteristics of the e-commerce sector;
- *a definition of the characteristics and statistical behaviour* of the e-commerce sector to measure the degree of efficiency and volatility of the sector, and analyse the economic implications thereof; and
- the study of the e-commerce sector from a portfolio selection perspective to determine the plausibility of the empirical findings from the proposed model (AEMM) and to *deduce strategic implications and propose policies* for dealing with investment portfolios that include the e-commerce sector.

1.6 The Research Methods – Financial Econometrics

As with most research done on stock markets, the behaviour of the Australian markets at a macro level is expressed by returns on an index for the study period and the behaviour of the e-commerce sector is represented by returns at the sector level. The research would initially involve a review of the evidence regarding the e-commerce stock phenomenon, tracing the market rise and volatility of this class of equity to identify the contributing variables that propel its rise and volatility. The ordinary least-squares methodology is adopted to estimate these variables and this approach is consistent with the broad structure of earlier models developed by researchers in the area of equity valuation (Keenan 1970). The traditional valuation models used for portfolio selection, such as the capital asset pricing model (Sharpe 1964; Lintner 1965b), the market model (Sharpe et al. 1995) and the mean-variance model (Markowitz 1952, 1959) are extensively discussed and, used to analyse and test the valuation of the Australian e-commerce sector in this book. These models use stock returns as a measure of value and consistent with these models this book will predominantly use the returns of e-commerce stocks (*e-stockret*) to measure and estimate value. According to Campbell, Lo and MacKinlay (1997), returns are statistically more attractive, in terms of stationarity and ergodicity, than prices, and are a scale-free summary of the investment opportunity. In this book, e-commerce stock returns are measured as the proportion of monthly changes in closing stock prices.

Key or strategic e-commerce variables and valuation methods from the perspective of the academic community, business consultants and financial intermediaries – the groups that contribute contemporaneously to e-commerce and stock valuation literature – will be identified through a review of the literature. The general conceptual literature on common equity valuation (Fuller and Hsia 1984; Sorenson and Williamson 1985; Ferguson 1997; Rivette and Kline 2000) and the development of the Internet as a business medium (Evans and Wurster 1999; Rayport and Sviokla 1999) will be examined and analysed. This will include a review of the financial models used in the valuation of equity investments and, in particular, the identification of elements or determinants entrenched in these models that may suggest relevance or capacity for the valuation of information technology based stocks. The underlying variables in these models and their ability to address a variable such as information technology, implied or expressed, will be investigated. The variables that influence e-commerce equity returns (i.e. value)[6] will be identified from an economic review involving macroeconomic, microeconomic, industrial organisation and fundamental security analyses.

In this research, a review based on empirical studies will be conducted to determine the relationship of relevant economic and capital market variables to stock valuation. Those variables (factors) that may have a major impact on the value of the e-commerce firm's equity will be identified, using parameters and formulas deduced from observed market behaviour such as realised prices (Keenan 1970) and by applying regression analysis. Secondary data collected will be analysed to assess the impact of identified e-commerce variables on equity value on a monthly basis, reflecting the nature and speed of Internet and e-commerce developments. The sample in this research consists of only pure-play e-commerce firms based on their primary activities (see Section 4.2 about sample size, study period and data). In data gathering, the secondary data sources will be collated according to the industrial sectors with e-commerce capabilities.

---

[6] As return on stocks comprises dividend yield and capital gain, in the case of Internet stocks and particularly those of e-commerce firms, investors are more concerned with only capital gain in the short term.

The identified variables are tested using correlation analysis and factor-loading procedures to determine their pervasiveness on e-commerce stock value. Based on the relationships established, the pervasive variables are then incorporated and tested in a multi-factor framework to develop a valuation model that best estimates the value of e-commerce stocks. Stationarity and cointegration procedures are also applied in the testing of the developed model for long-run economic relationships.

Analyses of the e-commerce stock returns pertaining to 'noise-trading' (Black 1986), volatility, efficient market and portfolio selection will be conducted to highlight and review idiosyncratic characteristics and behaviour. The studies carried out will be conducted along the lines of tests of weak form market efficiency in Fama (1965). This information and that derived from the developed valuation model will assist in deducing investment policies, macroeconomic and financial market implications, and strategies for e-commerce equity investment.

1.7 The Book Structure

The research in this book is generally structured to provide a critical review of the different theories of valuation of stocks, and presents an alternative hypothesis regarding e-commerce stock valuation and conducts econometric studies using Australian e-commerce data to support this hypothesis empirically. The research findings are then used in portfolio selection simulations to evaluate the properties of the e-commerce stocks for portfolio investment decision-making. The framework of this research is as follows: Chapter 2 provides a review of the development of the e-commerce sector and reviews the existing well-known theories of valuation of financial assets as well as the related issues of volatility and predictability. Chapter 3 presents the case for an alternative valuation model and proposes an improved model for the valuation of e-commerce stock. Chapter 4 lays out the theoretical and empirical evidence of existing valuation and econometric literature. This will provide both the foundation for the econometric methodology adopted in this research to develop, estimate and test the valuation model as well as the framework for analysing the e-commerce risk-return relationship, market efficiency and portfolio profile. E-commerce equity valuation forms the nexus for e-commerce investment decisions and financing decisions and this research commences in Chapter 5 with analysing the e-commerce value drivers under the existing market conditions in the study period. Empirical evidence to estimate the pervasive variables and test the valuation model developed in this study is also reported in Chapter 5. In Chapter 6, an analysis of the Australian e-commerce market in terms of volatility, returns and market efficiency is given and the results are analysed and interpreted. In Chapter 7, e-commerce stock returns are used to construct efficient portfolios and efficient frontiers, incorporating other assets and using existing portfolio principles and models as the framework. Chapter 8 states the major findings, areas for further work and the conclusions of this study.

This chapter provided a brief introduction to the background of e-commerce and the issues relating to the valuation of firms involved in using the Internet for business transactions. It also set out the aims and objectives and provided the context and structure for this research by defining the broad problems associated with these issues, which are elaborated in greater detail in Chapter 2. The developmental aspects of e-commerce and traditional valuation techniques are included in Chapter 2 to assist in the understanding of the valuation of an e-commerce investment. The e-commerce market is a relatively new sector of the Australian economy and related data is sparing and empirical research into the financial aspects of this sector is in early stages. In spite of the limitations of this research, the available data is scientifically tested to make a contribution to narrow the gap between theory and e-commerce equity valuation. Essentially, this research is highly exploratory and will rely fundamentally on relevant empirical evidence and existing methodologies or models for share analysis and valuation as discussed in Chapter 2.

CHAPTER 2

Financial Issues, Theory and Econometric Models

2.1 Introduction

The theory of finance is concerned with how individuals and firms allocate risky cash flows through time to achieve a desired objective. Invariably, financial decisions focus on cash, time and risk and the capital market is the medium through which financial assets are issued and traded. A financial asset (security) is a claim against some other economic unit and most financial claims arise when funds pass from surplus units to deficit units, the surplus units then acquire some sort of claim against the deficit units. This passing of funds enables the deficit units to make purchases that they otherwise could not afford and enables the surplus units to earn a financial return on their savings. Financial assets are generally discernible by the size of the cash flows they are expected to generate, the risk of the cash flows and their time horizon. The primary aim of corporate financial management is to maximise shareholder value (i.e. the value of the firm) and valuation forms the basis of financial decisions whether they are in investment decisions (what real assets should the firm acquire?) or financing decisions (how should funds be raised to acquired these assets?). Thus in corporate finance the value of the firm is modelled using the valuation of its financial assets rather than by a direct valuation of its real assets. For publicly traded firms, the valuation of these financial assets is inherent in the value of its stock. In applying valuation models to the e-commerce sector in Chapters 6 (Volatility and Return) and Chapter 7 (Portfolios and Financial Planning) the capital asset pricing model is used as the model for risk and beta as the measure of risk. The issues relating to market efficiency and predictability are also addressed in Chapter 6.

This chapter initially provides an overview of the Internet as a business medium in the market context to impart an understanding of its importance to the value of the firm, represented by its stocks. The traditional valuation models are reviewed and analysed to establish links between the determinants of stock prices suggested by the various theoretical approaches to e-commerce stock valuation. Since stock ownership represents a claim on an asset, investors engage in stock transactions to optimally distribute consumption over time. This produces an arbitrage condition where an investor would equate and make consumption decisions based on the marginal benefit of current to future consumption. The market value of the stock will be determined by the present discounted value (PV), adjusted for risk, of the expected income stream. The stock value can be described as the ratio of the dividend (incorporating growth) over the discount factor (risk-free interest rate plus an interest risk premium for holding stocks) and the negative of the nominal growth rate of dividends or earnings (detailed discussions in Section 2.5.2 below). Therefore, stock prices should rise (fall) as the risk-free rate or investor risk premium falls (rises), and/or the growth of earnings increases (decreases).

The practical limitation of this stock valuation approach is that it relies on future values of earnings and interest rates, both of which are unobserved. The determination of e-commerce stock value would thus require the analysis of expected returns and expectations about how a market change will impact on these estimates.

2.2 Financial Econometric Modelling

The empirical analysis of the e-commerce sector using financial econometric techniques (Mills 1999; Campbell, Lo, and MacKinlay 1997) is a relatively new area of research. The modelling techniques used in this book incorporate both univariate modelling techniques and multivariate modelling, including various time series regression techniques. The evaluation of the Australian e-commerce sector, in addition to the traditional descriptive statistics, also uses a variety of econometric models currently being used in the empirical analysis of financial markets (a discussion of the techniques is presented in Chapter 4).

The study of the distributional properties of e-commerce stock returns (Chapter 5) includes the use of recent techniques of autoregressive process (i.e. first order autoregressive or AR (1) process) for analysing and interpreting vectors that contain integrated and cointegrated variables. Though this book uses time series techniques extensively to identify the real economic factors that are e-commerce value-drivers, it also recognises the important role of cross-sectional modelling in empirical finance (as in the capital asset pricing model) and adopts a cross-sectional approach to specifying the pervasive factors of e-commerce stock return. The use of econometric techniques in valuation as applied to optimisation modelling in portfolio choice selection is also presented (Chapter 7).

2.3 Issues of the E-Commerce Stock Market

The era of increasing returns is upon us. Whereas diminishing returns hold sway in the traditional part of the economy – the processing industries, increasing returns reign in the newer part – the knowledge-based industries (Arthur 1996). New economy businesses are achieving market capitalisations that took old economy firms much longer to achieve. Different understanding of management techniques, strategies and government regulations are needed for the two economies (Bontis 1996). There is wide belief that information technology is a fundamental factor that will sustain the current rate of economic growth and high stock prices. De Long (1996) argues that the level of market valuation for stocks still reflects the underlying fundamentals and information technology is a major fundamental factor transforming the economy and generating a global economic boom. The challenge of this research is to establish and explain, through the use of observable measures, the correlation between stock returns and real activity as a result of information technology infusion in the economy (Figure 2.1). Investors' expectations of a firm's value based on the nascent development of e-commerce are essentially speculative and conjectural to economic performance.

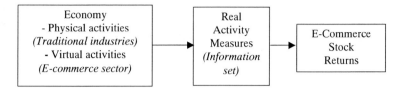

Figure 2.1   The Valuation Chain

The global market euphoria in e-commerce stocks raises the question of the underlying value of their market capitalisation, which appears contrary to conventional financial valuation wisdom (Desmet, Francis, Hu, Koller and Riedel 2000). The limitations of conventional approaches compel the use of current salient e-commerce and real economic activities, in an integrated and analytical manner, to visualise the economic logic behind this recent development. A review and investigation of the features, concepts and business models of e-commerce in the context of the financial theories of valuation and the stock market are necessary in order to capture the key elements. These elements will be analysed in the context of mainstream economic theory stressing the importance of financial activities to e-commerce developments in the stock market and the economy generally. The different approaches adopted to develop a coherent analytical framework will provide a detailed and comprehensive explanation of the different aspects of e-commerce development and, in turn, its stock price (returns).

2.4 Economic Theory of E-Commerce Equity Valuation

Innovation research in economics is extensive and increasing (Cohen and Levin 1989), stimulated primarily by the major role of innovation in the theory of economic growth. The study of information as a key economic variable has been given significantly more attention by disciplines other than economics (Arrow 1996). Information aspects of business have not received the same attention as the trilogy of capital, labour and resources – leading to a situation of uncertainty about the economic impact of information, as a key economic resource, for the exploitation of virtual business or e-commerce. The virtual world is one where many of the conventional constraints of physical economic processes (such as research and development (R&D), manufacturing, distribution and marketing) no longer apply and firms, big or small, can compete with anyone in the world just as easily.

Contrary to the conventional economic theory of diminishing returns developed in the nineteenth century, Arthur (1996) advocates the law of increasing returns. The foundations that the law of increasing returns is based upon rely on manipulating and exploiting the information and virtual aspects of a business. According to Arthur, increasing returns 'are the tendency for that which is ahead to get further ahead, for that which loses advantage to lose further advantage.' This holds true for industries that have no constraints on resources, such as high technology and knowledge-based industries. A business consists of both the physical and the virtual and while the physical may be subject to constraints, the virtual is not. Arthur (1996) defines the criteria for firms subject to increasing returns as those having made high investments in information systems in their operations. They are now using this information relatively cheaply. They are capable of locking in customers and networking by supplementing one firm's core strengths with those of another and creating a win-win situation for all. In equity valuation, the current market conditions call for a shift to new theories of the growth of firms. An assumption of the new growth theories should be the presupposition of the possibility of super normal profits in the hands of able management. The current trend of mega corporate mergers and acquisitions[7] is growing and will continue to be prevalent as strategic alliances continue to be struck to exploit e-commerce capabilities, including management and technical expertise. A parallel can be drawn between the present e-commerce firm and the neo-Schumpeter model of repeated innovation by a 'new theory' firm.

Schumpeter (1934) emphasised the important role played by the financial sector in economic growth, recently supported by King and Levine (1993). Schumpeter's theory of economic development promotes the causal relation between the financial and the real sectors. The benefits derived from the financial sector are the efficient intermediation between lenders and borrowers through capital mobilisation, risk management, project screening and monitoring and transaction cost reduction. These activities invariably contribute to market efficiency by addressing the problems of high transaction costs and information asymmetries (Pagano 1992), a situation exemplified and reinforced by electronic banking on the Internet. Therefore, the financial sectors disseminate information about the real market factors influencing economic growth and ultimately stock prices as reflected by financial variables. Fama (1970, 1990, 1991) conducted an extensive study of the relation between stock market returns and fundamental economic activities in the United States. Huang and Kracaw (1984), Chen, Roll and Ross (1986), Chen (1991), Pearce and Roley (1988), Fama (1991) and Wei and Wong (1992) have modelled the relation between asset prices and real economic activities using factors such as productivity, growth rate of gross national product, production rates, yield spread, inflation, unemployment and other real activity indicators.

The continued rapid growth of e-commerce could have significant effects on the structure and functioning of economies at the firm, sector and aggregate level. The effects of these changes are likely to be seen in prices, the composition of trade, labour markets and taxation revenue (Coppel 2000). The Australian Government estimated the economic impact on the level of national output through increased use and development of the Internet to be an annual 2.7 per cent increase.

---

[7] Example of recent mergers and acquisitions include the AOL-Time Warner merger in the US creating the largest firm in the world in terms of market capitalisation.

2.5 Emergence of the E-Commerce Sector

The Internet, originally called Arpanet, was first developed as an experimental computer network system in case of nuclear war. Academic and military research laboratories mainly used it as a messaging system until Tim Berners-Lee, an academic, developed the Worldwide Web (WWW), a multimedia method for displaying information and links from one site to another. The WWW is an Internet client-server hypertext[8] distributed information retrieval system and has developed a wide user base since its public introduction in 1991. The growth in use of the Internet in commerce can be traced from the early 1980s as depicted in (Figure 2.2) below.

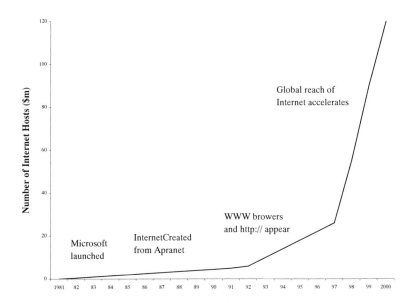

Figure 2.2 Growth of the Internet

Source: Hyndes et al. 1999

The information revolution is transforming the economy and people's lifestyles; and is expected to continue doing so. Knowledge products, such as software applications, comply with the law of increasing rather than diminishing returns and the more widely they are used

---

[8] A database system in which objects such as texts, pictures, music, programs, etc., can be creatively linked to each other.

the greater their value (Tapscott, Lowy and Ticoll 1998). The impetus for this transformation is the rapid advance made in the processing power of computer chips (Moore's Law)[9] and the falling cost of integrated circuits. In the future, it will become easier to communicate information and the amount of information exchanged between individuals and organizations will continue to increase. The information revolution requires firms to radically rethink how businesses are conducted and managed.

With rapid technological advances, there is a need to look at the macroeconomic conditions that are changing the way we manage our businesses and to appreciate the emergence of alternative contractual avenues or marketplaces for facilitating and governing transactions or interactions between individuals. The Internet is such an avenue and the implications this medium of transaction has on information costs will to a large extent explain the individual value of firms as they progressively adopt the advancing technologies for information management. The Internet allows firms to share information with their customers at virtually zero cost. Scott McNealy, the chief executive of Sun Microsystems, suggests four 'revolutions' the Internet would host being: e-commerce, messaging, telephony and entertainment.[10] In this era of the information revolution where there is no serious prohibitive barriers of entry, small firms can start to compete with large ones.

The attributes of the Internet as a business medium include the provision of a common platform for the integration and convergence of business systems to promote efficiency. It is also a powerful tool for facilitating international trade (Hyndes, Adam, Duffy and Bray 1999) by:
- reducing the impact of time and distance in marketing goods and services;
- allowing any item that can be digitised to be displayed in front of a rapidly growing international market;
- creating efficiency making international trade more effective;
- creating efficiencies in transport and distribution lowering overhead costs and allowing smaller firms to compete internationally.

The open structure of the Internet and low-cost connectivity facilitate integration of new and existing information and communication technologies offering consumers and businesses a new and powerful information system and a new form of communication (Coppel 2000). The Internet is essentially a free model of networking where firms are making substantial investments with the expectation of being paid and earning a return on these investments. This expectation remains largely unrealised at this stage, as most e-commerce firms are not yet profitable and many e-commerce firms are seeking and testing new business models to make e-commerce a viable business proposition. Firms are investing billions of dollars in developing cutting edge software and hardware to improve the capabilities and capacity of the Internet to support more efficient and effective communications between individuals and organizations. The level of investments is a definite reflection of confidence the firms have in the potential of this new business medium. This situation warrants a study of the business fundamentals that determine and drive these investments. As managers representing the firm

---

[9] In the 1960s Intel Corporation co-founder Gordon Moore projected that the density of transistors on a silicon chip would double every eighteen months.
[10] Speech to the Australian National Press Club on 25 September 2000.

are agents of the shareholders (Wilson 1968; Ross 1973) and maximising shareholder wealth is their primary objective, however contemporary agency theory (Jensen and Meckling 1990) espouses that the agent will not always act in the best interests of the pricipal, the general acceptability of investment decisions made by firms is reverberated in the stock prices.

The sophistication of capital markets today promotes the ease of raising monetary capital for start-up firms in the technology sectors. Many of the firms in which these investments are made have stock prices at 'undefined' price to earnings (P/E) ratios even though they have not made profits. In buying these shares, investors base their decisions on the firm's key asset, knowledge. It is this knowledge (the intellectual capital) that will provide the firm with the ability to operate successfully (and profitably) in the Internet business environment by gathering information about its customers, competitors and the market as a whole. The ability to fully exploit and manipulate the information derived from this knowledge and transform it into sales will provide the competitive edge for the firm and determine its business value.

The relevant value chain model in this context is to create value with information that describes and provides customers a series of value-adding activities connecting the firm's supply and demand sides (Rayport et al. 1999). Rayport et al. argued that the physical value chain is only part of the business and the other is a virtual value chain. All businesses compete in two worlds, a physical world of resources that is tangible and a virtual world of information, both of equal importance to the success of business. While the physical chain refers to the chain of activities from sourcing raw materials to production to the sale of goods to customers, the virtual value chain connotes the value that can be derived by using the information along this chain as follows:

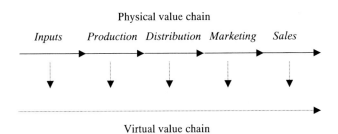

Figure 2.3 Physical Versus Virtual Value Chains

The measurement of knowledge poses a major obstacle for there is no commonly accepted "units" of knowledge and no public markets that meaningfully set its value. Drucker (1993) suggested that 'return on knowledge' would almost be impossible to measure rigorously. The value of all assets (in this case shares) must comply with the law of economics where investors choose to allocate their scarce resources (capital) in order to satisfy their wants (returns). One of the fundamental principles of economics is that value is created by scarcity, and at the moment the demand for e-commerce stocks appears to far exceed supply causing prices to escalate.[11] The proliferation of e-commerce stocks in the future may eventually satiate demand and cause stock prices to fall back into line with the general market (Kindleberger 1989). Siglienti, Tefertiller, Westrup and Wood (1999) concluded in their research that e-commerce stock prices are better explained by supply and demand than by long-term value. However, the distinction between firms in the new and the old economies may become more nebulous in the long term with Internet proliferation.

2.5.1 Valuation Principles of E-Commerce Stocks

The dynamics of increasing returns (Arthur 1996) suggests that involvement in the virtual market enables a firm to reap accelerated returns on investment. The initial capital investment in a virtual business is relatively small compared to traditional business and this investment is in fact not in technology but mainly for acquiring customer loyalty and support (Hagel and Armstrong 1997). The revenue growth trend of an increasing returns business is one that involves a gradual build up of revenues as the business develops followed by an accelerated increase and a fall in unit costs.

The evaluation done in this book for e-commerce has implications and ramifications for both New Economy and Old Economy firms. The firms used in this study are pure-play e-commerce firms, whether they are provider of e-commerce enabling services to other firms or exploiting e-commerce for their own business activity. Old Economy firms with e-commerce capability are also acknowledged in the study in this book as they too are affected in value to varying degrees by their involvement in e-commerce development. The benefits of the virtual economy favour both customers and vendor. The Internet enables customers to gain control of their own value as potential purchasers of goods and services by being able to better organise and manage their own information. This allows consumers to extract more value from vendors they interact with and the five elements that drive this value are distinctive focus, capacity to integrate content and communication, appreciation of member-generated content, access to competing vendors and commercial orientation (Hagel et al. 1997). The vendor benefits from market expansion through the network capabilities of the Internet and according to Hagel et al. (1997) the gains include reduction in search costs, increased propensity to spend, customer focus, ability to tailor and add value to products, lower capital investment in brick and mortar, broader geographic reach and disintermediation potential. These consumer-orientated innovations, resulting from aggressive intellectual property development in recent years, have altered the competitive environment of the traditional market structure and provided a potential for increasing the value of the firm. It can be implied that intellectual capital is an important integral part of these recent e-commerce sector developments and therefore constitutes the source and impetus of e-commerce market value.

---

[11] Over-subscription of Hong Kong's Tom.com by HK$144 billion and Melbourne.com are recent evidence of this phenomenon.

2.5.2 Implications of Intellectual Capital

Intellectual capital is defined as knowledge assets that can be broadly categorised into 'human capital (what people know), customer capital (who you know, and who knows and values you) and structural capital (how what you know is built into your business system),' according to Tapscott, Ticoll and Lowy (2000). While Tegart, Johnston and Sheehan (1998) sum up the importance of knowledge and people as the core resources in knowledge-based economies and that 'matching the education of the skills of the workforce [and Government policy]' are crucial for Australian industry to remain competitive in the global economy. The forces shaping the knowledge sector include the necessary pool of skilled workers able to continually contribute to the development of intellectual property.

The development of the Internet as a business medium for establishing market dominance and continuing profitability of firms has been driven by the growth of intellectual property. The Internet, where intellectual property in the form of information technology is most prominent, continues to provide the impetus for the development, trading, licensing, selling and joint venturing of intellectual property in the new economy. These activities in intellectual capital have been partially responsible for the recent market valuation of e-commerce stocks. The value of e-commerce stocks is affected by the level and rate of development of intellectual property in the economy. In spite of its growing importance, there is no absolute valuation method for intellectual property (Dabek 1999). The valuation of intellectual property is difficult due to the complexity associated with the identification and measurement of intangibles. This research addresses intellectual property in stock valuation by identifying, testing and incorporating variables, or their proxies, that are indicative of intellectual property contributions to real activity and hence the value of e-commerce stocks. As this research used macroeconomic proxies to represent the firm's activities, the intellectual qualities of the firms have been incorporated and tested using both macroeconomic and capital market factors (i.e. education spending and NASDAQ composite index) as intellectual property contributors to value.

In the context of e-commerce, information about customers is one of the most valuable intellectual assets for the firm. Such knowledge allows the firm to bypass the middlemen (disintermediation) and develop products and services specific to customer needs. One important aspect and foundation of the new economy is an open and competitive market that facilitates the diffusion of innovations. Strong competition and the associated rapid diffusion of innovations can reduce the returns to innovation and an appropriate framework of intellectual property rights is important to ensure that innovators receive an adequate return on their investment while at the same time encouraging the rapid diffusion of these innovations (OECD 2000). Lehman (1996) suggests that economic growth and competitiveness will be determined by the ability to create, own, preserve and protect intellectual property. The economic benefits from the proliferation of intellectual property, inherent in the development of the Internet, permeate the firm, industry and the general economy through lower production cost, shorter production cycle, improved productivity and higher return on investment and equity. Higher operating efficiencies due to technological innovation are translated into economic growth with low inflation, low unemployment and high corporate earnings. These are reflected in macro-based variables under efficient markets.

A model for measuring intellectual capital was developed by Skandia AFS when its top management realized the limitations of traditional management theory to address the growing importance of intellectual capital in shaping its business, which was becoming more service oriented and knowledge intensive. Skandia's management realized that in order to better manage its intellectual capital it needed to better understand and measure intellectual factors like individual talent, synergistic market relationships and the flow of competence. Figure 2.4 depicts Skandia's attempt in 1994 to visualize intellectual capital for better management.[12]

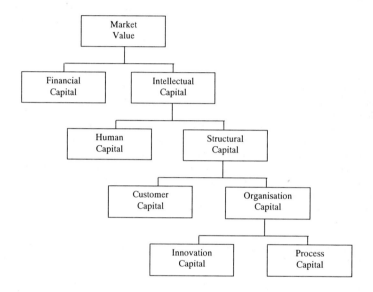

Figure 2.4   Skandia Market Value Scheme

2.6 General Valuation Models and Their Empirical Relevance: A Critical Review

What is driving the valuation of Internet companies is the fact that they are taking strategic positions in the post-industrial economy, which is where all future economic

---

[12] Reproduced from Edvinsson and Malone (1997).

growth is going to take place. (Stefan Rover, Chief Executive Officer, Banking, BROKAT Infosystems AG, 1999)

Modern financial management is largely concerned with the functioning of the firm in relation to optimal matching of the uses and sources of corporate funds that will maximise the firm's market value (Chew 1997). The value of a financial asset is the present value of the cash flows expected from that asset. To ensure that an investor does not pay more than the worth of the asset, the intrinsic value reflecting the cash flows from the asset has to be substantiated by economic reality. The idea of the rational investor and the efficient markets hypothesis (discussed below) underpin stock prices. They reflect the true value of economic fundamentals and market efficiencies preventing attempts by investors to make excess profits.

Coase's theory of the firm stresses that the impetus for the emergence of business corporations is the specialised institutional structure that comes into being to reduce the transaction costs (Coase 1937). With the advent and proliferation of information technology (IT) in global economies since the early 1990s giving birth to that cyber structure called 'The Internet', the strategic use of information technology within the firm will no doubt revive interests in its role of promoting cost efficiency. The theory of the firm expounds contractual relationships as a pervasive feature of economic life (Borland and Garvey 1994). New research into the tantalising effects of modern age information technology on the rules that govern exchange, vis-à-vis information exchange via the Internet, could provide the catalyst to illuminate the impact of this phenomenon on the value of a firm. This is the crux of this book and the study approach is presented in Chapter 3.

The phenomenon of e-commerce that is still evolving as a marketplace and developing in terms of business opportunities requires greater understanding to enhance quality investment and efficient allocation of funds. Like all new firms, e-commerce start-up firms face the same financial constraint of cost outflows preceding revenue inflows. They have to finance their start-up activities before earning any income from these activities. Research and development (intellectual property) expenditure constitutes one of the biggest costs for e-commerce firms. Therefore, they must have funds or sources of funds at the beginning of the business process. These funds may come from internal sources (owners' contributions), bank borrowings (credits) or potential investors (venture capital or strategic partners). Recent developments in the financial sectors, such as the venture capital industry, growth funds management and initial public offers (on ASX, NASDAQ and other regional hi-tech bourses), have eased this finance constraint.

The difficulty of valuing intellectual property compounds the problem faced with the measurement and evaluation of IT benefits. According to Remenyi, Money, and Sherwood-Smith (2000) 'the main reason for this is that despite the considerable amount of research conducted by academics and consultants so far no comprehensive or rigorous economics of information has been developed'. There is relatively more investment evaluation research done on manufacturing technology from a strategic cost management (SCM) perspective (Shank and Govindarajan 1992) and information technology from a capital budgeting perspective (Tam 1998; Panayi and Trigeogis 1998) than there is research done on the impact of technology on stock value in the secondary equity market. Shank and Govindarajan (1992) recognise that technology does pervade a firm's value chain and propose a value chain analysis approach for understanding the role of technology in competitive advantage. They elaborate that technology affects competitive advantage if it has a significant role in determining relative cost or differentiation and it also influences the other drivers of cost and uniqueness within a firm. The SCM perspective suggests a value chain analysis approach coupled with cost driver and competitive advantage evaluations of the firm to capture the diffusion and implications of new technology adoption in the industry. This approach would be relevant to firms adopting e-commerce capability, except the pervasiveness of e-commerce would be economy-wide and the value focus of each firm would be in the context of the overall chain of value creating activities in the economy of which it is only a part.

The fundamental principle of valuation under perfect competition is that the price of each share must be such that the rate of return, comprising of dividend plus capital gains per dollar invested, on every share will be the same throughout the market over any given interval of time (Miller and Modigliani 1961). The Miller and Modigliani proposition on share valuation has come under much criticism for its unrealistic assumptions of a perfect market. This proposition has some relevance to the valuation of e-commerce stocks when we consider the fact that these stocks are yet to pay any dividend. The market must therefore be concerned only with capital gain. The rate of return of some e-commerce stocks has performed better than "normal" (i.e. the market) rate of return and by investing his capital in e-commerce stocks the investor is expecting the earning power of these stocks, i.e. e-commerce firms, to yield more than normal return from opportunities in the new economy. This leads to a less distinct understanding of what the market capitalises or use as proxies for e-commerce stock valuation in the absence of dividends. The present value of e-commerce stocks is generally not considered to be a fair value measured against traditional financial benchmarks. As Porter (1980) emphasised, in a competitive market with free entry, firms cannot earn sustainable supranormal profits indefinitely because that would encourage other firms to enter and drive down prices.

Some of the important issues in the e-commerce stock market relate to the principles of valuation of e-commerce stock, the efficiency and volatility of the market, and the predictability of stock prices and returns (for a review of these issues and their empirical evidence relating to the general stock market see Cuthbertson (1997)). In order to facilitate a more profound appreciation of these valuation issues that relate to e-commerce stocks, it is imperative to review some of the conventional approaches to the valuation of stocks and their related theories. These issues and theories are addressed below.

2.6.1 Efficient Markets Hypothesis

The random walk hypothesis was developed postulating that stock price changes over time were comparable to a random series. This gave rise to a much larger theory known as the efficient market hypothesis (EMH). The mainstream concepts, issues and methods in financial economics are based on the theory of efficient market (see Cuthbertson (1997) for a review).

The EMH predicts that share prices fairly reflect, in an unbiased manner, all information that has been fully revealed to the market. The notion of market efficiency is usually attributed to "rationality" of traders with "homogeneous" information. The analysis of the EMH in relation to the e-commerce sector is important because it reveals market characteristics of the sector. The results from testing the EMH can assist in the identification of over or under valued e-commerce stocks and the trading strategies that could be adopted to earn profits, i.e. both fundamental and technical analysis.

The situation of noise trading implicates the concept of the EMH of an assumed world (Fama 1970, 1991). Are e-commerce (or technology) stocks really worth their market value or are the brokers 'noise-trading' (Black 1986) and over-hyping these shares to euphoric investors? The concept of noise trading is used to describe the behaviour of investors without access to inside information, but acting on the information they possess as though it is accurate information about fundamentals. Noise traders are not fully rational in their investment decisions and often overreact to fundamental news or are subject to systematic biases, such as positive feedback trading strategies, providing a reinforcing mechanism for market trends. This can cause large swings in the value of stocks traded on the market.

Under EMH conditions the share price is an unbiased estimate of its intrinsic value, where investment value is the present value of the share's future cash flows as estimated on average by well-informed and capable investors. If the share market is efficient then there are no financial gains from delaying an investment decision in the hope that the share price will improve (or deteriorate). The EMH holds:
- that the return of an investment is equal to its opportunity cost (allocative efficiency);
- that stocks are always in equilibrium;
- that it is impossible for an investor to consistently beat the market (informational efficiency); and
- that the market achieves Pareto efficient allocation of resources (Laffort 1989).

The EMH predicts that share prices fairly reflect all information that has been fully revealed to the market. The implicit assumption in the efficient market hypothesis is that there always exists a market for stocks to be transacted with little effort or cost. It states that the capital market is always in equilibrium where there is no pressure on stock price. As the stock price reflects all relevant information about the stock, this price must represent its fair market value. Then stock price only moves in response to new information that, intrinsically, is unpredictable. Hence stock price should be random and must follow a Markov process. Therefore, e-commerce stock prices must be fairly valued in market equilibrium. Fama (1970) mentioned three forms of market efficiency. The weak-form of the EMH states that all information contained in past price movements is fully reflected in current market price, and suggests that no investor analysing historical price data can expect to earn abnormal returns above the expected returns given the investment risk. The semi-strong form of the EMH states that current market prices reflect publicly available information. Under the semi-strong form of the EMH, it would be futile for investors to read financial reports or other published data because market prices would have adjusted to the information in them when it was first announced. With the semi-strong efficiency, investors can expect to earn the returns predicted by the Security Market Line (SML) and should not expect better returns unless they have information not publicly available. In the strong form, the current market prices reflect all pertinent information, whether publicly available or privately held. In the semi-strong form of the EMH, no investor can expect abnormal returns by analysing publicly available information and in the strong form, by analysing information from whatever source. Abnormal stock returns are computed as the difference between the return on a stock and its normal return. If the abnormal return is unforecastable using the chosen information set and is thus random, then the efficient market hypothesis is not rejected.

The basis of EMH is in the concept of a competitive market where an individual trader will not be able to affect share prices when buying or selling in such a market, as long as there are enough shares on issue. The traditional analysis of stock markets is based on the premise of the efficient market hypothesis. Empirical tests have shown that the EMH is valid in its weak and semi-strong form. Therefore, if stock prices under the EMH do seem to reflect public information, e-commerce stock prices must be fairly valued and in equilibrium. Information technology is interpreted as a fundamental factor transforming the real economy to high profit growth in the future (De Long 1996). In the context of EMH, this implies that the stock market reflects the future growth of the real economy because investors have incorporated this high growth expectation into their investment decisions and therefore fundamentally justify the stock prices.

Under real market conditions, many assumptions of the EMH, such as information symmetry, homogeneous rationale for information processing, supply-demand equilibrium and equal opportunities for borrowing and lending, are unlikely to be met. For example, different investors will form different probability assessments of the economic impact of the e-commerce sector or use different valuation models for determining expected returns. The supply of e-commerce stocks during the early days of the Internet was suggested to be substantially lower than market demand resulting in higher prices is another example. Share trading opportunities where persistent excess profits can be made for some time, thus contrary to the EMH, are referred to as stock market anomalies. They include the January and weekend effects, the small firm effect (Reinganum 1982, 1983) and winner's curse (DeBondt and Thaler 1985). It may be possible for prices to diverge from fundamental value occasionally; however, arbitrageurs (Shleifer and Summers 1990) or smart money would eliminate any divergence between actual and fundamental value to curb any excess returns as espoused by the EMH. De Long, Shleifer and Summers (1990) shows that irrational investors can survive in the market.

The valuation models for stock prices discussed in the next section are based on the principles of EMH – since if the valuation principles of these models are based on the assumptions that current market prices reflect all past information under the condition of information symmetry, then investors are unable to earn super normal profit.

2.6.2 Discounted Cash Flow Method

The most widely used valuation models for determining a firm's market value are based on the discounted cash flow (DCF) method (Chew 1997). The simple "efficient market model" of stock prices maintains that the actual price is the expected present discounted value of future dividends. Though there is no universally accepted definition of the term "efficient market model," the model does imply some form of expected present value relation (Shiller 1991). Like bond valuation, stock prices are determined as the present value of a stream of cash flows and the basic stock valuation equation is similar to the bond valuation equation (Brigham and Houston 1999) as follows:

$$V_B = \frac{INT}{(1 + K_d)^1} + \frac{INT}{(1 + K_d)^2} + ... + \frac{INT}{(1 + K_d)^N} + \frac{M}{(1 + K_d)^N}$$

where:
V_B =   the bond value;
INT =   the interest (coupon) payment;
M =   the face value of the bond;
N =   the maturity period; and
K_d =   the discount factor.

This value may be determined by capitalising either the dividends or the future earnings to which the original stockholders are or maybe entitled and the stock today is calculated as the present value (PV) of an infinite stream of dividends (the development of which is attributed to Gordon and Shapiro (1956)):

$$\text{Value of stock} = P_0 = \hat{PV} \text{ of expected future dividends}$$

$$= \frac{D_1}{(1 + K)^1} + \frac{D_2}{(1 + K)^2} + ... + \frac{D_\infty}{(1 + K)^\infty}$$

$$= \sum_{t = 1}^{\infty} \frac{D_t}{(1 + K)^t}$$

where:
D_t =   the dividend in period t;
K =   the discount factor; and

$\hat{PV}$ =   the current stock price.

The DCF method operates under the premise that the value of a firm is obtained by the sum of the present value of cash flows to be generated by the firm's existing assets and the present value of cash flows to be generated from future growth opportunities. The general limitations on the DCFM approach include:

(i)   implication of bias against longer term investments as a result of the difficulty in estimating the appropriate discount rate to be used in discounting future cash flows, i.e. the more distant cash flows are discounted more heavily making projects of this nature less attractive;

(ii)   the difficulty of estimating the growth rate in cash flow projections without the benefit of market comparables or positive earnings experience;

(iii)   the difficulty of setting the correct project life in the application of DCF techniques; and

(iv)   the assumption in the treatment of inflation in that the discount rate used implies that all costs and benefits rise at a general rate of inflation.

In the context of contemporary e-commerce stocks, the absence of positive cash flow poses a problem in adopting the DCF method for valuing a firm. Even if positive cash flows can be reasonably estimated in the absence of historical earnings, the extrapolation of growth on earnings estimates might be based on weaker foundations.

The most commonly used discounted cash flow (DCF) valuation approaches are those based on intrinsic financial attributes and earnings (Guatri 1994). The intrinsic method is based on present value of expected cash flows projected from data that is considered subjective and associated with specific strategic or management choices. The earnings method is generally characterised by the use of profits, dividends or free cash flows for valuing the firm. The use of future cash flows to determine stock prices is consistent with the randomness in security returns under the efficient market hypothesis (Campbell et al. 1997). This position is supported by the Law of Iterated Expectations (Samuelson 1965) and explained as follows: Consider the expectations of a random variable R (say representing returns) being extrapolated from these information sets, written as:[13]

$$E[R \mid I_t] \quad \text{or} \quad E[R \mid S_t]$$

where:

I_t and $S_t =$ are defined as information sets, where $I_t \subset S_t$ so all the information in I_t is also in S_t but S_t is superior because it contains extra information;

$E[R \mid I_t] =$ expectations of random variable R based on I_t; and

$E[R \mid S_t] =$ expectations of random variable based on S_t.

The Law of Iterated Expectations says that:

$$E[R \mid I_t] = E[E[R \mid S_t] \mid I_t]$$

---

[13] Referenced from and discussions found in detail in Campbell et al. (1997, pp. 23-24 and chapter 7).

where:

$E [E [R \mid S_t] \mid I_t] =$ forecast of random variable R based on the forecast of the forecast one could make of R with superior information.

Or if one has limited information I_t, the best forecast one can make of the random variable R is the forecast of the forecast that could be made of R if one were to possess superior information S_t.

This equation can be rewritten as:

$$E [R - E [R \mid S_t] \mid I_t] = 0$$

which says that one cannot use limited information I_t to predict the forecast error one would make if one had superior information S_t. If a stock price at time t, P_t is considered as the rational expectation and correlation to fundamental value V, conditional on information set I_t available at time t. This can be written as:

$$P_t = E [V \mid I_t] = E_t V$$

The same holds for subsequent periods, and so for period $t + 1$, P_{t+1} becomes:

$$P_{t+1} = E [V \mid I_{t+1}] = E_{t+1} V$$

Thus, the change in price over the next period is:

$$E_t [P_{t+1} - P_t] = E_t [E_{t+1} [V] - E_t [V]] = 0$$

and because $I_t \subset I_{t+1}$, so $E_t [E_{t+1} [V]] = E_t V$ by the Law of Iterated Expectations. This infers that realised changes are unforecastable given the information in set I_t. So, the use of the discounted present value model of a stock price is consistent with randomness in security returns.

In cases where the stream of dividends is expected to grow at a constant rate, the PV of expected future dividends equation is rewritten as follows:[14]

$$P_0 = \frac{D_0(1+g)^1}{(1+k)^1} + \frac{D_0(1+g)^2}{(1+k)^2} + \dots + \frac{D_0(1+g)^\infty}{(1+k)^\infty}$$

$$= \frac{D_0(1+g)}{k-g} = \frac{D_1}{k-g}$$

where:
g =   the growth rate;
D_0 = the dividend in period 0;
D_1 = the dividend in period 1; and
k =   the discount rate;

The dividend-based DCF model or the Dividend Discount Model (DDM) incorporating growth, referred to as the constant growth model or the Gordon[15] model, may create problems with valuation especially when the valuation of the discount rate k and the assumed dividend growth rate g are close, the result being highly sensitive to minor changes in the assumptions (FitzHerbert 1998). When they are equal, the valuation is infinite and would be unrealistic.

If e-commerce stock prices reflect the growth of the industry, then, the probability of this anomaly arising becomes more realistic. Entrenched in the above equation is k, which acts as proxy for the expected return required by equity investors. This proxy is normally estimated using the Capital Asset Pricing Model (CAPM) developed by Sharpe (1964) and Lintner (1965b). A frequently discussed issue in finance has been whether discount rates or expected returns are relatively constant and so allow the effective application of the CAPM in investment appraisal. Leroy and Porter (1981) and Shiller (1981a) suggested that stock prices were too volatile relative to the present value of dividends, discounted at a constant rate.

Estimating the expected returns for e-commerce stocks using the DCF model is a challenge because it is hard to find reliable estimates for key inputs, such as dividends, beta (see Section 2.6.4 below) and growth rate. The higher volatility of e-commerce stock prices (see Chapter 6) is likely to cause the parameters needed to estimate expected returns (i.e. dividends) to fluctuate and produce wide swings in these estimated expected returns. The high market valuation of e-commerce stocks seems to have reduced their expected returns. Empirical studies starting with Shiller (1981a) and Leroy and Porter (1981) have shown evidence that the variability of stock price indices cannot be accounted for by information regarding dividends alone since dividends do not vary enough to justify the price movement – the excess volatility problem. In addition, Grossman and Shiller (1981) show that the expected present discount rate model better explains price if the constant discount rate assumption underpinning it is relaxed.

---

[14] The derivation of the last term is presented in Extension to Chapter 28 of Brigham et al. (1999).
[15] After Myron J. Gordon, who helped to develop and popularise it.

2.6.3 Portfolio Theory

Asset pricing provided by different valuation models can be used to choose assets to hold in portfolio. Although the study of the trade-off between risk and return as the basis of efficient market resource allocation is formalised in the Capital Asset Pricing Model (CAPM) (Sharpe 1964; Lintner 1965b), the ideas originated and were developed historically by economists, including Hicks (1946), Markowitz (1952) and Tobin (1958), over a longer period of time.

A basic premise of economics is that all economic decisions are made in the face of trade-offs, because of the scarcity of resources. Markowitz (1952) identified the trade-off facing the investor as the risk versus the expected return of an asset. The return realised R, from holding a stock during period t, will be the sum of the dividends received plus capital gain or loss. The investment decision is not only on which stocks to invest, but how much or how to divide the investor's wealth amongst the investment options. Markowitz (1952) developed the mean-variance analysis in the context of selecting a portfolio of stocks.

The earlier method for evaluating investment choice is based on the expected monetary value (*EMV*). The principle underlying the *EMV* criterion is that multiplying the probability of the action by the payoff of that particular action derives the monetary value at a particular state of nature. If an investor has K possible investment actions or assets, where $k = 1, 2, ... , K$, and is faced with M states of nature, then the expected monetary value associated with k^{th} action, *EMV* (k), can be calculated by summing the monetary value over all states of nature as follows:

$$EMV(k) = \sum_{j=1}^{M} P_j M_{kj} \quad (k = 1, 2, ... , K)$$

where:

P_j = probability associated with state of nature j with $\sum_{j=1}^{M} P_j = 1$;

M_{kj} = return corresponding to the kth action and the jth state of nature; and

$EMV(k)$ = the expected monetary value of kth action.

The problem with the *EMV* criterion is that it does not take the element of risk into account but considers only the action with the highest absolute expected monetary value as the best choice. However, a relatively higher degree of risk may be associated with the preferred action using the *EMV* criterion and by accepting the action, the investor is expressing a preference for risk. To allow for risk in investment analysis it is imperative to understand individual investor's attitudes toward risk and there are two methods to evaluate risk, one is to employ utility analysis and the other uses mean and variance trade-off analysis.

Utility analysis (von Neumann and Morgenstern 1953) provides information about investors' attitudes toward risk and allows us to construct a risk profile for an individual or a group of investors. Utility measures the satisfaction an investor derives from the return associated with investment and the utility function, and a curve relating utility to payoff can be used to determine whether an investor is risk-averse, risk-neutral or a risk-seeker (Figure 2.5). A risk-averse investor has a concave utility function that shows utility increasing at a decreasing rate as return increases indicating a preference for small but certain return, compared to one that has a higher expected return but may involve a large but unlikely gain or a large but unlikely loss. A risk-neutral investor has a utility function that has an increasing utility at a constant rate. So for a risk-neutral investor every unit of increase in return has a constant increase in utility and such an investor uses the *EMV* criterion in decision making to maximise expected utility. A risk-seeking investor utility function is convex and has utility increasing at an increasing rate implying the investor is willing to accept investments having a smaller expected monetary value than an alternative where return is certain.

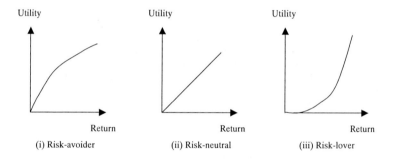

Figure 2.5 Types of Utility Functions

The choice of an investor in deciding alternative risk ventures may be regarded as a two-step process (Hanoch and Levy 1969). The investor first chooses an efficient set from the available portfolios, independently of his tastes or preferences. The second is to apply his individual preferences to this set to select the most desired portfolio.

The expected utility rule poses an implementation problem because it is difficult to estimate the investor utility function and the problem is compounded when a fund manager must act on behalf of many stockholders with different utility functions. Hence the more practical mean–variance decision criterion is used instead of the expected utility rule. The mean–variance rule assumes that the investor is risk- averse and the expected return, $E(R)$, measures an investment's profitability, whereas the variance or standard deviation (β) of returns measures its risk.

Markowitz (1952) explained that a stock's risk should be evaluated by its contribution to the risk of the entire portfolio of the investor, not just the variance of the return of the stock itself.

Hence for the investor to buy stock i, the expected rate of return on stock i must equate the sum of the imputed return on the portfolio and an allowance for risk or the risk discount (this relationship is represented by equation (7.9) and elaborated in section 7.2.3 of chapter 7). The variance of an individual firm's return is made up of both systematic risk and unsystematic risk. Unsystematic risk is firm-specific risk and caused by factors that surround an individual firm and are unique to the firm. Markowitz showed that if investors hold sufficient large, well-diversified portfolios, this unsystematic risk could be minimised or nearly eliminated (Elton and Gruber 1977). On the other hand, systematic risk or market risk cannot be avoided or diversified away and this is the risk that all stocks face because of economy-wide factors that affect all firms. The systematic risk was found to be proportional to the overall risk of the portfolio. Specifically, the risk of a stock was measured by its covariance with the portfolio. Markowitz showed that this risk is measured by the ratio of the stock's covariance to the market variance, or:

$$\frac{\text{Cov}(R_i, R_m)}{(\sigma_m)^2}$$

where:
R_i = the return of the stock i;
R_m = the market return;
$\text{Cov}(R_i, R_m)$ = the covariance for i^{th} stock with the market as a whole; and
$(\sigma_m)^2$ = the variance of the stock market.

The Markowitz theory of portfolio was expanded by Mossin (1996), Lintner (1965a) and Sharpe (1964) to develop the CAPM model based upon the theory that an asset must be priced so as to yield a return that compensates the investor for the additional risk assumed over the return from a risk-free investment. The additional return required for this additional risk assumed over the return of a risk-free investment is called the risk premium. The risk premium for investing in the risky market portfolio over risk-free investment is known as the market risk premium.

The prospects for each possible stock or portfolio (as represented by s in Section 2.5.4), could be depicted by two numbers – its mean, $E(R_p)$, the expected monetary value and $\sigma(R_p)$, the standard deviation of returns which measures its risk. The curve II' in Figure 2.6 above connects the set of all efficient portfolios and is described as the "efficient frontier". The efficient frontier has the property that no other portfolio has a smaller $\sigma(R_p)$ for the same $E(R_p)$. Any portfolio to the area to the right of the curve is considered of inferior quality. Sharpe (1964) also assumed that investors agree on the multivariate distribution of future prices and that there exists a single riskless interest rate (R_f) and $(K\text{-}1)$ risky assets. If the investor can borrow or lend at the risk-free rate of interest R_f, it would be possible to obtain a lower-risk portfolio than A. If the investor puts some money in a risk-free asset and the remainder in ordinary share portfolio M, the investor's expected return and risk is along the straight line joining R_f and M. M in their total portfolio. Portfolio M implies the market portfolio and essentially consists of all risky assets in the market. The best portfolio lies at the point where the straight line R_fN is tangent to II'. Any portfolio of R_f and risky portfolio, M, along this line clearly dominates those below it (i.e. line R_fB). The line R_fMN is called the capital market line (CML) as it represents all the total portfolios in which investors in the capital market might invest. It also assumes that investors are risk-averse individuals whose objective is to maximise wealth by selecting from a portfolio of assets from those available. The market risk premium is assumed to be exogenously determined.

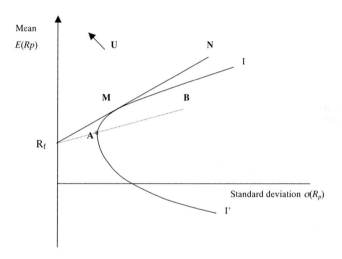

Figure 2.6 The Efficient Frontier in Mean-Deviation Space

The market risk premium can be expressed as the expected return of the market in excess of the risk-free rate:

$$E((R_m) - R_f)$$

where:
R_m = the return from investing in the market; and
R_f = the risk-free rate.

The CAPM model assumes that the risk premium must be sufficient to compensate investors for assuming the risk, or variance, of an investment in the market over a risk-free investment, one that has no variance. The market reward-to-risk ratio, or the market price of risk, is the ratio of the market risk premium to the variance of the market return, $(\sigma_m)^2$ and is expressed as:

$$= \frac{E((R_m) - R_f)}{(\sigma_m)^2} = \frac{E(R_m) - R_f}{(\sigma_m)^2}$$

The marginal price of risk for an individual stock is the incremental expected return on that stock divided by its systematic risk, that is, its covariance with the market, or represented by:

$$\frac{E((R_m) - R_f)}{\text{Cov}(R_i, R_m)}$$

Investors will purchase a stock as long as its marginal price of risk is greater than the market price of risk and sell it if it yields a return less than the market price of risk until equilibrium is reached for each stock as follows:

$$\frac{E((R_i) - R_f)}{\text{Cov}(R_i, R_m)} = \frac{E(R_m) - R_f}{(\sigma_m)^2}$$

By rearranging the terms, the ratio of the stocks' risk premium to the market premium is the same as the stocks' to market risk:

$$\frac{\text{Stocks' Risk premium}}{\text{Market risk premium}} = \frac{E(R_i) - R_f}{E(R_m) - R_f} = \frac{\text{Cov}(R_i, R_m)}{(\sigma_m)^2}$$

Multiplying the right hand side by $E(R_m) - R_f$, we obtain:

$$E(R_i) - R_f = \frac{\text{Cov}(R_i, R_m)}{(\sigma_m)^2} (E(R_m) - R_f)$$

The ratio of the risks $\dfrac{\text{Cov}(R_i, R_m)}{(\sigma_m)^2}$ is called β and is the systematic risk for asset i.

By substituting β into the above equation, we are able to derive the CAPM model:

$$E(R_i) - R_f = \beta_i(E(R_m) - R_f)$$

or $$E(R_i) = R_f + \beta_i(E(R_m) - R_f)$$

CAPM expressed in the $E(R_i) = R_f + \beta_i(E(R_m) - R_f)$ equation is known as the Security Market Line (SML) with gradient $(E(R_m) - R_f)$ and intercept R_f when $\beta_i = 0$. This is graphically represented below and for the market to be in equilibrium, all stocks must be on the security market line (Figure 2.7).

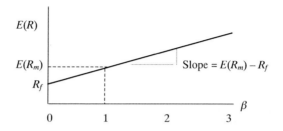

Figure 2.7 Security Market Line

The CAPM predicts a linear relationship between $E(R_i)$, the expected return on asset i and β_i, its beta or systematic risk. The CAPM implies that the market portfolio is the only relevant portfolio of risky assets. Hence the relevant risk measurement of any individual stock is its covariance with the market portfolio, that is, the systematic risk of the stock. Stocks with betas greater than 1 are more volatile than the market and have bigger risk premiums than the market, and vice versa. The CAPM incorporates the assumptions of both the efficient market hypothesis and portfolio theory.

E-commerce stocks are considered to be price volatile, hence risky assets and would require high expected returns $E(R_i)$. The attitude towards risk may not remain constant over time due to innovations in the financial markets. Woolridge (1995) and Blanchard (1993) find that the market risk premium required by investors on the stock market has declined substantially since the early 1980s.[16] This situation implies a decline in investors' risk aversion leading to lower discount rates and higher stock prices.

---

[16] See also article by Glassman, K. and Hassett (1999).

2.6.4 The Capital Asset Pricing Model

The CAPM foundation of much of the current research rests upon the following assumptions about the properties of investors' expectation for stock market returns (Fama 1970):
- the investor's objective is to maximise the utility of terminal wealth;
- investors make choices on the basis of risk and return;
- investors have homogeneous expectations of risk and return;
- there is symmetrical information distribution and it's free;
- investors have an identical investment time horizon;
- there are no taxes, transaction costs, restrictions on short selling or other market imperfections;
- there is a risk-free asset, and investors can borrow or lend unlimited amounts at the risk-free rate; and
- total assets quantity is fixed and all assets are marketable and divisible.

The CAPM is represented by the following equation and the derivation of the model is discussed below:

$$E(R_i) = R_f + \beta_i(E(R_m) - R_f)$$

where:
$E(R_i)$ = Expected return on investment;
R_f = Risk-free rate of return;
β = Investment's systemic risk; and
$E(R_m) - R_f$ = Expected risk premium in the market.

The CAPM is an economic model that predicts a trade-off between systematic risk, known as beta (β), and expected return under specific conditions. It is an economic model that restricts the parameters of statistical models to provide a more constrained normal return. Sharpe's (1964) version of the CAPM is the most widely recognised form and the model adopts the Markowitz (1952) "mean-variance paradigm" which assumes that each investor's expectations about the uncertain one-period rates of return (i.e. end-of-period cash proceeds divided by current price) on the asset can be characterised by a joint-normal distribution based on just two parameters, the mean and variance (or the standard deviation) of returns. The CAPM is a single-period model, hence does not have a time dimension. The CAPM defines risk as the covariability of the stock's return with the market returns or the volatility of the stock's returns relative to the volatility of the market portfolio's returns.

The CAPM is specified *ex ante* or before the event and it is a theory based on investors' unobservable beliefs about future returns on securities in equilibrium. The CAPM proves that the relationship between prices of assets in a general equilibrium, where the investors select assets to maximise the mean-variance utility, is linear. To derive the capital asset-pricing equation (the general equilibrium pricing relation) from the microeconomic foundations of portfolio choice, we start with the vector $s = (s_1, s_2,..., s_k)$ representing a portfolio where s denotes quantities of each of the K assets held in portfolio (the following CAPM model is based on the derivation in Brennan (1989) and discussion in Eichberger and Harper (1997)). The assets have returns in each period t denoted by r_{tk}, where $(t = 1, ..., T; k = 1, ..., K)$ and the value in each period depends on the quantity of each asset in the portfolio by the return from each asset:

$$V_t(s) = \sum_{k=1}^{K} r_{tk} \, s_k$$

The expected value of the portfolio s equals the sum of the expected returns from the individual assets weighted by the quantities of the assets held in the portfolio:

$$\mu(s) = \sum_{k=1}^{K} \mu_k \, s_k$$

Where μ_k is the expected return (μ_k = from asset k ($k =1, ..., K$). The variance of the value of the portfolio s is denoted by:

$$\sigma^2(s) = \sum_{k=1}^{K} s_k \cdot \sum_{j=1}^{J} s_j \, \sigma_{jk}$$

where:
s_j = the quantities of each of the J assets held in portfolio; and
σ_{jk} = the covariance between assets k and asset j.

When we differentiate $\mu(s)$ and $\sigma^2(s)$ with respect to asset s_H we get:

$$\mu_H(s) = \mu_H$$

where $\mu_H(s) = \partial\mu(s)/\partial s_H$ denotes the partial derivative of $\mu(s)$ with respect to s_H, and denoting the partial derivative of $\sigma^2(s)$ with respect to s_H by $\sigma_H^2(s) = \partial\sigma^2(s)/\partial s_H$,

$$\sigma_H^2(s) = 2 \text{ x } \left\{ \sum_{k=1}^{K} s_k \, \sigma_{Hk} \right\} = 2 \cdot \sigma(s, H)$$

where, $\sigma(s, H) = \sum_{k=1}^{K} s_k \, \sigma_{Hk}$ is the covariance between the return of the entire portfolio and the return of the single asset H.

In optimising the value of the asset portfolio of some investor $i \in (1, 2, \dots, I)$:

$$\text{Max } s = V^i(\mu(s), \sigma^2(s))$$

where $V^i(\mu(s), \sigma^2(s))$ represents ith consumer's utility function $V(\mu, \sigma)$ with increasing μ and decreasing σ, and:

$$\text{Subject to } \sum_{k=1}^{K} p_k \, s_k = \sum_{k=1}^{K} p_k \, \overline{s_k}.$$

where p_k is the price of kth asset.

Denoting $V^i_1 = \partial V^i / \partial \mu$ and $V^i_2 = \partial V^i / \partial \sigma^2$ the partial derivative of μ and σ^2, the first-order conditions for this problem are as following:

$$\{V^i_1(\mu(s), \sigma^2(s)) \cdot \mu_H(s)\} + \{V^i_2(\mu(s), \sigma^2(s)) \cdot \sigma_H^2(s)\} - \{\lambda \cdot p_H\} = 0 \quad (2.1)$$

(for $H = 1, \dots, K$), where λ is the Lagrange multiplier of the budget constraint, and:

$$\sum_{k=1}^{K} p_k \, s_k = \sum_{k=1}^{K} p_k \, \overline{s_k}.$$

The CAPM is derived from the first order condition of equation (2.1), at equilibrium and assuming that one of the assets is riskless. The first-order conditions implicitly defines share demand s^i_H in asset demand functions as follows:

$$s^i_H = f^i_H(p_1, \dots, p_K; \overline{s^i_1}, \dots, \overline{s^i_K}) \qquad \text{for all } H = 1, \dots, k$$

In an exchange market, the general equilibrium is a vector of asset prices
$p^* = (p^*_1, ..., p^*_K)$ together with a vector demand of asset demands for each investor
$i = 1, 2, ... , I$, $s^{*i} = (s^{*i}_1, ..., s^{*i}_K)$ such that:

$$\sum_{i=1}^{I} s^{*i}_k = \sum_{i=1}^{I} f^i_k(p^*_1, ..., p^*_k, \overline{s^i_1}, ..., \overline{s^i_K}) = \sum_{i=1}^{I} \overline{s^i_K} = S_k$$

where S_k is the aggregate quantity of the assets (shares) available in the market. If we take the
assets to be shares, then the quantity of shares demanded is in equilibrium with the available
supply.

To derive the CAPM equation from equation (2.1), assume asset K is risk-free, then
return $= r_{tK} = r$ for all $t = 1, ... , T$. The partial derivatives of the expected return and variance
function with respect to the changes in the size of asset K in the portfolio are:

$$\mu_K(s) = r$$

and:

$$\sigma^2_K(s) = \sigma(s, K) = 0$$

Substituting these values into the first-order conditions and choosing the riskless asset as
numeraire $p_K = 1$, we solve the K-th first-order condition for the Lagrange multiplier as:

$$\lambda = V^i_1(\mu(s^{*i}), \sigma^2(s^{*i})) \cdot r$$

where:
$V^i_1(\mu(s^{*i}), \sigma^2(s^{*i}))$ = represents ith consumer's utility function $V(\mu, \sigma)$ with increasing μ and
decreasing σ in asset s; and
r = the riskless pay-off (return).

Substituting for λ, $\mu_H(s)$ and $\sigma^2_H(s)$, the first $K-1$ first-order condition of equation (2.1)
becomes (and is similar in form to equation (7.8)):

$$V^i_1(\mu(s^{*i}), \sigma^2(s^{*i})) \cdot ((\mu_H - p^*_H \cdot r) + 2) \cdot V^i_1(\mu(s^{*i}), \sigma^2(s^{*i})) \cdot \sum_{j=1}^{K} s^{*i}_j \times \sigma_{Hj} = 0$$

Rewriting this equation as:

$$\Phi^i(s^{*i}) \cdot (\mu_H - p^*_H \cdot r) = \sum_{j=1}^{K} s^{*i}_j \cdot \sigma_{Hj}$$

where:

$$\Phi^i(s^{*i}) = -\frac{V^i_1(\mu(s^{*i}), \sigma^2(s^{*i}))}{2 \cdot V^i_1(\mu(s^{*i}), \sigma^2(s^{*i}))} = \left\{ \begin{array}{l} \text{marginal rate of substitution} \\ \text{along an investor's indifference} \\ \text{curve in } (\mu, \sigma) \text{ space.} \end{array} \right\}$$

The (μ, σ) space is presented in Figure 2.6 and under the assumption that $V(\mu, \sigma)$ is increasing in μ and decreasing in σ, for increasing utility the indifference curve of the investor moves in a north-westerly direction as indicated by the arrow **U** in Figure 2.6.

In equilibrium and over all investors:

$$\sum_{i=1}^{I} s^{*i}_k = S_k$$

$$\theta(s^*) \cdot (\mu_H - p^*_H \cdot r) = \sigma(S, H) \qquad\qquad (2.2)$$

where:

$$\theta(s^*) = \sum_{i=1}^{I} \Phi^i(s^{*i})$$

$$\sigma(S, H) = \sum_{j=1}^{K} S_j \, \sigma_{jH} = \begin{array}{l} \text{the covariance of asset } H \text{ with the aggregate of} \\ \text{assets } S = (S_1, ..., S_K). \end{array}$$

multiplying equation (2.2) by S_H and summing up over all risky assets $H = 1, ..., K\text{-}1$, we obtain:

$$\theta(s^*) \cdot \{\mu(S) - r \cdot V_0(S)\} = \sigma^2(S) \qquad\qquad (2.3)$$

where:

$$\mu(S) = \sum_{H=1}^{K} \mu_H \, S_H = \begin{array}{l} \text{the mean return on aggregate assets (market portfolio); and} \end{array}$$

$V_0(S) = \sum p_H A_H$ = the market value of the market portfolio.

Solving equation (2.3) for $\theta(s^*)$ and substituting into equation (2.2) we are able to obtain the CAPM equation for assets units:

$$\{\mu - r \cdot p^*_H\} = \frac{\sigma(S, H)}{\sigma^2(S)} \cdot \{\mu(S) - r V_0(S)\} \qquad (2.4)$$

In finance, the pay-off per unit of investment is measured by the expected rate of return under equilibrium represented by $(E)\mu_k = \mu_k / p^*_k$ and the optimal investment share in total expenditure on asset k, instead of optimal quantity of assets in investment. Expected investment in asset k is measured by, $(E)a^*_k = a^*_k \times p^*_k/V'_0$. Dividing equation (2.4) by p_H and $V_0(S)$ on the right hand side, we have:

$$(\hat{\mu}_H - r) = \frac{\hat{\sigma}(S, H)}{\hat{\sigma}^2(S)} \cdot (\hat{\mu}(S) - r) \qquad (2.5)$$

where:

$\hat{\mu}(S) = \mu(S) / V_0(S)$ = the average return on the market portfolio per unit of investment;

$\hat{\sigma}(S, H) = \sigma(S, H) / (p_H \times V_0(S))$ = the covariance between the asset H and the market portfolio per unit of investment; and

$\hat{\sigma}^2(S) = \hat{\sigma}^2(S) / V_0(S)^2$ = the variance of the market portfolio per unit of investment.

Replacing $\{\hat{\sigma}(S, H) / \hat{\sigma}^2(S)\}$ with β_H in equation (2.5), we have the familiar CAPM equation:

$$(\hat{\mu}_H - r) = \beta_H \cdot (\hat{\mu}(S) - r)$$

or:

$$\hat{\mu}_H = r + \beta_H \cdot (\hat{\mu}(S) - r) \tag{2.6}$$

where:

$\hat{\mu}_H$ = the expected return of a risky asset;

r = the riskless payoff;

β_H = the covariance of the return on the market portfolio with the risky asset H; and

$\hat{\mu}(S)$ = the expected return of the market portfolio.

Equation (2.6) is the familiar capital asset-pricing equation, which states that, in equilibrium, the expected return of each risky asset is equal to the riskless rate of return plus the difference between the expected rate of return on the market portfolio and the riskless rate for each individual risk class.

The CAPM is useful in measuring expected stock returns and three factors need to be determined in order to use the CAPM for estimating the required rate of return: the risk-free rate, the market risk premium and the systematic risk (β). The estimation of the beta line is done using the ordinary least-squares regression method. Theoretically, the best estimate of the risk-free rate would be the return on a zero-beta portfolio. The cost and complexity of such an exercise prohibits the construction of such a portfolio. There are three reasonable alternatives for estimating the risk-free rate using government securities: the rate for Treasury bills, the rate for ten-year Treasury bonds and the rate for thirty-year Treasury bonds. Harrington (1987) suggests that the most widely used proxies for the risk-free rate are the 30 or 90-day Treasury bill rates. The ten-year Treasury bond rate is recommended (Copeland, Koller and Murrin 1999) because it closely matches the cash flow duration of the company being valued and is a geometric weighted estimate of the expected short-term Treasury bill rates over the evaluation horizon. It is also consistent with the duration of the stock market index portfolio used for the estimation of the betas and market risk premiums. Finally, it is less sensitive to unexpected changes in inflation, and thus has a smaller beta and a lower liquidity premium than the thirty-year rate.

The standard procedure for estimating beta is to regress stock returns against market returns and to use the slope of the regression as the beta (Damodaran 1994). Copeland, Koller and Murrin (1991) recommends using 5 to 6 per cent market risk premium (Damodaran (1994) suggests 4.58% based on data from 1926 to 1990) for US companies. This rate is based on the long-run geometric average risk premium for the return on the SP 500 versus the return on long-term government bonds from 1926 to 1988. The geometric average rates of return provide a better measure of investor expected returns over long periods of time than arithmetic averages which are biased on the measurement period (Copeland, Koller and Murrin 1991; Damodaran 1994). The geometric mean is commonly used in finance for calculating average rate of returns as this method explicitly incorporates the concept of compound interest (Lee, Lee and Lee 2000). Many academics believe that because the CAPM is a single-period model, the simple arithmetic mean is appropriate (Harrington 1987). It is therefore prudent to use the geometric mean if investors evaluate investments as if the proceeds are to be reinvested and, the arithmetic mean if returns are viewed as a single holding period's return. In practice, the risk premium measurement periods should be of the longest possible historical period (Damodaran 1994), where any trend in premiums is absent over time.

The criticisms against the CAPM include the suggestion that since the market portfolio could never be observed, the CAPM could never be tested (Roll 1977) and that all tests of the CAPM were effectively joint tests of the model and the market portfolios used in the tests. Fama and French (1992) concluded no relationship exists between betas and returns between 1963 and 1990. Amihud, Christensen and Mendelson (1992) and Chan and Lakonisok (1992) subsequently refuted the Fama and French (various years) study and confirmed the positive relationship between betas and returns. The Chan and Lakonishok (1992) study confirmed the correlation from 1926 to 1982 and attributed the breakdown after 1982 to indexing which led the larger, lower beta stocks in Standard and Poor 500 to outperform smaller, higher beta stocks.

The adoption of the CAPM in this research poses the problem that only realised returns can be observed whilst CAPM refers to expected returns, which in turn should reflect all known information about e-commerce stocks. The evolving nature of the e-commerce sector creates a situation where information is dynamic with the constant introduction of unanticipated operating conditions in the industry, creating information surprises that cause e-commerce stocks to move in a magnitude or direction not predicted by the CAPM. The use of the CAPM has been limited recently due to doubts on the restrictions imposed by the CAPM on the market model, since these restrictions can be relaxed at little cost by using the market model (Campbell et al. 1997).

2.6.5 Consumption CAPM

The consumption CAPM (C-CAPM) is an inter-temporal model that determines equilibrium returns in a well-diversified portfolio on the basis of maximising the investor's expected utility, which depends on current and future consumption and subject to intertemporal budget constraint (Lucas 1978; Mankiw and Shapiro 1986). Breeden (1979) developed a model that measures a security's risk by its sensitivity to changes in investors' consumption. In the standard CAPM, the investors are concerned exclusively with the amount and uncertainty of their future wealth. The role of financial assets in the consumption CAPM is to smooth consumption over time by transferring purchasing power from one period to the next. Assets are accumulated or sold depending on the level of desired consumption and income and therefore an individual asset is preferred if its return is expected to be high and consumption is expected to be low. The systematic risk of the asset is therefore the covariance of the asset's return with respect to consumption compared to its covariance between the return and the market portfolio in the normal CAPM.

The principle of the consumption CAPM is incorporated in this research through the consideration and testing of those variables that underpin future consumption in a multivariate framework. Those risks that might affect future consumption are important to e-commerce stock valuation in terms of consumer behaviour and perception of the e-commerce sector as a viable consumer market. As such, this research also addresses the uncertainty about stock returns in relation to uncertainty about consumption. Like the consumption CAPM, the approach adopted in this research relies on "external" motives for investing – considering "real activity" variables as pervasive factors of e-commerce market value.

2.7 Tobin's q

The expectations of future profits are the basic determinant of investment activity and these expectations are supposed to be reflected in a firm's market value represented by its stock price. The Tobin's q (Tobin 1969) approach is defined as the ratio of the market value (V) of a firm to the replacement cost of its existing capital stock denoted by $P^i K$, representing P^i – the replacement cost and K – the existing capital level:

Tobin's $q = V/(P^i K)$

or:

$$\text{Tobin's q} = \frac{\text{market value of assets}}{\text{estimated replacement cost}}$$

The market value of the firm exceeds the value of its existing capital when investors' perceive its expected earnings as high or increasing. The firm can be worth less than its existing capital when its prospects are considered uncertain or low. Investment in new real capital is profitable if q exceeds one. Investment in new capital assets is then a function of q:

$$q_t = f(q_t)$$

The application of q theory to e-commerce stock in a situation of extremely high q ratios can be construed to portray under-investment in this sector resulting in bullishness on the stock.

Generally, the empirical studies done on q theory have failed to prove a significant relationship between business investment and changes in stock prices (Chirinko 1993), more so during periods of volatile stock prices (Blanchard 1993). Barro (1990) and Blanchard (1993) found the rate of return on the stock market explained investment better than q and other studies indicate movements of q being dominated by movements of stock price implying information content of q is already reflected in stock market data. As this research uses stock market data to analyse the e-commerce stock returns (i.e. movements of stock price) in the context of overall market return (i.e. S&P/ASX 200 share market index), the essence of the Tobin q model is essentially captured, under proxy, and consistent with recent empirical studies (Chirinko 1993; Blanchard 1993; Barro 1990).

2.8 Factor Models

Factor models or index models are "return-generating" (Sharpe, Alexander and Bailey 1995) statistical models that assume that the return on a stock is sensitive to the movements of various factors or indices. These factors and their sensitivities to stock returns need to be determined. The two main factor models are the one-factor market model and the multiple-factor models. Depending on the number of predicted variables, the techniques of simple or multiple regression analyses are used to define the return-generating process.

2.8.1 The Market Model

The market model is a well-known model in finance that assumes that the monthly rate of return on a stock (R_{it}) is linearly related to the monthly rate of return on the overall stock market (R_{mt}). In contrast to the Capital Asset Pricing Model, the Market Model (MM) is a statistical model linking *ex post* returns on a stock to those on the market. The MM relates the return of any stock to the return of the market portfolio. The MM states that a stock's return is a function of the return on one factor, the market index. The MM is usually expressed as:

$$R_{it} = \alpha_i + \beta_i R_{mt} + \varepsilon_{it}$$

where:
R_{it} = the return of stock i in period t;
α_i = the expected return if market return has a value of zero;
β_i = sensitivity of stock i to the market return;
R_{mt} = the rate of return on the market as a whole;
ε_{it} = the random residual return on stock i that is uncorrelated with prior residuals; and market returns. The residuals have mean of zero and variance (σ_i).

The error term ε_{it} is assumed to satisfy the requirements of the linear regression model and R_{mt} is taken to be the monthly rate of return on some major stock market index, such as the Australian All Ordinaries Index. The coefficient β_i, called the stock's beta coefficient, measures how sensitive the stock's rate of return is to changes in the level of the overall market. If $\beta_i > 1$ ($\beta_i < 1$), the stock's rate of return is more (less) sensitive to changes in the overall market than is the average stock.

The MM was developed by fitting, in the form of a separate Ordinary Least Squares (OLS) regression, each stock's price relatives on a market index of price relatives. In e-commerce stock valuation, the MM can be used to determine the level of stock return that is unrelated to the return on the market. The variable of interest would then be the stock return unrelated to general market return, represented by the regression residual from estimating the regression line and referred to as an abnormal return. By removing the portion of the return that is related to variation in the market's return, the variance of the abnormal return is reduced. The advantage of using the MM will rely on the R^2 of the MM regression. The higher the R^2 (the coefficient of determination),[17] the greater is the variance reduction of the abnormal return, and the larger the benefit (Campbell et al. 1997).

2.8.2 Multiple-Factor Model

The multiple-factor model is a "return-generating process" statistical model that describes how the return on a stock is produced by identifying major economic factors (variables) that systematically move the prices of all stocks. The multiple-factor model assumes that the return on a stock is sensitive to the movements of various factors. The model implies that the returns on two stocks will be correlated through common reactions to the factors specified in the model. Any unexplained return by the model is assumed to be unique to the stock and uncorrelated with the unique elements of returns on other stocks. The factors are the characteristics being measured and could be anything that can be objectively identified and scored.

Factor models potentially provide the benefit of reducing the variance of the abnormal return by explaining more of the variation in the normal return. This variance reduction is typically the greatest in cases where the sample firms have a common characteristic, in this case of e-commerce firms, when they are all members of one market sector or industry (considered as such) and are grouped into sectors under one market capitalisation group (Campbell et al. 1997, pp. 155-156).

As a rule of thumb, there should be a minimum of five (5) observations for every factor considered in a multivariate analysis (Page and Meyer 2000). The empirical relationships among the set of e-commerce economic factors identified will be established and evaluated using the data available for the period 1999 to 2000. The dependent factor in this case is the value of the stock and the independent factors are those economic variables that have a pervasive influence on the return of e-commerce stock. By summarising the interrelationships among the factors in a concise but accurate manner, the influence of these factors on the value of e-commerce stock can be conceptualised.

The specification of factors is done through two basic approaches, statistical and theoretical. The statistical approach is based on portfolios constructed from sample data (Lehmann and Modest 1988; Connor and Korajczyk 1988) and involves building factors from a comprehensive set of asset returns that is usually larger than the set of returns used to estimate

---

[17] In multiple regression model, R^2 measures the proportion of the total sample variation in the dependent variable that is explained by the independent variable.

and test the model. The theoretical approach for factor specification is based on arguments that the factors capture economy-wide systematic risks (Chen, Roll and Ross 1986; Fama and French 1993). Chen, Roll and Ross (1986) use macroeconomic variables as factors and Fama and French specify firm characteristics to generate factor portfolios.

In using the statistical approach, Lehmann and Modest (1988), and Connor and Korajczyk (1988) find little sensitivity to increasing the number of factors beyond five and Fama and French (1995) find that stocks require only three factors and that five factors are necessary when bond portfolios are included (Campbell et al. 1997, p. 240). Roll and Ross (1980) using factor analysis found that only three and possibly four factors explained the return generating process of US equities. Whilst Dhrymes, Friend and Gultekin (1984) suggested that the number of factors may depend on the number of securities in each portfolio.

The theoretical approaches for selecting factors generally fall into two categories of macroeconomic and financial market variables that are considered to capture the systematic risks of the economy (Chen, Roll and Ross 1986) and firm specific variables with explanatory power of differential sensitivity to the systemic risks.

2.8.3 Arbitrage Pricing Model

The Arbitrage Pricing Theory (APT) is a classic application of factor analysis and it assumes that in markets where there are arbitrage activities, all assets with similar characteristics trade at similar prices because the arbitrage activities will remove any mispricing. The APT (Ross 1976) is a multiple-factor model that is an alternative to the CAPM and measures the sensitivity of a company's stock return to a separate underlying factor in the economy. Ross's APT does not specify which portfolios are efficient, rather it assumes that each share portfolio depends partly on pervasive macroeconomic influences or factors (systematic risk) and partly on noise – events that are unique to that company (unsystematic risk) (Brealey et al. 2000). Thus only systematic risk is priced in the market and the factors are not identified in the model and must be ascertained through empirical research. Empirical study using the APT has suggested several fundamental factors that could influence returns and they are changes in forecast real GNP growth, inflation (both long and short-term), exchange rates, default risk (difference between the yield to maturity on Aaa and Baa-rated long term corporate bonds), short term real interest rate (difference between the yield on T-bills and the CPI) and interest yield spread (Elton, Gruber and Mei 1994).

Empirical evidence suggests that the APT explains expected returns better than the single factor CAPM (Chen 1983; Chen, Ross and Roll 1986; Berry, Burmeister and McElroy 1988). The APT expected rate of return is defined as:

$$E(R_{it}) = R_{rf} + \beta_1[E(F_{1t}) - R_{rf}] + \beta_2[E(F_{2t}) - R_{rf}] + , \dots , + \beta_k[E(F_{kt}) - R_{rf}] + e_{it}$$

where:
$E(R_{it})$ = the expected returns on asset i at time t;
R_{rf} = the risk-free return;

$E(F_{kt})$ = the expected rate of return of on a portfolio that mimics the kth factor at time t and is independent of all others;
β_k = the sensitivity of the stock return to the kth factor;
$[E(F_k) - R_{rf}]$ = the risk premium per unit of factor k risk;
k = number of factors; and
e_{it} = the idiosyncratic elements effecting asset i at time t.

The rationale behind the APT is, similar to the CAPM, that investors get rewarded for taking systematic risk. The CAPM is considered to be a variation of the APT with only one underlying factor measured by the market index. The measure of systematic risk in the APT is determined by an asset's sensitivity to various economic factors that affect all assets. The number and the identity of the factors are determined by historical returns and the APT relates expected returns to economic factors, with a beta specific to each factor. The parameters of the APT are estimated from a factor analysis on historical stock returns to yield the common economic factors that determine these returns, the risk premium for each factor and the factor beta for each stock. This approach is similar to that adopted in this research for the valuation of e-commerce stocks.

2.9 Expected Returns and Economic Fundamentals

The lack of historical financial information for the firms within the e-commerce sector and its rapid evolution makes it imperative to evaluate the sector at the macro level. Macroeconomic analysis is the first step in the process of security analysis as during periods of strong economic growth most firms report increased business activity and generate cash flows that can be paid out as dividends to shareholders or reinvested in the business to enhance future cash flows. The rates of return for these companies will subsequently be higher due to increase in dividends and rising stock prices. As a result the general economic conditions will affect performance of the firm. Macroeconomic analysis generally focuses on changes in macroeconomic conditions as a result of changes in government policies, market structure, technology, culture and other reasons. As these factors change, expectations about the performance of a particular firm, industry and economy will change and affect the investment weighting given to a particular sector. Officer (1973) studied the movements in aggregate stock market volatility and their relation to the volatility of macroeconomic variables. The advent of the Internet has been both pervasive and significant, affecting all market aspects including government policies, competition, lifestyle, costs and growth perception.

Economists have observed extreme sequences of price rises and offered fundamental explanations for their occurrence, including the "tulip mania" or the "south sea bubble" (Garber 1990), and thus show the existence of speculative bubbles caused by unobserved fundamentals is unproven. This implies that stock prices still reflect the underlying fundamentals. There is commonality in the view that the variations in expected returns are rational variations in response to market conditions (Patelis 1997; Chen 1991; Schwert 1990; Fama 1990; Fama and French 1989). Chen, Ross and Roll (1986) suggest that the following economic variables are highly correlated with the factors that come out of factor analysis: industrial production, shifts in the term structure, changes in default premium, changes in real interest rates and unanticipated inflation. These variables can be correlated with returns to produce a model of expected returns, with firm-specific betas calculated relative to each variable (Damodaran 1994). This research adopts the fundamental factor approach to estimate returns for e-commerce equity from an *ex post* perspective as there is uncertainty as to what the fundamental value really is in an *ex ante* sense (Stiglitz 1990).

A main disadvantage of using the macroeconomic multifactor model as opposed to the APT is the errors associated with identifying the factors. The factors in a model change over time, as will the risk associated with each economic factor and using the wrong factors or omitting a significant factor in a multifactor model can lead to inferior estimation of e-commerce stock value or returns. A summary of the monthly data associated with the identified factors and used in this research is presented in Appendix 2.1.

2.9.1 Financial/Capital Market Variables

Financial systems play crucial roles in pooling and mobilising individual saving to finance investment. They are instrumental in allocating finance to the activities generating the highest return and diversify and relocate risk among individual investors. The differences between financial systems with respect to debt versus equity funding, monitoring and risk management make them more relevant for different types of economic activities, in particular in the context of the new economy in the financing of new, innovative ventures. Black (1976) and Christie (1982) find that financial leverage partly explains movements in aggregate stock market volatility. Equity is more the dominant source of funding than debt in most new venture financing, including e-commerce business, due to the high risk and lack of collateral. To nurture growth in the ICT industry, countries like Australia have to stimulate venture capital either through public listing (also as a means of ensuring easy exit for venture capital) or government incentives.

2.9.2 Economic Variables

The fundamental value of a firm is the expected present value of the firm's future payouts if these expectations take all currently available information into account, consistent with the efficient market hypothesis. Thus future payout must ultimately reflect real economic activity as measured by, for instance, gross domestic product (GDP) (Shapiro 1988). Consequently, stock prices should react to these measures of real activity as stock prices are built on expectations of these activities. Barro (1990) and Fama (1990) support the argument that stock price should lead real activity.

2.9.3 E-Commerce Sector Variables

While real activity variables provide the indicators and underpinnings for economic performance of the general market, the variables that would signify potential growth impetus for the e-commerce sector are more specific and overt. The demographics of the Internet cannot be addressed by conventional physical sales and marketing that are constrained by geography for the number of consumers on the Internet is only constrained by the people who have access to it and make active use of it. The absence of earnings due to early-stage development of e-commerce made it imperative that surrogates are used for estimating a firm's potential earnings. This has resulted in e-commerce consultants and researchers using such indicators as web-based metrics (Hagel and Armstrong 1997; Bontis and Mill 2000; Demer and Lev 2000; Trueman, Wong and Zhang 2000a), "cash burn" rate (Demers and Lev 2000), research and development expenditure (Hand 1999; Amir and Lev 1996), revenue and expenses (Amir and Lev 1996; Bontis 2000; Demers and Lev 2000; Hand 1999; Trueman et al. 2000a). These "value-drivers" are fundamentally firm-specific indicators used to estimate and extrapolate its growth potential. This method of factor portfolios based on e-commerce sector-specific characteristics is consistent with the theoretical approach for factor selection mentioned in Section 2.8 above.

The popular web-based metrics are households with computers (customer base), Internet hosts (an often-cited indicator to measure the proliferation of e-commerce) and secure servers (an indicator used extensively by OECD to measure how wide the spread e-commerce is).

Aggressive research and development activity continues to be a defining characteristic for the success of a firm in the high technology industry. In the knowledge economy, as in most firms, the research and development (R&D) function is the source for the exploitation of the information revolution for e-commerce on the Internet. New virtual methods of creating products and services are replacing the traditional physical ways, at reduced costs and time taken for commercialisation of the new products. The Internet makes it possible for consumers to be linked to the firm's database and provides the mechanism for R&D feedback. The implications of R&D as a research tool and in promoting e-commerce development lie in the new ways in which businesses can be revolutionised on the Internet to enhance the value of the firm. A relatively higher level of R&D expenditure would produce greater expected benefits to the firm and economy.

While forecasting earnings is a fundamental approach to valuation of firms, the lack of historical earnings and rapid evolution of the e-commerce sector make firm-specific financial data limited in predictive quality. E-commerce is a new phenomenon in Australia and non-financial data such as that listed above does not have a long enough time series or is generally unavailable. Due to the relative infancy and high overseas reliance of the e-commerce sector in Australia, the valuation of firms in the sector may be best addressed through the use of factor analysis using macroeconomic variables that are deemed to be pervasive to e-commerce stock return for reasons explained above.

2.10 Other Financial Issues

The volatility and sources of volatility in the prices of corporate stocks have always intrigued researchers in finance as to whether the source of movements can be traced back, in a logical manner, to changes in economic fundamentals (Garber 1990; Chirinko 1993; Barro 1990; Blanchard 1993; Patelis 1997; Chen 1991; Schwert 1990; Fama 1990; Fama and French 1989). Empirical studies conducted that measure volatility (variance) of asset prices against simple market efficiency models include Leroy and Porter (1981), Shiller (1981a) and LeRoy and Parke (1992). Mandelbrot (1963) finds that market volatility is not constant over time and observes the "stylised fact" that market returns go through phases of high volatility for lengthy periods and for long periods show moderate patterns of volatility. Prices are instrumental in the efficient allocation of resources and guide economic activities. Persistent stock price movements that do not reflect changes in economic fundamentals will have implications for investors, corporate managers and regulators. The recent volatile movements in e-commerce stock prices may cause this class of asset to be under- or over-priced resulting in market inefficiency. This aspect of valuation will be explored in Chapter 6.

The predictability of return relates to what component of stock returns can be predicted given specific information and Shiller (1981a) shows evidence that the variability of stock price indices cannot be accounted for by information regarding dividend alone since dividends do not vary enough to justify the price movement. Fama and French (1988b), Flood, Hodrick and Kaplan (1986), and Poterba and Summers (1988) have shown that stock returns are more highly predictable when measured over periods of several years, rather than over shorter periods of a year or less. The condition of predictability in the financial markets is also relevant to other issues that are amenable to financial econometric analysis including market efficiency, portfolio choice selection, public policy formulation and the role of economic factors in the e-commerce sector.

2.11 Conclusion

This chapter has provided an account of the interplay between financial theory and practice. In the context of e-commerce stock valuation we highlight the limitations that mainstream financial models have in addressing the new economic phenomenon of e-commerce, where many firms in the sector are perceived to trade at market prices not supported by "intrinsic value". Though proxies and surrogates may be used in place of the normal financial information required in these models, this practice might not provide an ideal interpretation of the relevant market conditions thus rendering their results less convincing.

In this chapter, the various theories developed in the literature to help explain the asset pricing process in equity markets are discussed. The main models are the capital asset pricing model (CAPM), which asserts that beta is the only relevant factor that explains stock returns, and the arbitrage pricing theory (APT), which says that many factors, not just beta, are relevant in explaining asset return. While the CAPM is simple to use, the APT is considered a more superior model when the firm is sensitive to economic factors not well represented in the market index (Damodaran 1994). This logic augments the use of factor analysis in this research as the commercial development of e-commerce and the Internet generally is still very much in the early stages and the degree or magnitude of its pending success or failure is extremely sensitive to economic conjectures and interpretations. According to Damodaran (1994), the biggest intuitive block to the use of APT is its failure to specifically identify the factors driving expected returns. This makes it difficult to grasp the implications of the APT beta coefficients for the firm and how they change as the firm evolves, as would be the case with many e-commerce firms in such an innovative industry.

There is a high level of uncertainty and naivety surrounding the development of e-commerce and its impact on the market and global economies. This situation affects the behaviour of investors and, ultimately, market prices. The presence of uncertainty produces random fluctuations that require the use of statistical theory to estimate and test financial models that can intimately relate the uncertainty to normal market conditions (i.e. existing market models pricing of publicly traded stocks takes into account systematic risk only and unsystematic risk, firm- or industry-specific, is considered irrelevant and can be diversified away).

In addition to concentrating on developing a new e-commerce valuation model using the primary method of model-based statistical inference, the following chapters will test some of the existing models on e-commerce data to highlight some of the valuation issues and characteristics relating to e-commerce stocks in the context of financial theory in such areas as the EMH, returns, market volatility, predictability and portfolio selection.

CHAPTER 3

Multi-Factor Financial Econometric Model

3.1 Introduction

The objective of this chapter is to outline the limitations of the existing valuation practices or models in the context of e-commerce equities and propose a macro approach using market or economic indicators that take into consideration and reflect the idiosyncrasies, evolution and nascent development of the e-commerce sector as a market. For Australia, this approach is further justified by the lack of a significant database of financial performance necessary for microanalysis of e-commerce stock valuation. The chapter is structured to walk through the justifications for a new model, its process and related issues pertaining to the valuation of e-commerce stocks.

The methodology adopted in this research is one of real macro-economic variable analysis to overcome and address the difficulty of using firm-specific data due to the lack of a generally acceptable valuation approach for IP-intensive firms. It is a well-established finding that asset prices regularly react to fluctuations in macroeconomic variables (Fama 1981, 1990; Chen et al. 1986; Ferson and Harvey 1991, 1993). The approach adopted in this book is consistent with the fundamental financial proposition that market risk (systematic risk) explains why stocks have a tendency to move together and that the market only rewards investors for assuming market risk and therefore only beta matters for pricing.

The evaluation and measurement of a firm's total value or the price per share of its stock is one of the most interesting and challenging areas in finance, and according to Harrington (1987), the process of valuation is "vexingly difficult". The three parameters for determining value of a firm are:
1. The size of the expected returns;
2. The date that these returns will be received; and
3. The risk that the investor takes to obtain the returns.

The measure of risk (volatility) is the most difficult of the three parameters to estimate and incorporate into a valuation model and the most widely used valuation technique incorporating risk, is the portfolio valuation concept of the *capital pricing asset model* (CAPM). The risk factor is also addressed in the *discounted cash flow* (DCF) method using the discount rate as a measure of riskiness. Other models such as the *arbitrage pricing theory* (APT) suggest that there are many sources of risk that contribute to the returns of a stock or asset.

The positive market valuation of e-commerce firms, even when they have yet to earn a profit, suggests investors clearly expect the increasing economic importance of the e-commerce sector in generating revenue for these firms. The impetus of the high stock prices of e-commerce firms is a result of the market forecasting phenomenal growth in this sector and a robust business environment in the future. This condition is consistent with the high correlation between asset price fluctuations and business cycles in the industrialised world (IMF 2000). This should translate into strong earnings growth opportunities – but are these values too high? Though e-commerce firms have a number of advantages over traditional firms such as lower operating costs, the recent market consolidation[18] of e-commerce stocks indicates a reaction to market risks and conditions faced by this sector and investors are constantly studying to see how changing technology will end up transforming the market. The traditional approach of stock valuation is generally based on the recent earnings trend of the firm plus forecasts reflecting the economic prospects for the economy, industry and the firm. The valuation of e-commerce stocks based on current and likely future earnings performance poses a problem in that no past earnings or limited financial performance records are available for meaningful valuation and the process must therefore piece together information on forecasts of the overall economy and the conditions of the capital markets, to estimate or extrapolate a fair price. For many e-commerce firms, the emphasis is on long-term growth as opposed to current profitability.

Traditional asset pricing methodologies, such as those of Sharpe (1964), Lintner (1965b), Black (1972), Merton (1973), Ross (1976) and Breedan (1979) show that the expected return on a financial asset is a linear function of its betas or covariances with some systematic risk factors. The technique of factor analysis will be used to analyse data within the broader multivariate linear model developed in this research. In a linear model, the model may not give the best representation of the relationship between factors and variables and in cases where non-linear relationships are involved, no statistical analysis within the linear model will be adequate. Under such a condition, if a non-linear relationship is expected, then a variable might be transformed so that the relationship becomes linear.

3.2 Limitations of Current Models

The primary focus of corporate finance is the workings of the capital markets and the supply and pricing of capital assets and according to Brealey et al. (1999) 'it focuses on how companies invest in real assets and how they raise money to pay for these investments'. The basis of decision-making on investments are based on the valuation of both financial and real assets for 'today's capital investments decisions may determine the businesses that the firm is in 10, 20, or more years ahead' and a firm's success or failure depends in large part on its ability to find the capital it needs (Brealey 1999). In essence, the value of the firm is estimated from the present value of its earnings over all future periods and in order to manage a firm we need to value it. The central consideration of this postulate is the explicit recognition of the effects of all future periods (Chew 1997). The effects include investment decisions in

---

[18] April 2000 the market index dipped predominantly due to the fall of stocks in the e-commerce sector.

technology and industry and being inherently unpredictable the question arises as to whether the approaches adopted by market analysts in relation to e-commerce stock valuation are appropriate and reflect all future period effects.

The high and rising stock market valuations of Internet firms have come under much scrutiny recently with sceptics criticising that they do not make sense, either because the price to earning ratios (P/E) are too high or the firms do not have earnings to support them. The propositions by Fama (1995) and Lakonishok et al. (1994) in relation to value premium show firms with high book-to-market (B/M), earnings to price (E/P) or cash flow to price (C/P) value stocks, tend to have persistent low earnings. Firms with low B/M, E/P and C/P growth stocks, tend to have persistently high earnings. Lakonishok et el. (1994) argues that the market undervalues value stocks and overvalues growth stocks and when the market eventually corrects these pricing errors, the situation is reversed. Valuation of an e-commerce firm, as proposed by researchers at McKinsey (Desmet et al. 2000), should be based on other factors including customer relationship to customer-value analysis in relation to the virtual value chain (Rayport and Sviokla 1995).

The recent concerns (Fama and French 1992, 1993) raised about the validity of the CAPM based on the absence of historical relationship between stock returns and their market betas may render the CAPM a less effective model for valuing e-commerce stocks. Earlier concerns include the normative quality (what it should be and not what it is) and certain assumptions of the model also raised doubts about its effectiveness in measuring market reality. According to Mullins (1982) and Harrington (1987) other application problems of CAPM are:

- that betas estimated from historical data and used to calculate the expected returns are unstable through time and subject to statistical estimation errors;
- the return anomalies of the price-earnings-ratio (Basu 1977) and size effects (Banz 1981) make the CAPM a less appropriate model for general application;
- the theory provides no definitions of the risk-free rate of return (R_f) and market risk (R_m);
- the estimates of the risk-free rate and the expected return on the market are also subject to error; and
- the CAPM does not make distinctions among industry groups, which are known to have different betas, and adding industry factors could enhance CAPM's power.

Fama and French (1995) found two variables that are consistently related to stock returns, namely the firm's size and its market to book ratio. They established no relationship between a stock's beta and its return. The more general multi-beta models that encompass the CAPM and address its limitations are now more widely used as an alternative to the traditional CAPM. The CAPM is an *ex ante* model based on assumptions that the statistical process generating asset returns is stationary and that *ex post* rates of return are sample observations of the *ex ante* distributions These assumptions are necessary to make testing the CAPM possible. For the latter to be acceptable, the market must be information efficient where prices are generated by rational expectations. This position does not hold when the strong form of the EMH prevails and abnormal returns can be made from private information. The current evolutionary nature of e-commerce as a business medium tends to support the strong form of the EMH where relevant information may not be obvious to investors without intimate, clear and detailed knowledge of e-commerce potentials and therefore is not reflected in the stock price. Those investors with profound knowledge of and close involvement with e-commerce development are likely to have an information edge over the market and are thus able to earn abnormal returns from it. Under such circumstances, the use of the CAPM would render it inappropriate in the absence of an information efficient market.

The multi-beta models generalise the concept of risk under the traditional CAPM that market risk, risk that cannot be diversified away, underpins the pricing of assets. In the multi-beta model, market risk is measured using a series of risk factors that determine the behaviour of asset returns, whilst the CAPM measures risk only relative to market return. Empirical studies have identified several empirical systematic risk factors with relationship to security returns, including inflation, the bond term structure premium. The risk factors used in the multi-beta models are all non-diversifiable sources of risk.

The problems associated with using the CAPM in performance evaluation arise only with benchmarks based on equilibrium pricing models and those models that do not imply equilibrium, that is the absence of arbitrage possibilities, such as the Market Model, do not encounter these difficulties (Roll 1978; Peasnell, Skerratt and Taylor 1979; Appleyard, Strong and Walker 1982). The effects on the market valuation of an e-commerce business will have to depend on the state of various economic and market factors that decide the growth prospect for the firm.

The discounted cash flow models for stock valuation where future dividends are discounted at a constant rate poses two problems, the absence of earnings in the vast majority of e-commerce firms and the argument that stock prices are too volatile to be rational forecasts of future dividends discounted at a constant rate (Leroy and Porter 1981; Shiller 1981a). The absence of the earnings data required by and the limitations of traditional valuation models makes it imperative that proxies and alternative models be used to determine the value of stocks of many e-commerce firms. Since the value of common stocks reflects claims on future earnings, changes in real economic activity is likely to affect stock return (Schwert 1989). In the DCF model, changes in real economic activity are likely to cause expected cash flows, discount rates and growth forecasts to vary.

In this study, the multi-beta model is the preferred model for measuring e-commerce stock returns, whilst the CAPM will also be used to describe the market fundamentals and for comparison of results between the models. The multi-beta model will be used to test the firm's characteristics vis-à-vis market factors for the cross section of sample mean beyond the beta of the CAPM. The situation facing e-commerce stocks, as a reflection of the Internet as a business medium, is that it is still in a relatively early stage of development, untested, complex and not fully understood. The CAPM, with all its controversies, can offer a simple model that is easier to understand, test and use to abstract from the noisy complexity of the e-commerce stock scenario. It will be used to: describe what is occurring in regard to e-commerce stock volatility through analysis of the variability of past returns; also the findings will serve as the foundation for the forecast of the expected returns, and as a basis for constructing a more effective model.

The case with e-commerce stocks is such that in the absence of past earnings, the underlying principles of the DCF model suggest that an alternative valuation model capable of capturing the relevant variables of real economic activity could be a plausible proxy, as shown in Figure 3.1.

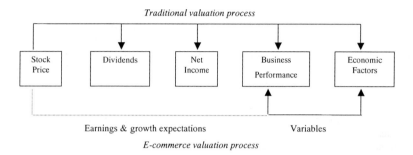

Figure 3.1 The Valuation Process

3.3 A Model for the E-Commerce Stock Market

From the above analyses (summarised in Section 3.2) it appears that there are theoretical limitations and insufficient empirical evidence for applying existing models to the valuation of e-commerce stocks. An appropriate model is proposed in this section.

A firm's market valuation reflects many aspects of its business such as its return on its assets, its market position, projected profitability and generally its overall performance. This market valuation would then reflect the firm's financial viability and could be used to raise funds. When firms assign any value to intangible assets in their financial reports they are normally reflected as goodwill (Ryan and Heazlewood 1995). When a firm's wealth is in its intellectual rather than physical assets, as is the case with most e-commerce firms, failing to report these intellectual assets means no recognition of their business potential. This creates the current market uncertainty and confusion in the valuation of e-commerce shares that could result in the inefficient allocation of capital.[19] The flexible nature of virtual business makes intellectual assets in an e-commerce firm difficult to value because it changes with investors' expectations, which are in turn influenced by and reflect the economic environment. One of the limitations of using the CAPM for e-commerce stock valuation is the CAPM assumption that all investors estimate risk and return according to the same, homogeneous expectations. Without a consensus, each investor could have different forecasts for variance and for mean return and the efficient portfolio for one investor could be quite different from that of another. As most e-commerce stocks do not yet declare dividends, it can be assumed that e-commerce

---

[19] The recent downturn, in April 2000, of hi-tech/e-commerce related stocks and the difficulty in raising capital for e-commerce start-ups are to a large extent due to the absence of generally accepted valuation techniques.

investors prefer capital gains to dividends, unlike those investors who prefer high-yield stocks to the high, longer-term potential e-commerce stocks. The varying preferences would result in investor-specific efficient frontiers instead of the single frontier of modern portfolio theory. Hence homogeneity may not be a realistic assumption, as a state of equilibrium relationship is not possible when investors have different sets of preferences for capital gains against dividends.

The nascent development, lack of historical earnings and the bullish expectations of the Internet as the preferred business medium have caused its volatility and therefore are major contributors to the difficulty of determining e-commerce stock price based on traditional corporate fundamentals. The recent price increases of e-commerce stocks that drove stock global markets to historically high levels in terms of price to earnings ratio have caused doubts among analysts about their fundamental justification.

The valuation process this research adopts to overcome this problem is to identify and test the key macroeconomic variables (factors) of real activity that have significant effect or impact on the market value of the e-commerce firms, and so influence their returns or prices. The reasons for taking the macro approach are three-fold. First is the sparsity of firm-specific data, second is the difficulty associated with measuring intellectual property which raises questions about consistency and accuracy of firm-specific data and finally, the strand of well-developed literature (Fama 1981, 1990; Chen et al. 1986; Ferson and Harvey 1991) which specifies a *priori* common real economic factors which may affect stock returns, and then investigate whether any such influence is significant. Therefore this study takes the approach to use macro-economic data for the following reasons:

(i)   The lack of a large pool of data on the Australian e-commerce sector;
(ii) The use of macroeconomic data may be more appropriate when there are still debates about how IP assets and IP-intensive firms should be valued (Dabek 1999) and see also Section 2.5.2 for write-up); and
(iii) The methodology adopted in this study is to use real macro-variables as proxies to test for value pervasiveness, which otherwise may be influenced by firm-specific characteristics, using a well-tested and generally accepted econometric model. The latest studies include Wongbanpo and Sharma (2002), which links stock market prices to macroeconomic fundamentals.

The approach is to quantify the impact of these variables on the tangible world in a predominantly intangible sector or industry. The key variables representing real activity or general business conditions and show high correlation with the e-commerce firms' market value, are selected and incorporated into the regression model to test for predictable variation of returns, *ex post*. This would enable the prediction of e-commerce stock prices based on movements in these factors. The level of stock returns that is unrelated to the selected variables would hence be represented by the regression residual (from estimating the regression line) and referred to as an abnormal return, consistent with the approach used in the Market Model. The proposed model for valuing e-commerce stocks thus involves two or more explanatory variables using the approach of multiple regression analysis and is depicted in the diagram below:

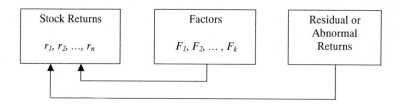

Figure 3.2 The Market Model

Studies of multi-stage real options on information technology infrastructure (Panayi and Trigeogis 1998) and real options generally (Amram and Kulatilaka 1999), may provide some leads or parallels to apply to Internet stock valuation. The Panayi study did show that options valuation could justify strategic investment decisions even if net present value (NPV) suggested otherwise.

3.4 A Linear Multi-Beta Model for Valuation of E-Commerce Stock

The advent of the virtual marketplace is a recent phenomenon and has brought with it a new business channel for which firms are still developing and evolving models to profitably exploit their opportunities. Similarly, pioneering attempts are being made to develop new and appropriate financial models (Desmet et al. 2000; Bontis and Mill 2000) for valuing e-commerce stocks. These first-generation valuation models are recent developments and are yet to be fully tested or generally accepted.

A regression model for Australia will be developed based on the multiple-factor modelling approach incorporating key or strategic variables (factors) and relevant elements of existing models (Desmet, Francis, Hu, Koller and Riedel 2000; Bontis and Mill 2000). The multi-period return regressions approach is chosen in this study because regression tests have proven that expected stock returns are time-varying rather than constant as assumed by the DCF model (Campbell et al. 1997). It is also a well-established finding that asset prices regularly react to fluctuations in macroeconomic variables (Fama 1981, 1990; Chen et al. 1986; Ferson and Harvey 1993).

In this paper, the linear multi-beta model is developed, using the method of ordinary least squares (OLS) for measuring e-commerce stock returns, whilst the CAPM will also be used to describe the market fundamentals and for comparison of results between the models. The CAPM proves that the relationship among prices of assets in a general equilibrium, where the investors select assets to maximise the mean-variance utility, is linear. Traditional asset pricing methodologies, such as those of Breeden (1979), Ross (1976), Black (1972), Lintner (1965b) and Sharpe (1964) show that the expected return on a financial asset is a linear function of its covariances with some systemic risk factors (e.g. CAPM). This approach is adopted in the development of the proposed model subject to statistical testing using Microsoft Excel software. The Australian model will be developed incorporating significant market variables and the multiple-factor model is selected for its ability to capture the essence of the fundamental economic and financial forces that affect security returns, in a concise and readily testable form. If there are k factors, a general representation of the multiple-factor model can be written as:

$$e\text{-}stockret_{it} = \alpha_i + (\beta_1)_i(F_1)_t + (\beta_2)_i(F_2)_t + \dots + (\beta_k)_i(F_k)_t + \varepsilon_{it}$$

where:
$e\text{-}stockret_{it}$ = the return of stock i in period t;
α_i = the expected value if each factor has a value of zero;
$(F_1)_t, (F_2)_t \dots (F_k)_t$ = the values of factors 1, 2 ... k with pervasive influence in period t;
$(\beta_1)_i$ & $(\beta_2)_i$ = sensitivities of stock i to the factors;
$(\beta_k)_i$ = the change in the return on stock i per change in factor k;
... = terms of the form $(\beta_k)_i(F_k)_t$ with k going from 3 to $k-1$ in period t; and
ε_{it} = random error term.

The purpose of the multifactor model estimate approach in this research is to capture the major market variables that systematically move the prices of all e-commerce stocks. Implicit in the construction of this model is the assumption that the values of two stocks will be correlated and move together only through common reactions to one or more of the factors specified in the model. This approach draws parallels from the time-series study conducted by Fama and French (1993), which identifies the factors that explain stock and bond returns.

Multifactor models became popular with the emergence of the arbitrage pricing theory (APT). The latter claims that if different stocks exhibit the same risk exposure to a common risk factor, then their returns must be consistent (Roll and Ross 1984). A main disadvantage of using this macroeconomic multifactor model, as opposed to the APT, is the errors associated with identifying the factors. The factors in a model change over time, as will the risk associated with each economic factor, and using the wrong factors or omitting a significant factor in a multifactor model can lead to an inferior estimation of e-commerce stock value or returns.

The specific model developed in this study is presented in Section 5.2 below (see page 97).

3.5 The Factors
E-commerce being an emerging industry in its nascent stage of development and would not be expected to have much in terms of supporting empirical evidence in relation to the range of factors to be tested and specified. This research adopts the theoretical approach to specifying factors. The variables used are based on empirical evidence from past studies done on equity markets, but not necessarily pertinent to e-commerce equity valuation (the latest research

along this strand of literature includes studies by Ferson and Harvey (1991), Kwon and Shin (1999); Fifield et al. (2002); Wongbangpo and Sharma (2002)). The variable factors to be analysed are classified into two categories of economic and capital market factors and the purpose is to identify the causality relation of these variables to e-commerce stock returns. The variable factors identified under each category are listed below and they will be tested within each e-commerce sector to determine the significance of their correlation to stock returns within each sector (time series) and across sectors (sectional analysis).

(1) Economic Factors

Economics variable	Regressor code
Industrial production	IP
Money supply (M1)	M1
Money supply (M3)	M3
Credit	CR
Exchange rate	FE
Capital imports	CI
Balance of payment	BOP
Education expenses	ED
Retail trade	RT
Consumer confidence (Westpac)	CC

(2) Capital Market Variables

Capital market variable	Regressor code
Market risk premium	MRP
Market capitalisation	MCAP
Yield spread	YS
Market return	MR
Risk-free rate	RF
SP/ASX 200	ASX

SP/ASX Banks	BKI
SP/ASX Industrial	IND.
Nasdaq	NAS
Dow Jones Industrial Average	DJ
Daily stock market turnover	MTURN
Dividend Yield	DIV
10-year Treasury bond rates	TB
3-month Treasury note rates	TN

This study selects macroeconomic and financial markets state variables closely related to e-commerce development. In addition, principal economic indicators such as GDP growth, money supply (*M1*) and industrial production are used as independent variables. Specifically, these categories are identified for their pervasiveness in influencing stock returns generally and e-commerce growth potential (thereby, cash flows).

The underlying theory of multi-factor models does not specify the number of factors that are required but the number should be reasonably small for the theory to be useful (Campbell et al. 1997). The approach used in this research is to repeat the estimation and test the model for various numbers of factors and observe the sensitivity of the tests to increasing number of factors (Lehmann and Modest 1988). Theoretically, the number of factors that is included in a model need not be more than five (Lehmann and Modest 1988; Connor and Korajczyk 1988; Fama and French 1993), and this research will work within this framework. The model assumes no hierarchical structure for the factors hence no orthogonalisation is done.

3.5.1 Capital Market Factors

As an important aspect of the development of the new economy, the capital market factors, especially those related to the equity funding activities, are crucial to the determination of e-commerce stock value and need to be analysed for correlation to stock returns. Roll (1977) and Roll and Ross (1994) studies indicated that stock returns were related to both the riskless rate and the market return. Others have suggested that stock returns over time were a function of returns on industry indexes such as the equity and bond indexes (Sharpe 1970; Sharpe et al. 1995).

The capital market factors identified for their pervasiveness to e-commerce market value and the rationale for their inclusion in the factor selection process of this research are as follows.

Market Risk Premium (*MRP*)

The era of financial innovations and new institutional arrangements in the Australian financial sector since deregulation in the 1990s has changed investor perception of risk. In the USA, studies have found the market risk premium required by investors on the stock market has declined significantly since the early eighties (Woolridge 1995; Blanchard 1993).

The view of risk derived from the extensive work in portfolio theory and capital market theory by Markowitz (1952) and Sharpe (1964, 1970) is that investors should use an external market measure of risk. It has been shown in the discussions on the "efficient frontier" of portfolio investment in Section 2.5.3 above that, all rational (risk-averse), profit maximising investors want to hold a completely diversified market portfolio of risky assets, and they borrow or lend to arrive at the desired risk level. The standard deviation of a portfolio is expected to eventually reach the level of the market portfolio, which means that all unsystematic risk has been eliminated and the only risk left in the portfolio is market risk or systematic risk, which is due to macroeconomic factors that cannot be eliminated. Consequently, the relevant risk measure for an individual stock is its co-movement or covariance with the market portfolio. This covariance is referred to as the stock's systematic risk and is the portion of the individual stock's total variance attributable to the variability of the total market portfolio. The relationships between e-commerce stock returns and the prevalent market risk premium in this research would help to highlight their volatility to fluctuations in the market risk premium and explain the risk premium for an e-commerce stock's return as a function of its systematic risk with the aggregate market portfolio of risky securities:

$$\text{E-stock risk premium} = f \text{ (systematic market risk)}$$

The *MRP* is calculated on a monthly basis for the study period by deducting the 3-month Treasury Note Yield from the annualised market returns (Appendix 2.2).

Market Capitalisation (*MCAP*)

Market capitalisation represents the total market value of listed domestic equities calculated at end-month for all equities listed on the Australian Stock Exchange main board, including preference shares and excluding overseas domiciled stocks compiled by the Reserve Bank of Australia (RBA) (Appendix 2.1). In the 1990s, many Australian companies increased their debt-equity ratios as a result of the more sophisticated and deregulated financial markets. There was increased activity in purchases of stocks by more established corporations in other companies, especially in information technology start-up businesses. The high demand for these stocks also made it easy for these corportions to raise large amounts of low-cost capital to finance e-commerce growth through mergers and acquisitions and as a result many start-up information technology companies have high-profile corporate shareholders that are able to offer powerful synergy in terms of finance and business growth. This situation perpetuates the valuation of information technology companies as they can use their high-value stocks to acquire reasonably priced companies.[20]

Siglienti et al. (1999) in his research suggested that e-commerce stock prices are better explained by supply and demand[21] than by long-term value. The increase in acquisition activity by corporations could be an explanatory variable to the high valuation of e-commerce stocks and the situation is compounded by the relative scarcity of this class of equity and competition from institutional investors. The important market indicator of equity value has not been completely ignored as its inherent qualities were captured in the use of market capitalisation as a variable, consistent with the methodology adopted in this research of one that focused on macro-economic variables as an alternative to firm-specific variables.

Managed Equity Funds (*MF*)
The recent evolution and proliferation of unit investment trusts and managed investment fund companies in Australia, have allowed investors a wider choice and more avenues to invest in the stock market with better risk management. These financial innovations help to reduce transaction costs and promote greater opportunities for portfolio diversification, thus lowering the market risk premium required by investors. These funds are not directly connected to financing real activities but trade in the financial sphere of the economy. The proliferation of managed funds has given retail investors more equity investment options and confidence, resulting in significant increases in stock market participation in recent years.

Australia used to have only about a million individual shareholders but in recent years, there have been several big initial public offers (IPO) to privatise government owned organisations such as Telstra. These floats have sharply increased the number of shareholders in Australia but the values of individual shareholders are still relatively smaller than the value of institutional shareholdings. There are some very large institutional shareholders such as AMP, National Mutual, Bankers Trust and the like, no one institution dominates the share market. This market situation promotes competition and helps to minimise the mispricing of shares, hence creating a fair value for those shares that are actively traded, as are the e-commerce shares. The levels of managed funds and their consistent superior performance[22] of beating the S&P/ASX 200's market returns would be a key factor in determining the value of these e-commerce shares as more investors enter the market.

Yield Spread (*YS*)
The yield spread represented by the return on long-term government bonds less return on 30-day Treasury bills has been identified by Elton, Gruber and Mei (1994) to have pervasive influence on market return. In this study, the yield spreads are calculated from the midpoints of the yields of predominant bid and offer quotations in each market as identified by the RBA. The monthly figures are the estimated yield at the close of business for the last business day of the month (Appendix 2.2).

---

[20] America On Line (AOL) – Time Warner merger, January 2000.
[21] See also Hand, J., forthcoming, 'The Role of Economic Fundamentals, Web traffic and Supply and Demand on the pricing of U.S. Internet Stocks', *European Finance Journal*.
[22] "Funds Defy Market as Returns Reach 32%", *The Age* Business Section, 23 October 2000.

Market Return (*MR*)
The typical investor in the market owns more than a few stocks and it would be onerous for him or her to follow each individual stock in order to determine the composite performance of the portfolio. There is an intuitive notion that most individual stocks move with the aggregate market (Reilly 1989). Thus if the overall market increased in value as measured by stock market indicator series, an individual's portfolio would also probably increase in value. The total market returns over a specified time period has traditionally been used as a benchmark to measure the performance of individual portfolios, and a basic assumption in finance is that an investor should be able to get a rate of return at least equal to the market return by randomly selecting a large number of stocks from the total market. The index as a proxy for the market portfolio used in estimating the market return is normally the key market index, such as the S&P/ASX 200.

Risk-free Rate (*RF*)
A traditional benchmark for measuring historical stock values is to use the price-earnings (P/E) ratio. As discussed in Chapter 2, P/E ratios are a function of the risk-free interest rate, the risk premium, and the expectations on earnings growth. Lower interest rates would lead to faster earnings growth due to reduced debt servicing expenditure and a lower discount factor for risk adjustment. An investor's nominal required rate of return on risk-free investment factors reflects changes in the price level or inflation. The inflation rate looks at the year-on-year growth rate of the general price level. In Australia and the US, almost all of the inflation rates were positive since World War II (Barro 1993). Elton, Gruber and Mei (1994) studied the change in forecasts of inflation and found they have a pervasive influence on cash flows and hence, stock value. Mascaro and Meltzer (1983), and Lauterbach (1989) argue that macroeconomic volatility is related to interest rates. As the risk free rate forms the basis for setting other general market interest rates, its movements would influence macroeconomic factors and subsequently affect aggregate stock market volatility.

S&P/ASX 200 (*ASX*)
The notion of the new economy is closely tied to the effects of technological progress, particularly the ICT that brings about stronger growth in the economy. It supposes a pervasive role for the application of ICT across wide sectors in the economy enabling and encouraging firms and individuals to make stronger use of the ICT network aspects. The stronger economic growth associated with the use of ICT is generated largely by better productivity or higher real GDP per capita. The full benefits of ICT use is only possible when firms, industries and markets make comprehensive structural changes to take advantage of higher productivity gains in the new economy. The nascent nature of the new economy requires a broad measure for the pervasiveness of ICT in the market: as most firms are only beginning to go through profound reorganisations to take advantage of the benefits. The S&P/ASX 200 index is a general market measure that reflects general market conditions vis-à-vis a specific firm's position in relation to ICT for e-commerce use. Using the S&P/ASX 200 also helps to alleviate the problems associated with measuring marginal gains in output and productivity from ICT, as both these factors would be reflected in the general market price index.
Interpreting and predicting the future trends of ICT and their impact on the performance of the firm is difficult when the recent past is yet to be fully appreciated. If we are to consider the efficient market hypothesis and the DCF method of stock valuation as appropriate for

measuring ICT pervasiveness in stock value, then, the current market price level must reflect the future earnings prospects of all firms in the market incorporating the benefits from ICT in e-commerce.

Companies listed on the ASX are divided into two broad sectors: Resources (16%) and Industrial (84%). This division reflects the Australian economy. The S&P/ASX 200 index is used in this research as the proxy for calculating market return. In accordance with RBA publications, all figures from April 2000 refer to the S&P/ASX 200 figures and prior to that, the All Ordinaries Index is used.

S&P/ASX Banks (*BKI*)

The growth and financial performance of the banking sector is closely tied to the effects of the technological progress associated with ICT, as the banking sector is in the forefront of ICT utilisation in their activities. The Internet has dramatically transformed commercial banking providing it with a whole host of new opportunities and increasingly, businesses and individuals are using the Internet for banking transactions. In Australia, virtually every leading bank has an Internet presence. On the Internet, customers can see their balances, transfer money, and research the bank's products. The market value of the banking sector represented by its index provides a good indication of the growth opportunities from embracing e-commerce and reflects the general trend of e-commerce adoption in the market.

S&P/ASX Industrial (*IND*)

This is a sector specific index of the Australian Stock Exchange and is representative of the broad industrial sector of the Australian economy.

NASDAQ Composite Index (*NAS*)

The NASDAQ composite index measures the market value of all U.S. domestic and foreign common stocks listed on the NASDAQ Stock Market. Price changes in each security affect a rise or fall in the index, in proportion to the security's market value. The composite includes the securities of more than 5,300 companies, which makes it the biggest single stock market in the world and is the fastest growing U.S. stock market (*Business Review Weekly* 16/7/99). The common stocks listed on the NASDAQ are part of one of eight industry specific sectors, each with its own index. The sectors are banking, biotechnology, computers, finance, industrial, insurance, telecommunications and transportations. The NASDAQ is the most successful financing source for the operations of U.S. high-tech small-capitalised stocks. Major Internet-based companies like Intel, Microsoft and MCI are listed on the NASDAQ and because companies prefer to go where their competitors are listed, it has been attracting more new economy companies. As a result of the recent growth in market capitalisation of the key technology and Internet stocks, NASDAQ now has many major and mid-capitalised stocks and its turnover volume has increased dramatically. Its movements have since become a main business barometer for the technology sector in the global equity market.

Dow Jones Industrial Average (*DJ*)

The Dow Jones Industrial Average is the best-known equity market price series consisting of 30 large, well known industrial stocks that are generally leaders in their industry (blue chips). The Dow Jones series is a priced-weighted average of the 30 stocks and consequently, a high-priced stock carries more weight than a low-priced stock (Reilly 1989). The Internet/technology-related stocks in the Dow Jones index are AT&T Corp., Honeywell International, Hewlett-Packard Co., IBM, Intel, Microsoft, SBC Communications and United Technologies Corp. These companies are leaders in the technology business and with their recent growth in market capitalisation, they would have a major influence on the movements of the index. Like the NASDAQ, investors and analysts look towards the movements of the Dow Jones Industrial Average for cues to the market performance of technology-based equities.

Stock Average Daily Turnover (*MTURN*)

The daily average turnover of equities in this study is the value of monthly equities turnover on the Australian Stock Exchange main board, divided by the number of trading days. As stock return volatility affects the underlying value of the securities, the relation between stock volatility and trading volume would shed light on return behaviour. There are three theories that predict a positive relation between volatility and volume (Schwert 1989). First, new information will cause both price and trading changes if investors have heterogeneous belief. Second, if price movements are the basis of stock trading decisions then large price movements will result in large trading volume. Third, in the case of illiquidity causing short-term price pressure in secondary trading markets, large trading volume will cause price movements.

Dividend Yield (*DIV*)

The hypothesis that dividend yields (Dividend/Price) forecast stock return is well documented (Dow 1920; Ball 1978) and evidence that dividends yields predict stock returns is in Rozeff (1984), Shiller (1984) and Fama and French (1988b). It often happens that when stock prices are low in relation to dividends, discount rates and expected returns are high and vice versa. In the context of e-commerce firms, where a majority are yet to make dividend payments, the positive stock price could be explained by the expectation of future returns (dividends plus high earnings growth) and low discount rates due to reduced risk aversion of investors. In using dividend yields as a variable in our analysis, the intention is to test the relation between e-commerce stock return and the variation in dividend yields of the general market. The definition of dividend is the end of the month Share Price Index-linked dividend yield (RBA). This important market indicator of equity return and therefore value is captured as a proxy variable of earnings, and together with market capitalisation they provide the ideal surrogate for the price-to-earnings ratio, consistent with the methodology adopted in this research of one that focused on macro-economic variables as an alternative to firm-specific variables.

Price/Earnings Ratio (*PE*)

The price to earnings (P/E) ratio shows how much investors are willing to pay per dollar of reported earnings. Basu (1977) finds that the market portfolio appears not to be mean-variance efficient when portfolios are formed on the basis of the price-earnings ratio of firms. In the study, firms with low P/Es have higher sample returns and firms with low P/Es have lower mean returns than that suggested by an efficient mean-variance market portfolio. Banz's (1981) study shows that low market capitalisation firms tend to have higher sample mean returns than that expected with a mean-variance efficient market portfolio. These findings contradict the concept of beta in the Sharpe-Lintner version of CAPM.

The P/E as a variable is not considered important to e-commerce stocks because the vast majority of these stocks have yet to have positive earnings though still command relative high market prices.

Market-to-Book Ratio
The market-to-book ratio is the ration of stock price to book value. The inherent difficulty of measuring intellectual property is the reason for not using the M/B ratio because the 'assets' (i.e. as reflected in book value) of e-commerce firms consist of predominantly intellectual property intensive assets such as patents and business models, which are not normally reflected on the balance sheet. The book value of an e-commerce firm therefore may not necessarily reflect the true intrinsic value of the firm and using this ratio may create an undervaluation bias of the e-commerce firms.

Fama and French (1992) found that book-to-market, market capitalisation and price earnings (P/E) ratios exerted considerable influence on US stock prices, the relationship disappeared once these factors were included in a cross-sectional model. It may therefore be prudent to omit this variable based on empirical evidence.

3.5.2 Economic Factors

Standard valuation models and the theory behind these models have certain implications that are empirically observable. If e-commerce stocks reflect economic fundamentals it would be justified to expect a close relation to future real activity. The effectiveness of government policy in managing and promoting economic growth, in this case by stimulating "new economy" industries, is an important consideration for investors whose confidence will affect the level of investments in the economy. The recent decline of the Australian dollar is a consequence of the old economy syndrome affecting Australia and the lack of initiatives by the government to advance the high-tech sector. The following economic indicators are considered relevant and pervasive to the determination of e-commerce market value.

Gross National Product (*GNP*)
Gross national product (*GNP*) measures the total output of goods and services of an economy. The GNP is the aggregate of consumer expenditures, investment (purchase of new capital goods), government purchases of goods and services, and net exports. Lee (1992), Barro (1990), Fama (1990) and Schwert (1990) found that aggregate annual stock return variations could be explained by future values of measures of aggregate real activity, such as GNP, in the United States. This result was later confirmed by studies conducted in other industrial countries using changes in stock prices instead of returns (Peiro 1996). Elton, Gruber and Mei (1994) identified that a change in forecasts of real GNP affects the cash flows or the rate (k) at which they are discounted.

The basis of the relation between stock returns and future economic growth rates of real activity is evident in the standard valuation models where the stock price of a firm equals the expected present value of the firm's future dividend payouts. These expectations are construed to reflect the fundamental economic factors and must, therefore, ultimately reflect real economic activity as measured by gross domestic production (GDP). Under these conditions, Morck, Shleifer and Vishy (1990) suggested that the stock market is a passive informant of future real activity as it reacts immediately to new information about future economic activity well before it occurs. These circumstances tend to intimately reflect the behaviour of investors in relation to e-commerce stocks where expected future real economic activity emanating from the use of the Internet in business, is being used to price these stocks in the absence of current or historical earnings. Coppel (2000) suggested that economic growth could rise with the proliferation of e-commerce transactions since they promote efficiency and subsequently productivity. The results of Fama (1990) show that stock returns are actually significant in explaining future real activity and monthly, quarterly and annual stock returns are highly correlated with future production growth rates. The study found that regressions done on past stock returns are significant in explaining current production growth rates and, conversely, future production growth rates are significant in explaining current stock returns. Schwert (1990) extended and confirmed Fama's study and found the correlations between future production growth rates and current stock returns to be robust in the extended period covered. Fama (1981, 1990) found that a longer length of time for which returns are calculated gives a higher degree of correlation between stock returns and future production growth rates. This is explained by the fact that not all information about future production becomes publicly known over a short time period but does over a longer time period as production activities actually take place.

The use of monthly data in this research will give a less detailed picture of the relationship between returns and production growth rates than if quarterly or annual data were to be used. However, this approach may be more appropriate for the e-commerce sector due to the rapidly evolving nature of Internet technology and the new economy and thereby provide a fair estimate of e-commerce stock returns.

Industrial Production (*IP*)

The industrial production index (*IP*) measures the change in output in manufacturing, mining, and electric and gas utilities. Output refers to the physical quantity of items unlike sales value that combines quantity and price. The index covers the production of goods and services for domestic sale and export. It excludes production in the agriculture, construction, transportation, communications, trade, financial service industries, government output and imports. The data for IP used in this study is from the OECD (Paris) database. Chen, Roll and Ross (1986) suggest that industrial production is one of the economic variables that is highly correlated with those factors derived from factor analysis.

Money Supply (*M1*)

Contrary to the assumption of equilibrium in the CAPM, in real economies, transactions take place sequentially and buyers and sellers cannot expect to exchange goods and assets such that the value of sales (realised returns) equals the value of purchases (expected rate of returns) (i.e. frictionless) for any two traders. Hence, trade of goods and assets is not pre-co-ordinated by a general equilibrium price system but by some form of obligation or credit or traders will settle the credit position by accepting some means of payment, such as money (medium of exchange). By depositing their money for a fee with a bank that agrees to hold it and pay it out on the depositor's instruction, the depositor has the liquidity of holding the medium of exchange without actually having to carry it. The bank can invest some of these funds to achieve a return that can be paid back as interest to the depositors. By investing the excess funds, the bank reduces the opportunity cost of holding money, and increases the overall level of investment in the economy.

The most popular definition of money, *M1*, serves to classify together the assets that serve commonly as a medium of exchange. *M1* is therefore the sum of currency held by the public and cheque deposits. In Australia and most countries today, cheque deposits account for the bulk of *M1*, for example the cheque deposits in Australia in were 69% of M1 in 1990. Money serves as a temporary abode of purchasing power and people can reduce their average holdings of cash only by incurring more costs.

There is a broader consensus recently that the availability of money (finance) influences the course of investment. Many investors face a finance constraint and this situation can only be relaxed by credit from banks and other financial institutions (Mayer 1994). Australia, with its well established and recent rapid growth of the financial sectors, offers the environment for the greater flow of funds for trading financial assets, including equity securities. In relation to secondary equity financing, these funds are made available to financial institutions like managed funds, individual investors and firms through margin lending for investment in stocks. This liquidity position is further enhanced by a corresponding growth of the real economy and a decreasing inflation rate (RBA).

The liquidity of the capital markets also indicates the flow of money into new e-commerce companies as equity. Sahlman (1999) suggests that the more money flows into the companies of the new economy, the better the new economy model works in reducing inefficiency and inflation, and as new economy companies grow stronger they put competitive pressure on existing players to bring prices and costs down.

An important implication of the growth of the digital economy is the means of payment for purchases of goods and services over the Internet. The typical means of payment will be some form of electronic cash and most money in the world economy has been digital for some time, transferred electronically from bank to bank, and computer to computer. By contrast, only a small proportion of the trillions in currencies circulating around the globe each day is actually in tangible form. Electronic money such as the smart card and digital cash has facilitated consumer spending and contributed to an increase in monetary aggregates and national income and wealth. Some electronic currencies exist independently with no backing by real money and are not dominated in units issued by a central bank (Tapscott, Lowy and Ticoll 1998). The problem becomes the difficulty to define and measure the domestic money supply.

The Reserve Bank of Australia (RBA) (www.rba.gov.au) defines the data for M1 used in this study as currency plus bank current deposits of the private non-bank sector.

Money Supply (*M3*)

M3 is a broader monetary aggregate that includes different types of financial assets and typically encompassing time deposits in excess of $100,000 and foreign currency accounts. The Reserve Bank of Australia defines *M3* as *M1* plus all other bank deposits of the private non-bank sector. In this research, the *M3* is used to represent a broader measure of money supply in the market, for the same reasons as *M1*, and to guage the level of liquidity in the market.

Credit (*CR*)
The globalisation of financial markets has facilitated capital flows between countries. This increasing capital mobility means that excess liquidity in one financial market can have an impact on the conditions in another local equity market. Recent study by Baks and Kramer (1999) suggests a relationship between liquidity and asset returns. Interest rates determine the cost of borrowing, the return to lending and reflect the level of liquidity in the market. A higher interest rate reduces the demand for money and the average growth rate of real money balances will be lower for countries in which the interest rate has increased, and vice versa for industrialised countries (Barro 1993). The neoclassical investment theory of Keynesian macroeconomics and Jorgenson (1971) regards the interest rate as a key variable to the explanation of investment. Real saving is the key variable determining investment and the level of real capital for investment can only be financed by a corresponding decrease in current consumption. Lucas (1972) promoted the macroeconomic theory of the rational expectations hypothesis that only misperceived or unanticipated monetary shocks can influence the real economy, as economic agents are able to predict (or anticipate) all other actions by the reserve bank. This theory was presented in the context of a frictionless model and its relevance to this study will depend on the importance of market frictions in the e-commerce stock sectors.

As the cost of capital, the interest rate is supposed to equal the marginal productivity of capital in equilibrium, which is achieved when all firms maximise their profits in competitive markets. This cost in equilibrium also reflects all necessary information allowing stock investors to choose an inter-temporally optimal investment path. Investment decisions are made on the basis of their profit expectations in an uncertain world and these profit expectations are the main determinants of investment. Expected profits (return *R*) are compared to the interest rate (discount factor *k*) to determine whether an investment is viable or not. Consequently, the expectations of changing interest rates may also have a large influence on stock prices. Chen, Roll and Ross (1986) argue that in selecting factors as proxies, consideration should be given to forces which will explain changes in the discount rate used to discount future cash flows and also to forces which influence cash flows themselves.

The credit aggregates used in this study are obtained from the RBA and include loans and advances by financial intermediaries plus total bank bills outstanding.

Interest Rates (see risk free rate above)
Peiro (1996), Fama (1990) and Barro (1990) find that stock returns may also be affected by interest rates. A decrease in interest rate, corresponding to the rate (k) used to discount future cash flows in valuation models of the stock market, can result in an increase in stock price (as well as production). Elton, Gruber and Mei (1994) found changes in Treasury bill returns affect the cash flows of the utilities they studied and the discount rate.

During the period 1997-2000, the interest rates in Australia were low and this has led to the decline in the discount factors, which investors use to discount expected cash flows in their stock market valuation models. The low discount rates are also a reflection of investors' confidence in the financial markets and consequently, they require a lower risk premium.

The level of capital expenditure on communication infrastructure and Internet application software development is likely to influence the future expansion of the Internet, and the extent to which the economy invests in network capacity is also likely to affect e-commerce transactions. Capital market activities are largely driven by interest rates and the levels of funds that flow into an industry sector, like e-commerce, reflect its investment growth. The Australian public capital markets have been receptive of new e-commerce equity issues as seen from the subscription rates of recent initial public offers. As in the US, for Australia the real threat to the economy may not be growth but the government putting an artificial stop to it by raising interest rates (Sahlman 1999).

Foreign Exchange Rate – US$ to AUS$ (*FE*)
As each country issues and uses its own currency, the exchange rate is used to convert the currency of one country into that of another for purposes of trade. Elton, Gruber and Mei (1994) found change in the value of the dollar relative to a basket of currencies to affect the cash flows of a firm. Since the early 1970s, after the U.S. raised the dollar price of gold to curb flows of gold out of the U.S. effectively ending the Bretton Woods System, many countries have allowed their currencies to float freely to clear the market for foreign exchange. The level of the exchange rate for a country is influenced by its balance of trade (current account balance), inflation (purchasing power parity) and ultimately the demand for the currency (Barro 1993).

The decline of the Australian dollar in October 2000 has largely been attributed to the strength of the U.S. economy and the flows of international capital to that country. An underlying rationale for the strength of the U.S. economy has been its relentless transformation to the new economy. On the contrary, Australia is still considered very much an old economy relying on its natural resources to drive growth.

Capital Imports/Productivity (*CI*)
The real business cycle model promoted by Kydland and Prescott (1982) states that nominal monetary shocks are quantitatively trivial and not necessary to explain the behaviour of the real economy. They proposed that the macro-economy is driven by exogeneous technology shocks that cause changes in productivity and are a factor in economic development. The prospect that e-commerce transactions will grow to dominate the economy is generating hype that, at the aggregate level, productivity will rise as a result of more efficient management of supply and distribution, lower transaction costs, low barriers to entry and improved access to information (Coppel 2000; OECD 2000a). Australia's technology consumption in the information technology and communication sector is predominantly through imports of high-tech equipment and technology transfers from countries in North America and Europe. The level of capital imports into Australia might suggest an intensity of technological development and growth in the economy that would invariably drive e-commerce stock value.

Balance of Payment (*BOP*)
The balance of payment statistics summarise all the economic transactions between residents of the home country and those of other countries. These transactions include trade in goods and services, transfer payments, loans and investment, both long- and short-term. The balance of payment reflects the net flow of goods and services and its performance affects the value of the home currency whether it is more or less favourable than expected. The relevant components of the balance of payment for e-commerce evaluation are the current account and capital account which measure the flows of goods and services and public and private investments and lending activities, all of which are important and related to development of the e-coommerce sector.

Education Expense (*ED*)
Soete (1997) suggests that information and communication technology investments are complementary with investment in human resources and skills. In the new economy or the knowledge-based economy, it is the production of innovative ideas, not goods, that is the source of economic growth. New educational policies need to be formulated to emphasise the role of information technology and entrepreneurship in the new economic framework. This can only be achieved through higher government expenditure to provide broad-base formal education on the role and importance of innovation systems, the requirement for infrastructure, as well as incentives that encourage investments in research and training to support the networks which can efficiently distribute knowledge and information (OECD 1996). In the US, the system of higher education has traditionally worked well to create and diffuse knowledge and to spawn a community of sophisticated engineers, entrepreneurs and managers. Yet a shortage of the technologically educated workforce exists and the shortage is likely to be compounded with the ever-increasing technological demands for talent (same case as Australia). The success of the new economy rests on major public investments in science and technical education, and on the broad improvement of the nation's primary and secondary school systems (Cohen, DeLong, and Zysman 2000). In Australia, the knowledge-based firm is altering the internal structure of organizations and placing new emphasis on continuous innovation and organisational learning which shifts the focus to the development of human capital and in turn places new demands on the education systems to train people with the necessary skills and competencies (Houghton and Sheehan 2000).

According to a recent survey of 6,000 employers in Australia, almost half are forced to employ information technology personnel from overseas because of a shortage locally.[23] Australian Government education expenditure may provide a lead as to whether investors perceive education spending as an important factor in e-commerce development and if so, whether the level is sufficient to ultimately influence the value and growth of those e-commerce firms.

Retail Trade (*RT*)
Retail trade represents the level of consumer spending in an economy. The level of retail consumption indirectly indicates the underlying fundamentals of the economy such as interest rates, consumer confidence and generally, real activities. The lack of monthly sales figures for electronic business-to-business (B2B) and business-to-consumer (B2C) transactions

---

[23] *The Australian*, 1/11/00, "IT Boom But No One Is Home".

necessitates the use of retail trade data as a proxy for these two major indicators of e-commerce business intensity. Retail expenditure, as reflected in retail trade, ultimately drives all business transactions whether it is from the traditional or electronic retail sectors of the customer value chain. Using this data to estimate the correlation between e-commerce stock value and e-commerce transaction levels would therefore be considered as parsimonious and appropriate under the circumstances. The explanatory/pervasive power of sales/revenue vis-à-vis the value of a firm in this research can be construed as being reflected in this real variable 'Retail Trade' to be used in the study.

Consumer Confidence (*CC*)
Consumer confidence contributes to the performance of the economy by increased spending which leads to better cash flows for the firm and subsequently higher investments. The persistence among consumers of confidence in an economy contributes to positive effects on the stock market, inclusive of e-commerce stocks.

3.6 Relationship between Economic Factors and Financial Markets

The implications of the EMH in e-commerce stocks relate to the efficient allocation of capital in that under the EMH market financing conditions, the firm's cost of capital is optimal. It follows that if markets are efficient there is no need to defer projects or for government intervention. The measure of volatility of the e-commerce stocks vis-à-vis other market benchmarks and statistical analysis is crucial as a further test of market efficiency for the allocation of financial resources. If the e-commerce prices do not reflect market fundamentals then resources will be misallocated and hence, volatility tests are joint test for informational efficiency. The predictability of e-commerce stock returns depends on the statistical analysis of the random walk hypothesis of the stock prices. If e-commerce stock prices were unpredictable, such tests would support the rational expectation element of the EMH that forecast errors should be zero on average and uncorrelated with any information available at the time the forecast was made. The EMH emphasises that it is impossible for investors to persistently make supernormal profits.

It is also argued that in the mainstream financial economics discipline it is possible to develop stock market models based on the EMH that assess the predictability and volatility path of stock prices and returns (Cuthbertson 1997). The financial econometric model developed in this study can also be applied to the analysis of financial market issues such as market efficiency, volatility, predictability and portfolio choice.

3.7 Conclusion

The ideal and ultimate stock valuation model is one that describes and represents the entire return-generating process. The lack of firm-specific financial performance indicators necessitates the use of an alternative approach to value the e-commerce firm. The Internet, through e-commerce, is causing a change in the fundamental structure of the traditional market as an avenue for business transactions. This structural change is pervasive and has fundamental economic and market implications, which need to be recognised and addressed using the appropriate analytical tools. In recognition of the fundamental economic evolution or revolution created by the Internet, this study adopts the multifactor modelling approach for e-commerce stock valuation through incorporating economic and financial/capital market variables that are sensitive to e-commerce stock valuation. A sample set of historical stock prices provides only a subset of all possible price outcomes in the market and is subject to estimation error or noise. Of all the possible relationships between economic variables and e-commerce stock prices, the key variables such as interest rates, productivity, GDP growth, market returns, e-commerce advertisement revenue, Internet hosts, secure servers, e-commerce market capitalisation and IT R&D expenditure are deemed as the factors most likely to have a pervasive influence on e-commerce stock value.

CHAPTER 4

Methodology and Financial Econometric Methods

4.1 Introduction

This chapter provides an overview of the methods and models, observations, design and procedures of this study. The broad methodology adopted in this study is as follows:

1. To identify and estimate factors that are most likely to pervade e-commerce stock value, and analyse the relation between e-commerce stock prices/returns and these factors.

2. To estimate the model by the standard multi-variate least squares methods using sample data for the Australian e-commerce sector (details of which are discussed below).

3. To develop a factor model for e-commerce stock returns and test the predictability of stock returns using the combined explanatory power of the factors (the results and findings are presented in Chapter 5).

4. To put the recent e-commerce stock price volatility and return into perspective by comparing their stock prices to various market measures, such as the S&P/ASX 200 index. This analysis will study the related issues of the volatility of e-commerce stock prices vis-a-vis returns and predictability against the general market and between sectors (see Chapter 6).

5. To analyse the risk implications of e-commerce stocks as applied to asset allocation in two and three-asset class portfolios, and in a mean-variance context of selecting a portfolio of common stocks (see Chapter 7).

The estimate of expected returns uses historical market data for individual firms, and is done from a portfolio perspective to determine the degree of volatility of these stocks to the market (Chapter 5). The estimate of returns and expectations about how market change will impact on these estimates is then analysed in Chapter 6, using a top-down approach starting at the market level and attempting to identify the movements in the market over the study horizon. The variables representing market movements are the real and financial factors such as interest rates, inflation, market indices and liquidity and is consistent with the framework of research done by Fama and French and others. The statistical methodology (analysing the connections between real and financial variables vis-à-vis e-commerce stock returns in this case) is to use fewer, but carefully selected, explanatory variables, in contrast with the traditional econometric approach, which uses numerous variables. Finally, the success of selecting shares for investment purposes is dependent on a range of forecasts and the increase in wealth of an equity portfolio is determined by the growth in share prices and the dividend return. In the context of selecting equity stocks, the investor must make a determination of the intrinsic value of the stocks relative to its current market value. The process of determining the intrinsic value and stock selection will be discussed in Chapter 7.

4.2 Sample Size, Data and Study Period

The study period in this study is from July 1999 to June 2000 and the period is selected for the following reasons:

- The global development and advent of e-commerce as a business channel in Australia;
- The proliferation of e-commerce equity fund raising;
- The growth in market capitalisation of e-commerce equity;
- The availability of data on public traded e-commerce firms; and
- The surge of public interest in e-commerce investment strategy.

The macroeconomic variables used are monthly data for the same period as the stock market data, selected from various sources such as the Australian Bureau of Statistics (ABS), financial web sites and the Reserve Bank of Australia.

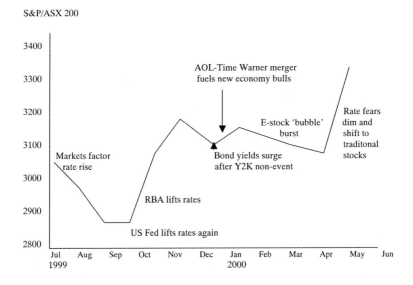

Figure 4.1 S&P/ASX 200 Index Trend: July 1999 to June 2000

Figure 4.1 above depicts the S&P/ASX 200 movements in the study period with summaries on the major market events. The valuation of e-commerce firms with several periods of negative stock returns, and firms with implicit negative growth rates, or firms that subsequently went bankrupt are included in the sample for analysis as these firms provide the underlying evidence as to how expectations are formed (Keenan 1970). This study examines the e-commerce stock return characteristics in the selected period on a diverse cross-section of firms and sectors. The period of the last two quarters of 1999 and initial two quarters of 2000 is significant in that it incorporates a diversity of events affecting e-commerce stocks, such as intense alliance activities, increased Internet-based initial public offers IPOs, increased e-commerce awareness and usage and the "bursting of the Internet bubble" in April 2000. To identify the key variables, the method will be to gather, manipulate and collate the data from the literature[24] contributing to the area of e-commerce development and e-commerce firm valuation.

4.2.1 Sample Size and Study Period

The use of pure-play e-commerce firms in this study is to provide pedigree of subject to avoid bias and complications in valuation if firms with traditional businesses are included in the analysis (see Section 2.5.1). The sample size in this research consists of eighteen pure-play e-commerce firms listed on the Australian Stock Exchange (ASX). The eighteen firms in the sample represent a relatively large proportion of the population of pure-play e-commerce firms listed on the ASX at the beginning of the study period. There were forty-five pure-play e-commerce firms identified as listed on the ASX in September 1999 with total market capitalisation of AUS$5,710.6 million.[25] There are twelve firms in the sample of this research, which belong to this list, and they represent 27 per cent of the listed firms identified. The other six firms (*MYC, PKT, BTB, AOL, WEB* and *WIN*) in this research were selected from ASX information available after the publication of the above article in the *Shares* magazine. The data used in this study comprise of 18 firms over the period July 1999 to June 2000 with 216 data points (18x12) across 10 industrial sectors overall. The firms were selected for the presence of a consistent and continuous time series of 12 months from July 1999 to June 2000. The use of pure-play e-commerce firms in this study is to provide pedigree of subject to avoid bias and complications in valuation if firms with traditional businesses are included in the analysis and this has also limited the number of e-commerce firms to be studied.

On the aggregate level, to capture the relationships between returns and the pervasive explanatory variables, the time series of returns data for the sectors are regressed on a cross-sectional pooling basis with the identified explanatory variables to capture individual differences in behaviour for estimation and inference purposes. This ensures the simulated parameters exhibit reasonable stability in different cross-sectional samples (Keenan 1970). The proxy for market return for the study period is calculated from the closing SP/ASX 200 index on the last trading day of the month in the period July 1999 to June 2000. The stock

---

[24] Including publications by corporations (e.g. prospectus and annual reports) and public institutions.

[25] In the article 'Surfing for fundamentals in the Internet sector', *Shares*, September 1999.

prices are the closing prices of the e-commerce firms on the last trading day in each month (Appendix 2.1).

The "downturn" or "market correction" of the e-commerce sector in April 2000 (see Figure 4.1 above) was confined strictly to the sector and not necessarily a broad market "structural change" according to the normal definition of a "bursting of the bubble". The unit root test and analysis leading subsequently to the differencing of the variables ensure that the data remains stationary to address and eliminate any bias due to "non-stationarity" and to enable the cointegration test to be carried out on a "stable" time series, in accordance with Perman's (1991) postulation. Perman (1991) noted that "if a vector times series is cointegrated, simple techniques may be employed to estimate consistently both long run equilibrium parameter vectors and the parameters associated with short-run dynamic adjustment process".

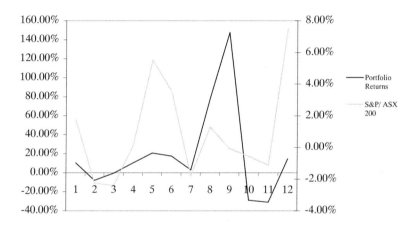

Figure 4.2 Study Period of S&P/ASX 200 and E-Commerce Portfolio Returns

Notes:
Study periods 1-12 correspond to July 1999 to June 2000.
Scale on left y-axis is for portfolio returns.
Scale on right y-axis is for S&P/ASX 200 returns.

Figure 4.2 depicts the returns patterns of the S&P/ASX 200 and the e-commerce portfolio time series over the study period. It can be seen that the study period covers the different events affecting e-commerce stocks including the rise from July 1999 to the subsequent global downturn beginning in February 2000 of e-commerce stocks. Inherently, the data for the study period provides a broad representation of the e-commerce market events.

4.2.2 Data Required and Processing

Generally, the identified variables are considered to have a pervasive influence on stock price or return. While some are already tested in empirical studies, others are intuitively idiosyncratic to e-commerce stock price or return. For instance, the US dollar to Australian dollar exchange rate is identified because the business of most major Australian firms is in the US-dollar area and predominant Internet-related transactions are US-dollar perceptive. The theoretical approach to factor specification is based on arguments that the factors capture economy-wide systematic risks (Chen, Ross and Roll 1986; Fama and French 1993). Chen, Roll and Ross (1986) use macroeconomic variables as factors and Fama and French (1993) specify firm characteristics to form factor portfolios. The desired approach includes the maximum amount of information from the original identified variables in as few derived factors as possible to keep the solution understandable. All the identified variables can be considered to have a pervasive influence on e-commerce stock price or return. The objective is to frugally describe the data. The final number of factors selected will manifest and represent the original factors to the degree that the factors are interrelated and it is possible to develop a relationship for each factor while still explaining a large number of variables. The task of deciding which variables should be included or excluded from the model will be done in a systematic way using the model building techniques used for identifying the best multiple regression model from a set of independent variables.

Data on economic and capital market variables will be gathered, collated, estimated, tested, evaluated and analysed in the research process according to the methodology specified.

4.2.3 Data Collection

The data collection will be from secondary sources. The data required for various economic values will be obtained from secondary sources such as the Australian Stock Exchange (www.asx.com.au), OECD datbases, Reserve Bank of Australia (www.rba.gov.au), and Australian Bureau of Statistics (www.abs.gov.au). Other organisations such as ASIC, MSCI, MLII and SPPR[26] and electronic web sites of Internet research and consulting firms (e.g. www.consult.com.au, www.internetstockreport.com and www.misq.org) are also rich source of data and information and will be constantly referred to during the process of this research. The period that data will be collected is from 1999 to 2000[27] to coincide with the emergence of public equity capital fund-raising in the e-commerce sector.

---

[26] ASIC: Australian Securities & Investment Commission; MSCI: Morgan Stanley's International Perspectives; MLII: Merrill Lynch Internet Index; SPPR: Australian Graduate School of Management's share market reports & share exchange publications.

[27] A period in which there was heightened e-commerce equity investment interest reflecting the active global e-commerce market developments.

4.3 Electronic Commerce Firms

The e-commerce firms in this study are selected from the population of pure-play e-commerce companies and from a variety of sectors listed on the Australian Stock Exchange. The definition of pure-play e-commerce firms are those firms whose business activities are exclusively Internet based, including those with a few embryonic Internet businesses, and those relying on their Internet expertise to provide the impetus for future growth. Table 4.1 presents the 18 e-commerce firms used in this study.

Table 4.1 E-commerce Firms Sample

	E-commerce firms	ASX code	Primary activities
1	My Casino	MYC	Casino, gaming
2	Sausage Software	SAS	Computer and office services
3	Solution 6	SOH	Computer and office services
4	Reckon Group	RKN	Computer and office services
5	Swish Group	SWG	Diversified media
6	Pocketmail	PKT	Equipment, services
7	131.shop.com	OTO	Equipment, services
8	B2B.Net.Technology	BTB	Health, medical services
9	Coms 21	CMZ	High technology
10	Etrade Australia	ETR	Miscellaneous financial services
11	AOL	AOL	Miscellaneous services
12	Candle	CND	Miscellaneous services
13	Liberty One	LIB	Other telecommunications
14	Spike Networks	SPK	Other telecommunications
15	Webjet	WEB	Retail
16	Travel.com	TVL	Retail
17	Ecorp	ECP	Retail, investments
18	Wine Planet	WIN	Retail

To avoid selection biases and promote representation, firms from a wide cross section of industries and with diverse characteristics are selected, subject to availability of stock data. In valuation terms, the pure-play e-commerce firms should characterise the fundamental quality of the group since their knowledge and experience help to minimise and mitigate risk exposure and this scenario helps in our factor analysis where the economic variables are determinants of valuation (returns), and adjusted for volatility or risk (β).

4.4 The Sectors

The stock prices of firms in the same industry or economic sector tend to move together in response to changes in prospects for that sector. The factors causing significant impacts within each sector are identifiable using the ordinary least-squares method. The starting point for estimating the key variables is to make a comprehensive study of the current market sectors in which e-commerce application is predominant. Once the e-commerce firms and the industry sectors (Table 4.2) they belong to are identified, the list of relevant economic and market factors identified from empirical study and contemporary e-commerce literature can be grouped and tested.

Table 4.2 Industrial Sectors

	Sector
1	Casino, gaming
2	Computer and office services
3	Diversified media
4	Equipment, services
5	Health, medical services
6	High technology
7	Miscellaneous financial services
8	Miscellaneous services
9	Other telecommunications
10	Retail/Retail Investment

The rapid growth of users and technology innovations and their diffusion largely drive the expansion of the Internet as an electronic infrastructure for commercial activities and information exchanges. In Australia, this growth has also been aided by the deregulation of the telecommunications sector and the pro-active involvement of governments in encouraging the use of the Internet by firms, individuals and government organisations. These policies have helped to proliferate and improve the quality of accessing the Internet, including lower cost.

This research will analyse key factors based on a three-tier structural study. The first is to conduct a factor analysis on the selected e-commerce firms (Table 4.1). These firms will then be analysed according to their industry sector classification on the Australian Stock Exchange. Finally, a portfolio analysis will be carried out on the stocks looking at their individual and collective risk behaviour and implications on portfolio selection. Such segregation of analysis reflects the general market structure under which contemporary e-commerce firms operate and the practices they adopt to embrace e-commerce.

4.5 Techniques

In steps (i) and (ii) (see Section 4.1), various valuation approaches will be used to estimate the returns (thus value) of e-commerce stocks by first identifying those with a pervasive influence on returns and then testing the selected factors for significance. Initially, traditional valuation models such as the Market Model (MM) using market indexes (as a factor) to estimate returns and the CAPM using market risk premium (as factors) will be used to test their accurateness in predicting returns. These results will be compared with and, where appropriate, incorporated into the multi-variate regression model using the ordinary least squares (OLS) approach based on the identified market factors having a pervasive influence on e-commerce stock value. The OLS produces unbiased estimators of the coefficient, β_F, for each factor in the model, and statistical inference on values of the population will be conducted using hypothesis testing. The null hypothesis (H_0) will be tested against a two-sided alternative (H_1), i.e.:

$$H_0: \quad \beta_F = 0 \qquad\qquad\qquad (4.1)$$
$$H_1: \quad \beta_F \neq 0 \qquad\qquad\qquad (4.2)$$

at the 20% significance level for this parameter in the research, where β_F is the factor coefficient. The rationale for using this alternative is to assume that each factor, F (the independent variable x), has a ceteris paribus effect on e-commerce stock returns (*e-stockret$_{it}$* or the dependent variable y). This is considered the prudent and relevant alternative in the context of e-commerce stock returns, as the sign of β_F for this class of securities is not well determined by theory or common sense (Wooldridge 2000). As the alternative is two-sided, the interest is in the absolute value of the t-statistic. The rejection rule for the null hypothesis (equation (4.1)), $H_0: \beta_F = 0$ against equation (4.2) (i.e. H_1) is:

$$|t_{\beta_F}| > c$$

where, $|\bullet|$ is the absolute value and c is the chosen critical value. The degree of freedom (df) for the general OLS problem with n observations and k independent variables is:

$$df = n - k - 1$$
$$\text{or} = n - (k + 1)$$
$$= \text{(number of observations)} - \text{(number of estimated parameters)}$$

and in this research df is equal to $(12) - (4) = 8$ for the estimated AEMM model in the study period. The larger significance level (20%) used for testing the hypotheses reflects the small sample size used in this study and the fact that it is harder to find significance with smaller sample sizes as the critical values are larger in magnitude and the estimators are less precise (Wooldridge 2000). The p-values for the t-statistics will also be computed for those factors that are considered pervasive to e-commerce returns to ascertain their degree of influence even if their β_F coefficients are statistically insignificant. According to Wooldridge (2000), "different researchers prefer different significant levels depending on the particular application and underlying agenda and there is no 'correct' significance level". By including those factors judged pervasive from their p-values, we attempt to tease out the characteristics of these explanatory variables for an area that is very much at a pioneering stage with very little information to rely on.

The identification and multiple regression analysis of the basic variables in terms of exogenous (independent) and endogenous (dependent) variables are done so that the incidence on the endogenous variables (returns) of a variation in the set of exogenous variables can be analysed, predicted and optimised using an objective function of the policy maker.

After identifying the significant factors, step (iii) (see Section 4.1) would be to test the predictability of the multi-variate model developed using the predictive power of these factors and a prognosis of the trend of e-commerce stock return performance and its structural aspects characterising the e-commerce sector, so that the sequential effects and constraints can be analysed with a view of addressing and managing risk in the context of the key factors identified.

In step (iv) (see Section 4.1), the approach is to measure and compare the degree of volatility of e-commerce stock returns against the general market and other traditional sectors. The standard CAPM valuation model will be used to compare actual e-commerce returns with expected returns estimated from using the model. This comparison will aid the appreciation and understanding of e-commerce stock price volatility and its magnitude using traditional valuation methods. The basic question to be addressed is the return volatility behaviour and characteristics of e-commerce stocks in relation to the general market, across sectors and as a group. This will be followed by a detailed analysis of the risk/return relationship and the asset pricing of the e-commerce stocks using traditional models.

The returns of the stocks are measured by simply dividing the returns expected of the stock (or in an *ex post* scenario, the difference in the stock price between periods t and $t - 1$ plus any dividend paid) by the $t - 1$ period stock price:

$$\begin{array}{l} \text{Expected} \\ \text{total} \\ \text{return} \end{array} = \frac{\text{Dividends}_t + (\text{Market price}_t - \text{Market price}_{t-1})}{\text{Market price}_{t-1}}$$

The CAPM is a simple model but in use it can produce diverse results and consistency and logic are the best criteria for using it (Harrington 1987). This study will explain the basis for selection of each variable used as proxy in the CAPM in the context of e-commerce conditions – consistency will be maintained for comparability. The risk-free rate used in this study will be the 90-day geometric mean of the Australian Treasury Notes rates and the market risk premium is based on the difference between the geometric means of the S&P/ASX 200 stock index returns and the Treasury Notes during the period 1992 to 1999.

Step (v) (see Section 4.1) involves the analysis of the e-commerce stock risk and return profile in a portfolio context. A better understanding of the underlying characteristics and behaviour of the volatility in e-commerce stock return would firstly, help to measure the effectiveness of the e-commerce factor model developed in Chapter 5; and secondly, assist those managing financial portfolios (portfolio selection analyses of e-commerce stocks are conducted in Chapter 7) and regulators to take actions that will minimise misallocation of resources.

4.5.1 Estimation

The multiple regression analysis of the e-commerce variable involves constructing and testing a valuation model of the relationship between e-commerce stock prices, the dependent (i.e. endogenous) variable, and one or more of the identified independent (i.e. exogenous) variables. The explanatory variables will first be tested for their pervasive influence on e-commerce sector returns by looking at the degree of correlation between returns and these explanatory variables. The research will initially find a set of five variables that are considered to have a pervasive influence on returns from the list of variables identified (Appendix 2.1). The correlation coefficient measures the strength of the relationship between two variables and the correlation coefficient will be calculated for each of the 23 variables with the individual stock's returns. The 5 variables with the highest correlation will be selected.

4.5.1.1 Multiple Regression Analysis

In multiple regressions, the objective is to identify the relationship between an exogenous variable and multiple endogenous variables and the starting point for the econometric analysis of a factor-pricing model is an assumption about the time-series behaviour of returns (Campbell et al. 1997). It is assumed that the models for asset returns conditional on the factor realizations are assumed to be independent over time (although maybe cross-sectionally correlated), identically distributed over time and normally distributed. A time-series approach, being perhaps the most intuitive to investors, is the method employed for multivariate co-integration. The time-series approach to estimate the multiple-factor model, at the firm and sector level, will be used to compare over time the stocks' returns to the predicted values of the key factors. In co-integration analysis, the relationship between the endogenous and exogenous variables is considered to be stationary. Fama and French (1993) adopted a similar approach in a time-series study using factors that explain stock and bond returns.

The relation between stock market returns and fundamental economic activities in the traditional economy has been widely researched, especially in the United States. However, the economic role of e-commerce with the advent of the Internet is relatively less clear. Specifically, how does the e-commerce sector of the stock market, hailed as the impetus of the new economy, respond to changes in the fundamental economic variables? In the past three years, with the rapid development of the e-commerce sector being the precursor to the new economy, the e-commerce sector of the Australian stock market has experienced tremendous growth, and also volatility, in both market value and trading volume. The Australian Stock Exchange is one of the most rapidly growing and relatively stable markets in the Asia Pacific region having gone through the Asian financial crisis unscathed. Recently, the number of e-commerce firms listed on the ASX has increased with the focus of attention on the new economy and the new opportunities that come with it. Australia is chosen for its similarity in economic dynamism to the US economy and its selection avoids the survivorship bias of the United States (Jorion and Goetzmann 1999). The structure of the Australian stock market differs from that of the United States in terms of investor profile and diversity of firms and industries. Even though the ASX is growing rapidly, the market capitalization of the Australian market is much smaller than the U.S. market. Owing to different investor perception of e-commerce development, the ASX response to economic variables and ASX price movements may be different from the U.S. market. The main purpose of this multivariate study (Gibbons 1982; Stambaugh 1982; Shanken 1985; Gibbons, Ross and Shanken 1989; Wood 1991) is to test whether current economic activities in Australia can explain e-commerce stock returns. This study proposes to test the degree of causality of economic variables on stock returns.

The first step is to develop multiple regression models based on key or strategic variables (factors) according to their significance in determining the returns of e-commerce stock over the relevant time period. The objective of the multiple regression approach is to identify the relationship between an exogenous variable (return), and multiple endogenous variables (real activity variables). The use of multiple regression models is to capture the major market indicators, as represented by the variables such as industrial production, interest rates, yields of corporate and government bonds, trade balance, foreign exchange, M1, inflation (Hardouvelis 1987; Keim 1985) and whether they are significant explanatory factors of e-commerce stock returns, which systematically move the prices of all e-commerce stocks. In addition, if economic variables are significantly priced in e-commerce stock returns, how significant are they compared to the general market or other non-e-commerce stocks? If there are no significant relations between macroeconomic variables and e-commerce stock returns, we are able to conclude that the ASX e-commerce stocks do not signal changes in real activities.

4.5.1.2 Factor Analysis

The cross-sectional approach will be used to measure the relationship between the variables and returns to investing in e-commerce stocks at a particular point in time. As the time-series model provides an explanation for the above empirical findings based on changes in firms risk through time, it should also relate to changes in sector-specific variables that empirically explain the cross-sectional variation in expected returns (Ferson and Harvey 1999). A cross-sectional study of the e-commerce stocks from different sectors would be more convincing in describing the explanatory variables. Empirical studies identified characteristics such as market value of equity, book to market value of equity and price-earnings ratio to be significant and generally, factor models with factor portfolios and broad base market portfolios, reflecting these characteristics, tend to effectively explain the cross-section of returns (Campbell et al. 1997). The results from the cross sectional analysis can be used to estimate an average relationship with the variable for a single point in time.

The technique of factor analysis involves the analysis of the structure of data within a multivariate framework for correlation between the variables. The process for factor model development from multivariate factor analysis involves testing the selected variables for significant correlation by relying on analysis of the variance/covariance matrix, which contains all the information on the degree to which the variables in use vary with each other, or the extent to which they duplicate or complement each other. In factor analysis, the structure of the relationship between the endogenous variables is investigated and unlike cointegration the relationships between the endogenous variables need not be stationary (Watsham and Parramore 1998). Implicit in the construction of this model is the assumption that the returns on two stocks will be correlated, that is, will move together only through common reactions to one or more of the factors specified in the model. Any abnormal returns by the model are assumed to be unique or specific to the stock and unrelated to unique elements on other stocks (Campbell et al. 1997). As a result, the factor model is selected and considered appropriate in this research for analysis of e-commerce stocks at the individual firm level and sector portfolios.

4.5.1.3 Stationarity and Cointegration Tests

Stationarity is a state of statistical equilibrium where a series of observations have the same distribution over time (an invariant distribution function). A series is thus stationary if its mean, variance and auto-covariances are independent of time. Stationarity is used in time series econometrics to test for stability of the relationship between two or more variables over time. A test of stationarity in a financial model helps detect the lack of the influence of time, i.e. the trend in the time series, and thus enables us to study the effects of the explanatory variables on the dependent variable. This enables a better understanding of the relationship when there is stationarity in the time series and the β does not change arbitrarily over time. The intuitive notion of weak dependence in a time series defines the concept behind a stationarity time series process and "weak dependence cannot be formally defined because there is no definition that covers all cases of interest" (Wooldridge 2000). According to Wooldridge, the crux of weak dependence is that it replaces the assumption of random sampling in implying that the law of large numbers and the central limit theorem hold. The approach for testing stationarity in this research is to use the autoregressive process, which assumes that the data being analysed is stationary (Watsham and Parramore 1998).

In the case of a stationary process, statistical summary numbers such as the mean, standard deviation and range that are computed on the basis of a limited sample, as in this research where the study period is for only 12 months (observations), are also sensible estimates of the same parameters for much longer samples, and can easily be converted into estimates for the population. By contrast, summary statistics computed from the sample of a non-stationary process tend to be misleading when applied to describe a longer period of the same process, let alone the population. If a time series needs to be differenced once in order to be transformed into a stationary series the original series is known to be "integrated of order one" or I(1) or generally known as "Difference Stationary Process" (DSP) and many time series are DSP (Nelson and Plosser 1982). If it has to be differentiated twice to become stationary it is known to be integrated of order two or I(2). An original series that is stationary and needs no differentiation is known to be integrated of order zero, I(0). Engle and Granger (1991) suggested that "in many cases (inventory accumulation, wealth etc), M_t is itself the difference between two or more I(1) series; e.g. $M_t = y_t - \lambda x_t$ (as in Savings = Income − Expenditure). If these *basic* series are cointegrated, M_t is I(0), so for $\delta = 0$, S_t is I(1) and could be cointegrated with x_t or y_t".

This study will use the cointegration test (Engle and Granger 1987) to investigate the relation between stock and their underlying macro-variables. If economic variables are significant and consistently priced in e-commerce stock returns, they should be cointegrated. This co-integration relation between e-commerce stock returns and the underlying factors is a necessary condition of the equilibrium model of stock market returns, steady-state equilibrium (Griffith, Hill and Judge 1993). Even though the time series in this research is relatively short, the application of the cointegration test is in recognition of and justified by the rapidly evolving nature of e-commerce firms compared to firms in traditional industries. The cointegration analysis presented is based on the Engle and Granger (1987) two-step estimation framework. This method consists of two stages: the unit-root test to determine their non-stationarity and, when the results indicate that the first-differenced series of each variable are stationary, a subsequent test to determine whether these two variables are cointegrated. Dickey and Fuller (1979, 1981) first introduced the test of the unit-root hypothesis. The test for unit root is initially done using the autoregressive process of order one AR(1) model (Wooldridge 2000):

$$y_t = \alpha + \rho y_{t-1} + \varepsilon_t, \tag{4.3}$$

where:

$t = 1,2,\ldots\ldots$

$y_0 =$ the first observed value

$\varepsilon_t =$ the martingale difference sequence with respect to

$\{y_{t-1}, y_{t-2}, \ldots\}$ of $E(\varepsilon_t / y_{t-1}, y_{t-2}, \ldots\ldots\ldots, y_0) = 0$

The null hypothesis is that y_t has a unit root:

$H_0: \rho = 1$

$H_1: \rho < 1$

Therefore, the testing of the null hypothesis, $H_0: \rho = 1$ in model (equation (4.3)) with the alternative hypothesis, $H_1: \rho < 1$, is in effect determining whether the time series y_t is *difference-stationary* or I(1) against *trend-stationary* or I(0), respectively.

By subtracting y_{t-1} from both sides of equation (4.3) and denoting $\theta = \rho - 1$, we derive equation (4.4) below as a working model for the unit root test:

$$\Delta y_t = \alpha + \theta y_{t-1} + \varepsilon_t \qquad\qquad\qquad (4.4)$$

The usual *t*-statistic for the estimated θ in the unit root model (equation (4.4)) will be used to carry out the test against the critical value at the 10% significant level. We reject the null hypothesis $H_0: \theta = 0$ against $H_1: \theta < 0$ if the *t*-statistic of the estimated θ is less than the critical value. We thus reject the null hypothesis if *t*-statistic of the estimated $\theta < -2.63$, the critical value for the 10% significance level (Banerjee et al. 1993). If an original time series is found to be non-stationary, and is said to be integrated of order one or I(1), it will have to be differenced once to be transformed into a stationary series. Differencing is the process of finding the change in the value of a variable in successive periods:

$$\Delta y_t = y_t - y_{t-1}$$

and the Δy_t series is the differenced series.

To test for unit root, in models with more complicated dynamics after the AR(1) model tested $\rho = 1$ and Δy is serially uncorrelated, Δy is allowed to follow an AR model by augmenting equation (4.4) with additional lags (Watsham and Parramore 1998, Wooldridge 2000). The following form of the augmented Dickey-Fuller test is used to test the unit-root hypotheses:

$$\Delta y_t = \alpha + \theta y_{t-1} + \gamma \Delta y_{t-1} + \varepsilon_t$$

where $|\gamma| < 1$. So when H_0: $\theta = 0$, Δy_t follows a stable AR(1) model, and under the alternative H_1: $\theta < 0$, y_t would follow a stable AR(2) model. For the dynamics to be completely modelled using the augmented DF test in terms of the lag length, Wooldridge (2000) suggests that there are no hard and fast rules to follow in any case.

Along with the null hypothesis that forecasts follow a random walk, the test for the significance of θ and γ uses the relevant critical values for the t-statistics of the coefficient on the lagged level as given in Banerjee et al. (1993). This study tests whether there are unit-roots in e-commerce stock returns, capital market and macro-economic variables.

This study will also investigate the causal relations between e-commerce stock prices and macroeconomic variables (Granger 1986; Granger and Newbold 1988). The second stage will test for cointegration between e-commerce stock prices and macroeconomic variables, known as the cointegrating regression:

$$y_t = \alpha + \beta x_t + u_t$$

where β is the coefficient of the estimated variable in the regression model.

This isolates the residual u_t in order to test whether or not they are stationary. If we add α and u_t to get z_t, then we have $y_t - \beta x_t = z_t$ and we shall test for the stationarity of z. If the z values are stationary, β will be the cointegrating vector. The Dickey-Fuller unit-root test will be used in this study to determine cointegration of the series by testing $\{z_t\}$. If the null hypothesis is rejected, we reject the unit-root in $\{z_t\}$ in favour of the I(0) alternative, then y_t and x_t are cointegrated. The test is to first estimate β (rather than test for a unit root in $\{z_t\}$) using the OLS estimator from the regression (Wooldridge 2000):

$$\hat{y}_t = \hat{\alpha} + \hat{\beta} x_t \qquad (4.5)$$

and if y_t and x_t are cointegrated the estimator $\hat{\beta}$ from equation (4.5) is consistent for β. The Dickey-Fuller test is applied to test the residuals (estimated μ) from equation (4.3) as follows:

$$\hat{\mu}_t = y_t - \hat{\alpha} - \hat{\beta} x_t$$

A regression of $\hat{\mu}_t$ on $\hat{\mu}_{t-1}$ will be done and compared with the t-statistic on $\hat{\mu}_{t-1}$ to the 10% significance level of the asymptotic critical value ($c = -3.04$) from Davidson and MacKinnon (1993). If the t-statistic is below the critical value, the evidence points towards $y_t - \beta x_t$ being I(0), which means that y_t and x_t are cointegrated.

If a pair of macroeconomic variable series is cointegrated, the bi-variate cointegrated system must have a causal ordering in at least one direction. Thus if the results show that the e-commerce stocks cause changes in the economic variables, it can be claimed that e-commerce stock price variability is fundamentally linked to economic variables and the change in e-commerce stock price lags or leads these economic activities (Granger 1986; Granger and Newbold 1988).

The presence of cointegration between e-commerce stock prices and underlying macro-economic variables will provide firm evidence that those economic variables are significant factors in explaining expected stock returns and there exists an interactive relation between them. The long-term equilibrium relationship of the cointegration process used to test the developed model does suggest and imply the predictive quality of the model. Engle and Granger (1991), states that 'if x_t, y_t are I(1) and cointegrated, there must be Granger causality in at least one direction, as one variable can help forecast the other'.

4.5.2 Evaluation

The final stage of the research will concentrate on whether any extrapolations can be made of the findings in the research in relation to improving and offering a more appropriate financial evaluation model for information technology investments. It will also attempt to explain the current information technology investment approaches, considerations and rationales, and from them, identify industry best practice relating to financing options and financial evaluation of e-commerce or information technology related equity investments.

4.5.3 Volatility and Expected Returns

In the analysis of stock investments, average rates of return and their betas and/or standard deviations are used to represent investments' profitability and risk, respectively. Volatility tests are a joint test of informational efficiency and that price equals fundamental value (Cuthbertson 1997). This study uses a triangulation of various volatility-return analyses, including the CAPM, to test the actual returns against the expected returns for e-commerce stocks on an individual and sector basis. The market model tests on the relationship between actual return and the market returns also tests the two elements of the EMH from the coefficient of determination (R^2) and analysis of the regression residual (risk decomposition) from the estimated regression line. The variance of rates of return can be decomposed into two components by the market model. The estimator of beta of the e-commerce equity is the slope coefficient in the excess-return market model, that is, the beta in the regression equation:

$$e\text{-}stockret_{it} = \alpha_{im} + \beta_{im}R_{mt} + e_{it}$$

where:

$i =$ the stock or asset sector;

$t =$ the time period, $t = 1, 2, \dots, T$;

$m =$ the market portfolio;

$e\text{-}stockret_{it} =$ the realised excess returns in time period t for e-commerce stock i;

$R_{mt} =$ the realised excess returns in time period t for the market portfolio; and

$e_{it} =$ random error term.

The S&P/ASX 200 Index serves as the proxy for the market portfolio, and the Australian Treasury bill rate proxies for the risk-free return. In the context of the stock market, the S&P/ASX 200 is now the benchmark index (but it is similar in composition to the All Ordinaries Index) that is used as an indicator of overall stock market performance and of current trends. It provides a performance benchmark for stock market cycles and an indicator of stock market reactions to economic events and situations. The S&P/ASX 200 is calculated on the basis of the aggregate market value (AMV) of a wide selection of companies quoted on the Australian Stock Exchange. The market value, or market capitalisation, of any company in the S&P/ASX 200 is the number of shares issued multiplied by the current market price per share in that company. The AMV of the S&P/ASX 200 Index is the sum of the market values of the companies included. The equation is estimated using the S&P/ASX 200 Index monthly data ($T = $ June 2000). Given an estimate of the beta, the return is calculated using a historical average for the excess return on the S&P/ASX 200 over Treasury Notes.

4.5.3.1 Market Model and Risk Decomposition

There are two means associated with the dependent variable, y_i, in regression analysis being the overall mean ($\bar{y}$) and conditional mean ($\hat{y}_i = a + bx_i$). From the two different means, the total deviation ($y_i - \bar{y}$) can be decomposed into unexplained deviation ($y_i - \hat{y}_i$) and explained deviation ($\hat{y}_i - y$) as:

$$y_i - \bar{y} = y_i - \hat{y}_i + \hat{y}_i - \bar{y}$$

$$\text{or:} \quad \sum_{i=1}^{n}(y_i - \bar{y})^2 = \sum_{i=1}^{n}(y_i - \hat{y}_i)^2 + \sum_{i=1}^{n}(\hat{y}_i - \bar{y})^2$$

Total Variation =	Unexplained	+	Explained
(SST)[28]	Variation (SSE)		Variation (SSR)

---

[28] SST = sum of squares total (total variation of y); SSE = sum of squares error; and SSR = sum of squares due to regression (explained variation of y).

The above equation is used to decompose the total risk associated with the e-commerce stocks from the analysis of variance (ANOVA) of the stock return to market return regression by dissecting it into systematic and unsystematic risks. The monthly rate of return for the individual e-commerce stocks and the market return for July 1999 to June 2000 are used to estimate the market model and the variance data is analysed to obtain the total risk (σ^2_i), systematic risk ($\beta^2_i\sigma^2_m$) and unsystematic risk (σ^2_{ei}) as follows:

$$\sigma^2_i = \beta^2_i\sigma^2_m + \sigma^2_{ei}$$

where:
σ^2_i = the variance of R_{it} (*e-stockret*$_{it}$);
$\beta^2_i\sigma^2_m$ = the variance of market rates of return; and
σ^2_{ei} = the residual of rates of return for the ith security.

Systematic or market risk is that part of the total risk that occurs from the basic variability of stock prices which represents tendency of stock prices to move together with the general market and cannot be eliminated by diversification. The unsystematic risk is the result of variations specific to the firm or industry and is that part of a stock's risk associated with random events; it can be eliminated by proper diversification.

The primary approach adopted for the valuation of e-commerce stocks in this research is through factor analysis using general market variables. Some e-commerce stocks or e-commerce stocks in specific sectors are sensitive to movements in the market while others may exhibit more independence and stability. A measure of the e-commerce stock's relative sensitivity to the market, assigned on the basis of its past performance, will highlight its systematic risk also referred to as relevant or market risk and will reflect the changes and fluctuations in general market conditions, behaviour and provide a context for the subsequent factor analysis.

4.5.3.2 Covariance and Correlation Analysis

The degree of relationship between the returns of e-commerce stocks among themselves and the market returns is measured and analysed in order to estimate stock return volatility, and the two alternatives used to determine the possibility of a linear association between any two series of stock returns are the covariance and correlation coefficient. The covariance between stocks X and Y can be defined as:

$$\text{Cov}(X, Y) = \sigma_{X,Y} = E[(X-\mu_X)(Y-\mu_Y)]$$

where μ_X and μ_Y are the means of X and Y, respectively.

The covariance derived is a statistical measure of the linear association between two returns of e-commerce stocks or the e-commerce stock returns and market returns. The sign of the covariance will reflect the direction of the linear relationship between the two random variables, i.e. the returns of stocks X and Y. The covariance is positive if the returns tend to move in the same direction and when the returns move in the opposite directions, the covariance is negative. In addition to measuring the direction of the relationship between returns, the test for volatility will also involve measuring the strength of the relationship using the correlation coefficient, which is obtained by scaling the covariance. The correlation coefficient ρ between X and Y is equal to the covariance divided by the product of the variables' standard deviations:

$$\rho = \frac{\sigma_{X,Y}}{\sigma_X \sigma_Y}$$

where:
ρ = the correlation coefficient;
σ_X = the standard deviation of X;
σ_Y = the standard deviation of Y; and
$\sigma_{X,Y}$ = the covariance of stocks X and Y.

and ρ is always less than or equal to 1.0 and greater than or equal to –1.0.

The process of measuring the degree of the selected e-commerce stock volatility will involve, firstly, analysing the standard deviations, betas, expected returns, covariances and correlation coefficients of the relevant stock and market returns in the study period. This analysis of volatility will provide an allusion of the risk profile. A stock with significant price or returns volatility does imply risk (Brigham and Houston 2000) because stock prices fluctuate due to uncertainty about the future, particularly future earnings. Thus companies with high betas have less predictable future earnings.

Secondly, the risk indicators will be analysed from a sector perspective to accentuate the sectorial risk characteristics of the stocks. This will allow an inference of the degree of risk associated with the various sectors of the e-commerce stocks, and allows a conjecture of the advancement and evolution of e-commerce as a marketing tool in that sector.

Finally, an analysis will be done for all the selected stocks, as a portfolio, in relation to the market to estimate the degree of volatility between the e-commerce related stocks from a portfolio perspective, to the general market. This analysis is intended to provide a proxy for a hypothetical e-commerce sector of pure-play e-commerce stocks across all industries to gauge its returns characteristics vis-à-vis the market portfolio. This will assist in our understanding when evaluating the reactions and pervasiveness of economic variables to the e-commerce portfolio in relation to the general market.

For factor selection of the e-commerce portfolio, the same process as used in Section 4.5.1 above is used thereby, determining the highest loadings or correlations between the stock returns and the factors. This approach recognises that a characterisation of a factor is typically based on loadings and the factors with the highest loadings represent higher degree of correlation between the stock returns and the factors (Drummen et al. 1992).

4.5.4 Portfolio Selection Analysis

The portfolio selection analyses to be conducted in this study are twofold (see Chapter 7). Firstly, hypothetical portfolios will be constructed based on the return characteristics of the e-commerce stocks and the market portfolio studied. These two types of stock will provide the portfolio options for identifying the selection behaviour of the two-asset portfolio. The objective is to find the efficient portfolios in a two-asset scenario to highlight the portfolio selection pattern and to assist portfolio fund managers with their decision-making when faced with a two-asset portfolio choice.

Secondly, in addition to the two-asset portfolio above, a risk-free asset such as cash will be introduced into the analysis and the selection behaviour of the three-asset portfolio will be evaluated. With the introduction of cash the problem of finding efficient portfolios is rather similar to a capital rationing problem. Here, we attempt to allocate a limited amount of capital in a combination of different assets to give the most efficient portfolios. The capital-rationing limit used will be the average monthly traded volume of the sample e-commerce stocks in the study period. The portfolio selection model (Thompson and Thore 1992) used in this analysis is one with a multiple solve statement for risk (λ) model for various assignments of λ. The solutions to this sequence with different values of λ will allow the pattern of the efficiency frontier of portfolios to emerge at different levels of risk. This will provide an insight into portfolio choice interactions between the e-commerce stocks and the other assets at varying degree of risk, from which ramifications and conclusions can be drawn to facilitate portfolio management decision-making.

4.6 Conclusion

Stock price volatility, and by extension stock returns volatility, does signify risk with the exception of stock that are negatively correlated with the market (Brigham 2000). The initial and crucial stage of the methodology adopted in this study is to unravel the risk profile of the selected e-commerce stocks and this is done in the next chapter. Various key risk indicators will be used to analyse the riskiness of the individual stocks compared with market risk. The aim is to understand the risk behaviour of the stocks and use that knowledge to help construct the valuation model while incorporating any significant risk features that might be uncovered in the process. The CAPM is used to estimate the level of expected returns, given that a risk factor is imputed for a particular stock, and Chapter 5 will discuss the relationship between risk and return and how risk and return interact to determine the market prices of e-commerce firms. The covariances and correlations coefficients are used to measure the strength of relationship between the stocks' returns and to determine the extent of co-movements between the comparable stocks.

The factor analysis approach for building the valuation model in Chapter 5 assumes no knowledge of the factor values or the stocks' sensitivities to those factors. The approach is used to determine the number of factors and the stocks' sensitivities, based on past market returns for the stocks.

CHAPTER 5

Financial Econometric Results and Factor Analyses

The most familiar interpretation for the large and unpredictable swings that characterize common stock price is that price changes represent the efficient discounting of new information. It is remarkable given the popularity of this interpretation that it has never been established what this information is about. (Grossman and Shiller 1981).

5.1 Introduction

These comments are familiar to the current market situation of e-commerce stocks, just as they were applicable to the equity markets of the 1970s and early 1980s. As presented in the preceding chapters, alternative models of expected returns give rise to different expressions for the determination of fundamental values and hence stock prices. Rational valuation models based on the widely accepted DCF methodology require earnings and discount rates as variables and they assume that only the arrival of new information or news about fundamentals affecting these variables will influence stock prices (Cuthbertson 1997). The absence of earnings and a generally accepted determinant of discount rates for the e-commerce sector necessitates proxies to act for these key variables, such as market interest rates acting as proxy for discount rates.

This chapter examines the value-relevance to e-commerce stock prices of the variables derived in the literature review process carried out in Chapter 2. This is achieved by examining in a contemporaneous setting the association between stock prices (or returns) and the significant value-driving variables as well as evaluating the inter-temporal association between any e-commerce adjusted estimates and subsequent stock returns. The contemporaneous analysis will indicate the extent of current recognition of the variables by investors or the market and the inter-temporal analysis may suggest either market efficiency or market failure to fully recognize the value relevance of the variables. This chapter will determine the macro factors that have a pervasive influence on e-commerce stock returns by identifying the established characteristics or covariances fit, which will also help to explain the behaviour of these returns.

5.2 Model Building

The problem of deciding which variables to include in the multiple regression equation is allied to deciding how to define the best model that explains the dependent variable, that is e-commerce stock return or valuation, using the smallest possible set of independent variables. The existing literature does not directly dispute the supposition that the return premia of stocks can be explained by a factor model but disputes whether there are pervasive factors that are associated with a particular class of securities and whether there are risk premia associated with these factors (Daniel and Titman 1997; Fama and French 1993, 1996; Lakonishok, Shleifer, and Vishny 1994). The crux of this study is hence to identify these pervasive factors that consistently influence e-commerce stock return and to investigate whether the returns of e-commerce stocks can be attributed to their factor loadings.

5.2.1 Factor Selection

This section focuses on choosing the set of independent variables to be considered in the valuation models. A set of five key variables is to be selected from the list of variables identified in Chapter 4.

The choice of factors in a regression model (i.e. the explanatory variables in the asset pricing model) can be done by one of the following ways. Incorporate one variable at a time (forward regression) and examine the R^2 value of the regression to determine the relevance of the variable. Alternatively, a set of all the identified variables can first be included in the model and eliminated one by one (backward regression), based on the R^2 value, leaving the ones that contribute to the highest R^2. Stepwise regression is a combination of the forward selection and backward elimination methods by running one-variable models and selecting the variable with the largest F or t-statistic. The difference in the methods is that stepwise regression can be used to consider combinations of variables when at least three variables have been included in the model. The process considers dropping previously included variables by using criteria similar to the ones used in back elimination. Some economic methods are also available for making this choice of regressors. In this study the factor selection approach is based on factor loadings, where we first determine the correlation coefficient of stock returns for each e-commerce sector and every economic variable. The correlation coefficient measures the strength of the relationship between e-commerce stock returns of each firm or sector and each of the identified economic variables. The correlation coefficients between the e-commerce firms and the variables are shown in the matrix in Appendix 5.1 and between the sectors and variables in Appendix 5.2. The economic variables of the pairs with the highest correlation will then be analysed and selected for the model only if they are considered appropriate and represent diversity in measuring e-commerce stock value.

The process for factor selection is initially based on computing the average correlation coefficients of the individual stock returns by sector (Appendix 5.2) and those variables with consistent high correlation coefficients and pervasiveness will be selected for inclusion in the valuation regression model (Appendix 5.3). By computing a frequency over a cross-section of the individual e-commerce stocks, the intent is to eliminate idiosyncrasies of individual stocks so that a general behaviour between the returns and variables can be established and aid in factor selection by highlighting the more pervasive factors. The results from Appendix 5.3 of the seven (7) most pervasive factors from the selection process are presented in Table 5.1 below.

The model building process continues by empirically testing whether the selected economic and capital market indicators presented in Table 5.1, are significant explanatory factors of e-commerce stock returns. The objective is to construct a valuation model, using regression analysis, with 3 to 5 factors that could parsimoniously estimate the value of e-commerce stocks traded on the Australian equity market. In addition, if the factors are significant and consistently priced in e-commerce stock returns, they should be cointegrated. If there are no significant relations between the factors and e-commerce stock returns, we can conclude that Australian e-commerce stock value does not reflect the real activities represented by these factors.

Table 5.1 Factors with Pervasive Influence on E-Commerce Stock Returns

Factor	Frequency Across Sectors	Average Correlation Coefficient
NASDAQ Composite Index (NAS)	4	14.10%
Industrial Production (IP)	5	25.56%
Balance of Payment (BOP)	4	13.80%
Consumer Confidence (CC)	4	26.43%
Foreign Exchange Rate (FE)	4	24.74%
Market Risk Premium (MRP)	6	34.55%
Market Return (MR)	6	34.27%

From Table 5.1, both *MRP* and *MR* are pervasive factors and they, fundamentally, measure the stock return from a market portfolio perspective. Therefore, it would be prudent to exclude one of these factors and in this case *MR*, which has a lower average coefficient than the *MRP*. Also, the *MRP* ($R_m - R_f$) is a more profound investment indicator as it measures market risk in relation to the risk free interest rate R_f. Industrial production (*IP*) is also selected for its pervasiveness and relatively higher correlation than other factors. The NASDAQ composite index (*NAS*) is selected for its strong correlation and the general perception that the NASDAQ represents the cradle of technological endeavours, where advances in the technological business sector are more than likely to originate from NASDAQ-listed companies. The *NAS* is also deemed to be a universal proxy of the technology sectors in respect to equity investment. Consumer confidence (*CC*) is an important element of the virtual community "for the benefits to customers flow from the very characteristics that define the virtual community" (Hagel and Armstrong 1997). The final factor to be included in the model for initial testing will be Foreign Exchange Rate (*FE*) being the one with a higher correlation to returns than the Balance of Payment (*BOP*) factor.

5.2.2 The Multifactor Regression Model – Results

The purpose of the multi-factor model development is to test the long-term relationship between e-commerce stock returns and the of macroeconomic variables using cointegration tests consistent with Engle and Granger (1991), which states that "if x_t, y_t are $I(1)$ and cointegrated, there must be Granger causality in at least one direction, as one variable can help forecast the other". A generic five-factor model, named the Australian E-Commerce Multifactor Model (AEMM) is presented here for consideration. Using the significant variables identified from the covariance and correlation coefficient analyses and on the basis of theoretical considerations in finance (as summarised previously), the model for estimation is as follows:

$$e\text{-}stockret_{i,t} = \alpha_i + (\beta_1)_i MRP_t + (\beta_2)_i IP_t + (\beta_3)_i NAS_t + (\beta_4)_i CC_t + (\beta_5)_i FE_t + \varepsilon_{it} \quad (5.1)$$

where:

$e\text{-}stockret_{i,t}$	= the return of e-commerce stock/sector i in period t;
α_i	= the expected value if each factor has a value of zero;
$(\beta_1)_i \dots (\beta_5)_i$	= sensitivities of the stock return to the factors;
MRP_t	= the value of market risk premium in period t;
IP_t	= the value of industrial production in period t;
NAS_t	= the value of the NASDAQ Composite Index in period t;
CC_t	= the value of consumer confidence in period t;
FE_t	= the rate of the Australian dollar against US dollar, and
ε_{it}	= random error term.

This is a linear model, which is developed following the usual practice of adopting linear models in stock pricing econometric modelling. The underlying hypothesis in this model is that this set of factors is important in determining and explaining the movements in e-commerce stock prices. The set of factors include the relevant forces influencing the Australian financial market represented by *MRP, IP* and *CC*, while the international factors representative of the global financial system are proxied by the NASDAQ and foreign exchange rate.

The AEMM is a static model, it has the limitation that time is not incorporated here. However, AEMM is relatively appropriate if it is assumed that investors are myopic (no systematic variations in the investment opportunity set) and the utility function of the investors is logarithmic (see Markowitz 1959; Ziemba and Vickson 1975; Mossin 1968). Empirical validity of these assumptions may be a subject of dispute, however, these assumptions have operational advantages. On the basis of these assumptions Markowitz (1959) has also justified the use of the one period mean-variance model for stochastic stock valuation and portfolio selection (Markowitz 1959).

This multifactor model differs from the traditional CAPM and the market model in that both are single-factor models. The estimated results, using the ordinary least squares principle, of the developed model for each sector are shown in Table 5.2 below (where *t*-statistic values appear in parentheses below the estimated coefficients):

Table 5.2 Estimated Equations of the Five-factor Model by Sector

Casino and Gaming *(CG)* – Appendix 5.4(2)

$$\textit{e-stockret}(\widehat{CG})_t = -21.8255 + 0.7447\textit{MRP}_t + 0.2459\textit{IP}_t - 0.0006\textit{NAS}_t - 0.1415\textit{CC}_t + 0.1898\textit{FE}_t$$
$$\quad\ (-1.1388)\qquad (0.8814)\qquad (-1.1082)\qquad (-0.9401)\qquad (-1.3073)\qquad (0.6330)$$

$R^2 = 0.2593$

Computer and Office Services *(COS)* – Appendix 5.4(2)

$$\textit{e-stockret}(\widehat{COS})_t = -2.4881 + 0.3416\textit{MRP}_t + 0.0088\textit{IP}_t + 0.0001\textit{NAS}_t + 0.0356\textit{CC}_t - 0.0470\textit{FE}_t$$
$$\quad\ (-0.6039)\qquad (1.8806)\qquad (0.1838)\qquad (0.4704)\qquad (1.5308)\qquad (-0.7284)$$

$R^2 = 0.8239$

Diversified Media *(DM)* – Appendix 5.4(2)

$$\textit{e-stockret}(\widehat{DM})_t = -1.8278 + 0.2301\textit{MRP}_t + 0.0196\textit{IP}_t + 0.0002\textit{NAS}_t + 0.0365\textit{CC}_t - 0.0926\textit{FE}_t$$
$$\quad\ (-0.4489)\qquad (1.2818)\qquad (0.4152)\qquad (1.3856)\qquad (1.5858)\qquad (-1.4537)$$

$R^2 = 0.7697$

Equipment and Services *(ES)* – Appendix 5.4(2)

$$\textit{e-stockret}(\widehat{ES})_t = -43.0254 + 0.6599\textit{MRP}_t + 0.2446\textit{IP}_t + 0.0005\textit{NAS}_t - 0.1546\textit{CC}_t - 0.5296\textit{FE}_t$$
$$\quad\ (-0.9575)\qquad (0.3331)\qquad (0.4702)\qquad (0.3212)\qquad (-0.6091)\qquad (0.7531)$$

$R^2 = 0.3443$

Health and Medical Services (*HMS*) – Appendix 5.4(2)

$$e\text{-}stockret(\; \hat{HMS}\;)_t = 71.8150 - 6.9365MRP_t - 0.3175IP_t + 0.0073NAS_t + 0.8038CC_t - 2.6109FE_t$$
$$(0.2879) \quad (-0.6309) \quad (-0.1099) \quad (0.8182) \quad (0.5705) \quad (-0.6689)$$

$R^2 = 0.2744$

High Technology (*HT*) – Appendix 5.4(2)

$$e\text{-}stockret(\; \hat{HT}\;)_t = -5.3726 + 0.1895MRP_t + 0.0517IP_t + 0.0000NAS_t - 0.0130CC_t + 0.0092FE_t$$
$$(-0.8990) \quad (0.7193) \quad (0.7471) \quad (0.0936) \quad (-0.3843) \quad (0.0986)$$

$R^2 = 0.3202$

Miscellaneous Financial Services (*MFS*) – Appendix 5.4(2)

$$e\text{-}stockret(\; \hat{MFS}\;)_t = -1.5770 - 0.0025MRP_t + 0.0275IP_t + 0.0001NAS_t + 0.0120CC_t - 0.0584FE_t$$
$$(-0.2301) \quad (-0.0083) \quad (0.3463) \quad (0.2280) \quad (0.3091) \quad (-0.5450)$$

$R^2 = 0.1445$

Miscellaneous Services (*MS*) – Appendix 5.4(2)

$$e\text{-}stockret(\; \hat{MS}\;)_t = 4.4975 - 0.2014MRP_t - 0.1554IP_t + 0.0008NAS_t + 0.0569CC_t - 0.0935FE_t$$
$$(0.4541) \quad (-0.4614) \quad (-1.3554) \quad (2.2194) \quad (1.0176) \quad (0.6034)$$

$R^2 = 0.5961$

Other Telecommunications (*OT*) – Appendix 5.4(2)

$$e\text{-}stockret(\; \hat{OT}\;)_t = -9.7822 + 0.4262MRP_t + 0.0528IP_t + 0.0000NAS_t - 0.0282CC_t - 0.1188FE_t$$
$$(-2.2661) \quad (2.2394) \quad (1.0556) \quad (0.0889) \quad (-1.1552) \quad (1.7586)$$

$R^2 = 0.7391$

Retail/Retail Investment (*RRI*) – Appendix 5.4(2)

$$e\text{-}stockret(\ \hat{RRI}\ )_t = 2.2943 + 0.2020MRP_t - 0.0705IP_t + 0.0003NAS_t + 0.0357CC_t + 0.0201FE_t$$
$$(0.4430) \quad (0.8848) \quad (-1.1756) \quad (1.7527) \quad (1.2199) \quad (0.2480)$$

$R^2 = 0.7117$

Portfolio Return (*PR*) – Appendix 5.4(2)

$$e\text{-}stockret(\ \hat{PR}\ )_t = -3.4032 - 0.1296MRP_t + 0.0064IP_t + 0.0006NAS_t + 0.0395CC_t - 0.0639FE_t$$
$$(-0.2548) \quad (-0.2201) \quad (0.0413) \quad (1.2703) \quad (0.5231) \quad (-0.3057)$$

$R^2 = 0.4812$

No serious econometric problems such as multicollinearity, heteroskadesticity and autocorrelation problems were evident from the interpretation of the results of the various tests conducted in this research. There are no exact linear relationships among the independent variables in the regression tests conducted in this study and for multicollinearity, the results from the covariance and correlation analsyses conducted on the independent variables suggest there are no estimates of β_j with R^2_j "close" to one, i.e. exact linear relationships among the independent variables. The conclusion on autocorrelation is derived from the augmented Dickey and Fuller (1979) ρ-tests and t-tests on regressions of time series on their lagged values (see Section 5.2.3 and Table 5.4) and the EMH regression (Section 6.10) analyses done on the e-commerce sectors. The time series model in this research deal with a relatively short period of data and is therefore not expected to experience an increasing variance over time or serious heteroskedasticity. The results from Table 5.2 above are summarised and statistically tested at the 20% significance level in Table 5.3 below.

Tables 5.3 summarises the important statistics of the estimated regression equations for the sectors with the coefficient of determination or R^2 shown in the last column. The statistical significance of the coefficient at the 20% level of significance is shown below each factor for statistical inference. The more liberal 20% significance level for testing the coefficient is used due to the small sample size ($n = 12$ monthly observations) and the fact that e-commerce is a new market phenomenon with the effects of the variables still relatively undiscovered and the hypothesis tests against a two-sided alternative at 20% significance level is appropriate to tease out any pervasive characteristics in the explanatory variables.

Table 5.3 Estimated Regression Equations (by Sector) and the t-Test

Sector	α	MRP_t β	IP_t β	NAS_t β	CC_t β	FE_t β	R^2
R(CG)$_t$	-21.8255	0.7447	0.2459	-0.0006	-0.1415	0.1898	0.2593
t-statistic	-1.1388	0.8814	1.1082	-0.9401	-1.3073	0.6330	
20% c =1.440							
p-value	0.2982	0.412	0.3102	0.3835	0.239	0.5501	
R(COS)$_t$	-2.2881	0.3416	0.0088	0.0001	0.0356	-0.0470	0.8239
t-statistic	-0.6039	1.8806	0.1838	0.4704	1.5308	-0.7284	
20% c =1.440		sign.			sign.		
R(DM)$_t$	-1.8278	0.2301	0.0196	0.0002	0.0365	-0.0926	0.7697
t-statistic	-0.4489	1.2818	0.4152	1.3856	1.5858	-1.4537	
20% c =1.440					sign.	sign.	
p-value	0.6693	0.2472	0.6924	0.2152	0.1639	0.1963	
R(ES)$_t$	-43.0254	0.6599	0.2446	0.0005	-0.1546	-0.5296	0.3443
t-statistic	-0.9575	0.3331	0.4702	0.3212	-0.6091	0.7531	
20% c =1.440							
R(HMS)$_t$	71.8150	-6.9365	-0.3175	0.0073	0.8038	-2.6109	0.2744
t-statistic	0.2879	-0.6309	-0.1099	0.8182	0.5705	-0.6689	
20% c =1.440							
R(HT)$_t$	-5.3726	0.1895	0.0517	0.0000	0.0130	0.0092	0.3202
t-statistic	-0.8990	0.7193	0.7471	0.0936	-0.3843	0.0986	
20% c =1.440							
R(MFS)$_t$	-1.5770	-0.0025	0.0275	0.0001	0.0120	0.0584	0.1445
t-statistic	-0.2301	-0.0083	0.3463	0.2280	-0.3091	-0.5450	
20% c =1.440							
R(MS)$_t$	4.4975	-0.2014	-0.1554	0.0008	0.0569	0.0935	0.5961
t-statistic	0.4541	-0.4614	-1.3554	2.2194	1.0176	0.6034	
20% c =1.440				sign.			
p-value	0.6657	0.6608	0.2241	0.0683	0.3482	0.5684	
R(OT)$_t$	-9.7822	0.4262	0.0528	0.0000	0.0282	0.1188	0.7391
t-statistic	-2.2661	2.2394	1.0556	0.0889	-1.1552	1.7586	
20% c =1.440	sign.	sign.				sign.	
p-value	0.0640	0.0664	0.3318	0.9321	0.2919	0.1291	
R(RRI)$_t$	2.2943	0.2020	-0.0705	0.0003	0.0357	0.0201	0.7117
t-statistic	0.4430	0.8848	-1.1756	1.7527	1.2199	0.2480	
20% c =1.440			sign.	sign.			
p-value	0.6733	0.4103	0.2843	0.1302	0.2683	0.8124	
R(PR)$_t$	-3.4032	-0.1296	0.0064	0.0006	0.0395	-0.0639	0.4812
t-statistic	-0.2548	-0.2201	0.0413	1.2703	0.5231	-0.3057	
20% c =1.440							
p-value	0.8074	0.8331	0.9684	0.251	0.6196	0.7701	

Notes:
Hypothesis test - two-sided.
Significance levels - 20%.
c = critical value.
sign. = statistically significant.

5.2.2.1 Casino and Gaming

In the regression equation the explanatory variables explain 25.93 per cent of the dependent variable as represented by R^2 in the study period. The relatively lower explanatory power for the casino and gaming sector may not be too surprising as there are probably other factors, which should influence the value of returns of an e-commerce gaming stock such as disposable income, variety of games on offer, minimum bet size, nature of gaming and others. These factors are probably included in the error term of the estimated regression equation. The predicted stock return for a casino and gaming stock if all the factors are set at zero (α), which is the value of the intercept –21.8255 and means that when the *MRP, IP, NAS, CC* and *FE* are zero, then the return on the *CG* stock would be negative 21.8255. This scenario is probable as when consumer confidence, market risk premium, industrial production and foreign exchange are stagnant, it conjures negative sentiments about the economy and a zero *MRP* would not encourage investors to invest in stocks (as opposed to a risk-free asset) causing stock prices and returns to fall. A stagnant economy is unlikely to encourage or generate *FE* activities causing it to be dormant. *FE* has a positive correlation with returns indicating that when the Australian dollar is strong, stock returns in this sector would improve. This means that firms in the sector favour a stronger Australian dollar because it could lead to higher virtual gaming on the Internet rather than having to rely on overseas visitors going to real casinos because they are discouraged by the stronger local currency. As a leading global indicator of technology, a latent *NAS* is unlikely to offer investors any leads about the market or sector and may cause a sell-down of the stocks. The negative *NAS* and *CC* coefficients are "wrong" as, intuitively, positive correlations would be more meaningful and we could conclude that these factors are statistically insignificant for determining the stock returns in this sector.

Using the t-test for statistical inference, the coefficients for all the factors of the *CG* equation are insignificant at the 20% level of confidence. The t-test for the coefficients failed to reject H_0 at both levels, thus all the factors are statistically insignificant in reference to the population parameters.

5.2.2.2 Computer and Office Services

In the regression equation the independent variables explain 82.39 per cent of the dependent variable as represented by R^2 in the study period. This is considered high in terms of explanatory power of the independent factors on the dependent variable in this sector. The predicted stock return when all factors are zero for the *COS* sector is –2.2881 and considered rather neutral to all the other factors having a zero value. The statistically significant *MRP* and *CC* at the 20% level partly contribute to the high coefficient of determination. A positively correlated *MRP* to returns means that a higher *MRP* would encourage stock investment and increase the demand for stocks in this sector. Likewise a positively correlated and heightened *CC* would increase value of stocks in this sector. A negative *FE* is also considered normal for this sector, as a weaker Australian dollar will make the export services from this sector more competitive. Together with the *DM, OT* and *RRI* sectors, the *COS* sector also manifests two (2) statistically significant explanatory factors at the 20% level, i.e. *MRP* and *CC*.

5.2.2.3 Diversified Media

The independent variables explain 76.97 per cent of the dependent variable in the regression equation as represented by R^2 in the study period. This is another sector with strong explanatory power in the independent factors for the dependent variable. The predicted stock return when all factors are zero for this sector is -1.8278 and is among the lowest of the sectors analysed in terms of absolute value. The level of the constant term is therefore considered rather neutral to all the other factors having a zero value. This means that stock returns in this sector are marginally negative when the independent factors have zero value. The statistically significant factors in this regression equation are *CC* and *FE* at the 20% level. The coefficients for *CC* is 0.0356 and *FE* is -0.0926; this effectively means that the stock returns of this sector increases by 3.56% and decreases by 9.26% when consumer confidence rises and foreign exchange value decreases by one unit, respectively. The signs of the coefficients can be explained in that higher *CC* leads to better business performance and lower FE means more competitive export business. Though the factors *MRP* and *NAS* are statistically insignificant at the 20% level in terms of t-statistic, their *p*-values are 0.2472 and 0.2152 (Table 5.3), respectively, hence we would observe only 24.72% and 21.52% of the t-statistics in all random samples for these factors when the null hypothesis is true. This is rather strong evidence against H_0 and signifies that both these factors do have a certain degree of pervasive influence on the sector returns despite their insignificant t-statistics.

5.2.2.4 Equipment and Services

The intercept for the *ES* sector is -43.0254 and for statistical inference, all the factors are statistically insignificant at the 20% level. R^2 is 34.43 per cent. The large *p*-values of the factors provide little evidence against H_0 and we can conclude that the null hypothesis is true.

5.2.2.5 Health and Medical Services

The intercept for the *HMS* sector is 71.8150 and for statistical inference, all the factors are statistically insignificant at the 20% level. R^2 is 27.44 per cent. This high value of the intercept of 71.8150 does confirm the trait of medical services in that they are a necessity regardless of economic conditions. This high intercept also signifies the stronger resilience of this sector to economic variations. The large *p*-values of the factors provide little evidence against H_0 and we can conclude that the null hypothesis is true.

5.2.2.6 High Technology

The R^2 for this sector is 32.02% and all factors are statistically insignificant at the 20% level. The intercept for this equation is -5.3726. The large *p*-values of the factors (Table A5.4/1) provide little evidence against H_0 and we can conclude that the null hypothesis is true.

5.2.2.7 Miscellaneous Financial Services

All factors in the estimated equation are statistically insignificant at the 20% level and the R^2 of 14.45% is low compared to the other sectors analysed. The large *p*-values of the factors (Table A5.4/1) provide little evidence against H_0 and we can conclude that the null hypothesis is true.

5.2.2.8 Miscellaneous Services

The *NAS* is a statistically significant factor in the estimated equation at the 20% level and is positively correlated (t-statistic 2.2194) to the returns of this sector. The NASDAQ being a leading market indicator for Internet related business development explains this relationship. Other factors with a high degree of influence on returns based on their *p*-values are *IP* (0.2241) and CC (0.3482). *IP* has a negative correlation (–0.1554) to returns whilst *CC* (0.0569) is positively correlated. The reason for the negative *IP* relation to returns may be due to the nature of the sector, miscellaneous services, which does not represent any major industrial group and therefore would render this factor statistically insignificant to the equation. *CC* has the "right" sign and from its *p*-value it does presume to have some relatively significant influence on returns. The R^2 for this equation is 59.61%.

5.2.2.9 Other Telecommunications

The statistically significant factors in this sector are the intercept and *MRP* coefficients at the 20%. The R^2 is 73.91%. The signs of the statistically significant factors as they explain *OT* stock returns are consistent with the other sectors analysed so far, except for those in the *HMS* and *RRI* sectors. Firstly, the intercept is negative and the rationale is similar to that given for the *CG* sector. Secondly, a positive correlation between *MRP* and sector returns defines the risk and return relationship between the variables (per *COS* sector). The *p*-values of the factors *CC* (0.2919) and *FE* (0.1291) tend to suggest relative strong influence on the sector returns. Intuitively, *CC* has a strong influence on the use of telecommunication services and a positively correlated *FE* is representative of the fact that Australia imports a high percentage of its telecommunication technologies and a strong Australian dollar make it cheaper and more viable for imports. These cheaper imports would translate to lower costs and thus better financial performance.

5.2.2.10 Retail/Retail Investment

The statistically significant factors at the 20% are the *IP* and *NAS* coefficients. A positive *IP* coefficient with the sector return is indicative of the strong traditional connection between retail activity and industrial production. A higher *IP* level provides the economic impetus for a stronger and more robust retail activity. From the regression equation, the *NAS* factor also has a positive correlation with retail sector returns. As a global growth indicator of the new economy, the *NAS* would have an influence on the confidence of consumers for retail spending, especially in the electronic retail sector of Australia. This is logical from the perspective that Internet or electronic-based business transactions are retail-based or retail-oriented, whether it is business-to-consumer (B2C) or business-to-business (B2B), they constitute the bulk of the commercial transactions in monetary terms. The NASDAQ is the development catalyst for this electronic business growth and therefore acts as an important proxy for the retail industry. The *CC* factor is statistically insignificant at the 20% level, but with a *t*-statistic of 1.2199 (and at 20% significance level $c = 1.440$) it may suggest a more important relationship. This relationship is evident from the *p*-value of *CC*; which is 0.2683 or in other words, we would observe only 26.83% of all random samples when the null hypothesis is true and this is relatively strong evidence against H_0. As a result, we conclude that *CC* constitutes a relatively significant factor for determining stock return in this sector. The R^2 for this model is 71.17% suggesting the explanatory factors significantly explain the independent variable.

5.2.2.11 E-Commerce Portfolio Return

The e-commerce portfolio return is an aggregate return of all the individual stock returns in the sectors and is representative of the average e-commerce stock return across all sectors in this study. The regression equation for the portfolio returns against the five factors did not identify any statistically significant coefficients at the 20% level. The R^2 for the *PR* is 48.12% and almost midway between the highest R^2 of 82.39% and the lowest R^2 of 14.45%. The portfolio has a negative return as shown by its intercept of -3.4032 when all the other factors are zero and is also negatively influenced by the factors *MRP* and *FE*. At the portfolio level, the only factor that suggests some pervasive influence on its returns is the *NAS* based on its *p*-value of 0.2510 (Table 5.3) meaning that we would observe only 25.10% of the t-statistic value in all random samples when the null hypothesis is true. This again is weak evidence to support the H_0 and we can conjure that the *NAS* factor does have a pervasive influence on the portfolio returns.

5.2.3 Stationary Test

The tests of stationarity or unit root tests are conducted on the factors that have been tested to be statistically significant at the 20% level in the estimated regression equations in Section 5.2.2 above. The factors to be tested are *MRP, IP, NAS, CC* and *FE* as they all have been tested to be statistically significant at the 20% level in at least one of the sectors in the regression analysis (Table 5.3). Our approach to testing for a unit root uses the autoregressive process of order one, or the AR(1) model and the results are presented in Table 5.4 below.

The statistics presented in Table 5.4 are extracts from Appendixes 5.5 to 5.9. The coefficients on MRP_{t-1}, NAS_{t-1}, CC_{t-1} and FE_{t-1} all show that their estimates of $\hat{\rho}$ are less than unity. While they are all less than unity, we need to test whether they are statistically less than one using the t-statistics on each of the factors. The 10% critical value is -2.63, therefore, we fail to reject H_0: $\hat{\rho} = 1$ against H_1: $\hat{\rho} < 1$ at the 10% level for all the four factors. The failure to reject a unit root concludes that the data do not provide strong evidence against H_0. However, *MRP* does provide a relatively stronger case against H_0 because its larger *t*-statistic of -2.3651, which is closer to the 10% critical value of -2.63 and the *p*-value of 0.0396 are not considered strong evidence to support the null hypothesis.

Table 5.4 Dickey-Fuller Test Summary

Factor	$\hat{\theta}$	$\hat{\rho}$	*t*-Statistic	Critical value*
MRP	**-0.9551**	0.045	-2.3651	-2.63
IP	0.1878	1.188	0.9768	-2.63
NAS	-0.2250	0.775	-1.2670	-2.63
CC	-0.1909	0.809	-1.0368	-2.63
FE	-0.2391	0.761	-1.5105	-2.63

*Critical value for 10% significance level from Banerjee, Dolado, Galbraith and Hendry (1993, p. 103) no time trend.[29]

IP_{t-1} has an estimate of ρ greater than one and where the roots are greater than one, it implies an explosive series with an exponential trend in its mean and such a situation is not usually considered (Wooldridge 2000). Watsham and Parramore (1997) suggest "such series are unlikely because economic pressure would stop the values becoming infinite".

Weakly dependent processes are said to be integrated of order zero, I(0), which means that nothing needs to be done to such series before using them in regression analysis: "averages of such sequence already satisfy the standard limit theorems" (Woolridge 2000). By using these explanatory variables which have a unit root in our regression analysis, it implies that the usual asymptotic approximations need not hold and one solution would be to use the first difference of the variables for our analysis (Wooldridge 2000). The use of the first difference data on the five-variable linear model (equation (5.1)) is conducted in the following section.

5.2.4 Regression Analysis Integrated of Order One

The cointegration tests conducted in this research are made with the qualification that there is "no time trend" (i.e. trend-free) in the data series. This assumption under the traditional theoretical framework for stocks that returns (or prices) follows a random walk behaviour,

---

[29] The critical value at 10% significance level for the smallest sample size of 25 is used as a proxy for this study with n = 12.

which cannot be said for most economic variables. Appendix 5.4(1) presents the summary results of the sectorial regression equations integrated of order one and the null hypothesis, H_0: $\beta = 0$, was tested against a two-sided alternative, H_1: $\beta \neq 0$ at the 20% significance level. A summary of the statistically significant explanatory variables for e-commerce stock return is presented in Table 5.5 below.

Table 5.5 Summary of Statistically Significant Explanatory Variables Integrated of Order One

Sector Δe-stockret	ΔMRP	ΔIP	ΔNAS	ΔCC	ΔFE
CG	SS		SS	SS	SS
COS	SS			SS	
DM	SS		SS	SS	SS
ES					
HMS	SS		SS	SS	SS
HT					
MFS		SS	SS	SS	SS
MS					
OT	SS			SS	SS
RRI			SS		
PR			SS	SS	SS
Frequency	5	1	6	7	6

Note: *SS* = statistically significant at the 20% significance level.

Table 5.5 shows the explanatory factors *MRP, NAS, CC* and *FE* are statistically significant across sectors when the first difference of the times series data for the variables is used for the estimation. The use of the first difference data highlights the pervasiveness of these four explanatory variables in determining e-commerce stock returns across sectors. In the portfolio return (*PR*), the first difference (*ΔPR*) for July 1999 was not used but maintained in the original order due to several of the stocks (7) not being listed prior to that time and regression tests done indicate no-significant impact on the estimates as a result of this procedure. However, in a portfolio context the use of the first difference data in regression analysis between the e-commerce stock return (*ΔPR*) and the five independent variables (*ΔMRP, ΔIP, ΔNAS, ΔCC* and *ΔFE*) confirms the pervasiveness of only three of these five explanatory variables in determining e-commerce stock return as shown in equation (5.2) below. The *t*-statistics from the regression estimation of equation (5.2) (as presented in Appendix 5.4(3)), indicate the pervasiveness of *NAS, CC* and *FE* to be strongest for the e-commerce portfolio at the 10% significance level, i.e.:

$$e\text{-}stockret(\Delta \hat{PR})_t = -0.2798 - 0.3836\Delta MRP_t - 0.1780\Delta IP_t + 0.0018\Delta NAS_t + 0.0979\Delta CC_t$$
$$\qquad\quad (-1.4433)\quad (-0.7958)\qquad (-0.8614)\qquad (2.7894)\qquad (1.9726)$$
$$\qquad\qquad\qquad\qquad\qquad\qquad\qquad\qquad significant\qquad significant$$
$$\qquad\quad - 0.4059\Delta FE_t \qquad\qquad\qquad\qquad\qquad\qquad (5.2)$$
$$\qquad\quad (-2.1373)$$
$$\qquad\quad significant$$

$R^2 = 0.4812$

From an e-commerce portfolio perspective these three explanatory variables have the strongest influence on e-commerce stock return across all the stocks and sectors evaluated in this study. They remain statistically significant even when we use a more stringent significance level of 10% ($c = 1.943$). Of the three pervasive factors, *NAS* and *CC* have a positive correlation and *FE* has a negative correlation with the return of the portfolio of e-commerce stocks.

When *IP*, the tested explosive series, was excluded from the equation in our regression estimation, the R^2 of the estimated regression equation for the e-commerce portfolio increased to 64.82% (Appendix 5.4(4)) from 48.12% (Appendix5.4(2)). The following equation is estimated:

$$e\text{-}stockret(\Delta \hat{PR})_t = -0.1867 - 0.1303\Delta MRP_t + 0.0014\Delta NAS_t + 0.0742\Delta CC_t - 0.3310\Delta FE_t$$
$$\qquad\quad (-1.1821)\quad (-0.3477)\qquad (3.2638)\qquad (1.8303)\qquad (-1.9977)$$

$R^2 = 0.6428$

Under this scenario the three factors considered statistically significant at the 10% significance level are *NAS, CC* (*CC*'s selection is based on *p*-value of 0.1099 meaning that only 10.99% of the *t*-statistic value are observed in all random samples when the null hypothesis is true) and *FE*. *MRP* had a *t*-statistic of 0.3749 and was insufficient to reject the null hypothesis. Also, the increase in R^2 of 0.61% (64.82% as opposed to the original 64.21% shown in Appendixes 5.4(4 & 5), respectively) with the inclusion of *MRP* in the regression equation, is only marginal and the variable is therefore dropped from our analysis.

When both *IP* and *MRP* are dropped from the regression equation, the R^2 is 64.21% (Appendix 5.4(5)). On the basis of the criterion of goodness of fit, the following equation (5.3) is considered appropriate and selected for analysing e-commerce stock price:

$$e\text{-}stockret(\Delta \hat{PR})_t = -0.1900 + 0.0013\Delta NAS_t + 0.0692\Delta CC_t - 0.3287\Delta FE_t \qquad (5.3)$$
$$\qquad\quad (-1.2772)\qquad (3.7657)\qquad (1.9345)\qquad (-2.1045)$$

$R^2 = 0.6421$

All three factors in the estimated equation are statistically significant at the 10% significance level and this validates the present model and confirms the evidence of their pervasiveness on the portfolio return of the e-commerce stocks.

5.2.5 Cointegration Test of Individual Factors

To test whether two series cointegrate, we have to hypothesise the value of β from equation (4.5) and use the process described in 4.5.1.3 for testing cointegration. The cointegration test is conducted on the dependent variable *e-stockret* with each of the three pervasive factors of *NAS, CC* and *FE* using the Dickey-Fuller test as follows:

$$e\text{-}stockret(\mathbf{PR})_i = \hat{\alpha} + \beta\hat{NAS}_i; \tag{5.4}$$

$$e\text{-}stockret(\mathbf{PR})_i = \hat{\alpha} + \beta\hat{CC}_i; \tag{5.5}$$

$$e\text{-}stockret(\mathbf{PR})_i = \hat{\alpha} + \beta\hat{FE}_i \tag{5.6}$$

A summary of the cointegration test results (Appendixes 5.10, 5.11 & 5.12) for the above equations are presented in Table 5.6 as follows. From Table 5.6, the t-statistic of $(\hat{\mu}_{i-1})$ for the explanatory variable NAS is below the asymptotic critical value of −3.04 at the 10% significance level, this is evidence that $y_t - \beta x_t$ (equation (4.5)) is an I(0) process for the cointegration series: *e-stockret* and *NAS*, and the variables are cointegrated. The t-statistics for *CC*: 2.75 and *FE*: 2.72 are above but are rather close to the critical value of −3.04. The *p*-values of *CC*: 2.1% and *FE*: 2.2% do not suggest a strong case to reject the I(0) process. Therefore, we can conclude that these economic variables are significant factors, albeit *NAS* being a stronger explanatory factor, in explaining expected e-commerce stock returns and there exists an interactive and long-term relationship between them.

Table 5.6 Cointegration Statistics of I(1) Processes

Cointegration Series	Critical Value*	t-statistic $(\hat{\mu}_{t-1})$	p-value	
Equation 5.4 (NAS)	−3.04	−3.1414	0.0105	cointegration
Equation 5.5 (CC)	−3.04	−2.7487	0.0205	no cointegration
Equation 5.6 (FE)	−3.04	−2.7149	0.0218	no cointegration

*Asymptotic critical values from Davidson and MacKinnon (1993) at the 10% significance level and no time trend.

A regression involving the first differences, Δy_t and Δx_t, for each of the equations (5.4) to (5.6), is run and the results are presented in Table 5.7.

Table 5.7 Cointegration Statistics of Series with First Differences

Cointegration Series	Critical Value*	t-statistic $(\hat{\mu}_{t-1})$	p-value	
Equation 5.4 (ΔNAS)	−3.04	−5.3614	.0003	cointegration
Equation 5.5 (ΔCC)	−3.04	−3.7237	.0040	cointegration
Equation 5.6 (ΔFE)	−3.04	−3.7076	.0041	cointegration

*Asymptotic Critical Values from Davidson and MacKinnon (1993) at the 10% significance level and no time trend.

From Table 5.7, the t-statistic of $(\hat{\mu}_{t-1})$ for the all the explanatory variables *NAS*, *CC* and *FE* are all below the asymptotic critical value of −3.04 at the 10% significance level (Appendixes 5.10(1), 5.11(1) and 5.12(1)). This is evidence that the $y_t - \beta x_t$ (equation (4.5)) is an I(0) process and that the variables are cointegrated for variables running a regression involving the first difference of their time series.

The bivariate framework is used in this study for testing cointegration. The reverse specification of equations (5.4), (5.5) and (5.6) have been conducted to complete the bi-directional cointegration test and the results are shown in Table 5.7a. Under the bivariate framework, the cointegrating regression equations with reverse specifications (thus completing the bi-directional test of the variables) can be described as follows:

$$NAS_i = \overset{\wedge}{\alpha} + \overset{\wedge}{\beta}e\text{-}stockret(PR)_i \qquad (5.4a)$$

$$CC_i = \overset{\wedge}{\alpha} + \overset{\wedge}{\beta}e\text{-}stockret(PR)_i \qquad (5.5a)$$

$$FE = \overset{\wedge}{\alpha} + \overset{\wedge}{\beta}e\text{-}stockret(PR)_i \qquad (5.6a)$$

A reverse specification for the equations (5.4a), (5.5a) and (5.6a) have been conducted and the results are shown in Table 5.7a.

Table 5.7a Reverse Specification Cointegration Test Results with First Difference Data

Reverse Specification Cointegration Series	Critical Value	t-statistic $(\overset{\wedge}{\mu_{t-1}})$	p-value	
Equation 5.4a (ΔNAS)	-3.04	0.2149	0.8341	no cointegration
Equation 5.5a (ΔCC)	-3.04	-1.5830	0.1445	no cointegration
Equation 5.6a (ΔFE)	-3.04	-0.5323	0.6061	no cointegration

*Asymptotic Critical Values from Davidson and MacKinnon (1993) at the 10% significance level and no time trend.

The results in Table 5.7a indicate that there is no cointegration between the variables in the reverse direction meaning that e-commerce returns have no long-term causal relation to the performance of ΔNAS, ΔCC or ΔFE and the relationship is uni-directional as discussed above.

5.2.6 Cointegration Test of the Four-Variable Model

From the previous section, the individual explanatory factors are cointegrated with the dependent variable of order one and using the Dickey-Fuller test for a unit root the linear combination of these three variables are also integrated of the same order. The following Table 5.8 presents the estimates of the cointegrating regression for e-commerce stock return of the first difference with a combination of three macroeconomic factors of the same order using the Dickey-Fuller and the Augmented Dickey-Fuller tests. The hypothesis tested is H_0: $\rho = 0$ (no cointegration). The numbers in parentheses below the estimated regression coefficients are t-statistics (Appendix 5.13 and 5.14). The t-statistics of the coefficient of the lagged cointegrated residuals are –4.6468, Dickey-Fuller test (DF) (Appendix 5.13 and Table

A5.13/5) and −1.1967, Augmented Dickey-Fuller test (ADF) (Appendix 5.14 and Table A5.14/2).

The extension of the Dickey-Fuller test, the augmented Dickey-Fuller test used for the cointegrating regression in this section includes lagged changes. With the small sample size in this study, the inclusion of lags will mean losing observations and the sample power of the test would be deteriorated. It would also be impractical to implement the ADF test with the suggestion that we might include twelve lags for monthly data (Wooldridge 2000). Therefore, the test for unit root using the ADF model will not be conducted for the four-variable model, instead; only the Dickey-Fuller (DF) test is used to test for cointegration of the variables.

Table 5.8 Cointegration Test Summary for the 4-Variable Model

$$e\text{-}stockret(\Delta \hat{PR})_t = -0.1900 + 0.0013\Delta NAS_t + 0.0692\Delta CC_t - 0.3287\Delta FE_t$$
$$(-1.2772) \qquad (3.7657) \qquad (1.9345) \qquad (-2.1045)$$

$$R^2 = .6421$$

Dickey-Fuller: $\Delta e_t = -1.3686 e_{t-1}$
$$(-4.6468)$$

$$R^2 = .6835$$

Augmented DF: $\Delta e_t = -0.9585 e_{t-1} - 0.4538\Delta e_{t-1} - 0.4326\Delta e_{t-2}$
$$(-1.1967) \qquad (-0.7046) \qquad (-1.0407)$$

The t-statistics of the DF test for unit root of the lagged cointegrated residuals is −4.6468, for the four-variable model. The result indicates that e-commerce stock return is cointegrated with the combination of the three macroeconomic variables at 5% significance level and no cointegration if the critical value at 1% significance level is selected. The presence of cointegration at the 5% significance level suggests that e-commerce stock return, with first difference, maintains a long-term equilibrium relationship with the set of macroeconomic variables (of the same level), as well as with the individual variables of Table 5.7. Therefore, individually and as a linear combination of the three variables, with first difference, they are integrated of order zero. The cointegrating relation of the linear combination of the three variables is interpreted as an equilibrium relationship.

5.3 Empirical Results

The purpose of the this study was to select the pervasive factors to include in a valuation model based on the multivariate regression framework and to investigate whether these factors, representing economic and financial markets activities, can explain e-commerce stock returns in Australian stocks on the basis of the response of the stock prices to fluctuations in the values of these factors. The following is the estimated regression model (equation (5.7)) that best explains Australian e-commerce stock returns in the study period:

$$e\text{-}stockret(\Delta \hat{PR})_t = -0.1900 + 0.0013\Delta NAS_t + 0.0692\Delta CC_t - 0.3287\Delta FE_t \quad (5.7)$$

where:

$e\text{-}stockret(\Delta \hat{PR})_t$	= the estimated portfolio return for e-commerce stock of order one in period t;
ΔNAS_t	= the value of the NASDAQ composite index of order one in period t;
ΔCC_t	= the value of consumer confidence of order one in period t; and
ΔFE_t	= the exchange of the Australian dollar against the US dollar of order one in period t.

This study used the cointegration test to investigate the relation between e-commerce stock returns and the underlying economic and financial variables. The cointegration analysis carried out was to test for unit-root to determine their non-stationarity and, when the results indicated that the first-differenced series of each factor of equation (5.7) are stationary, a subsequent test was done to determine whether these two factors are cointegrated. The cointegration test (Table 5.6) of the bi-variate model between the e-commerce stock return (*e-stockret*) and the individual macroeconomic factors indicates that the variable *NAS* is individually cointegrated with the e-commerce stock portfolio return (*PR*) of order zero, and *CC* and *FE* are not statistically significant at the 10% level but their *p*-values do not suggest strong evidence for rejection of the I(0) process for the non-cointegration alternative. This result is not unexpected in that the e-commerce stock return, like other financial assets, is normally a linear function of a combination of economic variables (Lintner 1965b; Ross 1976; Chung and Tai 1997). However, Table 5.6 reports that the *NAS* variable has a cointegrating relation with e-commerce return, because, intuitively the performance of the NASDAQ is synonymous with e-commerce development in the absence of more specific economic fundamentals.

From Table 5.7, all three factors are individually integrated to e-commerce portfolio return of order one implying the *e-stockret(PR)* equation, *e-stockret(ΔPR)*, and past ΔNAS, ΔCC and ΔFE have a significant explanatory power for current *e-stockret(ΔPR)* movement at the 10% significance level with R^2 of 0.6421 (Appendix 5.4(5)).

5.3.1 NASDAQ (*NAS*)

The technology-laden NASDAQ is the leading global indicator for the e-commerce market. The NASDAQ is the equity capital exchange on which major e-commerce related companies (e.g. Dell, Oracle, Cisco, Microsoft and Intel) and many thousands of smaller technology-based companies are listed and together they account for the bulk of network hardware and software support for the new economy.

The US is the largest source of Australian merchandise imports (telecommunications equipment and computers – A\$2.3 billion in 1999/2000) and foreign investment (A\$165 billion as at 30/6/99).[30] Australia has a relatively new e-commerce sector in a nascent market and relies both on technology[31] and capital transfers from the United States to provide impetus to sustain its growth. Most major US technology companies with a business presence in Australia would bring along these valuable resources. The Australian equity market long recognises this strategic contribution and investors factor this economic fundamental into equity valuation. The level and impact of contributions in this area depend on the performance of the NASDAQ, the exchange that many of these US firms are listed on and use as a benchmark for investment decision-making.

The AEMM model shows a positive relationship between the NASDAQ composite index and e-commerce stock return with a β coefficient of +0.0013 indicating a 0.13% percent change to stock return for every unit of change in the NASDAQ composite index.

5.3.2 Consumer Confidence (*CC*)

The *CC* factor measures the level of confidence individuals have on the performance of the economy. *CC* correlates closely with unemployment, inflation and real income growth.[32] The consumer-goods industries are closely linked to the expectations that the Internet would serve as the platform for future e-commerce development. This would happen at both the business-to-consumer (B-2-C) and business-to-business (B-2-B) levels, and the efficiency of the Internet would increase the intensity of business volume through better efficiency. However, the current proportion of business at the B-2-B level figures more prominently compared to B-2-C activity in the e-commerce sector.

Rising stock prices can also boost consumer confidence. In the context of e-commerce stocks, *CC* reflects the fundamental state of the economy such as: *CC* is a leading indicator for the business cycle; *CC* index releases contain information on consumer assessment of the present expectations for the future; and improved expectations for the future indicates higher consumer spending now and in coming months. These indicators of the economy will invariably influence the stock valuation of the evolving e-commerce sector, which in the

---

[30] Department of Foreign Affairs and Trade-Australia, www.dfat.gov.au
[31] Federal Government outsourcing of its IT functions to US companies is an example.
[32] www.dismal.com

absence of meaningful historical financial performance relies heavily on the public sentiment, perception and assessment of the economy for its viability.

The estimated multifactor AEMM regression model for the valuation of Australian e-commerce stocks indicates positive relationship ($\beta = +0.0692$) between ΔCC and the return of e-commerce stock. This implies that for every unit change of ΔCC factor, e-commerce stock return would change by 6.92%. Therefore, when business conditions are good and consumer confidence signals economic growth, the expectations of the development of e-commerce will be optimistic having a positive impact on e-commerce stock valuation.

5.3.3 Foreign Exchange (*FE*)

The relationship between the value of e-commerce stocks and the strength of the Australian dollar against the US dollar are twofold. Firstly, the significant trade between the US and Australia in computer technology merchandise which is considered fundamental to the development of the e-commerce sector and is mainly sourced from the US is nominated in US dollars; secondly, the recent flow of investments in the form of foreign direct investments (FDI) and managed-fund investment in the secondary equity market has been increasingly evident from the presence of several high profile US investment management funds companies (e.g. SSB Citigroup Asset Management).

Though Australia relies on imports of foreign technology to build its new economy competitiveness, it remains predominantly dependent on exports, especially of natural resources and tourism, to maintain economic growth. The export sector is sensitive to the strength of the Australian dollar and any fall in the value of the Australian dollar vis-à-vis US dollar would benefit exporters. The foreign equity investment position of Australia has increased fourfold since the June 1988 quarter to June 2000 quarter (Reserve Bank of Australia website) signifying the growing importance of equity as a source of foreign investment. Australian foreign direct investment is likely to be more active when Australian assets (including equities) are considered relatively cheap and the contribution to this, among other economic factors, is a weaker local currency. This currency relationship is depicted in the β coefficient of ΔFE (–0.3287) in the AEMM model. The effect of this situation is the reverse for importers of technology. Generally, the sensitivity of the Australian economy, hence the equity market, to the strength of its currency is explained by its export orientation and the rise in foreign equity investments. This also has a significant impact on the e-commerce sector as a relatively minor component of the overall market.

5.4 Conclusion

In general, these findings imply that the estimated factors are significant in predicting changes in e-commerce stock returns and it can be claimed that e-commerce stock returns variability is fundamentally linked to these factors. The systematic risk measured by the *NAS*, *CC* and *FE* factors in the estimated model explains more than half of the variance (56.62%) of the e-commerce portfolio return PR. Such systematic risk level is consistent with an empirical study done by Drummen, Martin, Zimmermann and Heinz (1992) where systematic risk explains almost half of the variance of European stocks. The estimated model therefore provides a better measure of e-commerce portfolio return compared to the average 17% systematic risk level measured by the market model using the S&P/ASX 200 as the market index in the study conducted in Chapter 6 of this book.

CHAPTER 6

Volatility, Predictability and Returns Issues

6.1 Introduction

The return on a stock is the sum of the dividends paid and possible price appreciation of the stock. The rate of return is the return divided by the initial market value of the stock. Common stock is equity capital, that is real capital, and equity is risky in that there is a risk that the value of the equity investment might deteriorate. The value of a stock may depreciate for two reasons:

- the market price of the stock may actually fall; and/or
- the firm fails to pay dividend.

The first kind of risk is called a price risk and the second kind is the dividend yield. The presence of risk subjects the return on a stock to random variation (volatility). It is stochastic. If the market price appreciates and the firm pays dividends, there might be a good return on the stock. If the market price falls and/or dividends are not issued, the net return may be low or even negative. The financial markets offer the possibility of trade-off between expected return, liquidity and risk.

The variance of market return is the general measure of stock market volatility. The purpose of volatility analysis in this chapter is to determine the volatility of e-commerce stocks and their associated returns according to financial theory using stock prices and the market stock index to measure volatility of individual stock and its variability to the market. In this chapter, the general market is widely used as a benchmark against which the volatilities of the e-commerce stocks will be compared. The use of the market model as a yardstick is based on the assumption of the rational behaviour of the broad equity market. The evaluation of volatility of e-commerce return is to determine whether price movements reflect changes in fundamentals. The implication is that if e-commerce stock returns (prices) are excessively more volatile than the market, then this constitutes a rejection of the efficient market hypothesis and that the e-commerce sector does not reflect the same economic fundamentals as the general market. In this chapter, three types of risk measured by beta, being market risk, sector risk and company risk, are analysed in the volatility study.

This chapter further analyses the volatility profile of the selected e-commerce stocks as to whether they are subject to systematic or unsystematic influence and hypothesises the association between e-commerce stock volatility and return. By removing the portion of the e-commerce return that is associated with the market's return, we are able to reduce the variance of the abnormal return. This will allow a better appreciation of the event effects of the e-commerce phenomenon on the equity market. Empirical studies relating changes in stock market volatility to movements in expected returns to stocks include those by Merton (1980), Poterba and Summers (1986), French, Schwert and Stambaugh (1987) and Bollerslev,

Engle and Wooldridge (1988). The traditional explanation for the risk-return relationship is that the higher returns are compensation for higher systematic risk (Fama and French 1993, 1996). This is in contrast to the suggestion by Lakonishok, Shleifer and Vishny (LSV) (1994) that low book-to-market, or growth stocks, which describes the e-commerce stocks scenario in the study period, are more glamorous than value stocks and thus attract naive investors who push prices and lower the expected returns of these securities. Furthermore, Lakonishok et al. (1994) argue that the return premia associated with the priced factors for growth stocks, are too large and their covariances with macro factors too low, in some cases negative, to be considered compensation for systematic risk. The approach adopted in this chapter seeks to put the volatility of e-commerce stocks into perspective by comparing their stock prices to various market benchmarks, such as the general market index, in this case the SP/ASX 200 Index. The stocks' systematic risk (β) will be analysed from the firm, industry and portfolio perspectives to profile their risk characteristics.

The market model approach is used to determine the betas of the selected stocks to gauge their relative volatility to general market stock movements. The CAPM will then be used to compare *ex post* e-commerce stock returns with expected returns estimated from using the model to examine the volatility of e-commerce stock prices over the study period and to assess market efficiency (e.g. Leroy and Porter 1981; Shiller 1981a, 1981b). Also Grossman and Shiller (1981) have compared the ex-post realised prices with the expected price and concluded that stock prices are too volatile to support efficient markets. Though the CAPM is an *ex ante* model, this comparison will aid the appreciation and understanding of e-commerce stock price volatility and its magnitude in relation to *ex-post* returns using this traditional valuation method. The CAPM is an *expectation* model and the CAPM analysis in this chapter describes what investors believe to determine e-commerce stock returns; the results provide a benchmark for highlighting the empirical behaviour of e-commerce stocks in relation to investor expectations. The risk-free rate used is the geometric mean of the 90-day Australian Treasury bill rates of 5.63% (Appendix 6.3) and the market risk premium is the difference between the geometric means of the S&P/ASX 200 stock returns (8.22%)[33] and 90-day Treasury bill rates (5.63%)[34] calculated to be 2.59%, being 8.22% minus 5.63% (Appendix 6.3), for the period from 1992 to 2000. The data pertaining to 90-day Treasury Notes is available from the Reserve Bank of Australia only from 1992 and the estimation period used should be of the longest possible historical period for the risk premium measurement (Damodaran 1994). The rationale for using the geometric mean is based on the assumption that investors will hold the e-commerce stocks for multi-periods for capital gains (being the sole return to e-stock investors in the absence of dividends), considering most e-commerce firms are recent start-ups selling ideas or products in the early stage of the product life cycle, and require relatively longer periods to establish a foothold in the market and reap the full

---

[33] Officer (1989) found the average rate of return on the AGSM value-weighted accumulation index over the ten-year period commencing 1978 was approximately 18.5 per cent per annum.
[34] This rate would be lower using the 3-month Treasury note yield (i.e. 5.28%) to coincide with the study period from July 1999 to June 2000 as shown in Appendix 6.1. The longer period is preferred in this research.

financial benefits. An analysis using the arithmetic means to calculate the expected returns $E(R_i)$ is also presented below for comparative reasons between the two types of mean.

6.2 Determining the Company Beta Values

The time series for betas is generally preferred to be the longest possible. However, in the absence of a longer times series for e-commerce returns it is only possible to measure this risk factor by comparing the calculated betas for e-commerce firms, using the single index market model, with the market beta or with the betas of other firms during the same period to gauge the degree of volatility. The company beta value is the risk of the individual e-commerce companies and is derived from the CAPM. The tendency of a stock to move up or down with the market is reflected in its beta coefficient, β. Beta is a key element of the CAPM. A stock that moves up and down in step with the general market is defined as an average stock and would have a beta of 1.0. For such a stock, if the market moves up by 5 per cent, the stock moves up by 5% and if the market falls by 5%, the stock likewise falls by 5%. Theoretically, it is possible for a stock to have a negative beta where the stock's returns would tend to rise when the returns on the other stocks fall. However, this may not be true as in practice market analyst firms like Value Line – which calculates more than 1700 stocks – has not found a negative beta (Brigham and Houston 2000). Empirical tests by Black, Jensen and Scholes (1972), Miller and Scholes (1972), Fama and MacBeth (1973), Blume and Friend (1973), Ball, Brown and Officer (1976) and Foster (1978) generally found that the relationship between betas and returns to be positive and linear. It is not impossible for a stock in a particular period to move in the opposite direction to the general market even if it has a positive beta and the main cause of this is normally company-specific factors.

The standard procedure for estimating company beta by regressing the stock returns of the selected e-commerce companies against market returns (Damodaran 1994) is adopted here and the slope of the regression, that is the beta, is presented in Table 6.1. The length of the estimation period is from July 1999 to June 2000 and the length of period is selected for three reasons: the limited availability of e-commerce market data; the selection of e-commerce firms with largely similar age to maintain comparability; and to minimise changes to risk characteristics had a longer period been used. The return interval used for estimating stock return is on a monthly basis to reduce bias in beta estimates due to non-trading. Betas obtained from regressions using monthly return intervals, compared to daily returns, are less likely to contain estimation errors and fewer tendencies of betas regressing toward the average of the overall market. However, several stocks (i.e. *My Casino, Pocketmail, B2B.Net* and *Wine Planet*) did not trade for several months in the selected period and the betas of these stocks are expected to show reduced correlation between stock returns and market returns due to non-trading.

Table 6.1 E-Commerce Firms' Betas: July 1999 to June 2000

	Company	Std. Deviation	Beta
1	My Casino	59.59%	0.03
2	Sausage Software	28.58%	5.29
3	Solution 6	38.43%	5.57
4	Reckon Group	19.54%	2.96
5	Swish Group	22.55%	4.05
6	Pocketmail	296.52%	3.70
7	131.shop.com	24.06%	4.81
8	B2B.Net.Technology	801.31%	-23.51
9	Coms 21	19.22%	1.46
10	Etrade Australia	19.57%	0.09
11	AOL	82.44%	6.24
12	Candle	11.25%	2.61
13	Liberty One	31.17%	-1.16
14	Spike Networks	45.45%	7.50
15	Webjet	29.67%	2.71
16	Travel.com	67.28%	2.81
17	Ecorp	33.03%	4.31
18	Wine Planet	56.22%	11.95

Source: From Appendix 6.4.

Figure 6.1 below depicts the volatility of the e-commerce firms' betas in relation to the market beta (equals 1); beta is shown on the y-axis. The numbers on the x-axis represent the e-commerce firms and correspond to those beside the firms in Table 6.1 above. Figure 6.1 shows that majority of the e-commerce stocks have betas greater than one and are thus more volatile than the market; and stocks *1 (My Casino)* and *10 (Etrade)* have betas less than one and are, therefore, less volatile than the market. The returns of the positive-beta stocks are expected to increase whenever the overall stock market rises. This implies that the return of most e-commerce stocks in this study is expected to rise when overall stock market return increases. *B2B.Net* and *Liberty One* are stocks with negative betas and the negativity implies that their stock return would tend to rise whenever the returns on other stocks fall. Both these firms are unlikely to have negative betas considering the nature of their businesses in health services and telecommunications, respectively. Traditionally, both these sectors have positive betas as their activities are perceived to have positive correlation with the performance of the mainstream business sectors, or the general market. The cause of the negative betas may be due to one or a combination of several reasons: the holding period or the length of time that the betas were calculated is not long enough to allow a statistically significant sample; the average market return during the period studied; and the interval choice within the holding period.

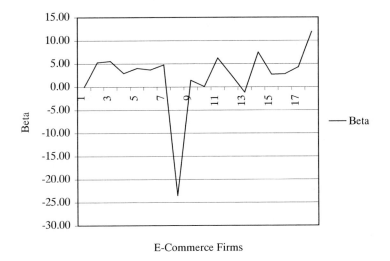

E-Commerce Firms

Figure 6.1 E-Commerce Firms' Betas

Due to the limited availability of data in the e-commerce sector, the length of time used for calculating the betas may be insufficient for both firms and, in the case of *B2B.Net* the non-trading period that caused the break in the time series may have contributed to the degree of correlation between the variables.

The standard deviation, σ, as shown in Table 6.1, measures the tightness of the probability distribution of returns for the e-commerce stocks. The smaller the standard deviation, the tighter the probability distribution of returns for the stock, and the lower the riskiness of the stock. In terms of return volatility measured by the standard deviation of the individual stocks, *Pocketmail* and *B2B.Net* have the highest standard deviations of 296.52 per cent and 801.31 per cent, respectively, but these extremities are likely due to the extended non-trading period of these stocks in the study period. Therefore, like their betas, the standard deviations of these stocks may not provide a fair representation of their state of volatility. The same can be said for *My Casino* and *Wine Planet* as a result of the lower correlation from non-trading periods. The standard deviations of *Candle* and *Coms 21* do tend to show some consistency with their low betas, with both having the lowest standard deviations and betas among the positive-beta stocks.

6.3 Risk Decomposition

The systematic and unsystematic risk profile shown in Table 6.2 indicates that the e-commerce stocks were to a large degree subject to unsystematic risk (82%) rather than systematic risk (18%) in the study period. This means that there was less of a tendency for the e-commerce stock prices to move together with the general market variability and this trend has also been evident for other stocks over the past few decades where there is an increase in idiosyncratic volatility relative to market volatility (Campbell et al. 2001). This situation can be explained by the higher return variability of the e-commerce stock portfolio where monthly σ equals 49.82 per cent (Appendix 6.6), compared to the general market where monthly σ is 3.13 per cent (Appendix 6.4).

The stock with the lowest total risk was *Candle* with 0.0132 compared with the highest of 65.765 for *B2B.Net*. Generally, stocks with higher total risks (i.e. *My Casino, Solution 6, Pocketmail, B2B.Net, AOL, Liberty One, Spike* and *Ecorp*) also had a relatively higher unsystematic risk component suggesting this class of stocks was more subject to variations peculiar to the firm and industry. Whilst stocks with lower total risk (*Sausage, Swish, 131.Shop* and *Candle*) had a higher percentage of systematic risk. In summary, the high level of total risk could be attributable to higher unsystematic risk of the individual e-commerce stocks, and stocks with lower total risk tend to move more in-tune with the general market. As the stocks under the high and low total risk categories are evenly represented by all sectors it is difficult to identify specific sectors that are peculiar to each risk category and we thus conclude that the total risk of the firms constitutes mainly unsystematic risk and is a consequence of firm-specific volatility.

Table 6.2 below exhibits the systematic and unsystematic risk components of the e-commerce firms in this study. It can be conjured from the total risk profile analysis above that the value of most Australian e-commerce stocks was driven by firm-specific conditions and development. This explains the wide market volatility (β_i) band for the positive-beta e-commerce stocks of between 0.03 and 11.95 or –1.16 to –23.51 if the negative-beta stocks are considered (Table 6.1). The total risk or stand-alone risk of an e-commerce stock is the sum of the market risk (systematic risk) and the firm-specific risk (unsystematic risk). From Table 6.2, the average firm-specific or unsystematic risk for the e-commerce stocks is 82%, while the systematic or market risk is 18%. This relationship in terms of the stock's total risk is depicted in Figure 6.2.

The market risk is that part of a stock security's stand-alone risk that cannot be eliminated by diversification while the firm-specific risk can be eliminated by proper diversification. In a portfolio context, the portfolio stand-alone risk can be reduced when more stocks are added to the portfolio and the portfolio standard deviation, σ_p, falls as a result. Almost half of the inherent riskiness or volatility of an individual stock, σ_i, or the standard deviation of a one-stock portfolio can be eliminated through proper diversification (Anderson and Leonardi 1982; Stokie 1982; Elton and Gruber 1987).

Table 6.2 Systematic and Unsystematic Risk Profile: July 1999 to June 2000

	Stock	Total Risk	Systematic Risk	Unsystematic Risk
1	My Casino	0.3807	0.0000	0.3807
		100.00%	*0.00%*	*100.00%*
2	Sausage	0.0851	0.0275	0.0577
		100.00%	*32.28%*	*67.72%*
3	Solution 6	0.1536	0.0304	0.1232
		100.00%	*19.81%*	*80.19%*
4	Reckon	0.041	0.009	0.032
		100.00%	*21.20%*	*78.80%*
5	Swish	0.0537	0.0161	0.0375
		100.00%	*30.09%*	*69.91%*
6	Pocketmail	9.1559	0.0134	9.1425
		100.00%	*0.15%*	*99.85%*
7	131.Shop	0.0598	0.0227	0.0371
		100.00%	*37.93%*	*62.07%*
8	B2B.Net	65.7650	0.5429	65.2221
		100.00%	*0.83%*	*99.17%*
9	Coms21	0.0401	0.0021	0.0380
		100.00%	*5.23%*	*94.77%*
10	Etrade	0.0421	0.0000	0.0421
		100.00%	*0.02%*	*99.98%*
11	AOL	0.6985	0.0383	0.6602
		100.00%	*5.48%*	*94.52%*
12	Candle	0.0132	0.0067	0.0065
		100.00%	*50.67%*	*49.33%*
13	Liberty One	0.1042	0.0013	0.1029
		100.00%	*1.26%*	*98.74%*
14	Spike	0.2133	0.0552	0.1580
		100.00%	*25.90%*	*74.10%*
15	Webjet	0.0935	0.0072	0.0863
		100.00%	*7.74%*	*92.26%*
16	Travel.Com	0.0409	0.0077	0.0332
		100.00%	*18.91%*	*81.09%*
17	Ecorp	0.1140	0.0183	0.0957
		100.00%	*16.01%*	*83.99%*
18	Wine Planet	0.3026	0.1403	0.1624
		100.00%	*46.35%*	*53.65%*
	All stocks average	*100%*	*17.77%*	*82.23%*

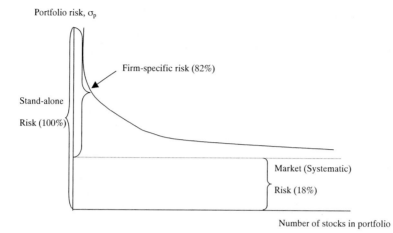

Figure 6.2 E-Commerce Stocks Stand-Alone Risk Profile

From Figure 6.2, it can be concluded that some of the risk inherent in individual e-commerce stocks can be eliminated through holding multiple stocks in a portfolio. If the average systematic risk of these e-commerce stocks is 18% of the total stand-alone risk and cannot be eliminated, the part of the stocks that represents diversifiable risk is 82% and a large part of this risk can be eliminated. The magnitude of the diversifiable risk eliminated through diversification depends on the correlation coefficient for the returns of the e-commerce stocks in the portfolio and from Appendix 6.9 most of the e-commerce stocks are positively correlated (except *My Casino*), but not perfectly so. Under such conditions, combining the stocks into portfolios will reduce but does not eliminate risk completely. The portfolio analysis of the e-commerce stocks will be carried out in Chapter 7.

The risk profile of the e-commerce stock is consistent with the market behaviour of the firms, which are subject to constant changes in corporate strategies reflecting, to a great extend, the nature of the "industry". The market knowledge of the many firms in this study that were involved in alliance negotiations with potentially strategic partners (i.e. *Sausage, Solution 6* and *Ecorp*) would influence investors' valuation of Internet firms. Recent studies[35] suggest a positive association between the announcements of an alliance and the market-to-book ratios of Internet stocks. The high unsystematic risk factor situation of the e-commerce market is compounded by the market's lack of a consensus on the value-drivers of e-commerce stocks, with different value-factors such as losses (Hand 1999), message-posting volume (Wysocki 1998) and unique visitors (Bontis and Mills 2000) being suggested.

---

[35] At the University of Rochester.

6.4 Expected Returns

The reason for the use of the mean-variance based asset pricing models to evaluate volatility in this section is due to the absence of significant earnings or dividend data for e-commerce firms necessary to apply the dividend-based volatility test models consistent with those adopted by Barsky and De Long (1993) or Shiller (1981a). Shiller's just mentioned study also rejects the widely held view that stock prices are determined by dividends in an efficient market, thus rendering the dividend-based models less appropriate in this study. The CAPM is used to study the e-commerce stock volatility in this section by comparing actual historical market e-commerce returns with the expected returns estimated from using the model, and the results provide a benchmark for highlighting the empirical behaviour of e-commerce stocks. It is common knowledge that stock returns are expected to exhibit a certain degree of volatility due to the arrival of new information about firms. The study of volatility here is essentially to examine whether e-commerce stock returns are excessively volatile as stock prices react to new innovations or information (i.e. fundamentals) pertaining to the e-commerce firm or market and how this volatility will likely affect future financial performance and hence stock return.

As investors demand a premium for bearing risk, then the higher the riskiness of a stock, the higher the expected return has to be to induce investors to invest in or hold the stock. The CAPM is an important tool used to analyse the relationship between risk and rates of return, and measures the relevant riskiness of an individual stock in terms of its contribution to the riskiness of a well-diversified portfolio. The CAPM is used to determine the expected return of an e-commerce company using the company specific betas in Table 6.1, with the geometric mean of 5.63 per cent (Appendix 6.3) being used as proxy for the risk-free rate calculated from the 90-day Australian Treasury note rates and the Australian market risk premium used

$((E(R_m) - R_f)$ is 2.59 per cent (Appendix 6.3). The CAPM (or the Security Market Line) equation using this data is as follows:

$$E(R_i) = R_f + \beta_i(E(R_m) - R_f)$$

$$E(r_i) = 5.63\% + \beta_i(8.22\% - 5.63\%)$$

or: $\quad E(r_i) = 5.63\% + \beta_i(2.59\%)$

The estimate expected returns $E(r_i)$ for the individual e-commerce firms are presented in Table 6.3 below.

Table 6.3 CAPM Estimated Expected Returns (geometric means): July 1999 to June 2000

	Company	Expected Return $E(r)$	Risk-free rate	Beta	Market risk premium
1	My Casino	5.71%	5.63%	0.03	2.59%
2	Sausage Software	19.33%	5.63%	5.29	2.59%
3	Solution 6	20.04%	5.63%	5.57	2.59%
4	Reckon Group	13.31%	5.63%	2.96	2.59%
5	Swish Group	16.13%	5.63%	4.05	2.59%
6	Pocketmail	15.20%	5.63%	3.70	2.59%
7	131.shop.com	18.07%	5.63%	4.81	2.59%
8	B2B.Net.Technology	-55.25%	5.63%	-23.51	2.59%
9	Coms 21	9.42%	5.63%	1.46	2.59%
10	Etrade Australia	5.87%	5.63%	0.09	2.59%
11	AOL	21.80%	5.63%	6.24	2.59%
12	Candle	12.39%	5.63%	2.61	2.59%
13	Liberty One	2.64%	5.63%	-1.16	2.59%
14	Spike Networks	25.05%	5.63%	7.50	2.59%
15	Webjet	12.66%	5.63%	2.71	2.59%
16	Travel.com	12.90%	5.63%	2.81	2.59%
17	Ecorp	16.79%	5.63%	4.31	2.59%
18	Wine Planet	36.58%	5.63%	11.95	2.59%

Wine Planet shows the highest expected return of the stocks estimated using the CAPM with an $E(r)$ of 36.58 per cent (Table 6.3). *B2B.Net* has a negative expected return of –55.25 percent due to its high negative beta of –23.51. The statistics of *B2B.Net* may not be unbiased due to the extensive non-trading period (from October 1999 to February 2000) of the stock. The individual expected returns for the portfolio range from 36.58 per cent (*Wine Planet*) to 2.64 per cent (*Liberty One*) or –55.25 per cent if we include *B2B.Net*. The average geometric expected return for these e-commerce stocks is 9.36% (Appendix 6.8). The graphic presentation of the relationship between risks, as measured by beta, and the CAPM estimated expected returns for the e-commerce firms is represented by the Security Market Line (SML) shown in Figure 6.3 below.

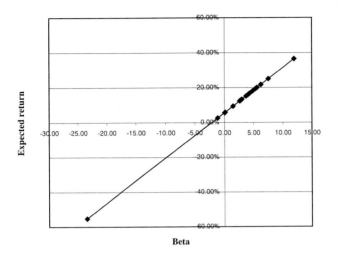

Figure 6.3 The E-Commerce Stock Security Market Line (geometric mean)

The CAPM is an equilibrium valuation model. It predicts that in equilibrium the expected excess return on an e-commerce stock should depend on its beta and the expected excess return on the market. As the excess return on the market portfolio is constant at a particular point in time, then the e-commerce stocks would have different expected returns only if their respective betas differ. Figure 6.3 above shows the expected return (geometric) of the e-commerce stocks against their beta values, from Table 6.3, on the SML. If an e-commerce stock persistently trades above the SML, then the stock is earning supernormal return given its risk class and is also in violation of the EMH. The excess-return chart below (Figure 6.4) suggests returns of the e-commerce portfolio to behave randomly and does not show persistent gains above the $E(R_p)$ of the e-commerce portfolio return on the CAPM's security market line of 11.22 per cent (i.e. $E(r_p) = 5.63\% + 2.16(2.59\%)$). In Figure 6.3, the axis ($x = 0$) about the excess returns represents the SML's expected return for the e-commerce portfolio of 11.22 per cent.

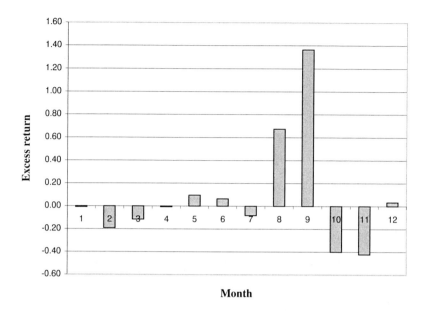

Figure 6.4 Excess Return Chart: E-Commerce Portfolio

Note: x-axis at 0 = 11.22% for the e-commerce $E(r_p)$ value.

Reilly (1989) suggests that the geometric mean is appropriate for long-run comparisons, while the arithmetic mean is more appropriate for estimating the premium for a given year. As the CAPM is a single period measure, the following analysis is done using the arithmetic mean. The CAPM equation and Table 6.4 below show the estimated expected returns for the individual companies using the arithmetic mean values for risk-free rate (5.73 per cent, see Appendix 6.3) and arithmetic market return (9.07 per cent, see Appendix 6.3).

$$E(R_i) = R_f + \beta_i(E(R_m) - R_f)$$

$$E(r_i) = 5.73\% + \beta_i(9.07\% - 5.73\%)$$

or: $\quad E(r_i) = 5.73\% + \beta_i(3.34\%)$

Table 6.4 CAPM Estimated Expected Returns (arithmetic means):
July 1999 to June 2000

	E-Commerce Firm	Expected Return $E(R)$	Risk-free rate	Beta	Market risk premium
1	My Casino	5.83%	5.73%	0.03	3.34%
2	Sausage Software	23.39%	5.73%	5.29	3.34%
3	Solution 6	24.32%	5.73%	5.57	3.34%
4	Reckon Group	15.63%	5.73%	2.96	3.34%
5	Swish Group	19.27%	5.73%	4.05	3.34%
6	Pocketmail	18.07%	5.73%	3.70	3.34%
7	131.shop.com	21.78%	5.73%	4.81	3.34%
8	B2B.Net.Technology	-72.78%	5.73%	-23.51	3.34%
9	Coms 21	10.61%	5.73%	1.46	3.34%
10	Etrade Australia	6.04%	5.73%	0.09	3.34%
11	AOL	26.58%	5.73%	6.24	3.34%
12	Candle	14.45%	5.73%	2.61	3.34%
13	Liberty One	1.87%	5.73%	-1.16	3.34%
14	Spike Networks	30.77%	5.73%	7.50	3.34%
15	Webjet	14.79%	5.73%	2.71	3.34%
16	Travel.com	15.11%	5.73%	2.81	3.34%
17	Ecorp	20.13%	5.73%	4.31	3.34%
18	Wine Planet	45.64%	5.73%	11.95	3.34%

When arithmetic mean values are used to calculate the CAPM expected return of the firms (Table 6.4), the same firms, *Wine Planet* and *B2B.Net* show the highest and lowest stock returns, respectively, as when the geometric mean values were used. However, the values of the respective returns, 45.64 per cent and −72.78 per cent, are more extreme compared to those calculated using the geometric mean values. The arithmetic average return of the stock is 13.42 percent (Appendix 6.8), which is relatively higher than the geometric average return of 9.61 per cent. The SML of the e-commerce stocks is depicted in Figure 6.5 below.

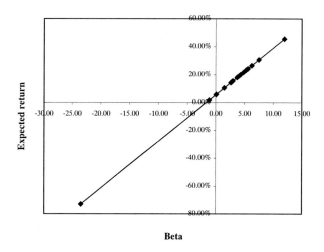

Figure 6.5 The E-Commerce Security Market Line (arithmetic mean)

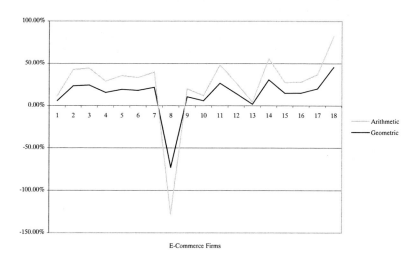

Figure 6.6 CAPM Expected Returns: Geometric vs Arithmetic Means

From Figure 6.6, the CAPM arithmetic expected returns for the e-commerce firms are more volatile than the geometric expected returns. The volatility of returns of the e-commerce stocks is high relative to the market as shown previously in Figure 6.1, thus the geometric mean is preferred in our analysis in this study to minimise the effects of extreme fluctuations in the data and also to take into consideration the fact that monthly data are used in this study which constitute a multi-period investment horizon, which is more appropriate in the context of e-commerce stock investment as discussed earlier.

6.5 Expected/Actual Returns versus Market Return

The geometric mean of the monthly market returns for the S&P/ASX 200 Index in the period July 1999 to June 2000 is 0.91 per cent per month (Appendix 6.2) or annualized at 10.96 per cent. The following Table 6.5 provides a comparison of the individual stock returns with their expected returns (calculated using the CAPM from Table 6.3) and the market return.

From Table 6.5, 8 out of the 18 stocks analysed (or 44% of the total) show a positive return in the study period from July 1999 to June 2000. Out of the 8 stocks with positive return, 7 outperformed the market return of 10.96%; with *B2B.Net* having the highest return in the period of 315.79%, which is an excess return of 304.83% over the market return for the period. *Sausage* outperformed the market by only 2.56% being the smallest of the stocks with excess return and *Candle* being the only stock from the positive-return group with a below-market performance of 6.86%. The remaining stocks (46%) in the portfolio had negative returns with *131.Shop*, having the largest negative return of –223.48%. The individual returns in the portfolio ranges from +315.79% to –223.48% or a spread of 539.27% suggesting the high degree of volatility of e-commerce stock returns vis-à-vis the market return (market spread equals 12.98%, Appendix 6.2). This implies that the geometric mean would be more appropriate for estimating e-commerce stock returns, as it is less sensitive to extreme values than the arithmetic mean.

Table 6.5 Comparison between Firm's Expected Return, Actual Return and
Market Return (geometric means): July 1999 to June 2000

	Company E-Commerce Firm	CAPM Expected Return $E(R)$	Actual Co. Return*	Market Return**	Overvalued/ Undervalued
1	My Casino	5.71%	179.97%	10.96%	Overvalued
2	Sausage Software	19.33%	13.52%	10.96%	Undervalued
3	Solution 6	20.04%	-7.39%	10.96%	Undervalued
4	Reckon Group	13.31%	-74.64%	10.96%	Undervalued
5	Swish Group	16.13%	-19.24%	10.96%	Undervalued
6	Pocketmail	15.20%	41.24%	10.96%	Overvalued
7	131.shop.com	18.07%	-223.48%	10.96%	Undervalued
8	B2B.Net.Technology	-55.25%	315.79%	10.96%	Overvalued
9	Coms 21	9.42%	-112.02%	10.96%	Undervalued
10	Etrade Australia	5.87%	-115.12%	10.96%	Undervalued
11	AOL	21.80%	168.49%	10.96%	Overvalued
12	Candle	12.39%	6.86%	10.96%	Undervalued
13	Liberty One	2.64%	-121.08%	10.96%	Undervalued
14	Spike Networks	25.05%	-35.75%	10.96%	Undervalued
15	Webjet	12.66%	43.51%	10.96%	Overvalued
16	Travel.com	12.90%	-42.59%	10.96%	Undervalued
17	Ecorp	16.79%	-6.79%	10.96%	Undervalued
18	Wine Planet	36.58%	73.91%	10.96%	Overvalued
Average return		11.59%	4.73%	10.96%	

* Geometric mean.
** Geometric mean, annualised.

The average actual e-commerce portfolio return of 4.73 per cent under-performed the market return of 10.96% in the study period (Table 6.5). In the study period, the actual market performance of 10.96 per cent, in comparison to the 11.59% average of the estimated CAPM expected returns for all the firms, would represent an undervaluation of the e-commerce portfolio by the market from an ex-post perspective (statistics from Table 6.5).

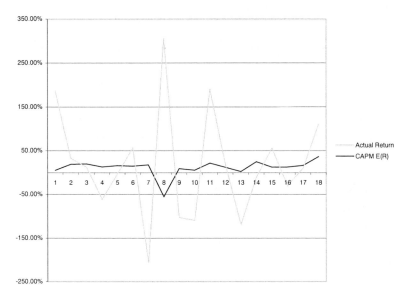

Figure 6.7 Individual Stock's Actual Return vs. CAPM Expected Return:
July 1999 to June 2000

Six (6) of the eighteen (18) stocks (33 per cent) in Table 6.5 are overvalued by the market relative to their CAPM expected returns. Figure 6.7 above depicts the two types of return for each of the eighteen e-commerce firms (shown on the *x*-axis) and also highlights the volatility of each firm's actual return to their respective CAPM expected return, E(R). *B2B.Net* is the highest overvalued stock, 370% above its E(R), while *Pocketmail* is the least overvalued at 26% above its expected return. The most undervalued stock is *131.Shop*. An overview of the mispricing between the actual returns and CAPM based expected returns on a sector basis, using geometric mean data, is presented as follows (the number of stocks is indicated in bracket for each sector).

Casino & gaming	(1)	Overvalued
Computer & office services	(3)	Undervalued
Diversified media	(1)	Undervalued
Equipment & services	(2)	Mixed
Health & medical services	(1)	Overvalued
High technology	(1)	Undervalued
Misc. financial services	(1)	Undervalued
Miscellaneous services	(2)	Mixed
Other telecommunications	(2)	Undervalued
Retail/retail investment	(4)	Mixed

Table 6.6 Comparison between Firm's Expected Return, Actual Return and
Market Return (arithmetic means): July 1999 to June 2000

	Company	CAPM Expected Return $E(R)$	Actual Co. Return*	Market Return**	Overvalued/ Undervalued
1	My Casino	5.83%	288.85%	23.32%	Overvalued
2	Sausage Software	23.39%	62.11%	23.32%	Overvalued
3	Solution 6	24.32%	76.14%	23.32%	Overvalued
4	Reckon Group	15.63%	-52.37%	23.32%	Undervalued
5	Swish Group	19.27%	8.61%	23.32%	Undervalued
6	Pocketmail	18.07%	826.00%	23.32%	Overvalued
7	131.shop.com	21.78%	-146.71%	23.32%	Undervalued
8	B2B.Net.Technology	-72.78%	2711.43%	23.32%	Overvalued
9	Coms 21	10.61%	-92.62%	23.32%	Undervalued
10	Etrade Australia	6.04%	-92.74%	23.32%	Undervalued
11	AOL	26.58%	401.70%	23.32%	Overvalued
12	Candle	14.45%	13.87%	23.32%	Undervalued
13	Liberty One	1.87%	-66.19%	23.32%	Undervalued
14	Spike Networks	30.77%	-35.75%	23.32%	Undervalued
15	Webjet	14.79%	99.52%	23.32%	Overvalued
16	Travel.com	15.11%	-9.10%	23.32%	Undervalued
17	Ecorp	20.13%	47.89%	23.32%	Overvalued
18	Wine Planet	45.64%	297.00%	23.32%	Overvalued

* Arithmetic mean.
** Annualised arithmetic mean.

Table 6.6 compares the CAPM expected returns and actual returns of the stocks with market returns in the study period using the arithmetic means. Eleven out of the 18 stocks analysed (or 61 per cent) show positive returns and out of these 11 positive-return stocks, 9 outperformed the market return of 23.32 per cent, with *B2B.Net* having the highest return in the period of 2711.43 per cent, an excess return of 2688.11 per cent over the market in the period. *Ecorp* outperformed the market by the lowest margin of 24.57 per cent, whilst, *Candle* and *Swish* are the only positive-return stocks in the portfolio with below-market performance. Seven stocks or 39 per cent of the portfolio have negative returns and *131.Shop* with −146.71 per cent, has the largest negative return. The individual stock returns in the portfolio ranges from +2711.43 to −146.71 per cent or a spread of 2858.14 per cent confirming the high degree of sensitivity to the extreme values of the stock returns when arithmetic mean is used instead of the geometric mean.

Table 6.6 shows that 50% of the stocks (9 stocks) were overvalued in the study period. An overview of the mispricing between the actual returns and CAPM based expected returns on a sector basis, using arithmetic mean data, is presented as follows (the number of stocks is indicated in bracket for each sector):

Casino & gaming	(1)	Overvalued
Computer & office services	(3)	Mixed
Diversified media	(1)	Undervalued
Equipment & services	(2)	Mixed
Health & medical services	(1)	Overvalued
High technology	(1)	Undervalued
Misc. financial services	(1)	Undervalued
Miscellaneous services	(2)	Mixed
Other telecommunications	(2)	Undervalued
Retail/retail investment	(4)	Mixed

6.6 Sector Returns

This section measures the average sector beta for the sectors studied. The sector beta is the average beta of all the e-commerce companies which are in the type of industry being measured. Tables 6.7 and 6.8 document the trade-off between risk and actual return for different sectors of the e-commerce stocks in the study period from July 1999 through June 2000. The e-commerce stocks were selected from a cross section of industries and Table 6.7 below presents the comparative betas, average returns and standard deviations. Excluding the stocks with extended non-trading periods (i.e. *My Casino, Pocketmail* and *B2B.Net*), the sector with the highest average[36] beta is the Retail/Retail Investment sector with 5.45 indicating the highest volatility of return vis-à-vis market. *Etrade*, the only stock represented in the Miscellaneous Financial Services sector had a beta of 0.09, which was the lowest making it the least volatile compared to the market. The Miscellaneous Financial Services sector also had the one of the lowest standard deviations (19.57%) among all sectors. The Miscellaneous Services sector had the highest average return of 87.68%, while the Equipment & Services sector had the lowest with –223.48% (i.e. excluding *Pocketmail*).

---

[36] Arithmetic average.

Table 6.7 Sector Actual Returns and Volatility

	Beta	Return*	Std. Dev.**	Total Risk
Casino & Gaming				
My Casino	0.03	179.97%	59.59%	0.3807
Computer & Office Services				
Sausage Software	5.29	13.52%	28.58%	0.0851
Solution 6	5.57	-7.39%	38.43%	0.1536
Reckon Group	2.96	-74.64%	19.54%	0.0407
Average	*4.61*	*-22.84%*	*28.85%*	*0.0931*
Diversified Media				
Swish Group	4.05	-19.24%	22.55%	0.0537
Equipment & Services				
Pocketmail	3.7	41.24%	296.52%	9.1559
131.shop.com	4.81	-223.48%	24.06%	0.0598
Average	*4.26*	*-91.12%*	*160.29%*	*4.6079*
Health & Medical Services				
B2B Net Technology	-23.51	315.79%	801.31%	65.7650
High Technology				
Coms 21	1.46	-112.02%	19.22%	0.0401
Miscellaneous Financial Services				
Etrade Australia	0.09	-115.12%	19.57%	0.0421
Miscellaneous Services				
Aussie On Line	6.24	168.49%	82.44%	0.6985
Candle	2.67	6.86%	11.25%	0.0132
Average	*4.46*	*87.68%*	*46.85%*	*0.3559*
Other Telecommunications				
Liberty One	-1.16	-121.08%	31.17%	0.1042
Spike Networks	7.5	-35.75%	45.45%	0.2133
Average	*3.17*	*-78.42%*	*38.31%*	*0.1588*
Retail/Retail Investment				
Webjet	2.71	43.51%	29.67%	0.0935
Travel.com	2.81	-42.59%	67.28%	0.0409
Ecorp	4.31	-6.79%	33.03%	0.114
Wine Planet	11.95	73.91%	56.22%	0.3026
Average	*5.45*	*17.01%*	*46.55%*	*0.1378*

*Geometric mean.
**Sample standard deviation.

The ranking order for all the sectors in terms of market volatility (β) with the corresponding average return and standard deviation is presented in Table 6.8 below

Table 6.8 Relative Market Volatility of Sectors and Trade-off Between Risk*
and Actual Return

	Sector	Beta	Return	Std. Dev.
1	Retail/Retail Investment	5.45	17.01%	46.55%
2	Computer & Office Services	4.61	-22.84%	28.85%
3	Miscellaneous Services	4.46	87.68%	46.85%
4	Equipment & Services	4.26	-91.12%	160.29%
5	Diversified Media	4.05	-19.24%	22.55%
6	Other Telecommunications	3.17	-78.42%	38.31%
7	High Technology	1.46	-112.02%	19.22%
8	Miscellaneous Financial Services	0.09	-115.12%	19.57%
9	Casino & Gaming	0.03	179.97%	59.59%
10	Health & Medical Services	-23.51	315.79%	801.31%

*Ranked in order of beta.

Table 6.8 shows that the e-commerce sectors had mixed returns and return volatility measured against the market and represented by beta, is generally higher for most sectors with the exception of Miscellaneous Financial Services ($\beta = 0.09$) and Casino & Gaming ($\beta = 0.03$). This indicates that the majority of e-commerce stock returns were more volatile than the market return in the study period. The Health & Medical Services sector had the highest return of 315 per cent and a negative beta of –23.51, whilst, Casino & Gaming sector had the second highest return but one of the lowest betas. Conversely, Retail/Retail Investment had the highest beta (i.e. 5.45) and a low return. From the perspective of risk-return relationship, the risk and return trade-off stated in Section 6.4 appears not to hold in these sample stocks in the study period.

The inconsistency in the risk–return relationship of the e-commerce sector (actual returns with sector betas), highlights the lack of correlation in price movements between the e-commerce stocks and market due to the high unsystematic risk element in the e-commerce sector, as shown in Figure 6.8 below.

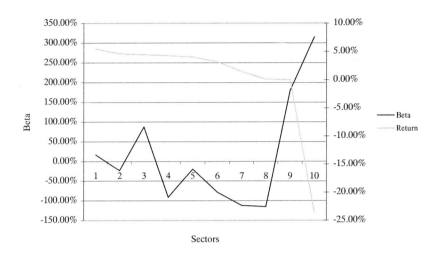

Figure 6.8 Beta-Actual Return by Sector

Note: Scale for beta on right y-axis

The above analyses confirm the general systematic risk level of the e-commerce stocks and that they move predominantly in a volatility sphere of their own, relatively independent of the market. Under the EMH conditions, the returns for the e-commerce stocks suggests these stocks did not reflect their fundamental value (V_t) during the study period resulting in returns that do not reflect the risk/return relationship and could be explained by the e-commerce stock attempting to adjust to market fundamentals. This situation implies that e-commerce prices (P_t) were generally above their fundamental value ($P_t > V_t$), due to the activities of irrational traders or noise trading and were adjusting towards V_t during the study period to reflect fundamentals.

6.7 Covariance Analysis

From Appendix 6.9, which shows the covariances for the e-commerce stock returns, *B2B.Net* has the highest variance of 54.8570 indicating it has the riskiest or most volatile returns of all stocks in the period, and the stock with the smallest risk is *Candle* with a variance of 0.0111. The high variance of *B2B.Net* is consistent with its high beta of –23.51 calculated using the market model.

With the exception of *My Casino*, which consistently registers a negative covariance against all the other stocks in the portfolio, the remaining e-commerce stocks display predominant positive covariance with each other. Of the 18 individual e-commerce stocks, the covariance ratios between them vary from −1.02 (*AOL-Candle*) to 1.37 (*AOL-Pocketmail*) and show a 90% low or negative (below 0.20) cross-sectional correlation. Sixty-five per cent of the ratios are positively correlated below 0.1000 (10%). This suggests that the behaviour of e-commerce stock returns is largely consistent or similar in characteristics among the stocks in the portfolio, albeit with a weaker correlation. The higher correlation of the e-commerce stocks is not surprising as the stocks contain much idiosyncratic noise and react rather uniformly to e-commerce-specific information.

In Appendix 6.10, which analyses the covariances of the stock prices, *Solution 6* shows the highest covariance of 15.1919 and hence the highest price volatility or risk. The stock with the lowest covariance is *Coms21* with 0.0042. The price covariance levels of the stocks appear to suggest consistency in price movements indicating similar price behaviour for the e-commerce stocks in the market during the period.

6.8 Correlation Coefficients

The analysis of the correlation coefficients of the e-commerce stock returns and prices, in Appendixes 6.9 and 6.10, seems to support and confirm the general returns and price behaviour of the stocks in the covariance study in Section 6.7. As the correlation coefficient measures the degree of association between two variables, it is a unit-free measure of the strength and the direction of the linear relationship between each pair of the e-commerce stocks. This is a more widely used and better measure than the covariance because the size of the correlation coefficient is not influenced by the values of the observations. For both returns and prices, the correlation coefficients of the e-commerce stocks, except for *My Casino*, show a consistently positive relationship between each other indicating a high level of association and volatility characteristics between the stocks.

The limitations of risky arbitrage (Cuthbertson 1997) may be insufficient to curb overpricing (or underpricing) of e-commerce stocks relative to fundamentals when there are a substantial number of noise traders in the market following the herd mentality (or *group behaviour*) and ignoring economic fundamentals. In order for this to happen, the noise traders must move in unison (Shiller 1989; Shleifer and Summers 1990) to be in a position to influence market prices, as is evident from the highly positive covariance and correlation across the e-commerce firms in the analyses above.

6.9 Portfolio Return versus Market Return

A portfolio is a collection of stocks (or securities) held by some economic entity or grouped together for some specific purpose. Forming portfolios through combining the e-commerce stocks and analysing their portfolio behaviour to uncover the systematic characteristics can largely attenuate the idiosyncratic noise. The purpose of portfolio analysis in this section is to test the volatility of returns of a portfolio of e-commerce stocks across several sectors against the general market returns. This will provide an indication and benchmark for the volatility of the e-commerce stock relative to the general market, whether they are more volatile or otherwise and if more, how much more volatile are they? The expected return of the e-commerce portfolio, $E(R_p)$ and the standard deviation of the portfolio σ_p, will be calculated and compared with expected return $(E(R_m))$ and the standard deviation σ_m, for market returns. Figure 6.9 below highlights the difference between the monthly e-commerce portfolio and market returns in the study period.

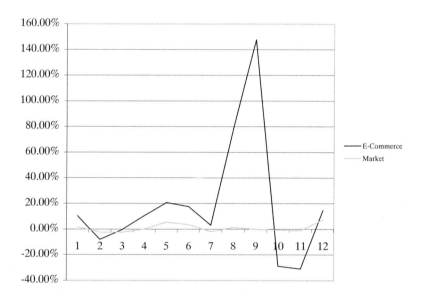

Figure 6.9 E-Commerce and Market Returns: July 1999 to June 2000

The e-commerce portfolio consists of the eighteen sample e-commerce stocks of this study, while the comparative monthly means and standard deviations (Appendixes 6.4 and 6.5) between the market and portfolio returns are presented in Table 6.9 below.

Table 6.9 Market versus Portfolio Monthly Return and Volatility:
July 1999 to June 2000

	Market	Portfolio
Mean Return	0.91%	10.56%
Standard Deviation	3.13%	49.82%

In analyzing the volatility of returns of the e-commerce stock portfolio relative to the market, the figures in Table 6.9 imply that the e-commerce stock volatility suggests investors are uncertain about the future, especially about future earnings. The e-commerce portfolio's standard deviation is 16 times higher than the market standard deviation indicating a much higher degree of volatility in the e-commerce stock portfolio return compared to the market return. Consistent with the risk and return tradeoff, the average return of the e-commerce stock portfolio is approximately 12 times higher than the market return in the study period.

The e-commerce portfolio beta of 2.16 (Appendix 6.7) suggests, on average, that there is a higher degree of volatility against market returns, but it is significantly lower than most of the individual betas of the e-commerce stocks in the portfolio. This result supports the theory that portfolio risk is lower than risk attached to a single stock and a substantial degree of the riskiness inherent in an individual stock can be eliminated if the stock is held in a portfolio, albeit one consisting of only e-commerce related stocks in diverse sectors in this instance. This portfolio risk may be further reduced if more stocks such as those in the old economy blue-chips are included in the portfolio, as blue chips stocks would generally have relatively lower betas compared to the highly volatile e-commerce stocks and while adding more stocks lowers portfolio risk.[37] Essentially, when partially correlated stocks are added to a portfolio, the riskiness of a portfolio will decline as the number of stocks in the portfolio increases. The extent to which adding stocks to a portfolio reduces its risk depends on the degree of correlation among the stocks. Portfolio selection may also be viewed in terms of identification of mispriced stocks that can be selected to increase portfolio returns while still maintaining an acceptable level of portfolio diversification. Even in a well-diversified portfolio, some risk still remains and this part of a stock's risk which cannot be diversified is called market risk. The study of optimal portfolio selection in relation to e-commerce stock characteristics will be conducted in Chapter 7.

The estimated portfolio expected return, $E(R_p)$, is 11.39% using the CAPM calculated as follows:

---

[37] Half of the riskiness inherent in an average individual stock can be eliminated if the stock is held in a well-diversified portfolio, which is one containing 40 or more stocks (Brigham and Houston 2000).

$E(r_p) = 5.63\% + 2.16(2.59\%)$

$E(r_p) = 11.22\%$

This figure is between the geometric average return of 9.61% and the arithmetic average return of 20.68%.

6.10 Efficient Market Hypothesis

The EMH predicts that share prices fairly reflect all information that has been fully revealed to the market and that stock price only moves in response to new information that, by definition, is unpredictable and should behave in a random manner. The prices of stocks are affected by investor perception and interpretation of conditions pertaining to the firm, industry and economy and such conditions are contained in a continuous stream of new information about investments concerning new technologies and new market opportunities. According to Cuthbertson (1997) the mainstream concepts, issues and methods in financial economics are based on the theory of efficient market (see for Section 2.6.1) and in this study, an original proposition of an efficient market is assumed.

For the e-commerce market analysed in this study, the three significant and pervasive factors that contain such information about e-commerce equity investment opportunities are reflected in the NASDAQ composite index (*NAS*), consumer confidence (*CC*) and foreign exchange strength (*FE*). The risk arises that new information may be left out of past information or that the pervasive factors, which influence e-commerce sector returns may change over time due to the fast changing technological and business environment of the virtual economy. Such a situation would result in systematic errors if future risk were to be deduced from past risk.

The three different forms of the EMH: weak, semi-strong and strong forms of market efficiency are normally tested in finance using regression and volatility based methods. The volatility test for EMH involves plotting the expected return of the e-commerce portfolio against its beta value on the SML with all actual returns to be distributed randomly around the line. Following the practice for testing market efficiency in the literature, asymptotic analysis can be used to test for the efficient market hypothesis (EMH) that information observable to the market prior to month t should not help to predict the return during the month t for the e-commerce sector return. If we use past information on y (representing e-commerce stock *return* in this study), the EMH is stated as (Wooldridge 2000):

$$E(y_t \,|\, y_{t-1}, y_{t-2}, \ldots) = E(y_t) \qquad\qquad (6.1)$$

If equation (6.1) is false, then past information can be used to predict the current return and under EMH conditions arbitragers will take advantage of such investment opportunities and the market will quickly move back into equilibrium again. The following AR(1) model is used as the alternative model to test equation (6.1):

$$y_t = \alpha + \beta y_{t-1} + \mu_t \qquad (6.2)$$

where the error μ_t has a zero expected value, given all past values of y:

$$E(\mu_t \mid y_{t-1}, y_{t-2}, \dots) = 0 \qquad (6.3)$$

The combined equations (6.2) and (6.3) imply that when the y lagged one period has been controlled for, no further lags of y affect the expected value of y_t and the relationship is considered to be linear:

$$E(\mu_t \mid y_{t-1}, y_{t-2}, \dots) = E(y \mid y_{t-1}) = \alpha + \beta y_{t-1}$$

The null hypothesis is stated as H_0: $\beta = 0$ against H_1: $\beta \neq 0$ and under the null hypothesis, stock returns are serially uncorrelated. This regression tests the weak form informational efficiency of the EMH by examining the autocorrelation coefficients between $return_t$ and $return_{t-1}$ to see if they are non-zero. If H_0 is not rejected, the inference is to confirm the weak form efficiency. The EMH does not specify the horizon over which return should be calculated and the period tested is the study period from July 1999 to June 2000.

Initially the weak form of the EMH is tested for market returns and the monthly returns of the S&P/ASX 200 in the study period are used as the proxy for the market. The average monthly return over the study period was 0.96% with the highest monthly return being 7.47% in June 2000 and the lowest of –2.40% in September 1999. The estimated AR(1) model (used in Appendix 6.15) is as follows with the t-statistics in parenthesis:

$$\hat{return}_t = \underset{(0.9586)}{0.0093} + \underset{(0.1161)}{0.0471 return_{t-1}}$$

$(n = 12,\ df = 10,\ R^2 = 0.0013)$.

The t-statistic for β coefficient on $return_{t-1}$ is 0.1161, and the H_0: $\beta = 0$ cannot be rejected against the two-sided alternative, at the 10% significance level with critical value 1.812. This estimate suggests that there is positive correlation ($\beta = +0.0471$) in the S&P/ASX from one month to the next but not strong enough to reject the efficient markets hypothesis.

Volatility, Predictability and Returns Issues

The estimates for the weak form of the EMH test by sector are summarised in Table 6.10 (see Appendix 6.15 for details) below.

Table 6.10 Summary of Results for Efficient Market Hypothesis Tests

Sector/$return_t$	α	$return_{t-1}$ β	R^2
Casino & gaming	**0.3080**	**-0.2154**	**0.0466**
t-statistic	*1.5486*	*-0.6992*	
Computer & office services	**0.0180**	**0.2540**	**0.0643**
t-statistic	*0.2358*	*0.8293*	
Diversified media	**0.0071**	**0.0832**	**0.0068**
t-statistic	*0.1055*	*0.2625*	
Equipment & services	**0.3048**	**-0.1128**	**0.0126**
t-statistic	*0.6745*	*-0.3579*	
Health & medical services	**2.5156**	**-0.1135**	**0.0129**
t-statistic	*1.0342*	*-0.3614*	
High Technology	**-0.0842**	**-0.1091**	**0.0121**
t-statistic	*-1.3801*	*-0.3505*	
Miscellaneous financial services	**-0.1039**	**-0.3255**	**0.1079**
t-statistic	*-1.7035*	*-1.0998*	
Miscellaneous services	**0.1416**	**0.2634**	**0.0621**
t-statistic	*1.1165*	*0.8137*	
Other Telecommunications	**0.0257**	**0.0573**	**0.0032**
t-statistic	*0.3802*	*0.1800*	
Retail/retail investments	**0.0599**	**0.1551**	**0.0169**
t-statistic	*0.7788*	*0.4149*	
Portfolio	**0.1658**	**0.1578**	**0.0250**
t-statistic	*1.0487*	*0.5061*	

From Table 6.10, the null hypothesis H_0: $\beta = 0$ cannot be rejected against the two-sided alternative, at the 10% significance level (critical value = 1.812) for the all sectors implying that the efficient markets hypothesis prevails. This suggests that e-commerce stock prices reflect all historical information regarding the underlying firm and the market responds immediately to new information regarding the firm. When informational efficiency does hold, the response to new information is manifested by an immediate change in price and hence information at time t cannot be used to help predict future returns of the e-commerce stocks. Nevertheless, the low R^2 associated with the efficiency tests should also be noted. The weak form efficiency is consistent for both the market return and the returns of the various e-commerce sectors tested. So if e-commerce stocks respond to new information immediately and each piece of new information is independent of previous information, then changes in their prices do follow the random walk and each change or innovation is independent of all previous changes. This characteristic can be reconciled with the dynamic nature of Internet development that is constantly changing as the virtual market evolves to incorporate new technologies, ideas and business models. Any piece of past information would be rendered irrelevant or obsolete, whilst new information is rapidly factored into the stock price by investors. These results are consistent with Praetz's (1969) Australian study on autocorrelations of returns that found some evidence of serial dependence. However, he concluded that the dependence was insufficient to earn abnormal profits and was therefore not able to reject the random walk hypothesis.

These results appear to be partially consistent with French and Roll's (1986) finding that returns (daily as opposed to monthly in their study) of individual securities have slightly negative autocorrelation. The estimates in Table 6.10 suggest that the sectors *CG, ES, HMS, HT,* and *MFS* have a negative correlation in their values (y_t and y_{t-1}) from one month to the next but it is not strong enough to reject the efficient markets hypothesis. The reasons for the difference could be due to the diversity of stocks and the use of daily return in the French and Roll's study. The sectors *COS, DM, MS, OT, RRI* and the e-commerce portfolio all have a positive correlation in their values from one month to the next and, also, are not strong enough to reject the null hypothesis. The returns of individual securities, especially from a diverse cross-section of industries with little homogeneity, are likely to have statistically insignificant autocorrelation (Campbell et al. 1997).

The EMH tests show that the markets pertaining to e-commerce stocks are efficient and prices do react instantaneously to new information. Fundamental analysis would be the trading strategy to follow for e-commerce stock investment to earn profits.

6.11 Conclusion

There is no certainty that history will repeat itself, however the returns of e-commerce stocks observed in the past can provide a valuable foundation for estimating e-commerce returns in the future. Similarly, the standard deviations of past returns provide useful insights into the risk profile of e-commerce stocks in different sectors. The risk-return relationship profile of the individual e-commerce stocks in the study period is such that when analysing the risk and actual return relationship, the volatility (σ) band is between 11% and 800%, while, actual return variability is between –224% and 316% (Appendixes 6.11 and 6.12). The bands are significantly reduced when the irregularly traded stocks are excluded from the group giving 11% to 83% (volatility) and –224% to 44% (actual returns), respectively. The volatility range of the e-commerce stocks is broad compared to the variation of monthly stock return for the

US between the 1857-1987 period of 2% to 20% (Schwert 1989). The excessive volatility against market return of the e-commerce stock returns can be explained by the high level of unsystematic risk element (low R^2) in the stocks as discovered in the regression analyses using the market model. This implies a low compliance of e-commerce returns to the market return in terms of their prices reflecting similar economic fundamentals. It is highly questionable that information is used consistently and therefore rationally and whether there is a lack of agreement (or general understanding) on the economic fundamentals that determine e-commerce valuation. This may be interpreted as a strong presence of event effects in e-commerce stock prices in the market.

The one-period autocorrelation coefficient of returns analysis for the e-commerce stocks conducted in this chapter provides inferences about the validity of the EMH. These regression analyses indicate that for e-commerce stock returns their *ex-post* real returns and excess returns are unpredictable and thus support the random walk hypothesis in relationship to these stocks.

The relationship between risk and expected return, calculated using the CAPM, shows that the estimated expected returns $E(R)$s, are between the –54% and 37% range (Appendixes 6.13, 6.14) indicating a significant reduction in the variation of expected return, compared to actual return, for the same risk level. By excluding the irregularly traded stocks, the band is further reduced to between 2% to 25%. Thus, the use of CAPM to estimate e-commerce expected return seems to substantially homogenise their stock returns by evening out extreme values prevalent in the actual returns and effectively narrowing the band of fluctuations. This is the result of several factors: the dominance of traditional stocks (value compared to growth stocks) in the Australian market indices thus giving a relatively lower market return (R_m); and the resulting small market risk premium, ($R_m - R_f$), which causes the e-commerce risk component of the CAPM, $\beta_{e\text{-}com}(R_m - R_f)$, to be substantially lower. The Dow Jones, which includes the high-capitalised Microsoft, Intel and other high technology stocks in its index or the NASDAQ composite index, would be more representative of the new economy. This situation further deteriorates the capability of the CAPM in valuing Australian e-commerce stocks. The violation of the EMH can be determined from the persistence of supernormal return in a stock for a given risk class using the CAPM. However, this violation of the EMH is determined under the assumptions that the CAPM is the "true model" (Cuthbertson 1997) of asset pricing and the joint hypotheses that investors are rational and that they all use the same equilibrium model, being the true model, for valuation.

The above discussions allude to the limitations of the CAPM as the true model for e-commerce stock valuation. This justifies the need for the improved AEMM model for determining the movement in e-commerce stock price.

At this stage, it would be premature to conclude whether e-commerce stock returns are mean reverting, that is higher returns are followed by lower returns in the future, due to the short study period (12 months). Fama and French's (1988a) univariate test finds evidence of mean reversion in stock returns by considering return horizons from one to ten years and found little or no autocorrelation, except for holding periods of between 2 and 7 years for which beta is less than 0 with the peak at holding period of 5 years when beta equals –0.5. Under such circumstances, it may not be meaningful at this stage to conduct a mean reverting study given the literature on the need for a longer investment horizon.

In a portfolio context, it may not be realistic to remove irregularly traded stocks from our analysis as trading suspension is one of the characteristics of listed e-commerce stocks in a very much evolving "industry" where there is still intense negotiations and storming and forming activities[38] to strike strategic alliances and test new business models. These corporate manoeuvres and market trials are expected to persist and a higher incident of trading suspensions for e-commerce stocks on the stock exchange is perhaps regular and should be addressed in model development.

From the covariance and correlation studies, the e-commerce stocks do covary and this reflects the fact that e-commerce firms tend to have similar characteristics or properties being subject to the same market conditions of Internet development. The e-commerce stock return movements in the study period supposedly reflect changes in investor perceptions of their intrinsic value due to shifts in economic conditions affecting the e-commerce market. The period July 1999 through June 2000 was a period in which investors were captivated and disappointed by e-commerce stocks. The second half of 1999 saw the continued market embrace of e-commerce stocks until the April 2000 price decline. Though July 1999 to June 2000 is, theoretically, an ideal study period considering the multitude of events happening within the period that could or would affect e-commerce stock valuation; the extremity of the events may contribute significantly to volatility. It is because of these circumstances that we need to be discreet in our use of the information on volatility for value estimation. The fact that e-commerce firms are subject to a relatively high level of unsystematic risk suggests that e-commerce sector return may react more aggressively to idiosyncratic economic factors than the traditional factors identified in other empirical studies.

---

[38] The recent on again/off again deal between Telstra and Pacific Century Cyberworks is a case in point.

CHAPTER 7

Portfolios and Financial Planning Models

7.1 Introduction

In Chapters 1 and 2, it was stated that the results of the AEMM valuation model would be used for portfolio choice analysis. The purpose is to use the static AEMM model results (see Section 5.2.2) to develop a portfolio choice profile for the e-commerce sector in Australia. This analysis will provide information about the plausibility and usefulness of the developed model in this book. A comparison will also be made between the portolfio choice results of the model with those based on historical data. The portfolio optimisation problem is to determine what proportion of the portfolio should be allocated to each type of asset so that the amount of expected return and the level of risk match the investor's objectives. The assumption in this analysis is that investors are risk averse and their main objective is to minimise risk in their portfolio selection.

Therefore, portfolio theory is an approach developed for the selection of risky assets. As an investor, the typical approach in equity investment is to hold a balanced portfolio of different stocks to provide some expected return (also known as diversification). The theory assumes investors choose between alternative portfolios on the basis of the expected return and risk of that return. It assumes that: the investor is risk averse; selects investment opportunities in terms of a probability distribution defined by expected return and risk (the mean-variance paradigm discussed in Section 7.2); behaves rationally; has an expected utility of increasing expected return and decreasing risk; and the capital market is perfect. In the evaluation of a mean-variance efficient portfolio, a risk-based pricing model offers a powerful insight (Pastor and Stambaugh 2000). Pastor and Stambaugh, in the context of the Sharpe-Lintner CAPM, the three-factor model of Fama and French (1993) and the characteristic-based model of Daniel and Titman (1997), find that models with fundamentally different expressions about economic determinants of expected returns often reach similar portfolio choices, in a market situation where mispricing uncertainty and share trading margin requirements are prevalent.

The intention in this chapter is to utilise the expected returns estimated by the AEMM for portfolio choice analysis (Section 7.3.1) and to compare the results with that generated using historical data in a two-asset portfolio choice context (Section 7.3.2). Different portfolio selection models with different characteristics are also used to test and compare the e-commerce portfolio results obtained in this research, to accentuate their investment quality in respect to portfolio choice. An analysis based on the classic capital asset pricing model (Section 7.5) is conducted to highlight the theoretical underpinnings of the model in a portfolio context for e-commerce sectors using historical data. This analysis also provides an opportunity to evaluate the CAPM as an appropriate model for valuation of e-commerce stock from a portfolio investment perspective. The other portfolio selection model used in this study to test e-commerce stock portfolio characteristics is the Sharpe's Diagonal Model (Thompson and Thore 1992) in Section 7.6. In Section 7.2, an overview on the development of the portfolio theory is presented emphasising the original Markowitz's (1952, 1959) mean-variance approach to portfolio selection and the CAPM, developed by Sharpe (1964) and Lintner (1965b), which captures economy-wide implications.

This analysis done in this chapter is in the context of the Australian market. The market portfolio if one is to carry it to the extreme should include all real and financial assets, which is realistically unobservable. The Australian e-commerce sector, being a small and at a nascent stage of development, is considered to have limited global impact. This precludes the use of a global market index in the simulation models and also avoids the difficulty of estimating a global riskfree rate (r_f). The simulation models developed were used to test the portfolio characteristics vis-à-vis e-commerce stock returns for the Australian market. From the data available on the e-commerce stocks analysed in this research, an attempt is made to construct an efficient e-commerce stock portfolio reflecting the past variability (July 1999 to June 2000) of returns, based on the assumption that the risk profile of these stocks remains unchanged over time, or at least over the short term. It would be possible to extrapolate future risk from historic risk if the underlying probabilistic structure of these stocks remains unaltered (Thompson and Thor 1992). Generally, where historical measures are used as a proxy for expected future returns, a longer time series may be a better indicator. Fama and French (1988a) and others found that long horizon returns (i.e. over several years) are more forecastable than short horizon (i.e. over a year or a month). Therefore, there are limitations on the results of this study that must be considered when the results are used for extrapolation.

7.2 Portfolio Theory and E-Commerce Stocks

The number and trade of e-commerce stocks continue to increase in the market place with the proliferation of e-commerce. Fund managers who include e-commerce stocks in their portfolios would seek to minimise risk for any given level of return. It is therefore imperative that we study the appropriate investment proportion of e-commerce stock in a portfolio given their risk profile evaluated in Chapter 6. The implications drawn from the portfolio selection analysis would also provide an indication of the investment trend for e-commerce stocks from a market perspective. This in turn allows an insight into and conjecture of the equity funding activities in this sector.

It is important to understand the response of individuals to the pricing of e-commerce stocks in the market, according to portfolio theory (Sharpe 1964; Lintner 1965a, 1965b; Mossin 1969; Fama 1968). However, the crux of this study is to construct a risk-return profile for e-commerce portfolio investment using the mean-variance approach showing an efficient frontier of optimal portfolios to suit individual investor's risk aversion. The mean-variance approach in portfolio analysis is based on a single period model of investment. At the beginning of the period, the investor selects the weights of the various asset classes in the portfolio. In selecting the asset weights, the sum of the weights must equal one. During the period, each portfolio asset generates a random return and at the end of the period, the investor's wealth would have been changed by the weighted average of the returns. The two important assumptions of portfolio theory are: firstly, that returns are normally distributed and the expected return and the standard deviation are sufficient to describe the returns, and secondly, investors are risk-averse.

The CAPM, developed by Sharpe (1964) and Lintner (1965b), captures economy-wide implications and was built on Markowitz's work to show that if investors have homogeneous expectations and optimally hold mean-variance efficient portfolios, the market portfolio will itself be a mean-variance efficient portfolio, in the absence of market frictions. Thus, the CAPM assumes that only the systematic risk exposure of each individual asset is relevant to portfolio construction. This theory is tested in Section 7.4 using the e-commerce sector returns. The Sharpe (1964) and Lintner (1965b) version of the CAPM assumes the existence of lending and borrowing at the risk free rate of interest and is tested incorporating e-commerce stocks as a portfolio choice in Section 7.3.2 below.

7.2.1 Markowitz Portfolio Theory

Modern portfolio theory proposed by Markowitz (1952, 1959), and still the most widely used, utilises the total risk of each individual asset (as opposed to the CAPM approach discussed above), as given by the following model. The principles of the Markowitz portfolio theory are discussed in this section (see also Eichberger et al. 1997; Campbell et al. 1997) and this approach will be applied to the portfolio analysis of e-commerce stocks in Sections 7.3, 7.4 and 7.5. The expected return for a portfolio, $E(R_p)$ and the variance of the portfolio are defined below:

$$E(R_p) \quad = \quad \sum_{i=1}^{n} x_i E(R_i) \tag{7.1}$$

and:

$$\sigma_p^2 \quad = \quad \sum_{i=1}^{n} x_i^2 \sigma_i^2 + \sum_{i=1}^{n} \sum_{j=1,i\neq j}^{n} x_i x_j \sigma_{ij} \tag{7.2}$$

where:
R_p = the return of the portfolio;
R_i = the return on security i;
σ_i = the standard deviation of the security i;
σ_{ij} = the covariance between securities i and j;
x_i = the investment proportions (or weights); and
σ_p^2 = the portfolio variance.

But $\sigma_{ij} = \rho_{ij}\sigma_i\sigma_j$, where ρ_{ij} is the correlation between securities i and j, then equation (7.2) can be rewritten as:

$$\sigma_p^2 = \sum_{i=1}^{n} \sum_{j=1}^{n} x_i x_j \, \sigma_{ij} \qquad (7.3)$$

For a portfolio with assets a to n, the matrix format can be written as:

$$\sigma_p^2 = [x_a x_b x_c \ldots x_n] \begin{bmatrix} \sigma_a^2 & \sigma_{ab} & \cdots & \sigma_{an} \\ \sigma_{ba} & \sigma_b^2 & \cdots & \sigma_{bn} \\ \cdot & \cdot & \cdots & \cdot \\ \cdot & \cdot & \cdots & \cdot \\ \sigma_{na} & \sigma_{nb} & \cdots & \sigma_n^2 \end{bmatrix} \begin{bmatrix} x_a \\ x_b \\ x_c \\ \cdot \\ x_n \end{bmatrix}$$

The individual variance in the variance-covariance matrix is multiplied by its respective proportion twice giving the proportions relating to variances a squared influence. Each covariance is multiplied once by the proportion for each asset in the pair of assets, hence there are two covariances in each pair, giving the two covariance $x_i x_j$.

The optimal allocation is that given by the solution to the following model (Markowitz 1952, 1959), and:

$$MAXIMISE \qquad \frac{E(R_p) - R_f}{\sigma_p}$$

where:
$E(R_p)$ = the expected portfolio return;
R_f = the risk-free rate, and
σ_p = the portfolio standard deviation;

subject to the constraints $\Sigma x_i = 1$ and $x_i \geq 0$ for all i.

From equations (7.2) and (7.3) above, it can be seen that the Markowitz model takes into consideration the variances of each pair of potential assets for the construction and determination of the overall risk of the portfolio. As will be seen in Section 7.4 below, not all efficient portfolios contain all assets. While there are infinitely many efficient portfolios, Markowitz showed that only a limited number of corner portfolios (determined by varying risk parameter, λ, the coefficient of variation, see Figure 7.4 and discussed below) are needed to identify all efficient portfolios.

To determine the locus of efficient portfolios, the stock portfolio return potential function $R_p - \lambda V$ is used where λ is always positive ($\lambda > 0$) (Thompson and Thore 1992). $R_p - \lambda V$ can be seen as the utility function of the investor, representing the expected return on the portfolio minus a risk allowance (the variance - V). R_p is defined by $E(R_p)$ in equation (7.1) and V by σ_p^2 equation (7.3). A large positive λ would mean higher risk aversion and vice versa. The optimal solution would thus be subject to the budget constraint B:

$$\text{Maximise} \quad R_p - \lambda V \tag{7.4}$$

$$\text{subject to} \quad \sum_{i=1}^{n} x_i E(R_i) \leq B$$

where:
R_p = stock portfolio return;
$x_i \geq 0$; and
$i = 1, \dots, n$.

The values of λ can be parametrically changed to allow the optimal solution to identify the locus of all the efficient portfolios. By inserting (7.1) and (7.3) into (7.4) the following quadratic programming problem is derived:

$$\text{Maximise} \quad z = \sum_{i=1}^{n} x_i E(R_i) - \lambda \sum_{i=1}^{n} \sum_{j=1}^{n} x_i x_j \sigma_{ij} \tag{7.5}$$

$$\text{subject to} \quad \sum_{i=1}^{n} x_i E(R_i) \leq B$$

where:
z = the maximand;
$x_i \geq 0$; and
$i = 1, \dots, n$.

The Markowitz model is used in Section 7.5 for two-asset portfolio analysis and the analysis is based on the assumption that investors will hold a combination of e-commerce stocks and a portion of stocks of the market portfolio that mimics the S&P/ASX 200. The data used to solve the portfolio optimisation problem include the expected returns on all assets, variances and co-variances of all asset returns and the assumptions are that investors have homogeneous expectations (agreement on the means and standard deviations and see the same efficient frontier of risky assets); that investors have a common single period time horizon for investment decision making; and that stocks are traded in a perfect market (no transaction or taxes).

The investors will also see the same capital market line (CML) with the introduction of the riskless asset later in the analysis. This will introduce the transformation line, which gives a linear relationship (Cuthbertson 1997) between expected return and portfolio risk for any two-asset portfolio consisting of a risky portfolio and risk-free asset.

7.2.2 The CAPM Implications of Portfolio Theory

This section addresses the theoretical implications for portfolio selection of both the classical capital asset pricing model based on a risk-free asset (Sharpe 1964; Lintner 1965a, 1965b; Mossin 1969) and the zero-beta CAPM (Black 1972). The construction of the efficient frontiers for e-commerce portfolios based on the CAPM is conducted for the e-commerce sectors analysed in this research, in Section 7.3 below.

The following procedures (based on the discussions in Benninga 2000), which are basic to the calculations of the CAPM, are used to derive the efficient frontier and the security market line. Let c be a constant, where $R - c$ denote the following vector:

$$R - c = \begin{bmatrix} E(r_1) - c \\ E(r_2) - c \\ : \quad : \\ : \quad : \\ E(r_N) - c \end{bmatrix}$$

Where the variable R represents the column vector of expected returns of N stocks, each would have an expected return $E(r_i)$ and is shown in the following notation

$$R \;=\; \begin{bmatrix} E(r_1) \\ E(r_2) \\ : \\ : \\ E(r_N) \end{bmatrix}$$

Let the vector z solve the system of linear equations $R - c = Sz$ and then this solution produces a portfolio x on the envelope of the feasibility set as follows:

$$z = S^{-1}(R - c)$$

$$x = (x_1, \ldots, x_n)$$

where:

$$x_i = \frac{z_i}{\displaystyle\sum_{j=1}^{n} z_j}$$

Intuitively, by picking a constant c to find an efficient portfolio x which is at a tangent to the feasible set, this provides a procedure for finding x and all envelope portfolios are also a result of this procedure. That is, for any x that is an envelope portfolio, there exists a constant c and a vector z such that:

$$Sz = R - c$$

and:

$$x_i = \frac{z}{\displaystyle\sum_{j=1}^{n} z_i}$$

Black (1972) proved that any two envelope portfolios are sufficient to construct the whole envelope and given any two envelope portfolios $x = \{x_1, \ldots, x_n\}$ and $y = \{y_1, \ldots, y_n\}$, all envelope portfolios are convex combinations of x and y. For any given constant a, the portfolio;

$$ax + (1-a)y = \begin{bmatrix} ax_1 + (1-a)y_1 \\ ax_2 + (1-a)y_2 \\ \vdots \quad \vdots \\ ax_n + (1-a)y_n \end{bmatrix}$$

lies on the efficient frontier. If y is any envelope portfolio, then for any other portfolio x, the following relationship exists:

$$E(r_x) = c + \beta_x \, (E(r_y) - c) \tag{7.6}$$

where:

$$\beta_x = \frac{\text{Cov}\,(x,\,y)}{\sigma^2_y}$$

Whilst, c is the expected return of a portfolio z whose covariance with $y = 0$:

$$c = E(r_z);$$

where: Cov $(y,\,z) = 0$.

Black's (1972) zero-beta CAPM proved that if y is on the envelope, then the regression of x on y portfolios gives a linear relationship and the Sharpe-Lintner security market line is replaced by an security market line (SML) where the role of the risk-free asset is represented by a portfolio with a zero beta with respect to the particular envelope y. If the market portfolio M (refer to Figure 2.6) is efficient, the SML holds with $E(r_z)$ and can be substituted for c in equation (7.6) above:

$$E(r_x) = E(r_z) + \beta_x \, (E(r_M) - E(r_z))$$

where:

$$\beta_x = \frac{\text{Cov}(x, M)}{\sigma^2_M} \quad ; \quad \text{Cov}(z, M) = 0$$

When there exists a risk-free asset, equation (7.6) above incorporates the security market line of the classic capital asset pricing model as follows:

$$E(r_x) = r_f + \beta_x (E(r_M) - r_f)$$

where:

$$\beta_x = \frac{\text{Cov}(x, M)}{\sigma_M}$$

The converse of equation (7.6) is also true for a portfolio y such that for any portfolio x, the following relation holds: and the portfolio y is an envelope portfolio:

$$E(r_x) = c + \beta_x (E(r_y) - c)$$

where:

$$\beta_x = \frac{\text{Cov}(x,y)}{\sigma_y}$$

This above approach for constructing the efficient portfolios and efficient frontier from the e-commerce sector-portfolios is applied in section 7.4. The e-commerce portfolio in this calculation is defined as the aggregate sector returns (Appendix 7.3) of all the e-commerce portfolio sectors studied in this research.

7.2.3 Kuhn-Tucker Conditions

In the portfolio analysis, the structure of an optimal portfolio will also be determined through the evaluation of the optimum points using the criteria known as the Kuhn-Tucker conditions. This approach also allows Lagrange multiplier techniques to be used when the constraints are inequalities rather than equalities. The optimal portfolios are those defined as having a minimum variance for a given level of risk (λ). The determination of optimum points, subject to constraints using Lagrange multipliers reveals a portfolio of minimum variance, where the portfolio range is a function of the covariances and asset weightings.

The conditions under portfolio selection are different from programming cases with separable concave objective function (or risk aversion function) and linear constraints. The conditions of separability no longer apply and we consider a non-linear programming problem (discussion in Thompson and Thore 1992):

Maximise $f(x_1, \ldots , x_n)$

subject to $Ax \leq b$
$x \geq 0$

where:
f = a concave function;
$A = (a_{ij})$ and $i = 1, \ldots , n$; and
$b = (b_j)$ and $j = 1, \ldots , n.$

The Kuhn-Tucker conditions involves the following partial derivatives:

$$\frac{\partial f}{\partial x_1}, \ldots , \frac{\partial f}{\partial x_n}$$

By defining the row vector of Lagrange multipliers as $u = (u_1, \ldots , u_m)$, the Kuhn-Tucker conditions thus become:

$$u^*_1 a_{11} + \ldots + u^*_m a_{m1} \geq \partial f^*/\partial x_1$$

$$\vdots$$

$$u^*_1 a_{1n} + \ldots + u^*_m a_{mn} \geq \partial f^*/\partial x_n$$

where:
$u^*_1, \ldots , u^*_m \geq 0$;
u^* = the value at the optimal point; and
f^* = the value at the optimal point for the concave function.

The following conditions also apply from the preceding:

$$[u^*_1 a_{11} + \ldots + u^*_m a_{m1} - \partial f^* / \partial x_1] \, x^*_1 = 0$$

$$\vdots$$

$$[u^*_1 a_{1n} + \ldots + u^*_m a_{mn} - \partial f^* / \partial x_n] \, x^*_n = 0$$

and are the same as:

$$A^* x^* \leq b, \qquad\qquad x^* \geq 0$$
$$u^*(b - A x^*) = 0$$

The Kuhn-Tucker conditions defined are:

$$u^* E(R_i)^0 \geq E(R_i) - 2\lambda \sum_{j=1}^{n} \sigma_{ij} x^*_j \qquad\qquad i = 1, \ldots, n \quad (7.7)$$

$$\{u^* E(R_i)^0 - E(R_i) + 2\lambda \sum_{j=1}^{n} \sigma_{ij} x^*_j\} \, x^*_i = 0 \quad i = 1, \ldots, n \quad (7.8)$$

By dividing (7.7) and (7.8) by $E(R_i)^0$, the current return of stock i, and rearranging the solved equations the final form of the Kuhn-Tucker conditions pertaining to portfolio selection is derived as in equation (7.9):

$$u^* + (2\lambda / E(R_i)^0) \sum_{j=1}^{n-1} \sigma_{ij} x^*_j \geq (E(R_i) / E(R_i)^0) \qquad\qquad (7.9)$$

The right hand side of this equation $(E(R_i)/E(R_i)^0)$, is the expected rate of return on stock i. The left hand side represents the total of the imputed rate of return on the portfolio incorporating an allowance (discount) for risk. When the risk allowance is excessive causing the left-hand side of the equation (7.9) to be greater than the right-hand side, then, the investor will not invest in stock i. For the investor to invest in stock i, the relation in equation (7.9) must hold as an equality.

7.3 Two Risky Assets Portfolio Choice Analysis

The portfolio choice scenario of two risky assets consisting of e-commerce stocks (represented by the AEMM and e-commerce portfolio returns) and market-stocks (S&P/ASX 200 index) is evaluated in this section. In Section 7.3.1, the AEMM estimated and S&P/ASX 200 returns are used to construct the efficient frontier. In Section 7.3.2, the historical e-commerce portfolio return data (Appendix 6.5) is used with the market returns for estimating the efficient frontier. The purpose is to compare the AEMM portfolio results with that derived by applying two-asset portfolio choice analysis on the e-commerce portfolio to determine the appropriateness of the AEMM as a model of the e-commerce sector in Australia.

7.3.1 Portfolio Choice Based on AEMM Estimated Returns and S&P/ASX 200 Stocks

The correlation between the AEMM and market returns is 0.4763 (Appendix 7.1), which shows a low degree of similarity in return behaviour between the two groups of data. Figure 7.1 below presents the efficient frontier with different proportions (from Appendix 7.1) of the two groups in the portfolio. The shape of the efficient frontier supports the traditional risk-return relationship in finance of Hicks (1946), Markowitz (1959) and Tobin (1958).

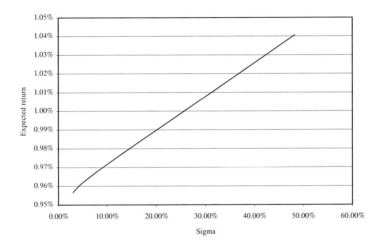

Figure 7.1 The Efficient Frontier: AEMM/Market Returns

Figure 7.2 depicts the relationship between expected return and the coefficient of variation (CV), which is the standardised measure of risk per unit of return, calculated as the standard deviation divided by the expected return (Appendix 7.1). The most efficient portfolio by measurement of CV would consist of no e-commerce stocks (Appendix 7.1, Table A7.1/2). Such a portfolio would represent the market portfolio, with a 3.00 per cent expected return and portfolio risk, σ_p, of 24.89 per cent. From Table A7.1/2, the level of expected return would only increase marginally, from 0.96 per cent to 1.04 per cent, when the σ_p increases from 3.00 per cent (no e-commerce stock portfolio) to 48.28 per cent (100% e-commerce stock portfolio). The risk-return profile of the portfolio choice of AEMM and market returns favours no investment in e-commerce stocks.

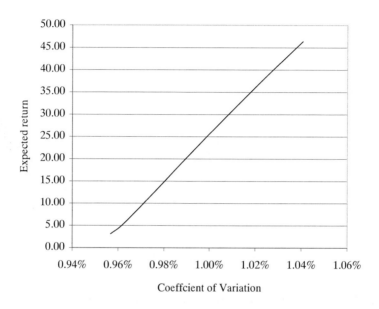

Figure 7.2 Efficient Frontier (AEMM/Market): Coefficient of Variation

7.3.2 Portfolio Choice Based on E-Commerce Stock Portfolio and S&P/ASX 200 Stocks

In this section the historical returns from the study period for the e-commerce stock portfolio and the market are used for building the efficient frontier. The correlation coefficient of these two risky assets is 0.1382 (Appendix 7.2) indicating a relative lower level of correlation between the two classes of stock compared to the analysis in Section 7.3.1. This implies a lower degree of comovement between the e-commerce stock portfolio returns to the market returns.

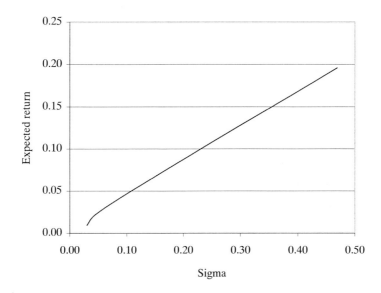

Figure 7.3 The Efficient Frontier: E-Commerce Stock Portfolio/Market Returns

Figure 7.3 depicts the different investment proportions between the two classes of stock. The risk-return behaviour of the portfolio standard deviation to expected return appears to be directly correlated with a greater proportion of e-commerce stock in the portfolio (Appendix 7.2). That is, a higher risk profile resulting from a greater proportion of e-commerce stock is compensated by higher expected return.

Figure 7.4 below shows the relationship between expected return and the CV (Table A7.2/3). The efficient portfolio measured by the coefficient of variation of the average e-commerce stocks and the average market stock would consist of 90% market stocks and 10% e-commerce stocks yielding an expected monthly return of 2.82% (or 33.84% annualised) with monthly σ of 5.73% and CV of 2.03 (Appendix 7.2).

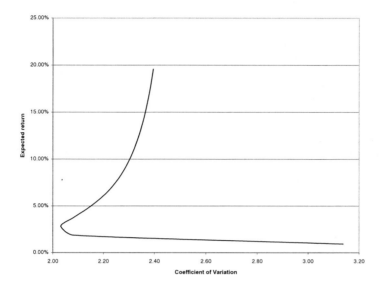

Figure 7.4 The Efficient Frontier (E-Portfolio/Market): Coefficient of Variation

On the basis of the CV criterion, the risk associated with an exclusive market-stock portfolio decreases with diversification by including 10 per cent e-commerce stocks from 3.14 to 2.03, and represents the efficient portfolio that offers the highest expected return at a given level of risk. After this point (CV = 2.03) any further diversification to include more e-commerce stocks to the portfolio progressively increases the level of CV at an increasing rate (Figure 7.4). Also from Figure 7.4, the downward sloping part of the envelope represents portfolios that are not efficient while portfolios on the rising part of the curve offer both a higher expected return and less risk (a lower coefficient of variation). The characteristics highlighted in this section confirm the high volatility nature of the e-commerce stocks under portfolio conditions. The portfolio selection process tested above allows for only 10% of the portfolio to be invested in e-commerce stocks, this percentage being the most efficient portfolio in terms of risk per unit of return.

7.4 Efficient Portfolios and Econometric Pricing Models

This section estimates the efficient portfolios and the efficient frontier for the e-commerce stock sectors analysed in this study, based on the principles of the classic capital asset pricing model presented in Section 2.6.4.

7.4.1 Efficient E-Commerce Sector Portfolios

In this section, there are $n = 10$ risky assets based on the 10 e-commerce sectors used in this study, each with expected return $E(R_s)$ (Appendix 7.3), where s represents the individual sectors. The risk-free rate (R_f), represented by the constant c, is the same risk-free rate used in our CAPM analyses in Chapter 6 of 5.63 per cent (the geometric mean), and the calculation for estimating the efficient frontier according to equation (7.6) is shown in Appendix 7.5. The method for calculating the variance-covariance matrix in this section involves using the excess return matrix (Appendix 7.4) and this approach underlies the security market line (SML). The objective of this section is to identify the set of feasible portfolios, consisting of the e-commerce sectors, represented by the area inside and to the right of the curved line in Figure 7.5 below. A feasibility portfolio is on the envelope of the feasible set with a minimum variance for a given return. The calculations for estimating the e-commerce envelope are presented in Appendixes 7.3 to 7.7.

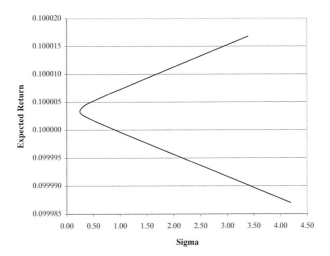

Figure 7.5 E-Commerce Sector Efficient Frontier

Figure 7.5 depicts the efficient frontier of the e-commerce sector envelope derived from the primary stock returns data for the e-commerce sectors. The convex combination of efficient portfolios x and y are represented by the envelope based on the data presented in Appendix 7.7. The set of efficient portfolios start with the portfolio $\sigma = .2549$ and $E(R) = 0.10000313$

with weight on x = 70 per cent and y = 30 percent (Appendix 7.7). The efficient portfolios consist of the weight on x being less than or equal to 70 per cent (i.e. $x \leq 70\%$ of total portfolio). The portfolios with weights of x greater than 70 per cent ($x > 70\%$), which are still on the envelope of the set of feasible portfolios are considered not efficient due to their lower expected returns. For each portfolio with greater than 70 per cent of x (downward sloping section of the envelope in Figure 7.5) a superior (efficient) portfolio can be found (with combinations that lie on the upward slope of the envelope) that gives a higher return for the same level of risk.

The conclusions we can draw from the analyses in this section pertaining to the investment quality of e-commerce stocks as a portfolio choice are that the e-commerce sectors are highly correlated and volatile. These findings are consistent with our earlier results (in Section 7.3). This is also evident from the efficient frontier in Figure 7.5, which shows only a narrow differential in expected return (from 0.10000313 to 0.10001181) with a corresponding wider band of risk (σ) of 1.8792 (from 0.2549 to 2.1341). The optimal portfolio with the lowest risk per unit of return, i.e. CV of 2.549 consists of 70 percent of x portfolio and 30% of y portfolio. We can therefore conclude that the right choice of e-commerce sectors in a portfolio can substantially reduce risk but has very little impact on expected return.

7.4.2 Testing the CAPM with the E-Commerce Sector Data

The CAPM's security market line postulates that the mean return of each asset should be linearly related to its beta. In the context of this research, if we are to assume that the historical data on stock return for the e-commerce sectors are representative of future returns, we can postulate that:

$$E(R_s) = \alpha + \Phi\beta_s + \varepsilon_s.$$

where:
$E(R_s)$ = the mean returns of the e-commerce sectors;
α = the constant term;
Φ = the coeffICENT of β_s;
β_s = the betas for the e-commerce sectors; and
ε_s = the error term.

We can test this hypothesis by regressing the mean returns on the betas for the e-commerce sectors. Appendix 7.8 shows the results of this regression that the SML is given by $E(R_s) = \alpha + \Phi\beta_s$, where α = 0.3266 and Φ = -0.0775. The R^2 of the regression is 90.98 percent. Thus the regression test yields the following SML:

$$E(r_s) = 0.3266 - 0.0775\beta_s \qquad (7.10)$$

The high R^2 (90.98%) and the t-statistics (Appendix 7.8) suggest that there is a relationship between expected return and portfolio β, albeit a negative or inverse relation. Under such conditions, the return on the market is $E(r_m) = 32.66\% - 7.75 = 24.91$ per cent (i.e. when $\beta = 1$). However, if we treat the constant in equation (7.10) as the risk-free rate, it would not realistically reflect the market risk-free rate. The inverse relationship between expected return $E(r)$ and the β coefficient in equation (7.10) appears to contradict the risk-return relation of portfolio selection to the extent that the constant remains positive.

Intuitively, this test of checking the CAPM by plotting the SML does not appear to be appropriate, despite the high statistical evidence (R^2) to support the relationship between expected return and portfolio beta. Several factors may contribute and they include non-homogeneity in the assessment of e-commerce returns, variances and co-variances, or the number of e-commerce assets (i.e. risky assets) may not be sufficient to fully test the model. The risky assets tested in this analysis are the e-commerce sectors only and in terms of all risky assets, they represent only a small proportion of all the stocks or risky assets in the market. Empirical tests done on the CAPM have successfully included risky assets such as real estate and bonds and its effectiveness is well documented (Pastor and Stambaugh 2000). From the preceding analysis, it appears that the CAPM is unsuitable for portfolio choice selection in the e-commerce sector. Therefore, this supports the multifactor model (AEMM) developed in this research as a better model for estimating e-commerce stock value, as the estimated independent factors (*NAS, CC* and *FE*) imply a wider systematic risk influence on other risky assets in the market.

7.5 Portfolio Choice and the Capital Market Line

In Sections 7.3.1 and 7.3.2 above, mean-variance analysis is used as a framework for asset allocation by drawing the efficient frontier in standard deviation-expected return space. With the opportunity to borrow and lend at the risk-free rate, the investor is no longer restricted to holding a portfolio that lies on the efficient frontier. It is possible for the investor to hold combinations of risky and risk-free assets according to their risk preference. Under such circumstances, the portfolio that maximises the probability of realised return can be estimated by the straight line (R_fN, the CML as depicted in Figure 2.6) passing through the expected return axis and is tangential, at point M, to the efficient frontier (II'). Points on the line to the right of M require borrowing at the risk-free rate and points to the left involve lending at the risk-free rate. If all investors in a particular market behave according to portfolio theory, then they must hold at least part of portfolio M in their total portfolio. Portfolio M implies the market portfolio and essentially consists of all risky assets in the market. The market portfolio is construed to be efficient, since investors only hold efficient portfolios, as it provides the maximum expected return for the relevant level of risk. In the context of this study, if the total value of the stocks in the e-commerce portfolio represents 10 per cent of the total market capitalisation of all stocks, then each investor's investment in the e-commerce portfolio stocks would be 10% of the investor's total investment in risky assets.

7.6 Portfolio Optimisation under Kuhn-Tucker Conditions

The analysis under the Kuhn-Tucker conditions will consider constrained optimisation within the context of a three-asset portfolio, being e-stocks, S&P/ASX 200 stocks and cash, based on data of the study period in this research. The computer program *PORTCHOICE* using the *GAMS* software (Brooke et al. 1997) is used to calculate the optimal portfolio choice. *PORTCHOICE* is a substantially modified version of the *PORTFOLIO* program provided in Thompson and Thore (1992). The details for programming using *GAMS* may be seen in Brooke et al (1997) and Thomson et al. (1992). The program selects the portfolios by solving a series of problems with different lambda (λ), representing risk aversion (equation (7.9)). The relevant *GAMS* program listing is presented in Appendix 7.10.

Monthly return data are used for this portfolio optimisation study. The monthly returns of the e-commerce stock are the average returns of the stocks in the e-commerce portfolio on the last business day of each month. The market stock's monthly returns are the returns of the S&P/ASX 200 market index on the last trading day of the month in the same period. The returns of these stocks are presented in Appendix 7.9[39]. The investment budget is $1.394 billion representing the monthly average total in monetary value of trade in the sample e-commerce stocks of this study, calculated by multiplying the average monthly turnover with the average of the high-low prices for each stock. The mathematical expectations of the stocks returns are the following:

E-Stock	($i = 1$)	19.59%
Market Stock	($i = 2$)	0.96%

and the covariance matrix is shown as follows:

	Portfolio	S&P/ASX 200
Portfolio	0.220093	
S&P/ASX 200	0.001946	0.000901

The expected returns are used as forecasts and the holding of cash is denoted by x_3. Thus the Lagrangian and the portfolio problem, incorporating the expected stock returns of the two assets and their covariances, to be optimised is presented in equation (7.11) below. Equation (7.11) is also the numerical specification of the equation (7.9) above.

---

[39] Actual returns have been rounded off to the nearest whole number to run this test.

Maximise:

$$19.95x_1 + 0.96x_2 + x_3 - \lambda(0.22x_1^2 + .0009x_1x_2 + .0019x_2x_1 + .0009x_2^2) \qquad (7.11)$$

subject to:

$$14.66x_1 + 7.47x_2 + x_3 = \$1,394,004,000$$
$$x_1, x_2, x_3 \geq 0$$

The risk parameter is denoted by λ and when λ is large, there is greater risk aversion. The results of a series of parametric tests for various values of λ are shown in Table 7.1 (Appendix 7.10).

Table 7.1 Optimal Solution[40]

λ	ESTOCK*	MKT STOCK*	CASH*	Expectation	Variance
0.0005	31.62	0	1,393,972	41.452	9836.148
0.0006	26.34	0	1,393,978	34.544	6830.658
0.0007	22.59	0	1,393,981	29.609	5018.444
0.0008	19.76	0	1,393,984	25.908	3842.244
0.0009	17.57	0	1,393,986	23.029	3035.848
0.0010	15.81	0	1,393,988	20.726	2459.037
0.0015	10.55	0	1,393,993	13.817	1092.906
0.0020	7.91	0	1,393,996	10.363	614.759

*$'000.

The general conclusion about the market-stock drawn from this parametric test is that it would not be a portfolio choice under all circumstances. This is largely due to its insignificant impact, in a portfolio context, in terms of the stock's relatively small expected return (0.96%) in relation to its risk (standard deviation = 3%). When risk aversion is less (i.e. λ is small) there is a tendency to purchase more of the riskier e-commerce stocks. When risk aversion is high (i.e. λ is large), the preference would be to hold more cash rather than the less risky market-stock, as the trade-off between the risk-return of the market-stock would tend to favour holding cash. This optimisation test confirms the riskiness of e-commerce stocks as an

---

[40] Summarised from GAMS output.

investment choice as manifested by the small amount allocated for investment in this highly volatile asset. When risk aversion is at its lowest in the test (i.e. $\lambda = 0.0005$), the amount invested in e-commerce stocks is only \$31,620 out of the sum of \$1.394 billion for investment (or 0.000023%). This suggests that the investor would rather choose to hold cash than to invest substantially in any of the two stocks when the e-commerce stock is too risky and volatile and the market-stock's return is too low for its risk level to be considered an advantage to holding cash. Conversely, the analysis suggests that the investor has to have relatively low risk aversion to remain invested in e-commerce stock.

The relationship between "expectation" and variance of the three-asset portfolio is depicted in Figure 7.3 (see Table 7.1 for details).

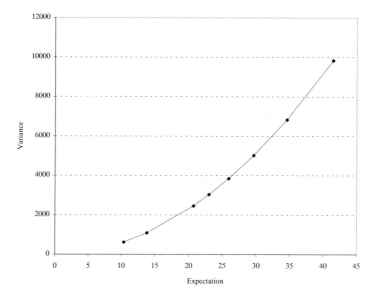

Figure 7.6 Efficient Frontier of the Three-Asset Portfolio

In a three-asset portfolio selection scenario consisting of one risk-free asset, the e-commerce stock becomes a portfolio choice in preference to the market stock. The trade-off in portfolio choice is between the riskless asset and the highly volatile e-commerce stock. The relevant optimal portfolios would consist of a very small proportion in e-commerce stock and mainly in cash. From Table 7.1, with increasing proportion of e-commerce stock in the optimal portfolios, from $\lambda = 0.0020$ to $\lambda = 0.0005$, we are able to see a four-fold increase in expected return but a sixteen-fold increase in portfolio risk. This confirms the earlier results that the inclusion of e-commerce stock in a portfolio leads to a disproportionate increase in portfolio risk.

7.7 Conclusion

In Section 7.3, under the two-risky-asset portfolio choice analysis, the CV is used as the selection benchmark where the preferred efficient portfolio is the one with the lowest CV. From the analysis using AEMM and market returns (Section 7.3.1) as portfolio choices, the lowest CV calculated is 3.14 implying the lowest risk per unit of return. The preferred efficient portfolio would consist of no e-commerce stocks. When the e-commerce stock portfolio and market returns are used in Section 7.3.2, the efficient portfolio with CV equal to 2.03 is optimal and consists of 90% market stock to 10% e-commerce stock. The individual standard deviation (σ) of the AEMM estimated returns data set equals 48.28% whilst it is 46.91% for the e-commerce stock portfolio. For the two-risky-asset portfolio analyses, the portfolio standard deviations with portfolio choices between AEMM returns/market stock and e-commerce stock portfolio returns/market stock are 24.89% and 23.71%, respectively. The expected return for the AEMM estimated data series is 1.04% and 19.59% for the e-commerce stock portfolio. The estimated returns for the two-asset portfolios would also mirror the wide discrepancy between the individual returns, being 1.00% for the portfolio with AEMM returns and 10.27% for the one with the e-commerce portfolio.

The portfolio analyses in this chapter are consistent with our earlier findings, in chapter 6, that the e-commerce sectors are highly correlated and volatile across sectors. The efficient frontiers constructed in Sections 7.3.1, 7.3.2 and 7.4.1 show highly consistent risk-return characteristic of only a marginal differential in expected returns with a corresponding bigger change in risk in the optimal portfolios. It can be concluded from this evaluation that the right choice of e-commerce sectors for equity portfolio investment can substantially reduce risk, with very little impact on expected return. Alternatively, the inclusion of an inappropriate choice of e-commerce sectors in a portfolio could substantially increase portfolio risk with only marginal contribution to the portfolio's expected return. In the three-asset portfolio context (see Section 7.6), the results reconfirm that the inclusion of e-commerce stock in a portfolio leads to a disproportionate increase in portfolio risk.

The above results are consistent with our earlier findings that the Australian e-commerce equity valuation is influenced to a greater degree by unsystematic factors (see Chapter 6). The AEMM incorporates the market pervasive factors (*NAS*, *CC* and *FE*) for estimating e-commerce stock return and these factors represent the systematic factors or variables which tend to permeate all e-commerce sectors in terms of equity valuation. If the AEMM were used to estimate the expected returns of e-commerce equity investment, then the expected return from such investment would be substantially lower than what the historical data suggests. The portfolio results from the analysis done in Section 7.3.1 reinforce this position by rejecting e-commerce stock from its portfolio choice due to its high unsystematic risk nature. Likewise, the portfolio findings in section 7.3.2 also suggest high aversion of e-commerce stock from the portfolio choice. This "similarity" indicates a high degree of consistency in using the AEMM for e-commerce portfolio findings and would suggest that the AEMM characterises the e-commerce sector in the market.

In Section 7.4, calculating the convex combination of two sector-portfolios (x and y) allows us to estimate the whole envelope of the feasible set from all the e-commerce sectors with the underlying propositions of the traditional capital asset pricing model. The suitability tests conducted in Section 7.4.2 on the CAPM as a model to measure e-commerce valuation suggests incompatibility at the present stage (during the study period) of e-commerce market development (with its inherent volatility as discussed in Chapter 6). This incompatibility is mainly the result of the CAPM being a model that predominantly addresses the systematic risk of the beta factor. Another plausible explanation for the CAPM being incompatible is that the e-commerce equity market, like the e-commerce sector, is still evolving rapidly through dynamic disequilibrium processes of adaptation and change and so does not remain in a state of equilibrium, whilst the CAPM is an equilibrium model. It should also be noted that CAPM/SML concepts (being an *ex ante* model) are based on expectations, yet betas are calculated using historical data. For e-commerce equity investment evaluation, with the rapid evolution of the sector, a company's historical data may not reflect investors' expectations about future riskiness.

The portfolio choice tests (Sections 7.3 and 7.6) conducted in this chapter show consistency in their results in respect to their considerable aversion against the selection of e-commerce stock. For the three-asset portfolio in Section 7.6, the less risky alternative would be to hold a substantial percentage of the investment sum in cash in all scenarios and the proportions of cash in the portfolio increases as risk aversion (λ) increases. The option of holding market-stock in the portfolio is ruled out with the introduction of a third asset in the form of cash for reasons stated above. This indicates and confirms that the rate of return on the portfolio and the allowance for risk must be balanced and holds as equality under the Kuhn-Tucker conditions.

The mean-variance analysis offers a powerful framework for portfolio selection but there are limitations that must be borne in mind when using this approach. The Markowitz model treats expected returns, standard deviations and correlations as population parameters and these population parameters are unlikely to be available in practice. Roy (1952) showed that even small estimation errors introduced could distort the optimisation results. So the use of mean-variance analysis in portfolio optimisation applications must be done with a sound understanding of the underlying market behaviour of the asset classes, in this case factoring e-commerce characteristics into the optimisation process, to enable efficient asset allocation. Hanoch and Levy (1969) suggest traditional portfolio analysis theory should incorporate the theory of the financial structure of the firm and its cost of capital, the multivariate utilities and distributions of consumption under uncertainty, and the general efficiency analysis of interdependent risks. This would enable a more relevant and comprehensive analysis of portfolio investment, rather than merely the choice among alternative, independent portfolios. The AEMM model developed in this study endeavours to fulfil some of these aspirations using a multivariate approach to value e-commerce stocks by capturing the effects of the underlying real economic factors and their inherent risks on valuation.

CHAPTER 8

Summary, Major Findings, Policy Implications and Conclusion

8.1 Summary

This study provides an econometric analysis on the volatility and return of e-commerce stocks in Australia between the period July 1999 to June 2000 in an attempt to identify financial and economic factors that might help to explain the value of e-commerce stocks in the absence of earnings. Studies are conducted of the relevant economic factors that might contribute to e-commerce equity value and correlation analysis is used to identify and estimate the pervasive factors. This is followed by the use of multifactor regression to model the relationship between value (return) and the pervasive macro factors. The pervasive factors are then tested for unit roots and the presence of unit roots necessitated the use of cointegration analysis.

The risk-return relationship of the e-commerce stocks under the market model and the CAPM are used to test e-commerce stock returns to better understand their risk characteristics. Effects of unsystematic risk, of a relatively new market structure posed by e-commerce can explain the extent of the differential in volatility. Econometric results generated from this study show that e-commerce portfolio return and the share market return, represented by the S&P/ASX 200 composite index, are positively related ($\beta = 2.16$, Appendix 6.7), regardless of a higher volatility for the e-commerce portfolio, represented by its beta. The higher volatility is compensated by a higher return for the e-commerce portfolio (e-commerce portfolio monthly return = 10.56% vs. monthly market return of 0.91%, refer to Table 6.9), thus maintaining the traditional risk-return relation. This relationship does not appear to hold when the actual return of the various e-commerce sectors are compared to their respective beta in Section 6.6. For the different sectors, a higher beta does not necessarily conjure higher actual returns in the study period. Figure 6.7 shows this lack of the relationship where e-commerce sectors with higher betas (sectors 1 to 5) actually had lower returns and the opposite is true for sectors 6 and 9. This casts some doubt on the appropriateness of using the CAPM as a valuation model for e-commerce stocks when the overall e-commerce sector is subject to such a high level of volatility due to unsystematic risk. This might render the market risk premium (*MRP*) estimate in the CAPM irrelevant and unsuitable for e-commerce equity valuation due to the sector's idiosyncratic market behaviour. The irrelevance of the *MRP* was manifested during the development of the AEMM when the *MRP* was excluded from the selection process using econometric analysis in Section 5.2.4.

The multifactor AEMM model supports the view that the Australian e-commerce sector is still very much influenced by offshore e-commerce developments or activities (NASDAQ and US\$/AUD exchange rate) as well as local consumer confidence. Finally, the e-commerce characteristics are extended to construct portfolios by the inclusion of other classes of stock and cash to determine the efficient frontiers and risk profiles of such portfolios.

8.2 Major Findings and Implications for Empirical Finance

This book conducts an empirical review on the development of e-commerce as a market and the implications of its development for the equity capital market as a main funding source for e-commerce business. The empirical analysis using a recent approach to econometric specification, including stationarity tests and cointegration modelling provide the identification of real economic factors that contribute to e-commerce equity value. This book also provides an empirical analysis of some other important issues in the e-commerce financial market such as market efficiency, volatility, predictability and portfolio choice selection. The issues and implications for empirical finance are discussed, explained and hypothesised in this section.

8.2.1 Systematic and Unsystematic Risks

The excessive volatility against market return of the e-commerce stock returns is attributed to the high level of unsystematic risk (low R^2) in the stocks as discovered in the regression analyses using the market model. The low compliance of e-commerce return to the market return reflects emphasis on different economic fundamentals in stock valuation. It appears doubtful that information for equity valuation can be used consistently and therefore rationally in the absence of an agreement (or general understanding) on the economic fundamentals that determine e-commerce valuation –therefore suggesting a strong presence of event effects in e-commerce stock prices in the market.

As the business activity of e-commerce firms becomes more established and stabilised, the level of unsystematic risk is expected to decrease while the riskiness of the stock is expected to reflect more the systematic risk or market risk. This can be explained by the fact that a firm's earnings become more stable and predictable as its business matures and it carves itself a niche in the market. It is consequently able to set clear objectives and direction for future growth. What then happens is that e-commerce firms become more like the traditional firms in the market that are sensitive and subject to market fundamentals. This can be seen from those firms (*Candle, Wine Planet, 131.Shop* and *Sausage*) with higher systematic risk being more established in their respective business sectors. This characteristic is consistent with the mean reverting behaviour of stock returns, that is, higher than average returns are followed by lower returns in the future (Fama and French 1988a; Poterba and Summers 1988). Initial above average e-commerce stocks could be due to the low information content of a relatively new class of stock in a euphoric new market which as time progresses, and more information about the e-commerce firm, industry and market becomes available and the industry establishes itself, the stock returns will adjust accordingly. In their studies, Fama and French (1988a) and Poterba and Summers (1988) find mean reversion in stock return over long horizons, in excess of 18 months. The 'normalisation' or mean reversion of the e-commerce stocks is probably going to take longer as e-commerce is still evolving with the Internet, and to become fully developed and universally accepted as an established market structure, may still be a while yet. The wide spread in actual return and the substantial difference compared to the required rate of return for the e-commerce stocks suggest the market for this class of stocks has not reached equilibrium.

8.2.2 Noise

The one-period autocorrelation coefficient of returns analysis for the e-commerce stocks supports the validity of the weak-form EMH. These regression analyses indicate that for e-commerce stock returns, their *ex-post* real returns and excess returns are unpredictable and thus confirm the random walk hypothesis in relationship to these stocks.

The proof of EMH shown by the tests, does not rule out the possibility of positive feedback traders or noise traders in the market for e-commerce stocks. Visual analysis of the return spread, betas and standard deviations for the e-commerce stocks appears to indicate more excessive volatility than would be suggested by the change in fundamentals (or the identified pervasive factors *NAS, CC* and *FE* in the AEMM) under the EMH. The EMH does not require all investors in the market to be efficient and well informed but that only sufficient smart money is invested to take advantage of arbitrage opportunities (Shleifer and Summers 1990). In the case of e-commerce stock trading, there can be a set of "noise" or irrational traders in the market who do not quote prices according to economic fundamentals. The lack of consensus among the arbitrageurs on the fundamental value of e-commerce stocks and that smart money may have a finite horizon due to credit constraints can restrict arbitrage activities and prevent e-commerce prices from reflecting their fundamental value. Under such circumstances, noise traders tend to dominate the market and herd mentality prevails, where investors act on sentiment rather than on the basis of fundamentals. Shiller (1989) and Shleifer and Summers (1990) studied such investor behaviour and find that individuals make systematic investment mistakes. They tend to take on excessive risk from over confidence and over reaction to new information and the projection of past price behaviour. Such conditions are readily applicable to the e-commerce stock sector with its high volatility and information turnover.

Volatility tests based on studies carried out by Shiller (1979, 1981a) and LeRoy and Porter (1981) would be instructive by measuring this excess volatility in a precise way and would constitute an area for future research, with a longer time series.

8.2.3 Volatility

The first difference of *estockret(ΔPR)$_t$* in the estimated equation (Equation 5.7) represents the change that occurs to the return of e-commerce equity returns as a covariation to the pervasive factors. This first-difference value of returns implies and measures the volatility of stock returns, and return volatility is a standard benchmark in risk-return relationship evaluation. Therefore the final estimated equation also implies and estimates the inherent risk profile for e-commerce returns.

The volatility of e-commerce stock returns appears to be consistent in terms of: the yield spreads, betas and standard deviations of the individual stocks; the systematic and unsystematic risk profile; and the EMH tests of the class of stocks examined in this study. Compared to the market, the yield spreads are excessively wide, while the standard deviations and betas are very much higher. The high degree of unsystematic risk profile together with the weak form efficiency of the stocks suggests a higher level of industry-specific information turnover reflecting the evolving nature and nascent stage of the e-commerce industry. This infers that e-commerce prices (hence returns) that alter by large amounts in the months of this study reflect the rapid changes in fundamentals of the industry. These changes may represent the opportunity sets for e-commerce firms and industry or more general structural market reform in response to Internet/ICT related developments. It is probably difficult at this stage to gauge whether the e-commerce market is excessively volatile relative to the general market, due to the lack of comparative and long-horizon earnings performance data for e-commerce firms, which could provide a yardstick against which to compare volatilities.

Lakonishok, Shleifer and Vishny (1994) suggest the return of growth stocks may be better explained by characteristics other than risk (volatility) and proposed an agency rationale, that, despite fund managers being aware of the expected returns of value stocks they still prefer growth stocks because they are easier to justify to investors. This explanation can equally apply to e-commerce stocks, which are considered growth stocks, and in the midst of Internet market euphoria, are driven partly by the surging NASDAQ composite index and heightened consumer confidence. It would be difficult for fund managers to ignore the noise and chance of higher returns despite knowing that the risk associated with these firms may be high by traditional standards and their earnings doubtful.

8.2.4 Valuation

The multifactor modelling approach is used in this book to explain the return-generating mechanism of shares consistent with the various theories that have been advanced (i.e. Sharpe 1964; Lintner 1965b; Mossin 1966; Ross 1976) and at the heart of these pricing theories is the notion that one or more pervasive factors are dominant source of covariation among asset returns. In this study the predictive quality of the CAPM is addressed and tested vis-à-vis the e-commerce data in Sections 6.5 and on the CAPM model in Section 7.4.2, which was found to be inappropriate due to the size of the risk-free factor in the estimated model.

The performance evaluation of the AEMM was conducted using the cointegration tests and the results confirmed through the long-term relationship of the variables. The relatively high R^2 results of the AEMM are an indicator of the robustness of the model as one of the techniques to estimate consistently both 'long-term equilibrium parameter vectors' and 'parameters associated with short-run dynamic adjustment processes' (Perman 1991). The long-term equilibrium relationship of the cointegration process used to test the developed model does suggest and imply the predictive quality of the model. This conclusion is consistent with Engle and Granger (1991) on cointegration and there must be Granger causality in at least one direction, as one variable can help forecast the other.

This high level of volatility caused by unsystematic risk, casts some doubts on the appropriateness of using the CAPM for e-commerce equity valuation. This position is based on: firstly, the insignificance or non-pervasive nature of the market risk premium (*MRP*) as shown by the econometric analyses (Section 5.2.4), and, secondly, the highly irregular behaviour of the e-commerce sector returns to their betas in the study period, which render the beta unsuitable for measuring e-commerce risk-return correlation. Therefore, the irrelevance of the *MRP* manifested during the development of the AEMM and the high market volatility (in the study period) of the e-commerce sector raises concerns about the suitability of the CAPM for e-commerce equity valuation when the sector is subject to erratic idiosyncratic market behaviour. This result is again confirmed in Section 7.3.2 where the mean return of each sector is regressed against beta to yield the security market line. Despite the high statistical evidence in support of the SML in this analysis, intuitive evaluation of the economic and financial implications of the estimated SML infers unrealistic conclusions.

The systematic risk measured by the ΔNAS, ΔCC and ΔFE factors in the estimated AEMM model, explains more than half of the variance (56.62%) of the e-commerce portfolio return ΔPR. The parameters in our regression of e-commerce stock returns, based on a set of predictive variables, appear to be weak when described by usual statistical measures. This is first evidenced by the low estimated systematic risk for e-commerce stocks that suggests e-commerce stocks to be in a unique universe. The use of a higher significance level for testing the null hypothesis for correlation between the dependent and the explanatory variables is another example. This suggests a weaker predictive quality for the variables. Nevertheless the selected pervasive factors do tend to explain a substantial part of the e-commerce portfolio return with an R^2 of 64.2% for the estimated three-factor model using the first difference data of the time series.

Like other stocks, e-commerce stock returns follow random walk behaviour and support the efficient markets hypothesis in the weak form. The absence of earnings due to early-stage development of e-commerce makes it imperative that surrogates are used for estimating a firm's potential earnings. This has resulted in e-commerce consultants and researchers having to rely on such indicators as: web-based metrics (Hagel and Armstrong 1997; Bontis and Mills 2000; Demers and Lev 2000; Trueman, Wong and Zhang 2000a); "cash burn" rate (Demers and Lev 2000); research and development expenditure (Hand 2000; Amir and Lev 1996); and revenue and expenses (Amir and Lev 1996; Bontis and Mills 2000; Demers and Lev 2000; Hand 2000; Trueman et el. 2000a). These "value-drivers" are fundamentally firm-specific indicators used to estimate and extrapolate its growth potential. This practice highlights the reliance of e-commerce valuation on the unsystematic risk (firm-specific risk) profile of the firm, which is very much idiosyncratic and sensitive to new technologies and market development.

8.2.5 Cointegration

In the study, all the three significant factors are individually integrated to e-commerce portfolio return of order one implying the $\Delta e\text{-}stockret(PR)$ (equation (5.3)), and past ΔNAS, ΔCC and ΔFE have significant explanatory power for current $\Delta e\text{-}stockret(PR)$ movement at the 10% significance level with R^2 of 0.6421 (Appendix 5.4(5)). The sets of variables are found to be non-stationary and are linked together in the long run, that is cointegrated. This finding provides a user of the AEMM model with a certain degree of confidence that these factors are relevant and suggests a longer term pervasive influence on e-commerce market value determination.

8.2.6 EMH and Predictability

The results of the weak-form EMH tests using the autocorrelation of returns data (by sectors) suggest the validity of that EMH for the returns of the e-commerce stocks in this study. This indicates the tests based on (*ex-post*) real returns cannot be used to predict excess returns. This essentially infers that e-commerce stock returns incorporate all relevant information immediately and price changes are a result of the arrival of new or unanticipated events. Statistically, the forecast errors are zero on average because the e-commerce prices only change on arrival of new information, which itself is a random variable and are uncorrelated with past information. This implies the efficiency of the capital markets for e-commerce stocks and their market values and returns are thus the outcome of a competitive market.

In relation to the preceding observations, the following set of alternative hypothesis regarding the current state of efficiency of the Australian e-commerce sector is offered:

The market sector is truly efficient and there is informational efficiency in the sector. This explanation has merit because in general the Australian equity market is efficient, as evidenced from the efficiency test of the S&P/ASX 200 index (Section 6.10), with the necessary sophisticated models and tools for information analysis. Presumably, efficient market performance is reinforced when this environment filters down to the sector level promoting informational efficiency and healthy competition in capital allocation.

The alternative is that the sector is truly inefficient (assuming that the current suite of tests is sufficient to address the state of efficiency). This scenario is plausible considering the returns volatility and lacklustre financial performance of the sector. Given that information about the sector may not be perfect or complete, the market mechanism failed to fully extract and digest its implications. As a result of the market's failure to factor in the full impact of new information, e-commerce stocks may be overvalued or undervalued. If this alternative is the correct, then the testable proposition is that the recent market rationalisation and diffusion of germane information on the sector should quickly remove any inefficiency in a relative short period of time[41]. However, if the sector is truly inefficient, but the current suite of tests only addresses a limited definition of efficiency, possible explanations for this are the limitation of

---

[41] Best done by event analysis around the performance announcements of e-commerce firms/sector.

the data examined in this research or the type of tests, in that the time series is too short for the tests to have sufficient power to distinguish an efficient market from an inefficient one. As the testable hypothesis implies, with better understanding of the behaviour of the e-commerce sector in terms of finance theories and analysis, the market efficiency of the sector should improve. Therefore market efficiency is a dynamic concept in which a market is supposed to move towards efficiency as information is revealed in the economy.

8.2.7 Portfolio Selection and the Valuation of E-Commerce Stocks

Despite the portfolio objectives of the investor, portfolio analyses conducted in this study on the e-commerce stocks are based on their risk-return behaviour between July 1999 and June 2000 tend to suggest a high degree of risk aversion towards these highly volatile stocks. Portfolio choice analyses of the two-risky-asset portfolio and a three-asset portfolio comprising of the e-commerce stock, market stock and cash, indicate that the efficient portfolios under different risk aversions would tend to minimise the holding of e-commerce stock. In the most efficient two-risky-asset portfolio, determined by the lowest coefficient of variation (CV), the percentage of e-commerce stock in the portfolio is 10% and the balance in market stock (90%). Whilst in the three-asset portfolio, the portion of the total investment sum in e-commerce stock is so marginal as to render it almost irrelevant as an investment choice. In such a portfolio, the prime holding would be in cash due to the marginal return of market stock in relation to holding cash for the relevant risk level.

The ideal strategy for investing in e-commerce stock, is no different from other stocks, is to maintain a mix of assets in the portfolio for diversification and shift the proportion of the investments into and out of asset classes (stocks) as the relative prospects of those asset classes change. The evolving nature and the high unsystematic risk element of the e-commerce sector will make appraisal or analysis of these stocks difficult, and trying to capitalise on short-term deviations from long-term trend could be a daunting task for investors. The analysis of e-commerce stocks in this study concludes a high degree of return volatility and offers three fundamental economic factors that are correlated to the return of Australian e-commerce equities. As economic conditions change over time factors affecting the pricing of e-commerce equities are likely to alter and investors need to predict correctly which are the relevant factors that influence price. The high risk-aversion towards e-commerce stocks tends to suggest that other economic factors underpinning risk-free or less risky assets may in the future become relevant and pervasive to e-commerce equity valuation. Such factors include the risk-free rate, 10-year Treasury Bonds, 3-month Treasury Notes and the S&P/ASX 200 (i.e. market and generally old-economy stocks that are considered less volatile).

The study on financial optimisation here is confined strictly to the prevailing market conditions (i.e. pertaining to e-commerce stock return, r_f and market index return) during the study period and within the context of the specified risk parameters. This portfolio position with zero weight on the market index is not expected to remain given the changing market conditions and investor's risk profile. Realistically, fund managers do make adjustments to their investment portfolio to reflect the existing market conditions (in this case changes in values of the pervasive factors) and the risk profile of their client. The ideal approach for portfolio selection to benefit from e-commerce equity investing would be some form of the industry-wide practice of tactical asset allocation (TAA) with a swing component within the equity asset class between e-commerce and other stocks. The level of investment in e-commerce stocks could be altered as economic conditions change; and in this case the conditions are delineated by the AEMM model developed here as one of the analytical tools to be employed.

8.3 Contributions of Study

The primary contribution of this exploratory study is to gain a financial insight into e-commerce equity valuation and provide a foundation for further research in the areas of portfolio management, corporate finance and public policy. Volatility and EMH analysis can assist fund managers, firms and governments in their decision-making by evaluating the precise implications of a projected policy upon the behaviour and characteristics of e-commerce firms.

8.3.1 Corporate Financing Implications

The implications from this research for corporate equity fund-raising are as follows:
- The volatility (thus low level of predictability) of e-commerce stocks would make pricing of initial public offers a daunting task for fund-raisers;
- Equity investment in the e-commerce sector might be construed as speculative given the findings on the volatility and return profile;
- The idiosyncratic factors influencing e-commerce stock value would make long-term valuation of e-commerce firms difficult creating a high degree of uncertainty in the market place of its investment value;
- High risk-aversion towards e-commerce stock as an investment choice would pose a challenge to corporate managers in equity fund-raising activity; and
- The EMH tests suggest that fundamental analysis would be the preferred approach for evaluating e-commerce investments.

The regression tests conducted for the valuation of Australian e-commerce stock return identified three pervasive factors suggesting these would better determine e-commerce stock returns than the traditional valuation models: the market model, the DCF model or the CAPM. It is prudent then for investors to monitor the trend of these factors to obtain an intimation of e-commerce stock valuation that is useful for formulating investment strategies.

8.3.2 Business Cycle Implications

Since asset price fluctuations have a high correlation with business cycles in industrialised countries (IMF 2000), this connection warrants a more definitive study into the interrelationships between e-commerce equity prices and business cycles. The volatility and high idiosyncratic nature of e-commerce equity return and its impact on the financial markets need to be further investigated from the perspective of asset pricing in a general equilibrium context (Cox, Ingersoll and Ross 1985). Also the idiosyncrasies of the e-commerce sectors need to be studied in more detail in the context of business cycles vis-à-vis the general market in terms of the three identified variables and other real factors, over time, using a general equilibrium model. Empirical studies by Schwert (1989), Fama and French (1988a, 1988b, 1989), and Poterba and Summers (1988) have established regularities in the cyclical behaviour of returns and return volatility. The approach adopted by Lucas (1978), Brock (1982) and Rouwenhorst (1995), where dynamic equilibrium models are used to analyse asset-pricing implications, is consistent with this form of business cycle analysis. The equilibrium models developed might incorporate the co-movement of returns or prices of e-commerce equities, consumption (CC), foreign exchange $(FE)^{42}$ and investment (NAS) over time, and possibly the analysis on the relative variability of these aggregates. For e-commerce equity investment, the crux of factor analysis in the business cycle context is to study the evolution of these factors and their impact on expected asset returns. The nascent development of e-commerce, and the current lack of e-commerce earnings data, heightens the need to establish and monitor those factors that influence its evolution and provide an insight into the relationship between these real economic factors and equity returns.

8.4 Public Policy Implications

The Internet, which spawned e-commerce, is a new market infrastructure in a nascent stage of development, and with its potential to pervade all facets of the economy, is probably too important to be left entirely to market forces. The results of this study (that e-commerce stocks have a high unsystematic risk profile) imply that the appropriate government action (Stiglitz 1993) is to enhance equity market efficiency in the e-commerce market as a means to minimise investment risk and/or encourage more adept and literal information dissemination about e-commerce market developments. Romer (1992) and Soete (1997) find the need for government intervention to sustain investment in knowledge and Lehman (1996) suggests that US economic growth in the next century depends on the government creating incentives for private sector investment in R&D and fostering and promoting of intellectual property.

If the market is efficient, there is the presumption that government intervention is necessary and according to Cuthbertson (1997) the outcomes of tests of the EMH can be used in public policy assessment of the desirability of mergers and acquisitions, short-termism, and regulation of financial institutions; which are all relevant and contemporary issues related to the development of e-commerce. Romer (1992) finds the need for government intervention to sustain the investment in knowledge and Lehman (1996) suggests that the government creating incentives for private sector investment in R&D and fostering and promoting

---

[42] A comprehensive study of the relationship between the business cycle and the exchange rate can be found in International Monetary Fund's publication, *"The Business Cycle, International Linkages, and Exchange Rates,"* World Economic Outlook, May 1998.

intellectual property will determine US economic growth in the next century. If the market is efficient, the current price reflects the intrisnsic value for the investment and if the financing conditions are optimal then firms should invest in e-commerce through internal expansion or mergers and acquisitions (Many firms are involved in e-commerce through internal development of e-commerce capabilities while others such as AOL-Time Warner and Telstra-Pacific Century Cyberworks prefer exploiting market opportunities through mergers and acquisitions or strategic alliances). The firm's cost of capital would also be at its optimal level under the EMH (Modigliani and Miller 1958, 1963).

8.5 Other Financial Market Issues

The implications of the financial econometric model results for other issues relevant to the financial markets are discussed below.

8.5.1 Real and Financial Sector Interaction and Economic Implications

The study of the relationship between financial intermediation and real economic activity is important to assess the potential role of improved financial intermediation in the process of economic development (Islam, Billington and Oh 2001). The relationships between the financial markets and real economic activity in the knowledge economy are not yet well explored. The relationship between financial markets in the knowledge economy has been studied using endogenous growth model although the application of this approach has not been fully explored (see Agenor and Montiel (1996) for a survey). The role of finance in economic growth via productivity growth is stressed and the adoption of some public policy to manage financial market is also implied by the general propositions of endogenous growth theory. According to Schreyer (2000), ICT investments contribute to economic growth and are inherently similar to other capital goods. The knowledge economy promotes innovation and provides the foundation for accelerated economic growth in the 21st century and e-commerce is an important technological development that can help to restructure the industrial economy towards the new economy. A rapidly changing economy in which ICT plays an increasingly important role in restructuring economic activities resulting in strong non-inflationary growth, robust stock market valuations and low unemployment are evidence of economic progress. Stock price movements have a close relationship to the rate of economic activities (Geske and Roll 1983 and Dhakal, Kandil and Sharma 1993).

Samih (2002) found that by using the lagged residuals of cointegration regression, past information can help to predict current stock returns. The cointegration tests and the results in this book imply an association between the factors and Engle and Granger (1991) states that if they are $I(1)$ and cointegrated, 'there must be Granger causality in at least one direction, as one variable can help forecast the other'. The three pervasive factors (NAS, CC and FE) identified in this study are therefore helpful in predicting e-commerce equity returns.

The accelerated rate of economic growth has modified the traditional structure and institutional basis of the economy and this has been accompanied by by-products of fundamental consequences such as globalisation, the emergence of the knowledge economy, and regional convergences and divergences of economic growth of different countries (Islam, Billington and Oh 2001; Sheehan and Tegart 1998). The important prerequisites of a knowledge-based economy relate to people and infrastructure (Oh, Islam and Bose 2002). The post industrial revolution era entails knowledge as well as increasing availability of material goods, services, and wealth for the strong growth of national economies. The important characteristics of the new market infrastructure of a knowledge economy are the increasing knowledge intensity of the economy, the rise of the online economy, the rising value of knowledge and market failures, and integrated international markets and globalisation (Sheehan and Tegart 1998), and with it the potential to pervade all facets of the economy. The results of this study that the e-commerce stocks have a high unsystematic risk profile imply that the appropriate government actions, for enhancing equity market efficiency in the e-commerce market as a means to minimise investment risk, would be more definitive public regulations and/or more adept and literal information dissemination about the e-commerce market development.

The findings in this book that pertains to real economic activity and financial markets imply that the NASDAQ composite index, consumer confidence and foreign exchange rate between the Australian dollar and U.S. dollar are significant factors in initiating changes in the e-commerce stock return and it can be claimed that e-commerce stock returns variability is fundamentally linked to these variables. Therefore there is a need for financial policy to cultivate participation in the e-commerce sector, taking into consideration these pervasive real economic factors, so that the sector operates according to the broader economic objective. This is consistent with studies of financial intermediation in the economy by Gurley and Shaw (1955, 1960) and Fry (1988), and endogenous growth theory where it is implied that financial intermediation may weaken the relationship between money and economic activity and may make the economy more dependent on the complex interaction between debts and assets in the economy, and the adoption of public policy is justified for proper financial management for economic development.

8.5.2 Financial Implications of E-Commerce Sector Volatility

The measure of volatility of the e-commerce stocks is crucial as a further test of market efficiency in the allocation of financial resources, for if the e-commerce prices do not reflect market fundamentals then resources will be misallocated and hence, volatility tests are joint tests for informational efficiency. The implications of the EMH in e-commerce stocks relate to the efficient allocation of capital in the sense that under the EMH market financing conditions and the firm's cost of capital are optimal. Therefore the degree of market efficiency helps determine the viability and optimality of e-commerce-related projects and also the need for government intervention.

The systematic and unsystematic risk profile of e-commerce stocks, as measured by the market index, indicates that unsystematic risk has a more profound influence (82%) than systematic risk (18%) on e-commerce stock returns (Oh 2001). Therefore e-commerce stocks have less of a tendency to move together with the general market variability. This is also illustrated by the higher return variability of the e-commerce stock portfolio (Oh 2001); where monthly standard deiviation (σ) is 49.82%, compared to the general market σ of 3.13%. Also, volatility measured against the market, represented by beta, is generally higher for most sectors. This indicates a more volatile market for e-commerce sector than the general market. From the perspective of risk-return relationship, the risk and return trade-off appears not to hold, which is consistent with the high unsystematic risk profile of e-commerce stock. This confirms the general systematic risk level of the e-commerce stocks and that they move predominantly in a volatility universe of their own, and relatively independent of the market (Oh 2001).

This infers that e-commerce prices (hence returns) that alter by large amounts reflect the rapid changes in fundamentals of the industry compared to the general market. These changes may represent the opportunity sets for e-commerce firms and industry or more general structural market reform in response to e-commerce related developments (Oh et al. 2002). It is probably difficult at this stage to gauge whether the e-commerce market is excessively volatile relative to the general market, due to the lack of comparative and long-horizon earnings performance data for e-commerce firms, which could provide a yardstick against which to compare volatilities.

The returns of growth stocks may be better explained by characteristics other than risk, i.e. volatility (Lakonishok, Shleifer and Vishny 1994) and an agency rationale is proposed, that, despite fund managers being aware of the expected returns of value stocks they still prefer growth stocks because they are easier to justify to investors. This explanation can equally apply to e-commerce stocks, which are considered growth stocks, and in the midst of Internet market euphoria, are driven partly by the surging NASDAQ composite index and heightened consumer confidence. The first difference of $estockret(\Delta PR)_t$ in the estimated equation (Equation 5.7) represents the change that occurs to the return of e-commerce equity returns as a covariation to the pervasive factors.

8.5.3 Predicitability of E-commerce Stocks and Investment Strategy

The strict random walk concept of stock prices suggests that stock returns are unpredictable. The predictability of e-commerce stock returns depends on the statistical analysis of the random walk hypothesis of the stock prices. If e-commerce stock prices were unpredictable, such a test would support the rational expectation element of the EMH that forecast errors should be zero on average and uncorrelated with any information available at the time the forecast was made. The EMH emphasises that it is impossible for investors to persistently make supernormal profits. The study of the predictability of e-commerce stocks is important since the e-commerce financial market has several special characteristics (Oh 2001, Oh and Islam 2002) such as volatility and returns, the high level of unsystematic risk and idiosyncratic factors that influence equity returns and their predictability in a portfolio context. The volatility in e-commerce stocks has made the valuation of e-commerce stock blurred and at best is an inconsistent measurement of e-commerce equity investment (Bontis et al. 2000). Since World War II the movements in stock prices were closely connected to the rate of economic growth and standard valuation models according to which stock prices are determined by market fundamentals could explain stock returns. But e-commerce stock prices are more troublesome and the question has been asked whether these stock prices can still be explained by fundamentals, or whether speculative bubbles and fads govern these prices. However, studies conducted on speculative bubbles have proved unsuccessful in testing directly for bubbles (Ahmed et al. 1997).

The existing literature on predictability of stock returns has focused on issues such as, Granger's anomaly (Samih 2002), model uncertainty (Avramov 2000), asset allocation (Kandel 1996) and dividends (Shiller 1981). The phenomenon of "noise-trading" (Black 1986) where the market value of e-commerce stocks is over-hyped to euphoric investors is a possible scenario of the sector. De Long (1996) advocates the current valuation of information technology related stocks, which e-commerce is a part, for information technology is a fundamental factor transforming the economy. There is a general acceptance that the variations in expected returns are rational variations in response to market conditions (Chen 1991; Schwert 1990; Fama 1989, 1990). The market value of e-commerce stock reflects this potential benefit from information technology and investors, optimistic about the new economy, factor this into their investment strategy. This implies that the predictability of e-commerce stock value is based on the potential outcomes and economic impacts of e-commerce, the forces underlying its development.

The market situation of e-commerce stocks, as a reflection of the Internet as a business medium, closely reflects a sector that is still in a nascent development stage, evolving and complex. Unlike the traditional approach of stock valuation, the meaningful valuation of e-commerce stocks therefore involves a process that pieces together information on forecasts of the overall economy and the conditions of the capital markets to project a fair price. For many e-commerce firms, the emphasis is on long-term growth as opposed to current profitability.

The results of the efficient market hypothesis test (Section 6.10) imply that for all the e-commerce sectors are informationally efficient in the weak form (at 10% significance level). This implies e-commerce stock prices reflect historical information underlying firm and the market responds immediately to new information regarding the firm. This characteristic can be reconciled with the dynamic nature of e-commerce development that is rapidly evolving, thereby contributing to volatility and hence problems in predictability. As the business activity of e-commerce firms becomes more established and stabilised, the level of unsystematic risk is expected to decrease while the riskiness of the stock is expected to reflect more the systematic risk or market risk. This can be explained by the fact that a firm's earnings become more stable and predictable as its business matures and it carves itself a niche in the market. It is consequently able to set clear objectives and direction for future growth. What then happens is that e-commerce firms become more like the traditional firms in the market that are sensitive and subject to market fundamentals. This characteristic is consistent with the mean reverting behaviour of stock returns, that is, higher than average returns are followed by lower returns in the future (Fama and French 1988; Poterba and Summers 1988). In their studies, Fama and French (1988) and Poterba and Summers (1988) find mean reversion in stock return over long horizons, in excess of 18 months. The 'normalisation' or mean reversion of the e-commerce stocks is probably going to take longer for two reasons: firstly e-commerce is still rapidly evolving as a market structure to become fully developed and universally accepted and, secondly due to its high technology turnover. The wide spread in actual return and the substantial difference compared to the required rate of return for the e-commerce stocks suggest the market for this class of stocks has not reached equilibrium. At this stage, it would be premature to conclude whether e-commerce stock returns are mean reverting, that is higher returns are followed by lower returns in the future, due to the shorter study period.

The predictability of e-commerce equity can partly be addressed by the systematic factors of *NAS*, *CC* and *FE* in the AEMM model. They explain more than half of the variance (56.62%) of the e-commerce portfolio return, indicating that 56.62% of Australian e-commerce stock variance is specified but individual stock may still vary from this benchmark. The AEMM only explains part of the e-commerce value ($R^2 = 64\%$) due to these systematic factors and it is likely investors continue to trade on noise, knowing that the risk associated with such practice may be high by traditional standards and their earnings doubtful (Oh 2001).

8.5.4 Portfolio Choice Management

The theory of portfolio choice management concerns the selection of risky assets. The typical approach in equity investment is to hold a balanced portfolio of different stocks to provide some expected return (also known as diversification). The theory assumes investors choose between alternative portfolios on the basis of the expected return and risk of that return. It assumes that: the investor is risk averse; selects investment opportunities in terms of a probability distribution defined by expected return and risk (the mean-variance paradigm discussed in Section 7.2); behaves rationally; has an expected utility of increasing expected return and decreasing risk; and the capital market is perfect. In the evaluation of a mean-variance efficient portfolio, a risk-based pricing model offers a powerful insight (Pastor and Stambaugh 2000). The simulation models developed in this book were used to test the portfolio characteristics vis-à-vis e-commerce stock returns and from the results, an attempt is made to construct an efficient e-commerce stock portfolio based on past variability of returns, with the assumption that the risk profile of these stocks remains unchanged over time, or at least over the short term. It would be possible to extrapolate or predict future risk from historic risk if the underlying probabilistic structure of these stocks remains unaltered (Thompson and Thor 1992).

The portfolio analyses conducted in this book on the e-commerce stocks suggest a high degree of risk aversion towards the highly volatile e-commerce stocks. The ideal strategy for investing in e-commerce stock is to proactively manage the portfolio to maintain a mix of assets in the portfolio for diversification and shift the proportion of the investments into and out of asset classes (stocks) as the relative prospects of those asset classes change. The evolving nature and the high unsystematic risk element of the e-commerce sector will make appraisal or analysis of these stocks difficult, and trying to capitalise on short-term deviations from long-term trend could be a daunting task for investors. The analysis of e-commerce stocks in this book concludes a high degree of return volatility and offers three fundamental economic factors that are correlated to the return of Australian e-commerce equities. As economic conditions change over time factors affecting the pricing of e-commerce equities are likely to alter and investors need to predict correctly which are the relevant factors that influence price. The high risk-aversion towards e-commerce stocks tends to suggest that other economic factors underpinning risk-free or less risky assets may in the future become relevant and pervasive to e-commerce equity valuation.

8.5.5 Globalisation, International Factors, Financial Liberalisation and the Changing Characteristics of Financial Markets

The financial sector plays an important role in macroeconomic management and the study of the role of financial intermediation in the knowledge intensive sector at the macroeconomic level can provide valuable insights into policy development in the new economy. There has been a fundamental change occurring in the behaviour of all developed economies due to globalisation, financial deregulation and the advent of the knowledge economy. In this book the international factors (*NAS* and *FE*) are found to be pervasive and significant for e-commerce equity value and we hypothesise that their characteristics have global-wide implications and inferences (Islam and Oh 2002a, 2002b). With the emergence of financial liberalisation, international factors are becoming crucial in determining value of securities in different financial markets and the impact of the relative influence of domestic and international factors in shaping the elements of the financial market is becoming more prominent.

The interdependent of financial markets and the shift to a knowledge-based economy have altered the financial landscape and made some international economic factors crucial in shaping future financial markets. This is characterised by a more open macroeconomy and the emergence of the knowledge-intensive sector that results in a distinct shift away from traditional manufacturing-based production to that of a service-based economy dependent upon innovative technology companies and highly skilled professional service.

8.6 Further Studies and Research

The issues that are important in studying e-commerce stock valuation may be discussed under the follows headings.

Microeconomic issues. The most immediate issue that needs to be addressed is the empirical implications of the efficient mean-variance allocation priorities of optimal portfolio choices in the e-commerce market (Markowitz 1959).

Macroeconomic issues. The impact of macroeconomic variables such as consumption, savings, and income on asset prices and portfolio optimal choices using a consumption beta model (Blanchard and Fisher 1989), specified within an open economy macro-dynamic framework, is also an area of interest for investigation.

Welfare economics issues. Welfare economics studies of the financial sector are also popular (see for example Hakansson 1987). A welfare economics study of the financial market addresses a wide range of issues including the following: Pareto efficiency or market failures of the financial markets, i.e. the possibilities of asymmetric information exchange; transaction and information costs; and issues in trading in the e-commerce market. Game theory models for addressing these issues are found to be appropriate.

Contagion. At the time of writing the book, the viability of an event study on contagion within the Australian e-commerce sector would be the difficulty with the limited data on e-commerce failures, due mainly to the nascent stage of development of the industry and the small number of pure-play e-commerce firms that existed in Australia during the period. The Australian e-commerce companies at this early lifecycle stage would not have experienced the full business cycle to enable a comprehensive contagion test.

Limitations and future studies. In this book, the above issues have not been addressed although their investigation would prove useful. These issues form the agenda for further research in finance by the authors. Future studies may also focus on statistical issues such as: the appropriate form of stochastic processes for asset price changes; the usefulness of the assumption of normal distribution and finding the alternatives, etc; and computational issues such as the numerical computation of continuous dynamic portfolio models of the e-commerce market (Tapierio 1998). A study on group behaviour of e-commerce investors, similar to that of Shiller (1989), would illuminate the extent of noise-trader behaviour or herd mentality in the e-commerce stock sector. Testing and hypothesis might perform better under non-linear specification (Hand 1999) rather than the linear approach to which the study in this book is restricted. This will involve a reformulation of the hypothesis and models of asset pricing to evince the effects of economic variables on first and second moments of returns. Due to the high degree of idiosyncratic or unsystematic risk in the e-commerce sector, no forecasting of future stock prices has been produced, and subsequently remains a task to be undertaken.

8.7 A Summary of Findings and their Implications for Other Regions

The empirical evidence generated by this study into the financial issues of Australian e-commerce stocks in the knowledge economy can be used to provide a theoretical foundation for formulating policies in other regions in the world. The following findings are relevant to e-commerce equity market development in these regions:

- The market model analyses highlight the excessive volatility of the e-commerce stock returns against market return, and was explained by the high level of unsystematic risk element (low R^2) in these stocks. This implies a low correlation of e-commerce returns to the market return in terms of their prices. This is interpreted as a strong presence of event effects in e-commerce stock prices in the market.

- Australian e-commerce stocks are subject to a higher unsystematic risk (82%) level than systematic risk (18%), measured by the S&P/ASX 200 market index.
- The fact that e-commerce firms are subject to a relatively high level of unsystematic risk suggests that e-commerce sector return may react more aggressively to idiosyncratic economic factors than the traditional factors identified in other empirical studies. This implies that investors may consider unsystematic risk as an important factor when determining e-commerce stock investments.

- From the covariance and correlation studies, e-commerce stocks do covary and this reflect the fact that e-commerce firms tend to have similar characteristics or properties (being subject to the same market conditions of Internet development).

- The following is the estimated regression model that best explains Australian e-commerce stock returns in the study period (Section 5.2.4):

$$e\text{-}stockret(\Delta \hat{PR})_t = -0.1900 + 0.0013\Delta NAS_t + 0.0692\Delta CC_t - 0.3287\Delta FE_t$$

The factor identification process in this study seeks to ensure that equity investments in the e-commerce sector will maximise financial return when these variables are included in the risk analysis – albeit the fact remains that changes will occur to the sensitivity (β) of each factor to return over time.

- In general, these findings imply that the NASDAQ composite index, consumer confidence and foreign exchange rate between the Australian dollar and US dollar are significant factors in predicting changes in e-commerce stock return and it can be claimed that the variability of the latter is fundamentally linked to these variables. The interpretation of macroeconomic variable dominance over financial variables can possibly be drawn depending on how we define Exchange Rate *(FE)*, FE has traditionally been treated as an macroeconomic variable and the definition of Consumer Confidence *(CC)* is more clear-cut, another macroeconomic factor, which is a proxy for consumption level in the economy. With two of the three value-pervasive variables in the estimated equation being macroeconomic variables (with NASDAQ-*NAS* the only capital market variable) it can be extrapolated that e-commerce returns are largely influenced by macroeconomic considerations consistent with other studies by Kwon and Shin (1999), Fifield et al. (2002) and Wongbangpo et al. (2002).

- The systematic risk measured by the *NAS, CC* and *FE* factors using the estimated model explains more than half of the variance (56.62%) of the e-commerce portfolio return, *PR*. This indicates that 56.62% of Australian e-commerce stock variance is specified but individual stock may vary from this benchmark.

- The proof of EMH shown by tests done does not rule out the possibility of positive feedback traders or noise traders in the markets for e-commerce stocks. Visual analysis of the return spread, betas and standard deviations for the e-commerce stocks appears to indicate excessive volatility, which is a characteristic of the e-commerce financial market as discussed above. The volatility is greater than would be suggested by the change in fundamentals (or pervasive factors *NAS*, *CC* and *FE*) under the EMH, and implicates noise effects.

- The findings of this research also have other financial market implications, extraplolated from the results of the econometric analysis, pertaining to the investment strategy, financial sector interaction, portfolio choice management, the role of international factors in e-commerce valuation and globalisation of financial markets.

In the midst of the Internet market euphoria, e-commerce stocks are perceived as growth stocks whose value is driven partly by the NASDAQ composite index, consumer confidence and strength of the Australian currency (AEMM). The systematic factors of the AEMM only explain part of the e-commerce value (i.e. $R^2 = 64\%$) and fund managers who ignore the noise would do so at the peril of missing the boat of higher returns while knowing that the risk associated with these firms may be high by traditional standards and their earnings doubtful. The trading approach may be to adopt an active tactical asset allocation strategy for risk management. Lakonishok, Shleifer and Vishny (1994) suggest the return of growth stocks may be better explained by characteristics other than risk and propose an agency rationale, that, while fund managers are aware of the expected returns of value stocks they may still prefer growth stocks because they are easier to justify to investors. This explanation can equally apply to e-commerce stocks.

The above results have relevance in other regions of the world (as mentioned earlier in this section) and takes the form of their implications suggesting interwined, however complex and apparently fragile relationship between financial activities and real economic performance and therefore points to the need for proactive government strategic intervention in the e-commerce sector for effective and efficient financial facilitation and development of this sector.

It may be noted that the case for Australia used in this book for analysing e-commerce equity market development can be extrapolated to other countries in the world, particularly the Asian region, for the following reasons:
- Australia and Asian countries are in the same geographic and economic region experiencing strong Internet growth and also at the same stage of e-commerce development;
- Like Australia, e-commerce market development in Asian countries relies on leads from developments in the e-commerce sector in the United States;
- Australia's established education system provides the impetus for intellectual property development, which is crucial and provides the foundation for the growth of e-commerce infrastructure and market;

- Australia's e-commerce development policies are formulated within the context of an industrialised and a free-market economy, these circumstances provide an ideal contrast to the pro-active and strategic interventionist role of Asian governments; and
- Using Australia as a benchmark study avoids the incident of survivorship bias associated with a U.S. study.

8.8 Conclusion

This investigation in this book of the financial issues of Australian e-commerce stocks has generated empirical data capable of providing a theoretical foundation for formulating policies in other regions in the world pertaining to e-commerce equity market development. From the recent global experience on the volatility of the e-commerce equity market, there is a need for more definitive public policy to cultivate investment decision-making in the e-commerce sector so that the sector operates efficiently in an economically and socially desirable manner. The accomplishment of social and economic objectives in relation to e-commerce development must therefore require a certain degree of government intervention, whether passive or pro-active, depending on the existing market conditions. Brainard and Tobin (1963) postulated that monetary policy had important real effects as it affects return on real capital and it also through such policy that government can influence the allocation of capital to the development of e-commerce. These problems are more evident due to the nascent and evolving nature of e-commerce development creating a situation of asymmetric information. The focus of public policy should be directed at minimising the problems of moral hazard and adverse selection in the e-commerce equity market. The implication, both business and government, is that investments in education and technology need to be fostered for firms and countries to remain in the forefront of the knowledge-based economic challenge (Oh, Islam and Bose 2002).

It is worth noting that in post industrial revolution era, knowledge (which forms the basis of e-commerce devlopment) as well as increasing availability of material goods, services, and wealth have contributed to the strong growth of the national economies. However, the accelerated rate of economic growth has modified the traditional structure and institutional basis of the economy. The important prerequisites of a knowledge-based economy relate to people and infrastructure. People require high levels of both academic and technical education and infrastructure has to be contemporary to ensure knowledge-based economic systems operate effectively. Governments have always pride themselves in being able to accelerate economic development. They have done so by investing extensively for the purpose of building new economic infrastructure and providing facilities necessary for economic growth. There is nothing new about government participation in economic life to help new industries and the electronic commerce (e-commerce) sector is no exception. Assistance can take the form of expenditure, tariff, incentives and subsidies to assist the industry to overcome financial difficulties in productive investments that facilitate and integrate economic activities, either on a long-term basis or to tie over short-term difficulties.

192   *Summary, Major Findings, Policy Implications and Conclusion*

In general, the findings in this book imply that the NASDAQ composite index, consumer confidence and foreign exchange rate are significant factors in predicting changes in e-commerce stock return and it can be claimed that e-commerce stock returns variability is fundamentally linked to these variables. The accomplishment of social and economic objectives in relation to e-commerce development must therefore require government intervention by observing the behaviour of these factors and ensuring that they are conducive to development in the sector. The focus of public policy should then be to create the right market environment for investors by minimising the problems of moral hazard, adverse selection and appropriate returns (in relation to risk understaken) in the e-commerce equity market.

It should be reiterated that the relatively high unsystematic risk of e-commerce firms suggests that e-commerce sector return may react more aggressively to idiosyncratic economic factors, including effective demand, market uncertainty, speculative investment, distribution and composition of national income, public policy and openness of domestic market to international finance and trade, than the traditional factors identified in other empirical studies. Therefore, investment evaluation and public policy formulation must take note of this important point in order to frame the right approach to address the situation.

Appendices

Appendix 2.1

Table A2.1/1 Monthly Data of Identified Variables

	1	2	3	4	5	6	7	8	9	10	11	12
	Stock	SP/	SP/	SP/			($ million)		($ million)		10-year	3-mth TN
	Returns	ASX 200	ASX Banks	ASX Ind.	NASDAQ	D. Jones	M1	M3	Credit	IP	T. Bond	Rf
1999 Jul-99	3020	6337	5253	2638	10655	117814	379273	592864	117.5	6.24	4.68
Aug-99	2952	6296	5116	2739	10829	118448	381502	597487	117.8	6.35	4.74
Sep-99	2881	6141	4928	2746	10336	120341	385025	602104	118.5	6.30	4.76
Oct-99	2885	6493	5028	2966	10730	119886	386643	607287	118.9	6.63	4.81
Nov-99	3044	6503	5294	3336	10878	120046	389879	612538	119.5	6.64	4.98
Dec-99	3153	6623	5403	4069	11497	121146	389581	611780	120	6.96	4.98
2000 Jan-00	3096	6432	5377	3940	10941	124044	392358	616895	119.7	7.16	5.12
Feb-00	3136	6254	5596	4697	10128	123395	394385	626952	119.2	6.65	5.45
Mar-00	3133	6112	5560	4573	10922	124590	396320	630597	118.3	6.36	5.47
Apr-00	3116	6705	5491	3861	10734	126172	399937	633019	116	6.39	5.73
May-00	3081	7184	5407	3401	10543	127709	404663	641751	114.4	6.27	5.88
Jun-00	3311	7431	5792	3966	10448	129611	409145	650418	112.8	6.16	5.83

Appendix 2.1

Table A2.1/1 Monthly Data of Identified Variables (cont.)

		13	14	15	16	17	18	19	20	21	22	23	24
		Yield						Fed. Gov.	($'000)	Westpac		MKt.	
		Spread	Mkt. Cap	Daily Turn.	Div. Yld.	Cap. Impts.	BOP	Edu. Exp.	R. Trade	Con'dence	Forex	Risk Prem.	Mkt. Return
1999	Jul-99	1.56	589003	1340	3.2	1925	-935	879	11969	113.8	57.1	0.16	1.72%
	Aug-99	1.61	577263	1105	3.3	2045	-1340	879	12141	109.7	56.0	-0.32	-2.25%
	Sep-99	1.54	568939	1076	3.5	2495	-1799	879	12198	114.2	57.0	-0.34	-2.40%
	Oct-99	1.82	590058	1166	3.5	2145	-747	864	12249	113.3	55.7	-0.03	0.14%
	Nov-99	1.66	625937	1348	3.3	2233	-1080	1056	12308	115.0	55.3	0.61	5.51%
	Dec-99	1.98	654998	1284	3.2	2078	-1059	675	12238	108.0	56.4	0.38	3.56%
2000	Jan-00	2.04	648568	1668	3.3	2328	-1219	1888	12076	111.1	56.0	-0.27	-1.79%
	Feb-00	1.20	658334	1666	3.3	2257	-873	816	12143	101.1	54.5	0.10	1.28%
	Mar-00	0.89	667225	1815	3.4	2245	-703	585	12183	99.6	53.1	-0.07	-0.08%
	Apr-00	0.66	653259	1580	3.3	2135	-764	725	12184	95.9	52.5	-0.13	-0.56%
	May-00	0.39	639504	1374	3.4	2318	-1445	1002	12248	93.7	51.4	-0.19	-1.12%
	Jun-00	0.33	681954	1761	3.3	2421	-1204	339	13151	100.3	53.3	0.84	7.47%

Appendix 2.1 (cont.)
Table A2.1/1 Monthly Data of Identified Variables (cont.)

Notes:

1   Stock returns for the firms.

2   Share price indices, 31 December 1979 = 500.

3   SP/ASX 200 Banks index

4   SP/ASX 200 industrial index

5   Nasdaq composite index

6   Dow Jones Industrial Average Index.

7   M1 - seasonally adjusted

8   M3 - seasonally adjusted

9   Credit figures seasonally adjusted.

10   (1995 = 100)

11   10-year Australian Treasury Bond rate.

12   The 3-month Australian Treasury Notes rate is used as the proxy for the risk-free rate, Rf.

13   Yield spread is calculated by deducting the 1-month TN yield from the 10-year Treasury bond return.

14   Market capitalisation of listed domestic equities in $'000.

15   Daily stock market turnover. $'000.

16   Dividend yield, percent per annum.

17   Merchandise trade - capital imports.

18   Balance of Payment balance.

19   Federal government spending in education. $ million.

20   Retail in trade in $'000. Current prices.

21   Wespac Melbourne Institute consumer sentiment index.

22   Foreign exchange, Trade Weighted Index, May 1970 = 100.

23   Market risk premium.

24   Market Returns .

Appendix 2.2

Table A2.2/1 Market risk Premium: July 1999 to June 2000

		S&P/ASX 200 Mkt. return (monthly)	S&P/ASX 200 Mkt. return (annualised)	3-month T. note yield	Market risk premium
1999	Jul-99	1.72%	20.61%	4.69%	15.92%
	Aug-99	-2.25%	-27.02%	4.74%	-31.76%
	Sep-99	-2.40%	-28.78%	4.77%	-33.55%
	Oct-99	0.14%	1.67%	4.87%	-3.20%
	Nov-99	5.51%	66.09%	5.01%	61.08%
	Dec-99	3.56%	42.77%	5.04%	37.73%
2000	Jan-00	-1.79%	-21.51%	5.39%	-26.90%
	Feb-00	1.28%	15.39%	5.66%	9.73%
	Mar-00	-0.08%	-0.92%	5.68%	-6.60%
	Apr-00	-0.56%	-6.70%	5.85%	-12.55%
	May-00	-1.12%	-13.40%	6.00%	-19.40%
	Jun-00	7.47%	89.66%	5.86%	83.80%

Source: RBA

Table A2.2/2 Yield Spread (*YS*)

		10-year Treasury bond	1-month Treasury note	Yield spread
1999	Jul	6.24	4.68	1.56
	Aug	6.35	4.74	1.61
	Sep	6.30	4.76	1.54
	Oct	6.63	4.81	1.82
	Nov	6.64	4.98	1.66
	Dec	6.96	4.98	1.98
2000	Jan	7.16	5.12	2.04
	Feb	6.65	5.45	1.20
	Mar	6.36	5.47	0.89
	Apr	6.39	5.73	0.66
	May	6.27	5.88	0.39
	Jun	6.16	5.83	0.33

Source: RBA

Appendix 2.3

Table A2.3/1 E-Commerce Stock Prices – July 1999 to June 2000

Month	131 Shop	AOL	B2N Net	Candle	Coms21	Ecorp	Liberty 1	My Casino	Pocket-mail	Reckon	Sausage	Solution 6	Spike	Swish	Travel .Com	Webjet	Wine P.	Etrade
Jul-99	$0.83	$0.03	$0.05	$3.50	$0.40	$2.43	$0.96	$0.10	$0.06	$1.69	$2.66	$4.45	$1.15	$0.30	$1.35	$0.07	$0.21	$4.83
Aug-99	$0.50	$0.04	$0.05	$3.52	$0.29	$1.98	$0.91	$0.07	$0.06	$1.30	$2.35	$4.05	$0.79	$0.27	$1.21	$0.08	$0.21	$5.81
Sep-99	$0.46	$0.03	$0.05	$3.30	$0.25	$2.01	$1.44	$0.09	$0.06	$1.23	$2.86	$5.47	$0.75	$0.21	$0.97	$0.10	$0.17	$4.42
Oct-99	$0.48	$0.03	$0.05	$3.52	$0.23	$2.17	$1.94	$0.08	$0.06	$1.45	$2.75	$6.88	$0.90	$0.21	$1.04	$0.14	$0.24	$4.19
Nov-99	$0.58	$0.04	$0.05	$3.74	$0.23	$2.61	$1.95	$0.10	$0.06	$1.84	$4.27	$11.10	$1.10	$0.30	$1.50	$0.14	$0.27	$4.25
Dec-99	$0.57	$0.04	$0.05	$4.02	$0.23	$3.81	$1.68	$0.20	$0.06	$1.75	$5.20	$16.60	$2.00	$0.29	$1.46	$0.19	$0.27	$3.72
Jan-00	$0.47	$0.12	$0.05	$3.65	$0.20	$4.25	$1.18	$0.20	$0.05	$2.05	$5.18	$10.20	$1.86	$0.30	$1.30	$0.24	$0.26	$3.00
Feb-00	$0.44	$0.34	$0.05	$3.59	$0.29	$7.27	$1.03	$0.20	$0.52	$1.77	$5.00	$8.18	$3.47	$0.38	$1.42	$0.24	$0.39	$3.09
Mar-00	$0.32	$0.30	$1.25	$3.35	$0.25	$5.35	$1.06	$0.20	$0.43	$1.56	$6.00	$10.65	$2.40	$0.44	$1.65	$0.28	$0.38	$4.05
Apr-00	$0.18	$0.13	$0.61	$3.30	$0.16	$3.00	$0.50	$0.56	$0.25	$1.10	$2.96	$5.24	$1.07	$0.37	$1.15	$0.14	$0.19	$2.40
May-00	$0.07	$0.07	$0.36	$2.60	$0.17	$2.09	$0.30	$0.54	$0.12	$0.72	$2.03	$3.02	$0.65	$0.23	$0.99	$0.08	$0.16	$2.05
Jun-00	$0.07	$0.15	$0.33	$3.15	$0.15	$2.27	$0.24	$0.46	$0.09	$0.78	$2.53	$3.25	$0.80	$0.24	$0.88	$0.12	$0.42	$1.79

Appendix 5.1

Table A5.1/1 Correlation

	My Casino	Sausage	Solution 6	Reckon	Swish	Pocket-mail	131.Shop	B2B.Net	Coms21	Etrade	AOL	Candle	Liberty one	Spike	Webjet	Travel.com	Ecorp	Wine Planet	Avg.	Portfolio
ASX 200	0.1488	0.0461	-0.2047	-0.0640	0.2558	0.1467	-0.0230	0.1606	0.1966	-0.0258	0.3854	0.2291	-0.6775	0.2252	0.0017	-0.0298	0.1587	0.4965	0.0792	0.2521
ASX Banks	0.0534	-0.1952	-0.2928	-0.0776	-0.2634	-0.2626	-0.1653	-0.3566	-0.0444	-0.3635	-0.0144	0.1468	-0.5364	-0.0512	-0.1286	-0.2828	-0.1590	0.4967	-0.1387	-0.4523
ASX Ind.	0.1085	-0.0533	-0.2963	-0.1389	0.2992	0.2734	-0.0956	0.2503	0.2696	0.0574	0.4010	0.1448	-0.6938	0.1706	-0.1041	0.0213	0.1194	0.4721	0.0670	0.3561
NASDAQ	0.1747	-0.0500	-0.2143	-0.1035	0.3738	0.4698	-0.0589	0.4168	0.4513	0.2044	0.4781	-0.1301	-0.5064	0.3344	0.0167	0.1358	0.3186	0.2182	0.1405	0.6075
D. Jones	0.3214	0.1749	0.3194	0.1760	0.0413	-0.5191	0.0532	0.1835	-0.3564	0.1178	-0.2128	0.0845	-0.1750	0.0393	0.2359	0.1624	-0.0496	-0.3218	0.0153	0.0039
M1	0.1142	-0.3454	-0.5375	-0.2790	-0.1734	-0.0008	-0.4012	0.1175	0.0692	-0.2039	0.1316	-0.2188	-0.6368	-0.1836	-0.2328	-0.3398	-0.2273	0.3492	-0.1666	0.0195
M3	0.1155	-0.2713	-0.4406	-0.2285	-0.0815	0.0181	-0.3216	0.0998	0.1376	-0.1523	0.1125	-0.1661	-0.6277	-0.1091	-0.2344	-0.2053	-0.1721	0.3961	-0.1184	0.0357
Credit	0.0898	-0.2757	-0.4419	-0.2571	-0.0341	0.0945	-0.3293	0.1732	0.1872	-0.0745	0.1427	-0.1746	-0.6220	-0.0890	-0.2389	-0.1616	-0.1498	0.4003	-0.0978	0.1325
IP	0.0325	0.3334	0.4049	0.3791	0.4078	0.2499	0.4087	0.0940	0.2529	0.2491	0.2150	-0.0924	0.3900	0.4117	0.3107	0.4624	0.4964	-0.4058	0.2556	0.3114
Rf	0.1628	-0.4355	-0.6044	-0.3977	-0.0823	0.1752	-0.4809	0.2097	0.2028	-0.0992	0.1460	-0.3410	-0.7233	-0.1735	-0.4083	-0.2208	-0.2007	0.2019	-0.1705	0.0437
T Note	0.1811	-0.4241	-0.5657	-0.4240	0.2457	0.1183	-0.4740	0.1508	0.1529	-0.1344	0.0649	-0.2662	-0.7078	-0.1908	0.4863	0.2924	-0.2420	0.2521	-0.0825	0.0691
Spread	-0.0672	0.3649	0.4246	0.5310	-0.2448	-0.0069	0.4894	-0.1957	0.0271	0.0748	0.2050	0.1198	0.4498	0.3734	-0.4865	-0.2923	0.4489	-0.2755	0.1078	-0.0292
Mkt. Cap	0.2152	-0.0511	-0.2588	-0.0605	0.2826	0.1998	-0.0857	0.2854	0.2794	0.0220	0.3702	-0.0019	-0.6915	0.2042	-0.0519	0.0531	0.1489	0.3477	0.0671	0.3674
Daily Turn.	0.0330	-0.0445	-0.3376	-0.0011	0.3751	0.2524	-0.0840	0.4591	0.1926	0.0987	0.4440	0.0038	-0.5566	0.0088	-0.0515	0.0628	0.0241	0.3400	0.0677	0.5223
Div. Yld.	-0.2114	-0.2350	-0.0333	-0.0748	-0.3492	-0.0383	-0.1678	0.1480	-0.0378	0.0604	-0.3140	-0.3762	0.5167	-0.2741	0.0189	-0.1208	-0.2748	-0.0749	-0.1021	0.0362
Cap. Impts.	-0.2229	0.1278	-0.1081	0.1179	-0.0548	0.0547	-0.0054	0.0175	0.1480	-0.2157	-0.1145	0.1999	-0.3091	0.1018	-0.0186	0.1563	-0.1390	0.3015	0.0203	0.0549
BOP	0.2591	-0.0994	0.0223	0.1061	0.4534	0.2157	0.1596	0.3908	0.0580	0.2073	0.0908	0.2904	-0.2346	0.1408	-0.0643	0.3642	0.0647	0.0586	0.1380	0.4764
Edu Exp	-0.1586	-0.0873	-0.3111	0.2889	0.0151	-0.0561	-0.0635	-0.2500	0.0486	-0.1797	0.3124	-0.4809	-0.1072	-0.1401	-0.0110	0.0139	0.0530	-0.3944	-0.0838	-0.2670
R Trade	-0.1588	0.2340	0.0896	0.2192	0.1146	-0.1344	0.2230	-0.0964	-0.0217	-0.0356	0.1786	0.4774	-0.1320	0.1523	0.3425	-0.0582	0.0498	0.8353	0.1266	-0.0402
Confidence	-0.2418	0.5973	0.6191	0.6993	0.2946	-0.1570	0.6782	-0.2412	-0.0962	0.0339	0.0751	0.3651	0.7002	0.2613	0.5369	0.3567	0.3313	-0.0558	0.2643	-0.1069
Forex	-0.1385	0.4950	0.5338	0.5043	0.1779	-0.0046	0.5960	-0.2592	-0.0501	-0.0159	0.1587	0.3776	0.6460	0.3826	0.5440	0.1511	0.4449	-0.0914	0.2473	-0.0723
Mkt. Risk Prem.	-0.0001	0.5930	0.4709	0.4834	0.5686	0.0381	0.6411	-0.0979	0.2372	0.0162	0.2433	0.7339	-0.1075	0.5302	0.2964	0.4553	0.4197	0.6966	0.3455	0.1367
Mkt. Return	0.0018	0.5865	0.4622	0.4778	0.5668	0.0402	0.6340	-0.0953	0.2392	0.0149	0.2449	0.7284	-0.1167	0.5269	0.2906	0.4518	0.4164	0.6980	0.3427	0.1382

Appendix 5.2

Table A5.2/1 Correlation Coefficients – E-Commerce Sector Returns and Variables

Variables	Casino & Gaming	Computers& Off. Services	Diversified Media	Equipment & Services	Health & Med. Serv.	High Technology	Misc. Fin. Services	Misc. Services	Other Telecomms.	Retail/ Retail Investments
ASX 200	14.88%	-7.42%	25.58%	6.18%	16.06%	19.66%	-2.58%	**30.73%**	-22.62%	15.68%
ASX Banks	5.34%	-18.85%	-26.34%	-21.40%	-35.66%	-4.44%	-36.35%	6.62%	-29.38%	-1.84%
ASX Ind.	10.85%	-16.28%	29.92%	8.89%	25.03%	**26.96%**	5.74%	**27.29%**	-26.16%	12.72%
NASDAQ	**17.47%**	-12.26%	37.38%	20.54%	**41.68%**	**45.13%**	**20.44%**	17.40%	-8.60%	17.23%
D. Jones	**32.14%**	22.34%	4.13%	-23.29%	18.35%	-35.64%	**11.78%**	-6.41%	-6.78%	0.67%
M1	11.42%	-38.73%	-17.34%	-20.10%	11.75%	6.92%	-20.39%	-4.36%	-41.02%	-11.27%
M3	11.55%	-31.34%	-8.15%	-15.17%	9.98%	13.76%	-15.23%	-2.68%	-36.84%	-5.39%
Credit	8.98%	-32.49%	-3.41%	-11.74%	17.32%	18.72%	-7.45%	-1.60%	-35.55%	-3.75%
IP	3.25%	37.25%	**40.78%**	**32.93%**	9.40%	**25.29%**	**24.91%**	6.13%	**40.09%**	21.59%
rf	16.28%	-47.92%	-8.23%	-15.29%	20.97%	20.28%	-9.92%	-9.75%	-44.84%	-15.70%
T Note	**18.11%**	-47.12%	24.57%	-17.79%	-19.57%	15.29%	-13.44%	-10.07%	-44.93%	19.72%
Spread	-6.72%	**44.02%**	-24.48%	24.12%	15.08%	2.71%	7.48%	16.24%	**41.16%**	-15.14%
Mkt. Cap	**21.52%**	-12.35%	28.26%	5.70%	**28.54%**	**27.94%**	2.20%	18.42%	-24.37%	12.45%
Daily Turn.	3.30%	-12.77%	**37.51%**	8.42%	**45.91%**	19.26%	**9.87%**	22.39%	-27.39%	9.39%
Div. Yld.	-21.14%	-11.44%	-34.92%	-10.30%	14.80%	-3.78%	6.04%	-34.51%	12.13%	-11.29%
Cap. Impts.	-22.29%	4.59%	-5.48%	2.47%	1.75%	21.57%	-11.45%	-5.46%	4.16%	9.08%
BOP	**25.91%**	0.97%	**45.34%**	18.76%	**39.08%**	5.80%	**20.73%**	19.06%	-4.69%	10.58%
Edu Exp	-15.86%	-3.65%	1.51%	-5.98%	-25.00%	4.86%	-17.97%	-8.42%	-12.36%	-8.46%
R Trade	-15.88%	18.09%	11.46%	4.43%	-9.64%	-2.17%	-3.56%	**32.80%**	1.02%	**29.24%**
Con'dence	-24.18%	**63.86%**	29.46%	**26.06%**	-24.12%	-9.62%	3.39%	22.01%	**48.07%**	**29.23%**
Forex	-13.85%	**51.10%**	17.79%	**29.57%**	-25.92%	-5.01%	-1.59%	26.81%	**51.43%**	**26.22%**
Mkt. Risk Prem.	-0.01%	**51.58%**	**56.86%**	**33.96%**	-9.79%	23.72%	1.62%	**48.86%**	21.14%	**46.70%**
Mkt. Return	0.18%	**50.88%**	**56.68%**	**33.71%**	-9.53%	**23.92%**	1.49%	**48.67%**	20.51%	**46.42%**

Appendix 5.3

Table A5.3/1 Frequencies of the Five Highest-Correlated Variables

Variables	Casino & Gaming	Computers & Off. Services	Diversified Media	Equipment & Services	Health & Med. Serv.	High Technology	Misc. Fin. Services	Misc. Services	Other Telecomms.	Retail/ Investments	Retail	Frequency
ASX 200								X				1
ASX Banks												0
ASX Ind.							X	X	X			3
NASDAQ	X				X	X	X					4
D. Jones					X	X						2
M1												0
M3												0
Credit												0
IP			X	X		X	X		X			5
rf												0
T Note	X											1
Spread		X							X			2
Mkt. Cap	X		X			X						3
Daily Turn.			X		X		X					3
Div. Yld.												0
Cap. Impts.												0
BOP	X		X		X		X					4
Edu Exp												0
R Trade				X						X		2
Con'dence		X						X	X	X		4
Forex		X		X					X	X		4
Mkt. Risk Prem.		X	X	X				X	X	X		6
Mkt. Return		X		X	X	X		X		X		6
											Total	50

Appendix 5.4

Table A5.4/1 Regression Summary (by sector) of *t*-Statistics and *p*-Values

Sector	α	MRP_t β	IP_t β	NAS_t β	CC_t β	FE_t β	R^2
R(CG)$_t$	-21.8255	0.7447	0.2459	-0.0006	-0.1415	0.1898	0.2593
t-statistic	*-1.1388*	*0.8814*	*1.1082*	*-0.9401*	*-1.3073*	*0.6330*	
20% c =1.440							
p-value	*0.2982*	*0.4120*	*0.3102*	*0.3835*	*0.2390*	*0.5501*	
R(COS)$_t$	-2.4881	0.3416	0.0088	0.0001	0.0356	-0.0470	0.8239
t-statistic	*-0.6039*	*1.8806*	*0.1838*	*0.4704*	*1.5308*	*-0.7284*	
20% c =1.440		significant			significant		
p-value	*0.5680*	*0.1091*	*0.8602*	*0.6547*	*0.1767*	*0.4938*	
R(DM)$_t$	-1.8278	0.2301	0.0196	0.0002	0.0365	-0.0926	0.7697
t-statistic	*-0.4489*	*1.2818*	*0.4152*	*1.3856*	*1.5858*	*-1.4537*	
20% c =1.440					significant	significant	
p-value	*0.6693*	*0.2472*	*0.6924*	*0.2152*	*0.1639*	*0.1963*	
R(ES)$_t$	-43.0254	0.6599	0.2446	0.0005	-0.1546	-0.5296	0.3443
t-statistic	*-0.9575*	*0.3331*	*0.4702*	*0.3212*	*-0.6091*	*0.7531*	
20% c =1.440							
p-value	*0.3753*	*0.7504*	*0.6548*	*0.7590*	*0.5648*	*0.4799*	
R(HMS)$_t$	71.8150	-6.9365	-0.3175	0.0073	0.8038	-2.6109	0.2744
t-statistic	*0.2879*	*-0.6309*	*-0.1099*	*0.8182*	*0.5705*	*-0.6689*	
20% c =1.440							
p-value	*0.7831*	*0.5514*	*0.9160*	*0.4445*	*0.5891*	*0.5284*	
R(HT)$_t$	-5.3726	0.1895	0.0517	0.0000	0.0130	0.0092	0.3202
t-statistic	*-0.8990*	*0.7193*	*0.7471*	*0.0936*	*-0.3843*	*0.0986*	
20% c =1.440							
p-value	*0.4033*	*0.4990*	*0.4832*	*0.9285*	*0.7140*	*0.9247*	
R(MFS)$_t$	-1.5770	-0.0025	0.0275	0.0001	0.0120	0.0584	0.1445
t-statistic	*-0.2301*	*-0.0083*	*0.3463*	*0.2280*	*-0.3091*	*-0.5450*	
20% c =1.440							
p-value	*0.8256*	*0.9936*	*0.7409*	*0.8272*	*0.7677*	*0.6054*	
R(MS)$_t$	4.4975	-0.2014	-0.1554	0.0008	0.0569	0.0935	0.5961
t-statistic	*0.4541*	*-0.4614*	*-1.3554*	*2.2194*	*1.0176*	*0.6034*	
20% c =1.440							
p-value	*0.6657*	*0.6608*	*0.2241*	*0.0683*	*0.3482*	*0.5684*	
R(OT)$_t$	-9.7822	0.4262	0.0528	0.0000	0.0282	0.1188	0.7391
t-statistic	*-2.2661*	*2.2394*	*1.0556*	*0.0889*	*-1.1552*	*1.7586*	
20% c =1.440	significant	significant				significant	
p-value	*0.0640*	*0.0664*	*0.3318*	*0.9321*	*0.2919*	*0.1291*	
R(RRI)$_t$	2.2943	0.2020	-0.0705	0.0003	0.0357	0.0201	0.7117
t-statistic	*0.4430*	*0.8848*	*-1.1756*	*1.7527*	*1.2199*	*0.2480*	
20% c =1.440			significant	significant			
p-value	*0.6377*	*0.4103*	*0.2843*	*0.1302*	*0.2683*	*0.8124*	
R(PR)$_t$	-3.4032	-0.1296	0.0064	0.0006	0.0395	-0.0639	0.4812
t-statistic	*-0.2548*	*-0.2201*	*0.0413*	*1.2703*	*0.5231*	*-0.3057*	
20% c =1.440							
p-value	*0.8074*	*0.8331*	*0.9684*	*0.251*	*0.6196*	*0.7701*	

Hypothesis test: Two-sided; Significance level = 20%; *c* = critical value

Appendices

Appendix 5.4(1)

Table A5.4(1)/1 Regression Summary (by sector) of *t*-Statistics and *p*-Values

Integrated of Order One

		MRP_t	IP_t	NAS_t	CC_t	FE_t	
Sector	α	β	β	β	β	β	R^2
R(CG)$_t$	**0.2935**	**1.3230**	**0.3928**	**-0.0018**	**-0.1805**	**0.7312**	**0.4492**
t-statistic	*0.7917*	*1.2295*	*0.9955*	*-1.4305*	*-1.9011*	*2.0140*	
20% c =1.440		*significant*		*significant*	*significant*	*significant*	
p-value	*0.4587*	*0.2649*	*0.3579*	*0.2025*	*0.1060*	*0.0906*	
R(COS)$_t$	**-0.0090**	**0.3044**	**0.0181**	**0.0002**	**0.0405**	**-0.0602**	**0.6760**
t-statistic	*-0.6039*	*1.8806*	*0.1838*	*0.4704*	*1.5308*	*-0.7284*	
20% c =1.440		*significant*			*significant*		
p-value	*0.9302*	*0.2583*	*0.8682*	*0.5797*	*0.1577*	*0.5537*	
R(DM)$_t$	**-0.1070**	**0.2060**	**-0.0725**	**0.0005**	**0.0560**	**-0.2073**	**0.8686**
t-statistic	*-1.7915*	*1.3877*	*-1.1384*	*2.6157*	*3.6656*	*-3.5435*	
20% c =1.440		*significant*		*significant*	*significant*	*significant*	
p-value	*0.1234*	*0.2146*	*0.2984*	*0.0398*	*0.0105*	*0.0122*	
R(ES)$_t$	**-0.3225**	**1.5809**	**0.1290**	**0.0008**	**-0.2037**	**0.1702**	**0.3389**
t-statistic	*-0.3340*	*0.6586*	*0.1253*	*0.2545*	*-0.8244*	*0.1799*	
20% c =1.440							
p-value	*0.7497*	*0.5346*	*0.9044*	*0.8076*	*0.4412*	*0.8631*	
R(HMS)$_t$	**-0.4337**	**-13.6508**	**-3.5158**	**0.0276**	**2.0207**	**-7.6074**	**0.4331**
t-statistic	*-0.9174*	*-1.1613*	*-0.6978*	*1.7497*	*1.6704*	*-1.6427*	
20% c =1.440		*significant*		*significant*	*significant*	*significant*	
p-value	*0.3943*	*0.2896*	*0.5114*	*0.1307*	*0.1459*	*0.1516*	
R(HT)$_t$	**-0.0278**	**0.2585**	**0.0567**	**-0.0001**	**-0.0279**	**0.0113**	**0.2262**
t-statistic	*-0.2024*	*0.7579*	*0.3881*	*-0.1264*	*-0.7951*	*0.0844*	
20% c =1.440							
p-value	*0.8463*	*0.4772*	*0.7113*	*0.9036*	*0.4568*	*0.9335*	
R(MFS)$_t$	**-0.1931**	**-0.2806**	**-0.1373**	**0.0009**	**0.0442**	**-0.2971**	**0.6456**
t-statistic	*-1.8604*	*-1.0874*	*-1.2418*	*2.4768*	*1.6662*	*-2.9223*	
20% c =1.440			*significant*	*significant*	*significant*	*significant*	
p-value	*0.1122*	*0.3186*	*0.2606*	*0.0480*	*0.1467*	*0.0266*	
R(MS)$_t$	**-0.0459**	**-0.1610**	**-0.1807**	**0.0008**	**0.0545**	**-0.0597**	**0.3268**
t-statistic	*-0.2095*	*-0.2954*	*-0.7734*	*1.1125*	*0.9712*	*-0.2780*	
20% c =1.440							
p-value	*0.8410*	*0.7777*	*0.4687*	*0.3085*	*0.3689*	*0.7903*	
R(OT)$_t$	**0.0434**	**0.4992**	**0.1051**	**-0.0001**	**-0.0487**	**0.1508**	**0.7228**
t-statistic	*0.4955*	*2.2949*	*1.1270*	*-0.5078*	*-2.1752*	*1.7595*	
20% c =1.440		*significant*			*significant*	*significant*	
p-value	*0.6379*	*0.0615*	*0.3028*	*0.6297*	*0.0725*	*0.1290*	
R(RRI)$_t$	**-0.0455**	**0.1310**	**-0.1032**	**0.0005**	**0.0292**	**-0.0549**	**0.6393**
t-statistic	*-0.4486*	*0.5194*	*-0.9543*	*1.6080*	*1.1264*	*-0.5526*	
20% c =1.440				*significant*			
p-value	*0.6695*	*0.6221*	*0.3768*	*0.1590*	*0.3030*	*0.6005*	
R(PR)$_t$	**-0.2798**	**-0.3836**	**-0.1780**	**0.0018**	**0.0979**	**-0.4059**	**0.6869**
t-statistic	*-1.4433*	*-0.7958*	*-0.8614*	*2.7894*	*1.9726*	*-2.1373*	
20% c =1.440				*significant*	*significant*	*significant*	
p-value	*0.199*	*0.4565*	*0.4221*	*0.0316*	*0.096*	*0.0764*	

Hypothesis test: Two-sided: Significance level = 20%; c = critical value

Appendix 5.4(2)

Table 5.4(2)/1 Five-Factor Model Sector Regressions

	Sector											MKt.	Factor			
	Casino & Gaming	Comp. & Off. Servs.	Diversified Media	Equipment & Services	Health & Medical	High Technology	Misc. Fin. Services	Misc. Services	Other Telecom.	Retail & Ret. Inv.	E-Com. Portfolio	Risk Prem.	IP	NASDAQ	Westpac Confidence	Forex
Jul-99	16.28%	15.79%	0.00%	0.00%	140.00%	-15.96%	-19.55%	5.95%	0.06%	-1.00%	10.40%	0.16	117.5	2638	113.8	57.1
Aug-99	-30.00%	-14.54%	-8.47%	-19.88%	4.17%	-26.58%	20.25%	15.29%	-15.68%	-3.06%	-7.91%	-0.32	117.8	2739	109.7	56.0
Sep-99	28.57%	17.12%	-22.22%	-4.00%	-10.00%	-13.79%	-23.90%	-20.30%	-2.24%	-5.29%	-0.32%	-0.34	118.5	2746	114.2	57.0
Oct-99	-6.67%	13.28%	-2.38%	2.18%	0.00%	-10.00%	-5.20%	9.34%	10.18%	23.84%	10.48%	-0.03	118.9	2966	113.3	55.7
Nov-99	19.05%	47.84%	46.34%	10.42%	0.00%	2.22%	1.43%	17.41%	11.12%	20.73%	20.74%	0.61	119.5	3336	115.0	55.3
Dec-99	100.00%	22.15%	-5.00%	-0.86%	0.00%	-2.17%	-12.47%	14.86%	40.84%	18.43%	17.58%	0.38	120	4069	108.0	56.4
Jan-00	0.00%	-7.26%	4.91%	-18.77%	0.00%	-11.11%	-19.35%	76.08%	-3.65%	6.61%	3.10%	-0.27	119.7	3940	111.1	56.0
Feb-00	0.00%	-12.35%	27.09%	488.48%	0.00%	42.50%	3.00%	97.01%	43.22%	33.36%	78.58%	0.10	119.2	4697	101.1	54.5
Mar-00	0.00%	12.81%	14.47%	-23.34%	2677.78%	-14.04%	31.07%	-9.20%	-15.41%	0.65%	147.66%	-0.07	118.3	4573	99.6	53.1
Apr-00	180.00%	-43.67%	-14.94%	-42.02%	-51.20%	-34.69%	-40.74%	-29.56%	-27.98%	-43.84%	-28.86%	-0.13	116	3861	95.9	52.5
May-00	-3.75%	-36.06%	-39.19%	-56.84%	-40.98%	3.13%	-14.58%	-31.01%	-19.82%	-25.03%	-31.01%	-0.19	114.4	3401	93.7	51.4
Jun-00	-14.81%	13.53%	8.00%	-11.78%	-8.33%	-12.12%	-12.68%	61.93%	11.44%	50.41%	14.66%	0.84	112.8	3966	100.3	53.3

Table 5.4(2)/2 Regression Statistics & ANOVA

Multiple R	0.5093	0.9077	0.8773	0.5868	0.5238	0.5658	0.3801	0.7721	0.8597	0.8436	0.6937
R Square	0.2593	0.8239	0.7697	0.3443	0.2744	0.3202	0.1445	0.5961	0.7391	0.7117	0.4812
Adjusted R Square	-0.3579	0.6771	0.5778	-0.2021	-0.3303	-0.2464	-0.5685	0.2596	0.5217	0.4715	0.0489
Standard Error	0.6856	0.1474	0.1457	1.6074	8.9219	0.2138	0.2451	0.3543	0.1544	0.1853	0.4779
Observations	12.0000	12.0000	12.0000	12.0000	12.0000	12.0000	12.0000	12.0000	12.0000	12.0000	12.0000

Intercept (Table 5.4(2)/2 - cont.)

Coefficients	-21.8255	-2.4881	-1.8278	-43.0254	71.8150	-5.3726	-1.5770	4.4975	-9.7822	2.2943	-3.4032
Standard Error	19.1655	4.1199	4.0718	44.9351	249.4084	5.9759	6.8521	9.9034	4.3168	5.1786	13.3589
t Stat	-1.1388	-0.6039	-0.4489	-0.9575	0.2879	-0.8990	-0.2301	0.4541	-2.2661	0.4430	-0.2548
P-value	0.2982	0.5680	0.6693	0.3753	0.7831	0.4033	0.8256	0.6657	0.0640	0.6733	0.8074
Risk Premium											
Coefficients	0.7447	0.3416	0.2301	0.6599	-6.9365	0.1895	-0.0025	-0.2014	0.4262	0.2020	-0.1296
Standard Error	0.8449	0.1816	0.1795	1.9810	10.9953	0.2635	0.3021	0.4366	0.1903	0.2283	0.5889
t Stat	0.8814	1.8806	1.2818	0.3331	-0.6309	0.7193	-0.0083	-0.4614	2.2394	0.8848	-0.2201
P-value	0.4120	0.1091	0.2472	0.7504	0.5514	0.4990	0.9936	0.6608	0.0664	0.4103	0.8331
Industrial Production											
Coefficients	0.2459	0.0088	0.0196	0.2446	-0.3175	0.0517	0.0275	-0.1554	0.0528	-0.0705	0.0064
Standard Error	0.2219	0.0477	0.0471	0.5203	2.8880	0.0692	0.0793	0.1147	0.0500	0.0600	0.1547
t Stat	1.1082	0.1838	0.4152	0.4702	-0.1099	0.7471	0.3463	-1.3554	1.0556	-1.1756	0.0413
P-value	0.3102	0.8602	0.6924	0.6548	0.9160	0.4832	0.7409	0.2241	0.3318	0.2843	0.9684
NASDAQ											
Coefficients	-0.0006	0.0001	0.0002	0.0005	0.0073	0.0000	0.0001	0.0008	0.0000	0.0003	0.0006
Standard Error	0.0007	0.0001	0.0001	0.0016	0.0089	0.0002	0.0002	0.0004	0.0002	0.0002	0.0005
t Stat	-0.9401	0.4704	1.3856	0.3212	0.8182	0.0936	0.2280	2.2194	0.0889	1.7527	1.2703
P-value	0.3835	0.6547	0.2152	0.7590	0.4445	0.9285	0.8272	0.0683	0.9321	0.1302	0.2510
Consumer Confidence											
Coefficients	-0.1415	0.0356	0.0365	-0.1546	0.8038	-0.0130	0.0120	0.0569	-0.0282	0.0357	0.0395
Standard Error	0.1083	0.0233	0.0230	0.2539	1.4090	0.0338	0.0387	0.0559	0.0244	0.0293	0.0755
t Stat	-1.3073	1.5308	1.5858	-0.6091	0.5705	-0.3843	0.3091	1.0176	-1.1552	1.2199	0.5231
P-value	0.2390	0.1767	0.1639	0.5648	0.5891	0.7140	0.7677	0.3482	0.2919	0.2683	0.6196
Forex											
Coefficients	0.1898	-0.0470	-0.0926	0.5296	-2.6109	0.0092	-0.0584	0.0935	0.1188	0.0201	-0.0639
Standard Error	0.2999	0.0645	0.0637	0.7032	3.9031	0.0935	0.1072	0.1550	0.0676	0.0810	0.2091
t Stat	0.6330	-0.7284	-1.4537	0.7531	-0.6689	0.0986	-0.5450	0.6034	1.7586	0.2480	-0.3057
P-value	0.5501	0.4938	0.1963	0.4799	0.5284	0.9247	0.6054	0.5684	0.1291	0.8124	0.7701

Appendix 5.4(3)

Table 5.4(3)/1 Five-Factor Model Sector Regression Results – Integrated of Order 1

	Sector											Factor				
	Casino & Gaming	Comp. & Off. Servs.	Diversified Media	Equipment & Services	Health & Medical	High Technology	Misc. Fin. Services	Misc. Services	Other Telecom. Services	Retail & Ret. Inv.	E-Com. Portfolio	MKt. Risk Prem.	IP	NASDAQ	Westpac Con'dence	Forex
Jul-99	-55.72%	3.12%	0.00%	-38.00%	153.00%	-18.96%	-1.55%	8.95%	0.06%	-1.00%	10.40%	-0.08	0.9	-48	0.1	-1.3
Aug-99	-46.28%	-30.33%	-8.47%	-19.88%	-135.83%	-10.62%	39.80%	9.34%	-15.74%	-2.06%	-18.31%	-0.48	0.3	101	-4.2	-1.1
Sep-99	58.57%	31.66%	-13.75%	15.88%	-14.17%	12.79%	-44.15%	-35.58%	13.44%	-2.23%	7.59%	-0.02	0.7	7	4.5	1.0
Oct-99	-35.24%	-3.84%	19.84%	6.18%	10.00%	3.79%	18.70%	29.63%	12.42%	29.13%	10.80%	0.30	0.4	220	-0.8	-1.3
Nov-99	25.72%	34.56%	48.72%	8.24%	0.00%	12.22%	6.63%	8.08%	0.94%	-3.11%	10.26%	0.64	0.6	370	1.6	-0.4
Dec-99	80.95%	-25.69%	-51.34%	-11.28%	0.00%	-4.39%	-13.90%	-2.56%	29.73%	-2.30%	-3.16%	-0.23	0.5	733	-6.9	1.1
Jan-00	-100.00%	-29.41%	9.91%	-17.91%	0.00%	-8.94%	-6.88%	61.23%	-44.49%	-11.83%	-14.48%	-0.65	-0.3	-129	3.0	-0.4
Feb-00	0.00%	-5.08%	22.18%	507.25%	0.00%	53.61%	22.35%	20.93%	46.87%	26.75%	75.48%	0.37	-0.5	756	-10.0	-1.5
Mar-00	0.00%	25.16%	-12.62%	-511.82%	2677.78%	-56.54%	28.07%	-106.20%	-58.62%	-32.71%	69.08%	-0.16	-0.9	-124	-1.5	-1.4
Apr-00	180.00%	-56.48%	-29.41%	-18.68%	-2728.98%	-20.65%	-71.81%	-20.37%	-12.57%	-44.49%	-176.52%	-0.06	-2.3	-712	-3.8	-0.6
May-00	-183.75%	7.61%	-24.25%	-14.82%	10.22%	37.82%	26.16%	-1.45%	8.16%	18.81%	-2.15%	-0.07	-1.6	-460	-2.1	-1.1
Jun-00	-11.06%	49.59%	47.19%	45.06%	32.65%	-15.25%	1.90%	92.93%	31.26%	75.44%	45.67%	1.03	-1.6	565	6.6	1.9

Table 5.4(3)/2 Regression Statistics & ANOVA

Multiple R	0.6702	0.8222	0.9320	0.5822	0.6581	0.4756	0.8035	0.5717	0.8502	0.7996	0.8288
R Square	0.4492	0.6760	0.8686	0.3389	0.4331	0.2262	0.6456	0.3268	0.7228	0.6393	0.6869
Adjusted R Square	-0.0098	0.4060	0.7590	-0.2119	-0.0392	-0.4187	0.3503	-0.2342	0.4918	0.3387	0.4261
Standard Error	0.9229	0.2441	0.1487	2.4034	11.7691	0.3415	0.2583	0.5458	0.2178	0.2526	0.4826
Observations	12.0000	12.0000	12.0000	12.0000	12.0000	12.0000	12.0000	12.0000	12.0000	12.0000	12.0000

Intercept (Table 5.4(3)/2 - cont.)

Coefficients	0.2935	-0.0090	-0.1070	-0.3225	-4.3367	-0.0278	-0.1931	-0.0459	0.0434	-0.0455	-0.2798
Standard Error	0.3707	0.0980	0.0597	0.9654	4.7273	0.1372	0.1038	0.2192	0.0875	0.1014	0.1939
t Stat	0.7917	-0.0913	-1.7915	-0.3340	-0.9174	-0.2024	-1.8604	-0.2095	0.4955	-0.4486	-1.4433
P-value	0.4587	0.9302	0.1234	0.7497	0.3943	0.8463	0.1122	0.8410	0.6379	0.6695	0.1990
Risk Premium											
Coefficients	1.1323	0.3044	0.2060	1.5809	-13.6508	0.2585	-0.2806	-0.1610	0.4992	0.1310	-0.3836
Standard Error	0.9209	0.2438	0.1485	2.4004	11.7544	0.3410	0.2580	0.5451	0.2175	0.2523	0.4820
t Stat	1.2295	1.2486	1.3877	0.6586	-1.1613	0.7579	-1.0874	-0.2954	2.2949	0.5194	-0.7958
P-value	0.2649	0.2583	0.2146	0.5346	0.2896	0.4772	0.3186	0.7777	0.0615	0.6221	0.4565
Industrial Production											
Coefficients	0.3928	0.0181	-0.0725	0.1290	-3.5158	0.0567	-0.1373	-0.1807	0.1051	-0.1032	-0.1780
Standard Error	0.3946	0.1045	0.0636	1.0289	5.0384	0.1462	0.1106	0.2337	0.0932	0.1081	0.2066
t Stat	0.9955	0.1732	-1.1384	0.1253	-0.6978	0.3881	-1.2418	-0.7734	1.1270	-0.9543	-0.8614
P-value	0.3579	0.8682	0.2984	0.9044	0.5114	0.7113	0.2606	0.4687	0.3028	0.3768	0.4221
NASDAQ											
Coefficients	-0.0018	0.0002	0.0005	0.0008	0.0276	-0.0001	0.0009	0.0008	-0.0001	0.0005	0.0018
Standard Error	0.0012	0.0003	0.0002	0.0032	0.0158	0.0005	0.0003	0.0007	0.0003	0.0003	0.0006
t Stat	-1.4305	0.5853	2.6157	0.2545	1.7497	-0.1264	2.4768	1.1125	-0.5078	1.6080	2.7894
P-value	0.2025	0.5797	0.0398	0.8076	0.1307	0.9036	0.0480	0.3085	0.6297	0.1590	0.0316
Consumer Confidence											
Coefficients	-0.1805	0.0405	0.0560	-0.2037	2.0207	-0.0279	0.0442	0.0545	-0.0487	0.0292	0.0979
Standard Error	0.0950	0.0251	0.0153	0.2470	1.2097	0.0351	0.0266	0.0561	0.0224	0.0260	0.0496
t Stat	-1.9011	1.6137	3.6656	-0.8244	1.6704	-0.7951	1.6662	0.9712	-2.1752	1.1264	1.9726
P-value	0.1060	0.1577	0.0105	0.4412	0.1459	0.4568	0.1467	0.3689	0.0725	0.3030	0.0960
Forex											
Coefficients	0.7312	-0.0602	-0.2073	0.1702	-7.6074	0.0113	-0.2971	-0.0597	0.1508	-0.0549	-0.4059
Standard Error	0.3631	0.0960	0.0585	0.9457	4.6312	0.1344	0.1017	0.2148	0.0857	0.0994	0.1899
t Stat	2.0140	-0.6271	-3.5435	0.1799	-1.6427	0.0844	-2.9223	-0.2780	1.7595	-0.5526	-2.1373
P-value	0.0906	0.5537	0.0122	0.8631	0.1516	0.9355	0.0266	0.7903	0.1290	0.6005	0.0764

Appendix 5.4(4)

Table A5.4(4)/1 E-Commerce Portfolio Returns: Four-Factor
(*MRP, NAS, CC* and *FE*) Sector Regression Model – Integrated of Order One

	Stock	MKt.		Westpac	
	Return	Risk Prem.	NASDAQ	Con'dence	Forex
Jul-99	10.40%	-0.08	-48	0.1	-1.3
Aug-99	-18.31%	-0.48	101	-4.2	-1.1
Sep-99	7.59%	-0.02	7	4.5	1.0
Oct-99	10.80%	0.30	220	-0.8	-1.3
Nov-99	10.26%	0.64	370	1.6	-0.4
Dec-99	-3.16%	-0.23	733	-6.9	1.1
Jan-00	-14.48%	-0.65	-129	3.0	-0.4
Feb-00	75.48%	0.37	756	-10.0	-1.5
Mar-00	69.08%	-0.16	-124	-1.5	-1.4
Apr-00	-176.52%	-0.06	-712	-3.8	-0.6
May-00	-2.15%	-0.07	-460	-2.1	-1.1
Jun-00	45.67%	1.03	565	6.6	1.9

Table A5.4(4)/2 Summary Output

Regression Statistics	
Multiple R	0.8051
R Square	0.6482
Adjusted R Square	0.4472
Standard Error	0.4737
Observations	12.0000

ANOVA

	df	SS	MS	F	Significance F
Regression	4.0000	2.8939	0.7235	3.2248	0.0844
Residual	7.0000	1.5705	0.2244		
Total	11.0000	4.4644			

	Coefficients	Standard Error	t Stat	P-value	Lower 95%	Upper 95%	Lower 95.0%	Upper 95.0%
Intercept	-0.1867	0.1579	-1.1821	0.2757	-0.5602	0.1868	-0.5602	0.1868
Risk Prem.	-0.1303	0.3749	-0.3477	0.7383	-1.0168	0.7561	-1.0168	0.7561
NASDAQ	0.0014	0.0004	3.2638	0.0138	0.0004	0.0024	0.0004	0.0024
Con'dence	0.0742	0.0405	1.8303	0.1099	-0.0217	0.1700	-0.0217	0.1700
Forex	-0.3310	0.1657	-1.9977	0.0859	-0.7227	0.0608	-0.7227	0.0608

Appendix 5.4(5)

Table A5.4(5)/1 E-Commerce Portfolio Returns: Three-Factor
(*NAS, CC* and *FE*) Sector Regression Model – Integrated of Order One

	Stock Return	NASDAQ	Westpac Con'dence	Forex
Jul-99	10.40%	-48	0.1	-1.3
Aug-99	-18.31%	101	-4.2	-1.1
Sep-99	7.59%	7	4.5	1.0
Oct-99	10.80%	220	-0.8	-1.3
Nov-99	10.26%	370	1.6	-0.4
Dec-99	-3.16%	733	-6.9	1.1
Jan-00	-14.48%	-129	3.0	-0.4
Feb-00	75.48%	756	-10.0	-1.5
Mar-00	69.08%	-124	-1.5	-1.4
Apr-00	-176.52%	-712	-3.8	-0.6
May-00	-2.15%	-460	-2.1	-1.1
Jun-00	45.67%	565	6.6	1.9

Table A5.4(5)/2 Summary Output

Regression Statistics

Multiple R	0.8013
R Square	0.6421
Adjusted R Square	0.5080
Standard Error	0.4469
Observations	12.0000

ANOVA

	df	SS	MS	F	Significance F
Regression	3.0000	2.8668	0.9556	4.7852	0.0341
Residual	8.0000	1.5976	0.1997		
Total	11.0000	4.4644			

	Coefficients	Standard Error	t Stat	P-value	Lower 95%	Upper 95%	Lower 95.0%	Upper 95.0%
Intercept	-0.1900	0.1488	-1.2772	0.2373	-0.5330	0.1530	-0.5330	0.1530
NASDAQ	0.0013	0.0003	3.7657	0.0055	0.0005	0.0021	0.0005	0.0021
Con'dence	0.0692	0.0358	1.9345	0.0891	-0.0133	0.1517	-0.0133	0.1517
Forex	-0.3287	0.1562	-2.1045	0.0685	-0.6888	0.0315	-0.6888	0.0315

Appendix 5.5

Table A5.5/1 Dickey Fuller Stationarity Test:
Market Risk Premium (*MRP*)

	MRP	Change y_t	y_{t-1}
Jul-99	0.16	-0.08	0.24
Aug-99	-0.32	-0.48	0.16
Sep-99	-0.34	-0.02	-0.32
Oct-99	-0.03	0.30	-0.34
Nov-99	0.61	0.64	-0.03
Dec-99	0.38	-0.23	0.61
Jan-00	-0.27	-0.65	0.38
Feb-00	0.10	0.37	-0.27
Mar-00	-0.07	-0.16	0.10
Apr-00	-0.13	-0.06	-0.07
May-00	-0.19	-0.07	-0.13
Jun-00	0.84	1.03	-0.19

Table A5.5/2 Summary Output

Regression Statistics

Multiple R	0.5989
R Square	0.3587
Adjusted R Square	0.2946
Standard Error	0.3936
Observations	12

ANOVA

	df	SS	MS	F	Significance F
Regression	1	0.8665	0.8665	5.5937	0.0396
Residual	10	1.5491	0.1549		
Total	11	2.4157			

	Coefficients	Standard Error	t Stat	P-value	Lower 95%	Upper 95%	Lower 95.0%	Upper 95.0%
Intercept	0.0614	0.1137	0.5397	0.6012	-0.1920	0.3148	-0.1920	0.3148
yt-1	-0.9551	0.4038	-2.3651	0.0396	-1.8548	-0.0553	-1.8548	-0.0553

Table A5.5/3 Estimate of ρ

$\hat{\rho} = 1 + \hat{\theta} = \quad 0.045 \quad$ (which is < 1)

Appendix 5.6

Table A5.6/1 Dickey Fuller Stationarity Test: Industrial Production (*IP*)

	IP	Change y_t	y_{t-1}
Jul-99	117.5	0.90	116.6
Aug-99	117.8	0.30	117.5
Sep-99	118.5	0.70	117.8
Oct-99	118.9	0.40	118.5
Nov-99	119.5	0.60	118.9
Dec-99	120	0.50	119.5
Jan-00	119.7	-0.30	120
Feb-00	119.2	-0.50	119.7
Mar-00	118.3	-0.90	119.2
Apr-00	116	-2.30	118.3
May-00	114.4	-1.60	116
Jun-00	112.8	-1.60	114.4

Table A5.6/2 Summary Output

Regression Statistics	
Multiple R	0.2951
R Square	0.0871
Adjusted R Square	-0.0042
Standard Error	1.0689
Observations	12.0000

ANOVA

	df	*SS*	*MS*	*F*	*Significance F*
Regression	1.0000	1.0902	1.0902	0.9541	0.3517
Residual	10.0000	11.4264	1.1426		
Total	11.0000	12.5167			

	Coefficients	*Standard Error*	*t Stat*	*P-value*	*Lower 95%*	*Upper 95%*	*Lower 95.0%*	*Upper 95.0%*
Intercept	-22.4781	22.6900	-0.9907	0.3452	-73.0345	28.0782	-73.0345	28.0782
yt-1	0.1878	0.1922	0.9768	0.3517	-0.2405	0.6160	-0.2405	0.6160

Table A5.6/3 Estimate of ρ

$\hat{\rho} = 1 + \hat{\theta} =$ 1.188 (which is > 1)

Appendix 5.7

Table A5.7/1 Dickey Fuller Stationarity Test: NASDAQ (*NAS*)

	NAS	Change y_t	y_{t-1}
Jul-99	2638	-48	2686
Aug-99	2739	101	2638
Sep-99	2746	7	2739
Oct-99	2966	220	2746
Nov-99	3336	370	2966
Dec-99	4069	733	3336
Jan-00	3940	-129	4069
Feb-00	4697	756	3940
Mar-00	4573	-124	4697
Apr-00	3861	-712	4573
May-00	3401	-460	3861
Jun-00	3966	565	3401

Table A5.7/2 Summary Output

Regression Statistics

Multiple R	0.3719
R Square	0.1383
Adjusted R Square	0.0521
Standard Error	439.4246
Observations	12

ANOVA

	df	SS	MS	F	Significance F
Regression	1	309872.7	309872.7	1.6048	0.2339
Residual	10	1930939.7	193094.0		
Total	11	2240812.4			

	Coefficients	Standard Error	t Stat	P-value	Lower 95%	Upper 95%	Lower 95.0%	Upper 95.0%
Intercept	889.351	630.733	1.410	0.189	-516.010	2294.712	-516.010	2294.712
y_{t-1}	-0.225	0.178	-1.267	0.234	-0.622	0.171	-0.622	0.171

Table A5.7/3 Estimate of ρ

$$\hat{\rho} = 1 + \hat{\theta} = \quad 0.775 \quad \text{(which is < 1)}$$

Appendices

Appendix 5.8

Table A5.8/1 Dickey Fuller Stationarity Test: Consumer Confidence (*CC*)

	CC	Change y_t	y_{t-1}
Jul-99	113.8	0.12	113.7
Aug-99	109.7	-4.17	113.8
Sep-99	114.2	4.51	109.7
Oct-99	113.3	-0.84	114.2
Nov-99	115.0	1.63	113.3
Dec-99	108.0	-6.92	115.0
Jan-00	111.1	3.04	108.0
Feb-00	101.1	-9.97	111.1
Mar-00	99.6	-1.50	101.1
Apr-00	95.9	-3.75	99.6
May-00	93.7	-2.14	95.9
Jun-00	100.3	6.62	93.7

Table A5.8/2 Summary Output

Regression Statistics	
Multiple R	0.3116
R Square	0.0971
Adjusted R Square	0.0068
Standard Error	4.7263
Observations	12.0000

ANOVA

	df	*SS*	*MS*	*F*	*Significance F*
Regression	1.0000	24.0137	24.0137	1.0750	0.3242
Residual	10.0000	223.3787	22.3379		
Total	11.0000	247.3924			

	Coefficients	*Standard Error*	*t Stat*	*P-value*	*Lower 95%*	*Upper 95%*	*Lower 95.0%*	*Upper 95.0%*
Intercept	19.3964	19.8295	0.9782	0.3511	-24.7866	63.5793	-24.7866	63.5793
y_{t-1}	-0.1909	0.1841	-1.0368	0.3242	-0.6012	0.2194	-0.6012	0.2194

Table A5.8/3 Estimate of ρ

$$\hat{\rho} = 1 + \hat{\theta} = \quad 0.809 \quad \text{(which is < 1)}$$

Appendix 5.9

Table A5.9/1 Dickey Fuller Stationarity Test:
Foreign Exchange (*FE*)

	FE	Change y_t	y_{t-1}
Jul-99	57.1	-1.30	58.4
Aug-99	56.0	-1.10	57.1
Sep-99	57.0	1.00	56.0
Oct-99	55.7	-1.30	57.0
Nov-99	55.3	-0.40	55.7
Dec-99	56.4	1.10	55.3
Jan-00	56.0	-0.40	56.4
Feb-00	54.5	-1.50	56.0
Mar-00	53.1	-1.40	54.5
Apr-00	52.5	-0.60	53.1
May-00	51.4	-1.10	52.5
Jun-00	53.3	1.90	51.4

Table A5.9/2 Summary Output

Regression Statistics

Multiple R	0.4310
R Square	0.1858
Adjusted R Square	0.1044
Standard Error	1.0806
Observations	12.0000

ANOVA

	df	SS	MS	F	Significance F
Regression	1.0000	2.6645	2.6645	2.2817	0.1618
Residual	10.0000	11.6780	1.1678		
Total	11.0000	14.3425			

	Coefficients	Standard Error	t Stat	P-value	Lower 95%	Upper 95%	Lower 95.0%	Upper 95.0%
Intercept	12.7920	8.7555	1.4610	0.1747	-6.7166	32.3006	-6.7166	32.3006
y_{t-1}	-0.2391	0.1583	-1.5105	0.1618	-0.5917	0.1136	-0.5917	0.1136

Table A5.9/3 Estimate of ρ

$$\hat{\rho} = 1 + \hat{\theta} = \quad 0.761 \quad \text{(which is} < 1)$$

Appendix 5.10

Table A5.10/1 Data for Cointegration Test of E-Commerce
Portfolio Return and NASDAQ (*NAS*)

	y_t Stock Return	x_t NAS
Jul-99	10.40%	2638
Aug-99	-7.91%	2739
Sep-99	-0.32%	2746
Oct-99	10.48%	2966
Nov-99	20.74%	3336
Dec-99	17.58%	4069
Jan-00	3.10%	3940
Feb-00	78.58%	4697
Mar-00	147.66%	4573
Apr-00	-28.86%	3861
May-00	-31.01%	3401
Jun-00	14.66%	3966

Table A5.10/2 Regression Summary Output / Cointegration Test of E-Commerce Portfolio
Return and *NAS*

Regression Statistics	
Multiple R	0.6075
R Square	0.3690
Adjusted R Square	0.3059
Standard Error	0.4082
Observations	12.0000

ANOVA

	df	SS	MS	F	Significance F
Regression	1.0000	0.9746	0.9746	5.8480	0.0362
Residual	10.0000	1.6665	0.1667		
Total	11.0000	2.6411			

	Coefficients	Standard Error	t Stat	P-value	Lower 95%	Upper 95%	Lower 95.0%	Upper 95.0%
Intercept	-1.2984	0.6291	-2.0640	0.0659	-2.7000	0.1032	-2.7000	0.1032
NASDAQ	0.0004	0.0002	2.4183	0.0362	0.0000	0.0008	0.0000	0.0008

Table A5.10/3 Dickey-Fuller Residual Test of E-Commerce
Portfolio Return and NASDAQ (*NAS*)

$\hat{\mu}t$	$= yt -$	$\hat{\alpha} -$	$\hat{\beta} x_t$	$\Delta \hat{\mu}_t$	$\hat{\mu}_{t-1}$
0.3472	0.1040	-1.2984	1.0552	0.3472	0.0000
0.1236	-0.0791	-1.2984	1.0957	-0.2236	0.3472
0.1967	-0.0032	-1.2984	1.0985	0.0732	0.1236
0.2166	0.1048	-1.2984	1.1866	0.0199	0.1967
0.1713	0.2074	-1.2984	1.3345	-0.0453	0.2166
-0.1535	0.1758	-1.2984	1.6277	-0.3249	0.1713
-0.2467	0.0310	-1.2984	1.5761	-0.0932	-0.1535
0.2055	0.7858	-1.2984	1.8787	0.4523	-0.2467
0.9459	1.4766	-1.2984	1.8291	0.7403	0.2055
-0.5345	-0.2886	-1.2984	1.5443	-1.4803	0.9459
-0.3721	-0.3101	-1.2984	1.3604	0.1624	-0.5345
-0.1414	0.1466	-1.2984	1.5864	0.2306	-0.3721

Table A5.10/4 Summary Output of DF Residual Test for
E-Commerce Portfolio Return and NASDAQ

Regression Statistics

Multiple R	0.7048
R Square	0.4967
Adjusted R Square	0.4464
Standard Error	0.4084
Observations	12.0000

ANOVA

	df	SS	MS	F	Significance F
Regression	1.0000	1.6463	1.6463	9.8685	0.0105
Residual	10.0000	1.6682	0.1668		
Total	11.0000	3.3145			

	Coefficients	Standard Error	t Stat	P-value	Lower 95%	Upper 95%	Lower 95.0%	Upper 95.0%
Intercept	0.0636	0.1203	0.5287	0.6086	-0.2045	0.3317	-0.2045	0.3317
μ_{t-1}	-1.0053	0.3200	-3.1414	0.0105	-1.7184	-0.2923	-1.7184	-0.2923

Appendix 5.10(1)

Table A5.10(1)/1 Data for Cointegration Test of E-Commerce
Portfolio Return and NASDAQ with First Difference

	Δy_t Stock Return	Δx_t NAS
Jul-99	10.40%	-48
Aug-99	-18.31%	101
Sep-99	7.59%	7
Oct-99	10.80%	220
Nov-99	10.26%	370
Dec-99	-3.16%	733
Jan-00	-14.48%	-129
Feb-00	75.48%	756
Mar-00	69.08%	-124
Apr-00	-176.52%	-712
May-00	-2.15%	-460
Jun-00	45.67%	565

Table A5.10(1)/2 Regression Summary Output / Cointegration Test of
E-Commerce Portfolio Return and NASDAQ with First Difference

Regression Statistics

Multiple R	0.6414
R Square	0.4114
Adjusted R Square	0.3525
Standard Error	0.5126
Observations	12.0000

ANOVA

	df	SS	MS	F	Significance F
Regression	1.0000	1.8366	1.8366	6.9894	0.0246
Residual	10.0000	2.6277	0.2628		
Total	11.0000	4.4644			

	Coefficients	Standard Error	t Stat	P-value	Lower 95%	Upper 95%	Lower 95.0%	Upper 95.0%
Intercept	-0.0843	0.1524	-0.5530	0.5924	-0.4239	0.2553	-0.4239	0.2553
NASDAQ	0.0009	0.0003	2.6437	0.0246	0.0001	0.0017	0.0001	0.0017

Table A5.10(1)/3 Dickey-Fuller Residual Test of E-Commerce
Portfolio Return and NASDAQ with First Difference

$\hat{\mu}_t$	$= y_t -$	$\hat{\alpha}$ $-$	$\hat{\beta} x_t$	$\hat{\Delta \mu}_t$	$\hat{\mu}_{t-1}$
0.2315	0.1040	-0.0843	-0.0432	0.2315	0.0000
-0.1897	-0.1831	-0.0843	0.0909	-0.4212	0.2315
0.1539	0.0759	-0.0843	0.0063	0.3436	-0.1897
-0.0057	0.1080	-0.0843	0.1980	-0.1596	0.1539
-0.1461	0.1026	-0.0843	0.3330	-0.1404	-0.0057
-0.6070	-0.0316	-0.0843	0.6597	-0.4609	-0.1461
0.0556	-0.1448	-0.0843	-0.1161	0.6626	-0.6070
0.1587	0.7548	-0.0843	0.6804	0.1031	0.0556
0.8867	0.6908	-0.0843	-0.1116	0.7280	0.1587
-1.0401	-1.7652	-0.0843	-0.6408	-1.9268	0.8867
0.4768	-0.0215	-0.0843	-0.4140	1.5169	-1.0401
0.0325	0.4567	-0.0843	0.5085	-0.4443	0.4768

Table A5.10(1)/4 Summary Output of Dickey-Fuller Residual Test
of E-Commerce Portfolio Return and NASDAQ with First Difference

Regression Statistics	
Multiple R	0.8613
R Square	0.7419
Adjusted R Square	0.7161
Standard Error	0.4486
Observations	12.0000

ANOVA

	df	SS	MS	F	Significance F
Regression	1.0000	5.7847	5.7847	28.7445	0.0003
Residual	10.0000	2.0125	0.2012		
Total	11.0000	7.7972			

	Coefficients	Standard Error	t Stat	P-value	Lower 95%	Upper 95%	Lower 95.0%	Upper 95.0%
Intercept	-0.0004	0.1295	-0.0033	0.9974	-0.2890	0.2881	-0.2890	0.2881
μ_{t-1}	-1.4840	0.2768	-5.3614	0.0003	-2.1007	-0.8673	-2.1007	-0.8673

Appendix 5.11

Table A5.11/1 Data for Cointegration Test of E-Commerce
Portfolio Return and Consumer Confidence (CC)

	y_t Stock Return	x_t CC
Jul-99	10.40%	113.8
Aug-99	-7.91%	109.7
Sep-99	-0.32%	114.2
Oct-99	10.48%	113.3
Nov-99	20.74%	115.0
Dec-99	17.58%	108.0
Jan-00	3.10%	111.1
Feb-00	78.58%	101.1
Mar-00	147.66%	99.6
Apr-00	-28.86%	95.9
May-00	-31.01%	93.7
Jun-00	14.66%	100.3

Table A5.11/2 Regression Summary Output / Cointegration Test of
E-Commerce Portfolio Return and Consumer Confidence

Regression Statistics

Multiple R	0.1069
R Square	0.0114
Adjusted R Square	-0.0874
Standard Error	0.5110
Observations	12.0000

ANOVA

	df	SS	MS	F	Significance F
Regression	1.0000	0.0302	0.0302	0.1155	0.7409
Residual	10.0000	2.6110	0.2611		
Total	11.0000	2.6411			

	Coefficients	Standard Error	t Stat	P-value	Lower 95%	Upper 95%	Lower 95.0%	Upper 95.0%
Intercept	0.9177	2.1284	0.4312	0.6755	-3.8247	5.6600	-3.8247	5.6600
Con'dence	-0.0068	0.0200	-0.3399	0.7409	-0.0513	0.0377	-0.0513	0.0377

Table A5.11/3 Dickey-Fuller Residual Test of E-Commerce
Portfolio Return and Consumer Confidence (*CC*)

$\hat{\mu}_t$	$= y_t -$	$\hat{\alpha}$	$\hat{\beta} x_t$	$\Delta \hat{\mu}_t$	$\hat{\mu}_{t-1}$
-0.0396	0.1040	0.9177	-0.7741	-0.0396	0.0000
-0.2511	-0.0791	0.9177	-0.7457	-0.2115	-0.0396
-0.1445	-0.0032	0.9177	-0.7764	0.1066	-0.2511
-0.0423	0.1048	0.9177	-0.7706	0.1023	-0.1445
0.0715	0.2074	0.9177	-0.7818	0.1137	-0.0423
-0.0072	0.1758	0.9177	-0.7347	-0.0786	0.0715
-0.1313	0.0310	0.9177	-0.7554	-0.1241	-0.0072
0.5557	0.7858	0.9177	-0.6876	0.6870	-0.1313
1.2363	1.4766	0.9177	-0.6774	0.6806	0.5557
-0.5544	-0.2886	0.9177	-0.6519	-1.7907	1.2363
-0.5905	-0.3101	0.9177	-0.6373	-0.0361	-0.5544
-0.0888	0.1466	0.9177	-0.6823	0.5017	-0.5905

Table A5.11/4 Summary Output of DF Residual Test of
E-Commerce Portfolio Return and Consumer Confidence

Regression Statistics

Multiple R	0.6560
R Square	0.4304
Adjusted R Square	0.3734
Standard Error	0.5061
Observations	12.0000

ANOVA

	df	SS	MS	F	Significance F
Regression	1.0000	1.9353	1.9353	7.5551	0.0205
Residual	10.0000	2.5616	0.2562		
Total	11.0000	4.4969			

	Coefficients	Standard Error	t Stat	P-value	Lower 95%	Upper 95%	Lower 95.0%	Upper 95.0%
Intercept	0.0000	0.1461	-0.0002	0.9999	-0.3256	0.3256	-0.3256	0.3256
μ_{t-1}	-0.8624	0.3138	-2.7487	0.0205	-1.5615	-0.1633	-1.5615	-0.1633

Appendix 5.11(1)

Table A5.11(1)/1 Data for Cointegration Test of E-Commerce
Portfolio Return and Consumer Confidence with First Difference

	Δy_t Stock Return	Δx_t CC
Jul-99	10.40%	0.1
Aug-99	-18.31%	-4.2
Sep-99	7.59%	4.5
Oct-99	10.80%	-0.8
Nov-99	10.26%	1.6
Dec-99	-3.16%	-6.9
Jan-00	-14.48%	3.0
Feb-00	75.48%	-10.0
Mar-00	69.08%	-1.5
Apr-00	-176.52%	-3.8
May-00	-2.15%	-2.1
Jun-00	45.67%	6.6

Table A5.11(1)/2 Regression Summary Output / Cointegration Test of
E-Commerce Portfolio Return and Consumer Confidence with First Difference

Regression Statistics

Multiple R	0.0701
R Square	0.0049
Adjusted R Square	-0.0946
Standard Error	0.6665
Observations	12.0000

ANOVA

	df	SS	MS	F	Significance F
Regression	1.0000	0.0220	0.0220	0.0494	0.8285
Residual	10.0000	4.4424	0.4442		
Total	11.0000	4.4644			

	Coefficients	Standard Error	t Stat	P-value	Lower 95%	Upper 95%	Lower 95.0%	Upper 95.0%
Intercept	0.0228	0.1982	0.1151	0.9106	-0.4189	0.4645	-0.4189	0.4645
Con'dence	0.0094	0.0424	0.2224	0.8285	-0.0850	0.1039	-0.0850	0.1039

Table A5.11(1)/3 Dickey-Fuller Residual Test of E-Commerce
Portfolio Return and Consumer Confidence with First Difference

$\hat{\mu}t$	$= yt -$	$\hat{\alpha}$ $-$	$\hat{\beta}xt$	$\hat{\Delta}\mu t$	$\hat{\mu}t-1$
0.0803	0.1040	0.0228	0.0009	0.0803	0.0000
-0.1664	-0.1831	0.0228	-0.0395	-0.2467	0.0803
0.0108	0.0759	0.0228	0.0423	0.1772	-0.1664
0.0927	0.1080	0.0228	-0.0075	0.0819	0.0108
0.0648	0.1026	0.0228	0.0150	-0.0280	0.0927
0.0105	-0.0316	0.0228	-0.0649	-0.0543	0.0648
-0.1958	-0.1448	0.0228	0.0282	-0.2063	0.0105
0.8260	0.7548	0.0228	-0.0940	1.0218	-0.1958
0.6821	0.6908	0.0228	-0.0141	-0.1439	0.8260
-1.7523	-1.7652	0.0228	-0.0357	-2.4344	0.6821
-0.0246	-0.0215	0.0228	-0.0197	1.7277	-1.7523
0.3719	0.4567	0.0228	0.0620	0.3964	-0.0246

Table A5.11(1)/4 Summary Output of Dickey-Fuller Residual Test of
E-Commerce Portfolio Return and Consumer Confidence with First Difference

Regression Statistics

Multiple R	0.7622
R Square	0.5810
Adjusted R Square	0.5391
Standard Error	0.6561
Observations	12.0000

ANOVA

	df	SS	MS	F	Significance F
Regression	1.0000	5.9687	5.9687	13.8660	0.0040
Residual	10.0000	4.3046	0.4305		
Total	11.0000	10.2733			

	Coefficients	Standard Error	t Stat	P-value	Lower 95%	Upper 95%	Lower 95.0%	Upper 95.0%
Intercept	-0.0056	0.1897	-0.0293	0.9772	-0.4281	0.4170	-0.4281	0.4170
μ_{t-1}	-1.1792	0.3167	-3.7237	0.0040	-1.8848	-0.4736	-1.8848	-0.4736

Appendix 5.12

Table A5.12/1 Data for Cointegration Test of E-Commerce
Portfolio Return and Foreign Exchange (*FE*)

	y_t Stock Return	x_t *FE*
Jul-99	10.40%	57.1
Aug-99	-7.91%	56.0
Sep-99	-0.32%	57.0
Oct-99	10.48%	55.7
Nov-99	20.74%	55.3
Dec-99	17.58%	56.4
Jan-00	3.10%	56.0
Feb-00	78.58%	54.5
Mar-00	147.66%	53.1
Apr-00	-28.86%	52.5
May-00	-31.01%	51.4
Jun-00	14.66%	53.3

Table A5.12/2 Regression Summary Output / Cointegration
Test of E-Commerce Portfolio Return and Foreign Exchange

Regression Statistics

Multiple R	0.0723
R Square	0.0052
Adjusted R Square	-0.0942
Standard Error	0.5126
Observations	12.0000

ANOVA

	df	SS	MS	F	Significance F
Regression	1.0000	0.0138	0.0138	0.0526	0.8232
Residual	10.0000	2.6273	0.2627		
Total	11.0000	2.6411			

	Coefficients	Standard Error	t Stat	P-value	Lower 95%	Upper 95%	Lower 95.0%	Upper 95.0%
Intercept	1.2332	4.5243	0.2726	0.7907	-8.8475	11.3138	-8.8475	11.3138
Forex	-0.0189	0.0824	-0.2294	0.8232	-0.2026	0.1648	-0.2026	0.1648

Table A5.12/3 Dickey-Fuller Residual Test of E-Commerce
Portfolio Return and Foreign Exchange (*FE*)

$\hat{\mu}_t$	$= y_t -$	$\hat{\alpha}$ $-$	$\hat{\beta} x_t$	$\Delta \hat{\mu}_t$	$\hat{\mu}_{t-1}$
-0.0500	0.1040	1.2332	-1.0792	-0.0500	0.0000
-0.2539	-0.0791	1.2332	-1.0584	-0.2039	-0.0500
-0.1591	-0.0032	1.2332	-1.0773	0.0948	-0.2539
-0.0757	0.1048	1.2332	-1.0527	0.0834	-0.1591
0.0194	0.2074	1.2332	-1.0452	0.0950	-0.0757
0.0086	0.1758	1.2332	-1.0660	-0.0108	0.0194
-0.1438	0.0310	1.2332	-1.0584	-0.1524	0.0086
0.5827	0.7858	1.2332	-1.0301	0.7265	-0.1438
1.2470	1.4766	1.2332	-1.0036	0.6643	0.5827
-0.5296	-0.2886	1.2332	-0.9923	-1.7765	1.2470
-0.5718	-0.3101	1.2332	-0.9715	-0.0423	-0.5296
-0.0792	0.1466	1.2332	-1.0074	0.4926	-0.5718

Table A5.12/4 Summary Output of DF Residual Test
of E-Commerce Portfolio Return and Foreign Exchange

Regression Statistics

Multiple R	0.6514
R Square	0.4243
Adjusted R Square	0.3667
Standard Error	0.5068
Observations	12.0000

ANOVA

	df	SS	MS	F	Significance F
Regression	1.0000	1.8931	1.8931	7.3706	0.0218
Residual	10.0000	2.5684	0.2568		
Total	11.0000	4.4615			

	Coefficients	Standard Error	t Stat	P-value	Lower 95%	Upper 95%	Lower 95.0%	Upper 95.0%
Intercept	-0.0014	0.1463	-0.0094	0.9927	-0.3274	0.3246	-0.3274	0.3246
$\mu_{\tau-1}$	-0.8499	0.3131	-2.7149	0.0218	-1.5475	-0.1524	-1.5475	-0.1524

Appendices

Appendix 5.12(1)

Table A5.12(1)/1 Data for Cointegration Test of E-Commerce
Portfolio Return and Foreign Exchange with First Difference

	Δy_t Stock Return	Δx_t Forex
Jul-99	10.40%	-1.3
Aug-99	-18.31%	-1.1
Sep-99	7.59%	1.0
Oct-99	10.80%	-1.3
Nov-99	10.26%	-0.4
Dec-99	-3.16%	1.1
Jan-00	-14.48%	-0.4
Feb-00	75.48%	-1.5
Mar-00	69.08%	-1.4
Apr-00	-176.52%	-0.6
May-00	-2.15%	-1.1
Jun-00	45.67%	1.9

Table A5.12(1)/2 Regression Summary Output / Cointegration Test of
E-Commerce Portfolio Return and Foreign Exchange with First Difference

Regression Statistics

Multiple R	0.0128
R Square	0.0002
Adjusted R Square	-0.0998
Standard Error	0.6681
Observations	12.0000

ANOVA

	df	SS	MS	F	Significance F
Regression	1.0000	0.0007	0.0007	0.0016	0.9684
Residual	10.0000	4.4636	0.4464		
Total	11.0000	4.4644			

	Coefficients	Standard Error	t Stat	P-value	Lower 95%	Upper 95%	Lower 95.0%	Upper 95.0%
Intercept	0.0092	0.2069	0.0443	0.9655	-0.4519	0.4702	-0.4519	0.4702
Forex	-0.0072	0.1764	-0.0406	0.9684	-0.4002	0.3859	-0.4002	0.3859

Table A5.12(1)/3 Dickey-Fuller Residual Test of E-Commerce Portfolio Return and Foreign Exchange with First Difference

$\hat{\mu}_t$	$= y_t -$	$\hat{\alpha}$	$- \hat{\beta} x_t$	$\Delta \hat{\mu}_t$	$\hat{\mu}_{t-1}$
0.0854	10.40%	0.0092	0.0094	0.0854	0.0000
-0.2002	-18.31%	0.0092	0.0079	-0.2857	0.0854
0.0739	7.59%	0.0092	-0.0072	0.2741	-0.2002
0.0894	10.80%	0.0092	0.0094	0.0155	0.0739
0.0905	10.26%	0.0092	0.0029	0.0011	0.0894
-0.0329	-3.16%	0.0092	-0.0079	-0.1234	0.0905
-0.1569	-14.48%	0.0092	0.0029	-0.1240	-0.0329
0.7348	75.48%	0.0092	0.0108	0.8917	-0.1569
0.6715	69.08%	0.0092	0.0101	-0.0633	0.7348
-1.7787	-176.52%	0.0092	0.0043	-2.4502	0.6715
-0.0386	-2.15%	0.0092	0.0079	1.7401	-1.7787
0.4612	45.67%	0.0092	-0.0137	0.4998	-0.0386

Table A5.12(1)/4 Summary Output of Dickey-Fuller Residual Test of E-Commerce Portfolio Return and Foreign Exchange with First Difference

Regression Statistics

Multiple R	0.7608
R Square	0.5789
Adjusted R Square	0.5368
Standard Error	0.6572
Observations	12.0000

ANOVA

	df	SS	MS	F	Significance F
Regression	1.0000	5.9379	5.9379	13.7461	0.0041
Residual	10.0000	4.3197	0.4320		
Total	11.0000	10.2577			

	Coefficients	Standard Error	t Stat	P-value	Lower 95%	Upper 95%	Lower 95.0%	Upper 95.0%
Intercept	-0.0071	0.1901	-0.0375	0.9708	-0.4308	0.4165	-0.4308	0.4165
μ_{t-1}	-1.1844	0.3194	-3.7076	0.0041	-1.8961	-0.4726	-1.8961	-0.4726

Appendix 5.13

Table A5.13/1 Cointegration Tests of the Four-Factor Model
$e\text{-}stockreturn(\Delta PR)_t = \alpha + \beta\Delta NAS_t + \beta\Delta CC_t + \beta\Delta FE_t + \varepsilon_t$

$e\text{-}stockreturn(\Delta PR)_t = -0.1900 + 0.0013\Delta NAS_t + 0.0692\Delta CC_t - 0.3287\Delta FE_t$

Table A5.13/2 Regression Summary Output of the Four-Factor Model

Regression Statistics

Multiple R	0.8013
R Square	0.6421
Adjusted R Square	0.5080
Standard Error	0.4469
Observations	12.0000

ANOVA

	df	SS	MS	F	Significance F
Regression	3.0000	2.8668	0.9556	4.7852	0.0341
Residual	8.0000	1.5976	0.1997		
Total	11.0000	4.4644			

	Coefficients	Standard Error	t Stat	P-value	Lower 95%	Upper 95%	Lower 95.0%	Upper 95.0%
Intercept	-0.1900	0.1488	-1.2772	0.2373	-0.5330	0.1530	-0.5330	0.1530
NASDAQ	0.0013	0.0003	3.7657	0.0055	0.0005	0.0021	0.0005	0.0021
Con'dence	0.0692	0.0358	1.9345	0.0891	-0.0133	0.1517	-0.0133	0.1517
Forex	-0.3287	0.1562	-2.1045	0.0685	-0.6888	0.0315	-0.6888	0.0315

Table A5.13/3 Residual Output of the
Four-Factor Model Regression

Observation	Predicted Return	Residuals
1.0000	0.1810	-0.0770
2.0000	0.0139	-0.1970
3.0000	-0.1980	0.2739
4.0000	0.4717	-0.3637
5.0000	0.5396	-0.4370
6.0000	-0.0636	0.0320
7.0000	-0.0208	-0.1240
8.0000	0.6066	0.1482
9.0000	0.0030	0.6878
10.0000	-1.1936	-0.5716
11.0000	-0.5797	0.5582
12.0000	0.3866	0.0701

Table A5.13/4 Regression Data for
the Residuals with One Lag

Δe_t	=	βe_{t-1}
-0.0770		0.0000
-0.1200		-0.0770
0.4708		-0.1970
-0.6376		0.2739
-0.0733		-0.3637
0.4690		-0.4370
-0.1560		0.0320
0.2722		-0.1240
0.5397		0.1482
-1.2594		0.6878
1.1298		-0.5716
-0.4881		0.5582

Table A5.13/5 Regression Summary Output of the Four-Factor Model

Regression Statistics	
Multiple R	0.8267
R Square	0.6835
Adjusted R Square	0.6518
Standard Error	0.3716
Observations	12.0000

ANOVA

	df	SS	MS	F	Significance F
Regression	1.0000	2.9824	2.9824	21.5924	0.0009
Residual	10.0000	1.3812	0.1381		
Total	11.0000	4.3637			

	Coefficients	Standard Error	t Stat	P-value	Lower 95%	Upper 95%	Lower 95.0%	Upper 95.0%
Intercept	-0.0022	0.1073	-0.0201	0.9844	-0.2412	0.2369	-0.2412	0.2369
$\varepsilon_{\tau-1}$	-1.3686	0.2945	-4.6468	0.0009	-2.0249	-0.7124	-2.0249	-0.7124

Appendix 5.14

Table A5.14/1 Cointegration Test of the Four-Factor Model
– Augmented Dickey Fuller Test

$$\Delta e_t \quad = \alpha \quad + \quad \beta e_{t-1} \quad + \quad \beta \Delta e_{t-1} \quad + \quad \beta \Delta e_{t-2}$$

e_t	Δe_t	e_{t-1}	Δe_{t-1}	Δe_{t-2}	e_{t-2}
-0.0770	-0.0770	0.0000	0.0000	0.0000	0.0000
-0.1970	-0.1200	-0.0770	-0.0770	0.0000	0.0000
0.2739	0.4708	-0.1970	-0.1200	-0.0770	-0.0770
-0.3637	-0.6376	0.2739	0.4708	-0.1200	-0.1970
-0.4370	-0.0733	-0.3637	-0.6376	0.4708	0.2739
0.0320	0.4690	-0.4370	-0.0733	-0.6376	-0.3637
-0.1240	-0.1560	0.0320	0.4690	-0.0733	-0.4370
0.1482	0.2722	-0.1240	-0.1560	0.4690	0.0320
0.6878	0.5397	0.1482	0.2722	-0.1560	-0.1240
-0.5716	-1.2594	0.6878	0.5397	0.2722	0.1482
0.5582	1.1298	-0.5716	-1.2594	0.5397	0.6878
0.0701	-0.4881	0.5582	1.1298	-1.2594	-0.5716

Table A5.14/1 Summary Output & ANOVA for the Augmented
Dickey-Fuller Test for Cointegration of the Four-Factor Model

Regression Statistics	
Multiple R	0.8500
R Square	0.7225
Adjusted R Square	0.6184
Standard Error	0.3891
Observations	12.0000

ANOVA

	df	SS	MS	F	Significance F
Regression	3.0000	3.1528	1.0509	6.9431	0.0129
Residual	8.0000	1.2109	0.1514		
Total	11.0000	4.3637			

	Coefficients	Standard Error	t Stat	P-value	Lower 95%	Upper 95%	Lower 95.0%	Upper 95.0%
Intercept	0.0007	0.1145	0.0065	0.9949	-0.2634	0.2649	-0.2634	0.2649
e_{t-1}	-0.9585	0.8010	-1.1967	0.2657	-2.8056	0.8885	-2.8056	0.8885
Δe_{t-1}	-0.4538	0.6440	-0.7046	0.5010	-1.9388	1.0312	-1.9388	1.0312
Δe_{t-2}	-0.4326	0.4156	-1.0407	0.3285	-1.3910	0.5259	-1.3910	0.5259

Appendix 6.1

Table A6.1/1 Risk-free Rate Estimation – July 1999 to June 2000

	1-month T. Notes	3-month T. Notes	6-month T. Notes	3-year T. Bond	5-year T. Bond	10-year T. Bond
Jul-99	4.68	4.69	4.70	5.53	5.82	6.24
Aug	4.74	4.74	4.71	5.77	6.02	6.35
Sep	4.76	4.77	4.77	5.60	5.88	6.30
Oct	4.81	4.87	4.90	6.08	6.31	6.63
Nov	4.98	5.01	5.05	6.18	6.41	6.64
Dec	4.98	5.04	5.14	6.47	6.70	6.96
Jan-00	5.12	5.39	5.56	6.82	7.01	7.16
Feb	5.45	5.66	5.97	6.52	6.64	6.65
Mar	5.47	5.68	5.95	6.38	6.40	6.36
Apr	5.73	5.85	6.04	6.43	6.45	6.39
May	5.88	6.00	6.18	6.20	6.24	6.27
Jun	5.83	5.86	5.96	5.97	6.05	6.16
Total	62.44	63.56	64.92	73.95	75.93	78.11

Source: RBA

Table A6.1/2 Geometric and Arithmetic Means

	1-month Treasury Notes	3-month Treasury Notes	6-month Treasury Notes	3-year Treasury Bonds	5-year Treasury Bonds	10-year Treasury Bonds
Arithmetic mean:	5.20	5.30	5.41	6.16	6.33	6.51
Geometric mean:	5.19	5.28	5.38	6.15	6.32	6.50

Appendix 6.2

Table A6.2/1 Stock Market Average Rate of Return: July 1999 to June 2000

		SP/ASX	Market			
		200	Return		Geomean calculations	
1999	Jul-99	3020	1.72%	1	1.0172	1.0172
	Aug-99	2952	-2.25%	1	0.9775	0.9943
	Sep-99	2881	-2.40%	1	0.9760	0.9704
	Oct-99	2885	0.14%	1	1.0014	0.9718
	Nov-99	3044	5.51%	1	1.0551	1.0253
	Dec-99	3153	3.56%	1	1.0356	1.0618
2000	Jan-00	3096	-1.79%	1	0.9821	1.0428
	Feb-00	3136	1.28%	1	1.0128	1.0562
	Mar-00	3133	-0.08%	1	0.9992	1.0554
	Apr-00	3116	-0.56%	1	0.9944	1.0495
	May-00	3081	-1.12%	1	0.9888	1.0378
	Jun-00	3311	7.47%	1	1.0747	1.1153
	Total		23.32%			1.0091

Source: RBA

Table A6.2/2 Arithmetic and Geometric Monthly/Annual Stock
Market Return for the Period July 1999 to June 2000

	Monthly returns	Annualised
Arithmetic mean of returns:	1.94%	23.32%
Geometric mean of returns:	0.91%	10.96%

Appendix 6.3

Table A6.3/1 Historical Returns of Stocks and Treasury Notes:
1992 to 2000

1992 to 2000 (monthly)	Stocks	3-Mth. T. notes
Arithmetic mean	0.76%	5.73
Geometric mean	0.68%	5.63

1992 to 2000 (annualised)	Stocks
Arithmetic mean	9.07%
Geometric mean	8.22%

Appendix 6.3(1)

Table A6.3(1)/1 Data for Monthly Stock Returns (S&P/ASX 200) and

3-Month Treasury Note Yield

		S&P/ASX 200	90-Day T. Notes
1992	jan	-0.02	
	feb	-0.01	
	mar	-0.02	
	apr	0.05	
	may	0.01	
	jun	-0.02	
	jul	-0.02	5.55
	aug	-0.04	5.46
	sep	-0.04	5.59
	oct	-0.04	5.54
	nov	0.02	5.71
	dec	0.07	5.76
1993	jan	-0.01	5.75
	feb	0.05	5.69
	mar	0.04	5.24
	apr	0.01	5.06
	may	0.03	5.07
	jun	0.00	5.10
	jul	0.06	4.96
	aug	0.06	4.62
	sep	0.00	4.70
	oct	0.08	4.69
	nov	-0.05	4.67
	dec	0.08	4.72
1994	jan	0.06	4.71
	feb	-0.06	4.70
	mar	-0.06	4.75
	apr	0.01	4.72
	may	0.01	4.75
	jun	-0.04	5.01
	jul	0.04	5.33
	aug	0.03	5.52
	sep	-0.04	5.81
	oct	0.01	6.44
	nov	-0.08	7.10
	dec	0.01	7.90
1995	jan	-0.04	8.32
	feb	0.05	8.05
	mar	-0.01	8.04

	apr	0.08	7.76
	may	-0.01	7.57
	jun	0.00	7.45
	jul	0.05	7.46
	aug	0.01	7.49
	sep	0.00	7.45
	oct	-0.03	7.43
	nov	0.04	7.41
	dec	0.02	7.30
1996	jan	0.04	7.31
	feb	0.00	7.39
	mar	-0.03	7.42
	apr	0.04	7.38
	may	-0.02	7.37
	jun	-0.01	7.33
	jul	-0.03	7.39
	aug	0.04	6.81
	sep	0.01	6.78
	oct	0.03	6.64
	nov	0.02	6.37
	dec	0.02	6.01
1997	jan	0.00	5.72
	feb	0.01	5.80
	mar	-0.01	5.91
	apr	0.03	5.87
	may	0.05	5.69
	jun	0.04	5.24
	jul	0.00	5.11
	aug	-0.05	4.84
	sep	0.07	4.71
	oct	-0.11	4.76
	nov	0.00	4.88
	dec	0.06	4.96
1998	jan	0.02	4.91
	feb	0.02	4.91
	mar	0.02	4.88
	apr	0.01	4.81
	may	-0.02	4.84
	jun	-0.02	4.98
	jul	0.01	4.94
	aug	-0.08	4.96
	sep	0.04	4.85
	oct	0.02	4.70
	nov	0.05	4.70
	dec	0.01	4.57
1999	jan	0.03	4.65

feb	0.00	4.67
mar	0.03	4.67
apr	0.05	4.63
may	-0.06	4.68
jun	0.02	4.69
jul	0.02	4.69
aug	-0.02	4.74
sep	-0.02	4.77
oct	0.00	4.87
nov	0.06	5.01
dec	0.04	5.04
jan	-0.02	5.39
feb	0.01	5.66
mar	0.00	5.68
apr	-0.01	5.85
may	-0.01	6.00
jun	0.07	5.86
Total	*77.09%*	*549.62*

Appendix 6.4

Table A6.4 /1 E-Commerce Firm & Market Return Data, Means and Risk Estimates

Month	Market Returns	My Casino	Sausage	Solution 6	Reckon	Swish	Pocket-mail	131 Shop	B2N Net	Cons21	Etrade	Aussie Online	Candle	Liberty One	Spike	Webjet	Travelcom	Ecorp	Wine Planet
Jul-99	1.72%	16.28%	20.23%	27.14%	0.00%	0.00%	0.00%	0	140.00%	-15.96%	-19.55%	-3.23%	15.13%	0.12	0.00%	-4.00%	0.00%	0.00%	0.00%
Aug-99	-2.25%	-30.00%	-11.55%	-8.99%	-23.08%	-8.47%	0.00%	-39.76%	4.17%	-26.58%	20.25%	30.00%	0.57%	-0.05	-31.30%	16.67%	-10.37%	-18.52%	0.00%
Sep-99	-2.40%	28.57%	21.57%	35.16%	-5.38%	-22.22%	0.00%	-8.00%	-10.00%	-13.79%	-23.90%	-35.90%	-4.69%	0.58	-5.06%	16.67%	-19.83%	1.52%	-19.51%
Oct-99	0.14%	-6.67%	-3.75%	25.69%	17.89%	-2.38%	0.00%	4.35%	0.00%	-10.00%	-5.20%	12.00%	6.67%	0.35	20.00%	37.76%	7.22%	7.96%	42.42%
Nov-99	5.51%	19.05%	55.27%	61.34%	26.90%	46.34%	0.00%	20.83%	0.00%	2.22%	1.43%	28.57%	6.25%	0.01	22.22%	3.70%	44.04%	20.28%	14.89%
Dec-99	3.56%	100.00%	21.78%	49.55%	-4.89%	-5.00%	0.00%	-1.72%	0.00%	-2.17%	-12.47%	22.22%	7.49%	-0.14	81.82%	32.14%	-2.54%	45.98%	-1.85%
Jan-00	-1.79%	0.00%	-0.38%	-38.55%	17.14%	4.91%	-20.00%	-17.54%	0.00%	-11.11%	-19.35%	161.36%	-9.20%	-0.30	-7.00%	29.73%	-10.96%	11.42%	-3.77%
Feb-00	1.28%	0.00%	-3.47%	-19.77%	-13.80%	27.09%	983.33%	-6.38%	0.00%	42.50%	3.00%	195.65%	-1.64%	-0.13	86.56%	0.00%	9.23%	71.26%	52.94%
Mar-00	-0.08%	0.00%	20.00%	30.15%	-11.71%	14.47%	-18.27%	-28.41%	2677.78%	-14.04%	31.07%	-13.24%	-5.15%	0.03	-30.84%	16.67%	16.20%	-26.41%	-3.85%
Apr-00	-0.56%	180.00%	-50.73%	-50.79%	-29.49%	-14.94%	-41.18%	-42.86%	-51.20%	-34.69%	-40.74%	-57.63%	-1.49%	-0.53	-55.42%	-51.79%	-30.30%	-43.93%	-49.33%
May-00	-1.12%	-3.57%	-31.26%	-42.36%	-34.55%	-39.19%	-52.00%	-61.67%	-40.98%	3.13%	-14.58%	-40.80%	-21.21%	-0.39	-39.25%	-40.00%	-13.91%	-30.43%	-15.79%
Jun-00	7.47%	-14.81%	24.41%	7.58%	8.61%	8.00%	-25.00%	1.45%	-8.33%	-12.12%	-12.68%	102.70%	21.15%	-0.20	23.08%	41.98%	-11.62%	8.77%	162.50%
Returns - Arithmetic Mean																			
Monthly		24.07%	5.18%	0.0634	-0.0436	0.0072	0.6891	-0.1223	225.95%	-0.0772	-0.0773	0.3348	0.0116	-0.0552	0.0088	8.29%	-0.0076	0.0399	0.2475
Annualised		288.85%	62.11%	0.7614	-0.5237	0.0861	8.2689	-1.4671	2711.43%	-0.9262	-0.9274	4.0173	0.1387	-0.6619	0.1053	99.52%	-0.091	0.4789	2.97
Returns - Geometric Mean																			
Monthly	0.91%	15.00%	1.13%	-0.0062	-0.0622	-0.016	0.0344	-0.1862	26.32%	-0.0934	-0.0959	0.1404	0.0057	-0.1009	-0.0298	3.63%	-0.0355	-0.0057	0.0616
Annualised	10.96%	179.97%	13.52%	-0.0739	-0.7464	-0.1924	0.4124	-2.2348	31.58%	-1.1202	-1.1512	1.6849	0.0686	-1.2108	-0.3575	43.51%	-0.4259	-0.0679	0.7391
Variance & Standard Deviation																			
Variance	0.10%	35.51%	8.17%	0.1477	0.0382	0.0508	8.7923	0.0579	6421.02%	0.037	0.0383	0.6797	0.0127	0.0972	0.2066	8.80%	0.4527	0.1091	0.316
Std. Dev.	3.13%	59.59%	28.58%	0.3843	0.1954	0.2255	2.9652	0.2406	801.31%	0.1922	0.1957	0.8244	0.1125	0.3117	0.4545	29.67%	0.6728	0.3303	0.5622

Table A6. 4/2 Market Model Regression Statistics

Multiple R	0.0016	0.5865	0.4622	0.4778	0.5668	0.0402	0.6340	0.0953	0.2393	0.0149	0.2449	0.7284	0.1175	0.5269	0.2907	0.4519	0.4164	0.6980
R Square	0.0000	0.3439	0.2137	0.2283	0.3213	0.0016	0.4020	0.0091	0.0573	0.0002	0.0600	0.5305	0.0138	0.2777	0.0845	0.2042	0.1734	0.4873
Adjusted R Square	-0.1000	0.2783	0.1350	0.1512	0.2534	-0.0982	0.3422	-0.0900	-0.0370	-0.0998	-0.0340	0.4836	-0.0848	0.2054	-0.0071	0.1246	0.0907	0.4360
Standard Error	0.6170	0.2401	0.3510	0.1791	0.1937	3.0237	0.1927	8.0760	0.1950	0.2052	0.8125	0.0807	0.3208	0.3976	0.2937	0.1822	0.3094	0.4029
Observations	12	12	12	12	12	12	12	12	12	12	12	12	12	12	12	12	12	12

ANOVA

Intercept

Coefficients	0.2404	0.0012	0.0102	-0.0720	-0.0316	0.6537	-0.1957	2.4844	-0.0912	-0.0782	0.2750	-0.0134	-0.0441	-0.0177	0.0570	-0.0459	-0.0013	0.0346
Standard Error	0.1869	0.0728	0.1063	0.0543	0.0587	0.9161	0.0584	2.4469	0.0591	0.0622	0.2462	0.0245	0.0972	0.1205	0.0890	0.0552	0.0937	0.1221
t Stat	1.2861	2.3099	0.0960	-1.3264	-0.5386	0.7136	-3.3530	1.0153	-1.5431	-1.2571	1.1172	-0.5486	-0.4538	-0.1472	0.6401	-0.8315	-0.0142	0.2831
P-value	0.2274	0.9875	0.9254	0.2142	0.6019	0.4918	0.0073	0.3339	0.1538	0.2373	0.2900	0.5953	0.6597	0.8859	0.5365	0.4251	0.9890	0.7829

X Variable - Market Return

Coefficients	0.0292	5.2887	5.5653	2.9643	4.0540	3.6960	4.8047	23.5072	1.4618	0.0931	6.2443	2.6108	-1.1547	7.4978	2.7144	2.8069	4.3103	11.9492
Standard Error	5.9351	2.3099	3.3761	1.7233	1.8633	29.0858	1.8533	77.6866	1.8758	1.9744	7.8159	0.7766	3.0862	3.8242	2.8255	1.7523	2.9763	3.8761
t Stat	0.0049	2.2896	1.6484	1.7201	2.1757	0.1271	2.5926	-0.3026	0.7793	0.0471	0.7989	3.3617	-0.3742	1.9606	0.9607	1.6019	1.4482	3.0828
P-value	0.9962	0.0450	0.1303	0.1162	0.0546	0.9014	0.0268	0.7684	0.4539	0.9633	0.4429	0.0072	0.7161	0.0784	0.3594	0.1403	0.1782	0.0116

Risk

Systematic	0.0000	0.0275	0.0304	0.0086	0.0161	0.0134	0.0227	0.5429	0.0021	0.0000	0.0383	0.0067	0.0013	0.0552	0.0072	0.0077	0.0183	0.1403
Unsystematic	0.3807	0.0577	0.1232	0.0321	0.0375	9.1425	0.0371	65.2221	0.0380	0.0421	0.6602	0.0065	0.1029	0.1580	0.0863	0.0332	0.0957	0.1624

Appendix 6.5

Table A6.5/1 Data on E-Commerce Portfolio Returns: July 1999 to June 2000

Month	131 shop	AOL	B2N Net	Candle	Coms21	Ecorp	Lib. One	My Casino	Pocket-mail	Reckon	Sausage	Solution 6	Spike	Swish	Travel-Com	Webjet	Wine P.	Etrade	Portfolio Returns
Jul-99	0	0.03	1.4	0.15	-0.16	0.00	0.12	0.16	0.00	0.00	0.20	0.27	0.00	0.00	0.00	-0.04	0.00	-0.20	0.1040
Aug-99	-0.4	0.3	0.04	0.01	-0.27	-0.19	-0.05	-0.30	0.00	-0.23	-0.12	-0.09	-0.31	-0.08	-0.10	0.17	0.00	0.20	-0.0791
Sep-99	-0.08	0.36	-0.1	-0.05	-0.14	0.02	0.58	0.29	0.00	-0.05	0.22	0.35	-0.05	-0.22	-0.20	0.17	-0.20	-0.24	-0.0032
Oct-99	0.04	0.12	0	0.07	-0.10	0.08	0.35	-0.07	0.00	0.18	-0.04	0.26	0.20	-0.02	0.07	0.38	0.42	-0.05	0.1048
Nov-99	0.21	0.29	0	0.06	0.02	0.20	0.01	0.19	0.00	0.27	0.55	0.61	0.22	0.46	0.44	0.04	0.15	0.01	0.2074
Dec-99	-0.02	0.22	0	0.07	-0.02	0.46	-0.14	1.00	0.00	-0.05	0.22	0.50	0.82	-0.05	-0.03	0.32	-0.02	-0.12	0.1758
Jan-00	-0.18	1.61	0	-0.09	-0.11	0.11	-0.30	0.00	-0.20	0.17	0.00	-0.39	-0.07	0.05	-0.11	0.30	-0.04	-0.19	0.0310
Feb-00	-0.06	1.96	0	-0.02	0.43	0.71	-0.13	0.00	9.83	-0.14	-0.03	-0.20	0.87	0.27	0.09	0.00	0.53	0.03	0.7858
Mar-00	-0.28	0.13	26.78	-0.05	-0.14	-0.26	0.03	0.00	-0.18	-0.12	0.20	0.30	-0.31	0.14	0.16	0.17	-0.04	0.31	1.4766
Apr-00	-0.43	0.58	-0.51	-0.01	-0.35	-0.44	-0.53	1.80	-0.41	-0.29	-0.51	-0.51	-0.55	-0.15	-0.30	-0.52	-0.49	-0.41	-0.2886
May-00	-0.62	0.41	-0.41	-0.21	0.03	-0.30	-0.39	-0.04	-0.52	-0.35	-0.31	-0.42	-0.39	-0.39	-0.14	-0.40	-0.16	-0.15	-0.3101
Jun-00	0.01	1.03	-0.08	-0.21	-0.12	0.09	-0.20	-0.15	-0.25	0.09	0.24	0.08	0.23	0.08	-0.12	0.42	1.63	-0.13	0.1466
																		Total	2.3509

Table A6.5/2 E-Commerce Portfolio Returns Means

	Monthly	Annual
Arithmatic mean:	19.59%	235.09%
Geometric mean:	10.56%	126.74%

238 Appendices

Appendix 6.6

Table A6.6/1 Mean and Standard Deviation of E-Commerce Portfolio Returns: July 1999 to 2000

Month	Portfolio Returns	$(x - \bar{x})$	$(x - \bar{x})^2$
Jul-99	0.1040	-0.0056	0.0000
Aug-99	-0.0791	-0.1887	0.0356
Sep-99	-0.0032	-0.1128	0.0127
Oct-99	0.1048	-0.0048	0.0000
Nov-99	0.2074	0.0978	0.0096
Dec-99	0.1758	0.0662	0.0044
Jan-00	0.0310	-0.0786	0.0062
Feb-00	0.7858	0.6762	0.4572
Mar-00	1.4766	1.3670	1.8686
Apr-00	-0.2886	-0.3982	0.1586
May-00	-0.3101	-0.4197	0.1762
Jun-00	0.1466	0.0370	0.0014
			2.7304

Table A6.6/2 E-Commerce Portfolio Means

Arithmetic mean:	19.59%
Geometric mean:	10.56%

Table A6.6/3 E-Commerce Portfolio Variance

Variance = s^2	0.25

Table A6.6/4 E-Commerce Portfolio Standard Deviation

Standard Deviation	49.82%
Annualised SD	597.86%

Appendix 6.7

Table A6.7/1 Data on E-Commerce Portfolio and
Market Returns: July 1999 to June 2000

Month	Portfolio Return	Market Return
Jul-99	10.40%	1.72%
Aug-99	-7.91%	-2.25%
Sep-99	-0.32%	-2.40%
Oct-99	10.48%	0.14%
Nov-99	20.74%	5.51%
Dec-99	17.58%	3.56%
Jan-00	3.10%	-1.79%
Feb-00	78.58%	1.28%
Mar-00	147.66%	-0.08%
Apr-00	-28.86%	-0.56%
May-00	-31.01%	-1.12%
Jun-00	14.66%	7.47%
Total	235.09%	

Table A6.7/2 E-Commerce Portfolio and Market
Returns Regression Summary Output

Regression Statistics

Multiple R	0.138194
R Square	0.019098
Adjusted R Square	-0.078993
Standard Error	0.508981
Observations	12.000000

ANOVA

	df	SS	MS	F	Significance F
Regression	1.000000	0.050438	0.050438	0.194694	0.668425
Residual	10.000000	2.590613	0.259061		
Total	11.000000	2.641051			

	Coefficients	Standard Error	t Stat	P-value	Lower 95%	Upper 95%	Lower 95.0%	Upper 95.0%
Intercept	0.175239	0.154215	1.136327	0.282318	-0.168374	0.518852	-0.168374	0.518852
X Variable 1	2.160360	4.896094	0.441242	0.668425	-8.748820	13.069540	-8.748820	13.069540

Appendix 6.8

Table A6.8/1 Means of CAPM Estimated Expected Returns

	Geo-Returns	Arith. Returns	Geomean calculations:		
My Casino	5.71%	5.83%	1	1.06	1.06
Sausage	19.33%	23.39%	1	1.19	1.26
Solution 6	20.04%	24.32%	1	1.20	1.51
Reckon	13.31%	15.63%	1	1.13	1.72
Swish	16.13%	19.27%	1	1.16	1.99
Pocketmail	15.20%	18.07%	1	1.15	2.30
131	18.07%	21.78%	1	1.18	2.71
B2B	-55.25%	-72.78%	1	0.45	1.21
Coms 21	9.42%	10.61%	1	1.09	1.33
Etrade	5.87%	6.04%	1	1.06	1.40
AOL	21.80%	26.58%	1	1.22	1.71
Candle	12.39%	14.45%	1	1.12	1.92
Liberty One	2.64%	1.87%	1	1.03	1.97
Spike	25.05%	30.77%	1	1.25	2.47
Webjet	12.66%	14.79%	1	1.13	2.78
Travel.com	12.90%	15.11%	1	1.13	3.14
Ecorp	16.79%	20.13%	1	1.17	3.67
Wine Planet	36.58%	45.64%	1	1.37	5.01
Total		241.50%			1.09

Table A6.8/2 E-Commerce Portfolio
CAPM Estimated Means

Arithmetic mean	13.42%
Geomean	9.36%

Appendix 6.9

Table A6.9/1 Covariance Matrix (Returns): Jul '99 to Jun '00

	131 shop	AOL	B2N Net	Candle	Coms21	Ecorp	Lib. One	My Casino	Pocketmail	Reckon	Sausage	Solution 6	Spike	Swish	Travel. Com	Webjet	Wine P.	Etrade
131 shop	0.0519																	
AOL	0.0599	0.5864																
B2N Net	-0.2453	-1.0149	54.8570															
Candle	0.0117	-0.0120	-0.0341	0.0111														
Coms21	0.0120	0.0855	-0.1410	-0.0011	0.0343													
Ecorp	0.0474	0.1681	-0.6431	0.0087	0.0447	0.0959												
Lib. One	0.0346	-0.0397	0.2356	0.0125	0.0001	0.0177	0.0868											
My Casino	-0.0169	-0.1733	-0.6013	0.0144	-0.0320	-0.0295	-0.0594	0.3178										
Pocketmail	0.1033	1.3659	-1.9224	0.0193	0.4227	0.5823	-0.0254	-0.2220	7.6252									
Reckon	0.0364	0.0526	-0.1465	0.0055	0.0029	0.0250	0.0219	-0.0295	-0.0627	0.0349								
Sausage	0.0494	0.0383	0.3813	0.0079	0.0106	0.0397	0.0421	-0.0526	-0.0373	0.0360	0.0732							
Solution 6	0.0608	-0.0505	0.5901	0.0199	0.0032	0.0384	0.0732	-0.0272	-0.1715	0.0375	0.0844	0.1308						
Spike	0.0661	0.1934	-0.7816	0.0129	0.0574	0.1283	0.0230	-0.0201	0.7115	0.0314	0.0545	0.0657	0.1824					
Swish	0.0336	0.0888	0.3162	0.0073	0.0161	0.0355	0.0046	-0.0241	0.2334	0.0248	0.0363	0.0325	0.0440	0.0454				
Travel.Com	0.0250	0.0282	0.4219	0.0077	0.0152	0.0232	0.0144	-0.0365	0.1058	0.0192	0.0342	0.0417	0.0307	0.0323	0.0345			
Webjet	0.0385	0.0949	0.2166	0.0025	0.0028	0.0410	0.0409	-0.0777	-0.0392	0.0349	0.0465	0.0545	0.0579	0.0202	0.0133	0.0790		
Wine P.	0.0538	0.2145	-0.4074	-0.0183	0.0280	0.0643	0.0058	-0.1355	0.3229	0.0394	0.0493	0.0294	0.0997	0.0412	0.0159	0.0800	0.2652	
Etrade	0.0011	0.0263	0.8716	0.0012	0.0076	0.0059	0.0116	-0.0636	0.1003	0.0009	0.0165	0.0216	0.0077	0.0173	0.0205	0.0198	0.0162	0.0351

Table A6.9/2 Correlation Coefficients (Returns): Jul '99 to Jun '00

	131 shop	AOL	B2N Net	Candle	Coms21	Ecorp	Lib. One	My Casino	Pocket-mail	Reckon	Sausage	Solution 6	Spike	Swish	Travel.Com	Webjet	Wine P.	Etrade
131 shop	1.0000																	
AOL	0.3435	1.0000																
B2N Net	-0.1453	-0.1789	1.0000															
Candle	0.4873	-0.1484	-0.0436	1.0000														
Coms21	0.2833	0.6032	-0.1029	-0.0581	1.0000													
Ecorp	0.6722	0.7089	-0.2804	0.2662	0.7796	1.0000												
Lib. One	0.5159	-0.1758	0.1080	0.4017	0.0022	0.1935	1.0000											
My Casino	-0.1313	-0.4014	-0.1440	0.2417	-0.3070	-0.1687	-0.3576	1.0000										
Pocketmail	0.1642	0.6460	-0.0940	0.0662	0.8270	0.6809	-0.0313	-0.1426	1.0000									
Reckon	0.8548	0.3680	-0.1060	0.2800	0.0851	0.4326	0.3983	-0.2799	-0.1215	1.0000								
Sausage	0.8018	0.1849	0.1903	0.2770	0.2126	0.4737	0.5282	-0.3450	-0.0500	0.7128	1.0000							
Solution 6	0.7378	-0.1823	0.2203	0.5202	0.0478	0.3431	0.6869	-0.1333	-0.1717	0.5558	0.8629	1.0000						
Spike	0.6791	0.5914	-0.2471	0.2868	0.7255	0.9698	0.1827	-0.0834	0.6033	0.3940	0.4718	0.4250	1.0000					
Swish	0.6911	0.5445	0.2004	0.3241	0.4095	0.5376	0.0738	-0.2005	0.3968	0.6233	0.6303	0.4219	0.4837	1.0000				
Travel.Com	0.5899	0.1980	0.3066	0.3951	0.4419	0.4023	0.2631	-0.3485	0.2061	0.5529	0.6796	0.6210	0.3873	0.8157	1.0000			
Webjet	0.6011	0.4410	0.1040	0.0845	0.0547	0.4706	0.4944	-0.4903	-0.0505	0.6645	0.6115	0.5355	0.4826	0.3376	0.2546	1.0000		
Wine P.	0.4587	0.5439	-0.1068	-0.3358	0.2940	0.4033	0.0383	-0.4668	0.2271	0.4099	0.3543	0.1580	0.4531	0.3753	0.1664	0.5526	1.0000	
Etrade	0.0264	0.1834	0.6279	0.0616	0.2194	0.1021	0.2105	-0.6018	0.1938	0.0261	0.3261	0.3189	0.0967	0.4321	0.5898	0.3758	0.1679	1.0000

Appendix 6.10

Table A6.10/1 Covariance Matrix (Prices): Jul '99 to Jun '00

	131 Shop	AOL	B2N Net	Candle	Coms21	Ecorp	Liberty 1	My Casino	Pocketmail	Reckon	Sausage	Solution 6	Spike	Swish	Travel.Com	Webjet	Wine P.	Etrade
131 Shop	0.0454																	
AOL	-0.0073	0.0105																
B2N Net	-0.0380	0.0196	0.1234															
Candle	0.0515	-0.0025	-0.0439	0.1122														
Coms21	0.0117	-0.0004	-0.0064	0.0082	0.0043													
Ecorp	0.0126	0.1398	0.1407	0.1658	0.0137	2.4703												
Liberty 1	0.0790	-0.0177	-0.0738	0.1336	0.0105	0.0372	0.3078											
My Casino	-0.0311	0.0040	0.0253	-0.0375	-0.0081	-0.0146	-0.0745	0.0301										
Pocketmail	-0.0083	0.0147	0.0298	-0.0040	0.0005	0.2030	-0.0196	0.0050	0.0238									
Reckon	0.0652	0.0043	-0.0378	0.1119	0.0129	0.3235	0.1514	-0.0468	0.0053	0.1619								
Sausage	0.0599	0.0767	0.1337	0.2545	0.0043	1.6609	0.2832	-0.0578	0.1000	0.3846	1.7455							
Solution 6	0.3092	0.0462	0.0041	0.9856	0.0021	2.9050	1.4045	-0.2269	0.0573	1.1196	4.3377	15.1919						
Spike	0.0290	0.0670	0.0483	0.1177	0.0122	1.2727	0.0642	-0.0226	0.0978	0.1954	0.8929	1.7787	0.6736					
Swish	0.0000	0.0053	0.0149	0.0052	0.0006	0.0816	-0.0048	0.0011	0.0084	0.0105	0.0615	0.0929	0.0404	0.0047				
Travel.Com	0.0246	0.0091	0.0212	0.0469	0.0065	0.2309	0.0518	-0.0161	0.0155	0.0711	0.2500	0.6519	0.1306	0.0120	0.0541			
Webjet	-0.0003	0.0051	0.0096	0.0087	-0.0004	0.0914	0.0079	-0.0011	0.0066	0.0154	0.0827	0.1724	0.0467	0.0032	0.0102	0.0045		
Wine P.	-0.0036	0.0065	0.0091	0.0054	-0.0006	0.0827	-0.0044	-0.0006	0.0072	0.0053	0.0589	0.0843	0.0421	0.0027	0.0061	0.0035	0.0072	
Etrade	0.1876	-0.0417	-0.1003	0.1834	0.0568	-0.3041	0.3582	-0.1731	-0.0396	0.1972	0.0116	0.5717	-0.0706	-0.0038	0.0946	-0.0124	-0.0281	1.3145

Appendix 6.10

Table A6.10/2 Correlation Coefficient (Prices): Jul '99 to Jun '00

	131 Shop	AOL	B2N Net	Candle	Coms21	Ecorp	Liberty 1	My Casino	Pocket-mail	Reckon	Sausage	Solution 6	Spike	Swish	Travel.Com	Webjet	Wine P.	Etrade
131 Shop	1.0000																	
AOL	-0.3374	1.0000																
B2N Net	-0.5076	0.5444	1.0000															
Candle	0.7216	-0.0736	-0.3728	1.0000														
Coms21	0.8354	-0.0643	-0.2762	0.3737	1.0000													
Ecorp	0.0378	0.8698	0.2549	0.3149	0.1330	1.0000												
Liberty 1	0.6684	-0.3115	-0.3786	0.7189	0.2886	0.0426	1.0000											
My Casino	-0.8404	0.2239	0.4149	-0.6454	-0.7119	-0.0535	-0.7735	1.0000										
Pocketmail	-0.2533	0.9338	0.5502	-0.0780	0.0525	0.8366	-0.2287	0.1859	1.0000									
Reckon	0.7611	0.1049	-0.2675	0.8306	0.4907	0.5115	0.6781	-0.6702	0.0846	1.0000								
Sausage	0.2128	0.5679	0.2882	0.5752	0.0499	0.7999	0.3863	-0.2518	0.4901	0.7236	1.0000							
Solution 6	0.3724	0.1159	0.0030	0.7549	0.0083	0.4742	0.6495	-0.3353	0.0953	0.7139	0.8424	1.0000						
Spike	0.1656	0.7982	0.1676	0.4283	0.2261	0.9866	0.1409	-0.1583	0.7716	0.5919	0.8235	0.5560	1.0000					
Swish	0.0019	0.7589	0.6198	0.2281	0.1447	0.7594	-0.1257	0.0912	0.7953	0.3799	0.6807	0.3485	0.7202	1.0000				
Travel.Com	0.4964	0.3846	0.2593	0.6017	0.4295	0.6320	0.4015	-0.3993	0.4311	0.7602	0.8138	0.7194	0.6843	0.7523	1.0000			
Webjet	-0.0224	0.7420	0.4064	0.3870	-0.1002	0.8670	0.2126	-0.0951	0.6379	0.5715	0.9328	0.6593	0.8482	0.7043	0.6509	1.0000		
Wine P.	-0.2011	0.7440	0.3067	0.1907	-0.1112	0.6196	-0.0939	0.0390	0.5467	0.1538	0.5253	0.2548	0.6044	0.4636	0.3084	0.6125	1.0000	
Etrade	0.7683	-0.3556	-0.2491	0.4776	0.7562	-0.1687	0.5631	-0.8695	-0.2235	0.4276	0.0077	0.1279	-0.0750	-0.0482	0.3550	-0.1611	-0.2888	1.0000

Appendix 6.11

Table A6.11/1 E-Commerce Stocks' Risk – Actual Return
Comparison

	Volatility (Std. Dev.)	Actual Return
My Casino	59.59%	179.97%
Sausage	28.58%	13.52%
Solution 6	38.43%	-7.39%
Reckon	19.54%	-74.64%
Swish	22.55%	-19.24%
Pocketmail	296.52%	41.24%
131	24.06%	-223.48%
B2B	801.31%	315.79%
Coms 21	19.22%	-112.02%
Etrade	19.57%	-115.12%
AOL	82.44%	-168.49%
Candle	11.25%	6.86%
Liberty One	31.17%	-121.08%
Spike	45.45%	-35.75%
Webjet	29.67%	43.51%
Travel.com	67.28%	-42.59%
Ecorp	33.03%	-6.79%
Wine Planet	56.22%	73.91%

Appendix 6.12

Figure A6.12 Graph of E-Commerce Risk-Actual Return Profile

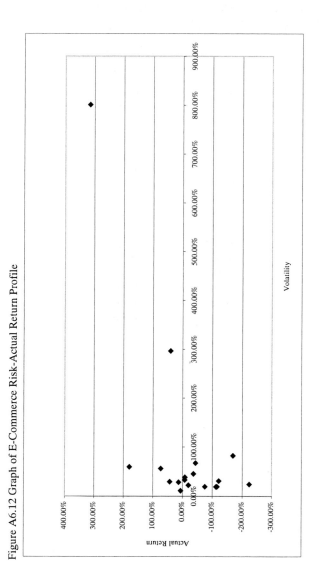

Appendix 6.13

Table A6.13/1 E-Commerce Stocks: Risk-Expected Return
Comparison: July 1999 to June 2000

	Volatility (Std. Dev.)	Expected Returns*
My Casino	59.59%	5.94%
Sausage	28.58%	19.35%
Solution 6	38.43%	20.06%
Reckon	19.54%	13.43%
Swish	22.55%	16.21%
Pocketmail	296.52%	15.29%
131	24.06%	18.12%
B2B	801.31%	-54.07%
Coms 21	19.22%	9.60%
Etrade	19.57%	6.11%
AOL	82.44%	21.79%
Candle	11.25%	12.69%
Liberty One	31.17%	2.92%
Spike	45.45%	24.99%
Webjet	29.67%	12.79%
Travel.com	67.28%	13.03%
Ecorp	33.03%	16.86%
Wine Planet	56.22%	36.34%

(* using the CAPM)

Appendix 6.14

Figure A6.14/1 E-Commerce Stocks: Risk-Expected Return Profile

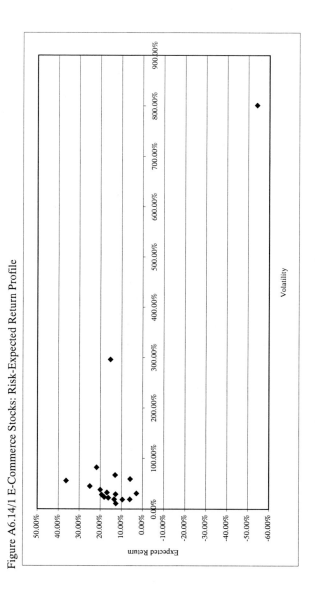

Appendix 6.15

Table A6. 15/1 Estimation of the AR (1) Model to Test the Weak-Form of the Efficient Market Hypothesis by Sector

	S&P/ASX 200	Market Return	Market Return$_{t-1}$	C&G Return	C&G Return$_{t-1}$	COS Return	COS Return$_{t-1}$	DM Return	DM Return$_{t-1}$
Jul-99	3020	1.72%	2.37%	16.28%	72.00%	15.79%	12.67%	0.00%	0.00%
Aug-99	2952	-2.25%	1.72%	-30.00%	16.28%	-14.54%	15.79%	-8.47%	0.00%
Sep-99	2881	-2.40%	-2.25%	28.57%	-30.00%	17.12%	-14.54%	-22.22%	-8.47%
Oct-99	2885	0.14%	-2.40%	-6.67%	28.57%	13.28%	17.12%	-2.38%	-22.22%
Nov-99	3044	5.51%	0.14%	19.05%	-6.67%	47.84%	13.28%	46.34%	-2.38%
Dec-99	3153	3.56%	5.51%	100.00%	19.05%	22.15%	47.84%	-5.00%	46.34%
Jan-00	3096	-1.79%	3.56%	0.00%	100.00%	-7.26%	22.15%	4.91%	-5.00%
Feb-00	3136	1.28%	-1.79%	0.00%	0.00%	-12.35%	-7.26%	27.09%	4.91%
Mar-00	3133	-0.08%	1.28%	0.00%	0.00%	12.81%	-12.35%	14.47%	27.09%
Apr-00	3116	-0.56%	-0.08%	180.00%	0.00%	-43.67%	12.81%	-14.94%	14.47%
May-00	3081	-1.12%	-0.56%	-3.75%	180.00%	-36.06%	-43.67%	-39.19%	-14.94%
Jun-00	3311	7.47%	-1.12%	-14.81%	-3.75%	13.53%	-36.06%	8.00%	-39.19%

Source: RBA

Table A6. 15/2 Regression Statistics

Multiple R	0.0367	0.2159	0.2537	0.0827
R Square	0.0013	0.0466	0.0643	0.0068
Adjusted R Square	-0.0985	-0.0487	-0.0292	-0.0925
Standard Error	0.0329	0.6025	0.2631	0.2343
Observations	12	12	12	12
ANOVA				
Intercept				
Coefficients	0.0093	0.3080	0.0180	0.0071
Standard Error	0.0097	0.1989	0.0763	0.0676
t Stat	0.9586	1.5486	0.2358	0.1055
P-value	0.3604	0.1525	0.8184	0.9181
Return$_{t-1}$				
Coefficients	0.0471	-0.2154	0.2540	0.0832
Standard Error	0.4060	0.3081	0.3063	0.3168
t Stat	0.1161	-0.6992	0.8293	0.2625
P-value	0.9099	0.5004	0.4263	0.7983

Table A6. 15/3 Estimation of the AR (1) Model to Test the Weak-Form of the Efficient Market Hypothesis by Sector

	ES Returns	ES Return$_{t-1}$	HMS Return	HMS Return$_{t-1}$	HT Return	HT Return$_{t-1}$	MFS Return	MFS Return$_{t-1}$
Jul-99	0.00%	38.00%	140.00%	-13.00%	-15.96%	3.00%	-19.55%	-18.00%
Aug-99	-19.88%	0.00%	4.17%	140.00%	-26.58%	-15.96%	20.25%	-19.55%
Sep-99	-4.00%	-19.88%	-10.00%	4.17%	-13.79%	-26.58%	-23.90%	20.25%
Oct-99	2.18%	-4.00%	0.00%	-10.00%	-10.00%	-13.79%	-5.20%	-23.90%
Nov-99	10.42%	2.18%	0.00%	0.00%	2.22%	-10.00%	1.43%	-5.20%
Dec-99	-0.86%	10.42%	0.00%	0.00%	-2.17%	2.22%	-12.47%	1.43%
Jan-00	-18.77%	-0.86%	0.00%	0.00%	-11.11%	-2.17%	-19.35%	-12.47%
Feb-00	488.48%	-18.77%	0.00%	0.00%	42.50%	-11.11%	3.00%	-19.35%
Mar-00	-23.34%	488.48%	2677.78%	0.00%	-14.04%	42.50%	31.07%	3.00%
Apr-00	-42.02%	-23.34%	-51.20%	2677.78%	-34.69%	-14.04%	-40.74%	31.07%
May-00	-56.84%	-42.02%	-40.98%	-51.20%	3.13%	-34.69%	-14.58%	-40.74%
Jun-00	-11.78%	-56.84%	-8.33%	-40.98%	-12.12%	3.13%	-12.68%	-14.58%

Source: RBA

Table A6. 15/4 Regression Statistics

Multiple R	0.1125	0.1136	0.1102	0.3285
R Square	0.0126	0.0129	0.0121	0.1079
Adjusted R Square	-0.0861	-0.0858	-0.0867	0.0187
Standard Error	1.5279	8.0604	0.1996	0.1939
Observations	12.0000	12.0000	12.0000	12.0000
ANOVA				
Intercept				
Coefficients	0.3048	2.5156	-0.0842	-0.1039
Standard Error	0.4518	2.4323	0.0610	0.0610
t Stat	0.6745	1.0342	-1.3801	-1.7035
P-value	0.5153	0.3254	0.1976	0.1193
Return$_{t-1}$				
Coefficients	-0.1128	-0.1135	-0.1091	-0.3255
Standard Error	0.3153	0.3141	0.3114	0.2959
t Stat	-0.3579	-0.3614	-0.3505	-1.0998
P-value	0.7279	0.7253	0.7332	0.2972

Table A6. 15/5 Estimation of the AR (1) Model to Test the Weak-Form of the Efficient Market Hypothesis by Sector

	MS Returns	MS Return$_{t-1}$	OT Returns	OT Return$_{t-1}$	RRI Returns	RRI Return$_{t-1}$	Portfolio Return	Portfolio Return$_{t-1}$
Jul-99	5.95%	-2.00%	0.06%	0.00%	-1.00%	0.00%	10.40%	0.00%
Aug-99	15.29%	5.95%	-15.68%	0.06%	-3.06%	-1.00%	-7.91%	10.40%
Sep-99	-20.30%	15.29%	-2.24%	-15.68%	-5.29%	-3.06%	-0.32%	-7.91%
Oct-99	9.34%	-20.30%	10.18%	-2.24%	23.84%	-5.29%	10.48%	-0.32%
Nov-99	17.41%	9.34%	11.12%	10.18%	20.73%	23.84%	20.74%	10.48%
Dec-99	14.86%	17.41%	40.84%	11.12%	18.43%	20.73%	17.58%	20.74%
Jan-00	76.08%	14.86%	-3.65%	40.84%	6.61%	18.43%	3.10%	17.58%
Feb-00	97.01%	76.08%	43.22%	-3.65%	33.36%	6.61%	78.58%	3.10%
Mar-00	-9.20%	97.01%	-15.41%	43.22%	0.65%	33.36%	147.66%	78.58%
Apr-00	-29.56%	-9.20%	-27.98%	-15.41%	-43.84%	0.65%	-28.86%	147.66%
May-00	-31.01%	-29.56%	-19.82%	-27.98%	-25.03%	-43.84%	-31.01%	-28.86%
Jun-00	61.93%	-31.01%	11.44%	-19.82%	50.41%	-25.03%	14.66%	-31.01%

Source: RBA

Table 6. 15/6 Regression Statistics

Multiple *R*	0.2492	0.0568	0.1301	0.1580
R Square	0.0621	0.0032	0.0169	0.0250
Adjusted *R* Square	-0.0317	-0.0964	-0.0814	-0.0725
Standard Error	0.4182	0.2338	0.2650	0.5075
Observations	12.0000	12.0000	12.0000	12.0000
ANOVA				
Intercept				
Coefficients	0.1416	0.0257	0.0599	0.1658
Standard Error	0.1268	0.0677	0.0769	0.1581
t Stat	1.1165	0.3802	0.7788	1.0487
P-value	0.2903	0.7117	0.4541	0.3190
Return$_{t-1}$				
Coefficients	0.2634	0.0573	0.1551	0.1578
Standard Error	0.3237	0.3181	0.3737	0.3117
t Stat	0.8137	0.1800	0.4149	0.5061
P-value	0.4348	0.8607	0.6869	0.6237

Appendices

Appendix 7.1

Table A7.1/1 AEMM Return Estimates

$$e\text{-}stockret(\Delta \hat{PR})_t = -0.19 + 0.0013\Delta NAS + 0.0692\Delta CC - 0.3287\Delta FE$$

Month	$e\text{-}stockret(\Delta \hat{PR})_t$	α	ΔNAS	ΔCC	ΔFE
Jul-99	18.18%	-0.19	-48	0.1	-1.3
Aug-99	1.22%	-0.19	101	-4.2	-1.1
Sep-99	-19.82%	-0.19	7	4.5	1.0
Oct-99	46.80%	-0.19	220	-0.8	-1.3
Nov-99	53.32%	-0.19	370	1.6	-0.4
Dec-99	-7.62%	-0.19	733	-6.9	1.1
Jan-00	-1.86%	-0.19	-129	3.0	-0.4
Feb-00	59.39%	-0.19	756	-10.0	-1.5
Mar-00	0.52%	-0.19	-124	-1.5	-1.4
Apr-00	-118.13%	-0.19	-712	-3.8	-0.6
May-00	-57.18%	-0.19	-460	-2.1	-1.1
Jun-00	37.67%	-0.19	565	6.6	1.9

Mean	1.04%
Variance	25.43%
Standard deviation	48.28%

Table A7.1/2 Data & Risk Profile for 2-Risky-Asset Portfolio
Consisting of AEMM Estimates and S&P/ASX 200 Returns

	Proportion of E-commerce Stock =	0.5	
	Returns		
		S&P/	2-Asset
Month	e-stockret($\Delta \hat{PR}$)$_t$	ASX 200	Portfolio
Jul-99	18.18%	1.72%	9.95%
Aug-99	1.22%	-2.25%	-0.51%
Sep-99	-19.82%	-2.40%	-11.11%
Oct-99	46.80%	0.14%	23.47%
Nov-99	53.32%	5.51%	29.42%
Dec-99	-7.62%	3.56%	-2.03%
Jan-00	-1.86%	-1.79%	-1.83%
Feb-00	59.39%	1.28%	30.33%
Mar-00	0.52%	-0.08%	0.22%
Apr-00	-118.13%	-0.56%	-59.35%
May-00	-57.18%	-1.12%	-29.15%
Jun-00	37.67%	7.47%	22.57%
Mean	1.04%	0.96%	1.00%
Variance	25.43%	0.10%	6.76%
Standard deviation	48.28%	3.00%	24.89%

Proportion	Sigma	Expected Return	Coefficient of Variation
	24.89%	1.00%	
0	3.00%	0.96%	3.14
0.05	4.53%	0.96%	4.71
0.1	6.56%	0.97%	6.80
0.15	8.75%	0.97%	9.03
0.2	11.00%	0.97%	11.30
0.25	13.29%	0.98%	13.60
0.3	15.60%	0.98%	15.88
0.35	17.91%	0.99%	18.16
0.4	20.23%	0.99%	20.43
0.45	22.56%	0.99%	22.69
0.5	24.89%	1.00%	24.93
0.55	27.23%	1.00%	27.15
0.6	29.56%	1.01%	29.36
0.65	31.90%	1.01%	31.54
0.7	34.24%	1.02%	33.72
0.75	36.58%	1.02%	35.87
0.8	38.92%	1.02%	38.01
0.85	41.26%	1.03%	40.13
0.9	43.60%	1.03%	42.24
0.95	45.94%	1.04%	44.33
1	48.28%	1.04%	46.40

Table A7.1/3 Correlation Coefficient – AEMM Estimates & S&P/ASX 200

	e-stockret(ΔPR)$_t$	S&P/ASX 200
e-stockret(ΔPR)$_t$	1	
S&P/ASX 200	0.476342228	1

Appendix 7.2

Table A7.2/1 Risk Profile –Data for Two Risky Asset Portfolio
Consisting of E-Commerce and S&P/ASX 200 Stocks
Proportion of E-Stock =   0.5

	Returns		
	E-Stock	S&P/	2-Asset
		ASX	Portfoli
Month	Portfolio	200	o
Jul-99	10.40%	1.72%	6.06%
Aug-99	-7.91%	-2.25%	-5.08%
Sep-99	-0.32%	-2.40%	-1.36%
Oct-99	10.48%	0.14%	5.31%
Nov-99	20.74%	5.51%	13.13%
Dec-99	17.58%	3.56%	10.57%
Jan-00	3.10%	-1.79%	0.66%
Feb-00	78.58%	1.28%	39.93%
Mar-00	147.66%	-0.08%	73.79%
Apr-00	-28.86%	-0.56%	-14.71%
May-00	-31.01%	-1.12%	-16.07%
Jun-00	14.66%	7.47%	11.07%
Mean	19.59%	0.96%	10.27%
Variance	24.01%	0.10%	5.62%
Standard deviation	46.91%	3.00%	23.71%

Table A7.2/2 Correlation Coefficient of E-Commerce and

S&P ASX 200 Portfolios

	E-Commerce Portfolio	S&P/ASX 200
E-Commerce Portfolio	1	
S&P/ASX 200	0.138207	1

Table A7.2/3 Portfolio Risk Profile – Two Risky Asset Portfolio
Consisting of E-Commerce and S&P/ASX 200 Stocks

Proportion	Sigma	Exp. Return	Coefficient of Variation
	23.71%	10.27%	
0	3.00%	0.96%	3.14
0.05	3.93%	1.89%	2.08
0.1	5.73%	2.82%	2.03
0.15	7.81%	3.75%	2.08
0.2	10.00%	4.68%	2.14
0.25	12.24%	5.62%	2.18
0.3	14.51%	6.55%	2.22
0.35	16.80%	7.48%	2.25
0.4	19.10%	8.41%	2.27
0.45	21.40%	9.34%	2.29
0.5	23.71%	10.27%	2.31
0.55	26.02%	11.21%	2.32
0.6	28.34%	12.14%	2.33
0.65	30.66%	13.07%	2.35
0.7	32.98%	14.00%	2.36
0.75	35.30%	14.93%	2.36
0.8	37.62%	15.86%	2.37
0.85	39.94%	16.80%	2.38
0.9	42.27%	17.73%	2.38
0.95	44.59%	18.66%	2.39
1	46.91%	19.59%	2.39

Appendix 7.3

Table A7.3/1 Monthly Stock Returns/Means/Standard Deviations/Betas of E-Commerce Sectors

	Casino & Gaming	Comp. & Off. Serv.	Div. Media	Equip & Services	Health & Medical	High Technology	Misc. Fin Serv.	Misc. Serv.	Other Telcom.	Retail & Ret. Inv.	S&P/ ASX 200
1999 Jul	16.28%	15.79%	0.00%	0.00%	140.00%	-15.96%	-19.55%	5.95%	0.06%	-1.00%	1.72%
Aug	-30.00%	-14.54%	-8.47%	-19.88%	4.17%	-26.58%	20.25%	15.29%	-15.68%	-3.06%	-2.25%
Sep	28.57%	17.12%	-22.22%	-4.00%	-10.00%	-13.79%	-23.90%	-20.30%	-2.24%	-5.29%	-2.40%
Oct	-6.67%	13.28%	-2.38%	2.18%	0.00%	-10.00%	-5.20%	9.34%	10.18%	23.84%	0.14%
Nov	19.05%	47.84%	46.34%	10.42%	0.00%	2.22%	1.43%	17.41%	11.12%	20.73%	5.51%
Dec	100.00%	22.15%	-5.00%	-0.86%	0.00%	-2.17%	-12.47%	14.86%	40.84%	18.43%	3.56%
2000 Jan	0.00%	-7.26%	4.91%	-18.77%	0.00%	-11.11%	-19.35%	76.08%	-3.65%	6.61%	-1.79%
Feb	0.00%	-12.35%	27.09%	488.48%	2677.78%	42.50%	3.00%	97.01%	43.22%	33.36%	1.28%
Mar	0.00%	12.81%	14.47%	-23.34%	-51.20%	-14.04%	31.07%	-9.20%	-15.41%	0.65%	-0.08%
Apr	180.00%	-43.67%	-14.94%	-42.02%	-40.98%	-34.69%	-40.74%	-29.56%	-27.98%	-43.84%	-0.56%
May	-3.75%	-36.06%	-39.19%	-56.84%	-8.33%	3.13%	-14.58%	-31.01%	-19.82%	-25.03%	-1.12%
Jun	-14.81%	13.53%	8.00%	-11.78%	0.00%	-12.12%	-12.68%	61.93%	11.44%	50.41%	7.47%
Mean	24.06%	2.39%	0.72%	26.97%	225.95%	-7.72%	-7.73%	17.32%	2.67%	6.32%	0.96%
Variance	31.73%	6.17%	4.61%	197.04%	5484.95%	3.36%	3.51%	15.54%	4.57%	5.95%	0.09%
Standard Dev.	56.33%	24.83%	21.46%	140.37%	740.60%	18.33%	18.74%	39.42%	21.38%	24.40%	3.00%
Beta	0.03	4.61	4.05	4.25	-23.51	1.46	0.09	4.43	3.74	5.45	

Regressing the means on the betas:

Intercept	0.3267
Slope	-0.0775
R-squared	91.00%

Appendix 7.4

Table A7.4/1Excess Return Matrix of E-Commerce Sectors by Month

	Casino & Gaming	Comp. & Off. Serv.	Div. Media	Equip & Services	Health & Medical	High Technology	Misc. Fin Serv.	Misc. Serv.	Other Telcom.	Retail & Ret. Inv.
1999 Jul	-0.0778	0.1572	-0.0067	-0.2697	1.3961	-0.1470	-0.1999	0.0054	-0.0261	-0.0520
Aug	-0.5406	-0.1461	-0.0914	-0.4685	0.0378	-0.2532	0.1981	0.0988	-0.1835	-0.0726
Sep	0.0451	0.1705	-0.2289	-0.3097	-0.1039	-0.1253	-0.2434	-0.2571	-0.0491	-0.0949
Oct	-0.3073	0.1321	-0.0305	-0.2479	-0.0039	-0.0874	-0.0564	0.0393	0.0751	0.1964
Nov	-0.0501	0.4777	0.4567	-0.1655	-0.0039	0.0348	0.0099	0.1200	0.0845	0.1653
Dec	0.7594	0.2208	-0.0567	-0.2783	-0.0039	-0.0091	-0.1291	0.0945	0.3817	0.1423
2000 Jan	-0.2406	-0.0733	0.0424	-0.4574	-0.0039	-0.0985	-0.1979	0.7067	-0.0632	0.0241
Feb	-0.2406	-0.1242	0.2642	4.6151	26.7739	0.4376	0.0256	0.9160	0.4055	0.2916
Mar	-0.2406	0.1274	0.1380	-0.5031	-0.5159	-0.1278	0.3063	-0.1461	-0.1808	-0.0355
Apr	1.5594	-0.4374	-0.1561	-0.6899	-0.4137	-0.3343	-0.4118	-0.3497	-0.3065	-0.4804
May	-0.2781	-0.3613	-0.3986	-0.8381	-0.4137	0.0439	-0.1502	-0.3642	-0.2249	-0.2923
Jun	-0.3887	0.1346	0.0733	-0.3875	-0.0872	-0.1086	-0.1312	0.5652	0.0877	0.4621

Appendix 7.5

Table A7.5/1 Transpose of Excess Return Matrix for E-Commerce Sectors

	Jul	Aug	Sep	Oct	Nov	Dec	Jan	Feb	Mar	Apr	May	Jun
C&G	-0.0778	-0.5406	0.0451	-0.3073	-0.0501	0.7594	-0.2406	-0.2406	-0.2406	1.5594	-0.2781	-0.3887
COS	0.1572	-0.1461	0.1705	0.1321	0.4777	0.2208	-0.0733	-0.1242	0.1274	-0.4374	-0.3613	0.1346
DM	-0.0067	-0.0914	-0.2289	-0.0305	0.4567	-0.0567	0.0424	0.2642	0.1380	-0.1561	-0.3986	0.0733
E&S	-0.2697	-0.4685	-0.3097	-0.2479	-0.1655	-0.2783	-0.4574	4.6151	-0.5031	-0.6899	-0.8381	-0.3875
H&M	1.3961	0.0378	-0.1039	-0.0039	-0.0039	-0.0039	-0.0039	-0.0039	26.7739	-0.5159	-0.4137	-0.0872
HT	-0.1470	-0.2532	-0.1253	-0.0874	0.0348	-0.0091	-0.0985	0.4376	-0.1278	-0.3343	0.0439	-0.1086
MFS	-0.1999	0.1981	-0.2434	-0.0564	0.0099	-0.1291	-0.1979	0.0256	0.3063	-0.4118	-0.1502	-0.1312
MS	0.0054	0.0988	-0.2571	0.0393	0.1200	0.0945	0.7067	0.9160	-0.1461	-0.3497	-0.3642	0.5652
OT	-0.0261	-0.1835	-0.0491	0.0751	0.0845	0.3817	-0.0632	0.4055	-0.1808	-0.3065	-0.2249	0.0877
R&RI	-0.0520	-0.0726	-0.0949	0.1964	0.1653	0.1423	0.0241	0.2916	-0.0355	-0.4804	-0.2923	0.4621

Table A7.5/2 Variance-Covariance Matrix for the E-Commerce Sectors

	C&G	COS	DM	E&S	H&M	HT	MFS	MS	OT	R&RI	Mean Return	Mean minus constant
C&G	3.8078	-0.4395	-0.2850	-1.4380	-7.2308	-0.3813	-0.7654	-1.0308	-0.1268	-0.8364	0.2406	0.1843
COS	-0.4395	0.7465	0.3787	-0.2514	3.9681	0.0479	0.1340	0.2024	0.3073	0.4580	0.0239	-0.0324
DM	-0.2850	0.3787	0.5528	1.6071	3.9422	0.1924	0.2077	0.5910	0.2663	0.3887	0.0072	-0.0491
E&S	-1.4380	-0.2514	1.6071	23.6444	-13.1091	2.5804	0.6001	4.2811	2.3266	1.7117	0.2697	0.2134
H&M	-7.2308	3.9681	3.9422	-13.1091	719.2480	-3.4608	8.2419	-3.5992	-4.6389	-0.6907	2.2595	2.2032
HT	-0.3813	0.0479	0.1924	2.5804	-3.4608	0.4534	0.1530	0.3957	0.3392	0.2526	-0.0772	-0.1335
MFS	-0.7654	0.1340	0.2077	0.6001	8.2419	0.1530	0.5014	0.0312	0.0441	0.1642	-0.0773	-0.1336
MS	-1.0308	0.2024	0.5910	4.2811	-3.5992	0.3957	0.0312	2.0350	0.6354	0.8829	0.1732	0.1169
OT	-0.1268	0.3073	0.2663	2.3266	-4.6389	0.3392	0.0441	0.6354	0.5486	0.4790	0.0267	-0.0296
R&RI	-0.8364	0.4580	0.3887	1.7117	-0.6907	0.2526	0.1642	0.8829	0.4790	0.7198	0.0632	0.0069

Constant 0.0563

Appendix 7.6

Table A7.6/1 Calculating the Efficient Frontier

z	x		z	y
0.9073	0.5876		0.3110	-0.9981
2.0886	1.3526		0.8169	-2.6218
-2.4327	-1.5755		-1.0508	3.3721
0.1913	0.1239		0.1750	-0.5617
-0.0073	-0.0047		-0.0001	0.0003
0.8934	0.5786		-0.3068	0.9846
1.1815	0.7652		0.2070	-0.6642
1.0259	0.6644		0.2827	-0.9072
-3.3704	-2.1827		-1.3826	4.4370
1.0665	0.6907		0.6360	-2.0410
1.5441			-0.3116	

Transpose x

0.5876	1.3526	-1.5755	0.1239	-0.0047	0.5786	0.7652	0.6644	-2.1827	0.6907

Transpose y

-0.9981	-2.6218	3.3721	-0.5617	0.0003	0.9846	-0.6642	-0.9072	4.4370	-2.0410

Mean (x)	0.1817		Mean (y)	-0.6213
Var(x)	0.1177		Var(y)	2.1744
Sigma(x)	0.3430		Sigma(y)	1.4746

Cov(x,y)	0.1177
Corr(x,y)	0.2326

Proportion of x 0.3

x	y	Portfolio
0.5876	-0.9981	-0.5224
1.3526	-2.6218	-1.4295
-1.5755	3.3721	1.8878
0.1239	-0.5617	-0.3560
-0.0047	0.0003	-0.0012
0.5786	0.9846	0.8628
0.7652	-0.6642	-0.2354
0.6644	-0.9072	-0.4357
-2.1827	4.4370	2.4511
0.6907	-2.0410	-1.2215
	Mean	0.1000
	Variance	1.4397
	St. dev.	1.1999

Appendix 7.7

Table A7.7/1 Data Table for Efficient Frontier Graph

Proportion of x	Sigma 1.1999	Return 0.1000
-0.4	3.3890	0.10001677
-0.3	3.0749	0.10001553
-0.2	2.7610	0.10001429
-0.1	2.4473	0.10001305
0	2.1341	0.10001181
0.1	1.8214	0.10001057
0.2	1.5098	0.10000933
0.3	1.1999	0.10000809
0.4	0.8935	0.10000685
0.5	0.5962	0.10000561
0.6	0.3331	0.10000437
0.7	0.2549	0.10000313
0.8	0.4662	0.10000190
0.9	0.7538	0.10000066
1	1.0571	0.09999942
1.1	1.3658	0.09999818
1.2	1.6768	0.09999694
1.3	1.9890	0.09999570
1.4	2.3020	0.09999446
1.5	2.6155	0.09999322
1.6	2.9293	0.09999198
1.7	3.2433	0.09999074
1.8	3.5575	0.09998950
1.9	3.8718	0.09998826
2	4.1863	0.09998702

Appendix 7.8

Table A7.8/1 The E-Commerce Sector
Data for Testing the CAPM

	Mean	Beta
C&G	24.06%	0.03
COS	2.39%	4.61
DM	0.72%	4.05
E&S	26.97%	4.25
H&M	225.95%	-23.51
HT	-7.72%	1.46
MFS	-7.73%	0.09
MS	17.32%	4.43
OT	2.67%	3.74
R&RI	6.32%	5.45

Table A7.8/2 Summary Output/ANOVA of Regression of the Means
on Betas to Test the CAPM with The E-Commerce Sector Data

Regression Statistics

Multiple R	0.9539
R Square	0.9098
Adjusted R Square	0.8986
Standard Error	0.2236
Observations	10.0000

ANOVA

	df	SS	MS	F	Significance F
Regression	1.0000	4.0367	4.0367	80.7301	0.0000
Residual	8.0000	0.4000	0.0500		
Total	9.0000	4.4367			

	Coefficients	Standard Error	t Stat	P-value	Lower 95%	Upper 95%	Lower 95.0%	Upper 95.0%
Intercept	0.3266	0.0708	4.6116	0.0017	0.1633	0.4899	0.1633	0.4899
Beta	-0.0775	0.0086	-8.9850	0.0000	-0.0974	-0.0576	-0.0974	-0.0576

Critical value at 10% significance (two-sided test)   1.8600*
  *(for $n = 10$; $k = 2$; $df = 8$)

Appendix 7.9

Table A7.9/1 Risk Profile of a Portfolio with
E-Commerce, S&P/ASX 200 Stocks and Cash

	Actual Return	
	E-Stock	S&P/
Month	Portfolio	ASX 200
Jul-99	10%	2%
Aug-99	-8%	-2%
Sep-99	0%	-2%
Oct-99	10%	0%
Nov-99	21%	6%
Dec-99	18%	4%
Jan-00	3%	-2%
Feb-00	79%	1%
Mar-00	148%	0%
Apr-00	-29%	-1%
May-00	-31%	-1%
Jun-00	15%	7%
Expected Return	19.59%	0.96%

Table A7.9/2 Covariance Matrix of E-Commerce Portfolio and
SAP/ASX 200

	E-Comm. Portfolio	S&P/ASX 200
E-Comm. Portfolio	0.220093	
S&P/ASX 200	0.001946	0.000901

Table A7.8/1 Portfolio Optimisation Problem
Max:
$$19.95x_1 + .96x_2 + x_3 - \lambda(.22x_1^2 + .0009x_1x_2 + .0019x_2x_1 + .0009x_2^2)$$

Subject to:
$$14.66x_1 + 7.47x_2 + x_3 = 10,000$$
$$x_1, x_2, x_3 \geq 0$$

Appendix 7.10

GAMS Program Listing - Input and Output Data

GAMS 2.25.085 386/486 DOS   01/04/80 15:44:13 PAGE   1
General Algebraic Modeling System
Compilation

1	* The GAMS Program PORTCHOICE to solve the optimal portfolio choice problem to determine optimal value and allocation of e-commerce stocks discussed in Chapter Seven.
2	
3	*2 aggregate stocks are ESTOCK = e-commerce stock, MKT = market stock
4	
5	SETS
6	I 2 aggregate stocks / ESTOCK, MKT /
7	N months / 1*12 /
8	
9	ALIAS (I,J) ;
10	
11	TABLE P(I,N) prices of stocks
12	1 2 3 4 5 6 7 8 9 10 11 12
13	ESTOCK 10 -8 0 10 21 18 3 79 148 -29 -31 15
14	MKT 2 -2 -2 0 6 4 -2 1 0 0 -1 7
15	
16	PARAMETER EXPV(I) expected price of stock I;
17	EXPV(I) = SUM(N,P(I,N))/12;
18	DISPLAY EXPV;
19	
20	PARAMETER COVM(I,J) covariance matrix showing variance and covariance between stocks I and J;
21	COVM(I,J) = SUM(N, (P(I,N) - EXPV(I))*(P(J,N) - EXPV(J))/12);
22	DISPLAY COVM;
23	
24	SCALAR LAMBDA risk attitude;
25	LAMBDA = 0.0005;
26	
27	VARIABLES
28	UTILITY objective function to be maximized;
29	
30	POSITIVE VARIABLES
31	CASH cash in the sector
32	Y(I) investment in stock I
33	EXPP mathematical expection of portfolio
34	VARP variance of portfolio;
35	
36	EQUATIONS
37	OBJECTIVE

```
38            DEFEXPP
39            DEFVARP
40            ECSMCAP;
41
42            OBJECTIVE..   UTILITY =E= EXPP+CASH-LAMBDA*VARP;
43            DEFEXPP..     EXPP =L= SUM(I,EXPV(I)*Y(I));
44            DEFVARP..     VARP =G= SUM((I,J),COVM(I,J)*Y(I)*Y(J));
45            ECSMCAP..     SUM(I,P(I,"12")*Y(I))+CASH =L= 856225;
46
47
```

GAMS 2.25.085 386/486 DOS   01/04/80 15:44:13 PAGE   2
General Algebraic Modeling System
Compilation

```
48            MODEL PORTCHOICE /ALL/;
49
50            SOLVE PORTCHOICE MAXIMIZING UTILITY  USING NLP;
51
52            display CASH.l, Y.l, EXPP.l, VARP.l;
53
54            LAMBDA=0.0006;
55            SOLVE PORTCHOICE  MAXIMIZING UTILITY  USING NLP;
56
57            LAMBDA=0.0007;
58            SOLVE PORTCHOICE  MAXIMIZING UTILITY  USING NLP;
59
60            LAMBDA=0.0008;
61            SOLVE PORTCHOICE  MAXIMIZING UTILITY  USING NLP;
62
63            LAMBDA=0.0009;
64            SOLVE PORTCHOICE  MAXIMIZING UTILITY  USING NLP;
65
66            LAMBDA=0.0010;
67            SOLVE PORTCHOICE  MAXIMIZING UTILITY  USING NLP;
68
69            LAMBDA=0.0015;
70            SOLVE PORTCHOICE MAXIMIZING UTILITY  USING NLP;
71
72            LAMBDA=0.0020;
73            SOLVE PORTCHOICE  MAXIMIZING UTILITY  USING NLP;
```

GAMS 2.25.085 386/486 DOS   01/04/80 15:44:13 PAGE   4
General Algebraic Modeling System
Symbol Listing

SETS

```
I        2 aggregate stocks
J        Aliased with I
N        months
```

PARAMETERS

COVM	covariance matrix showing variance and covariance between stocks I and J
EXPV	expected price of stock I
LAMBDA	risk attitude
P	prices of stocks

VARIABLES

CASH	cash in the sector
EXPP	mathematical expection of portfolio
UTILITY	objective function to be maximized
VARP	variance of portfolio
Y	investment in stock I

EQUATIONS

DEFEXPP
DEFVARP
ECSMCAP
OBJECTIVE

MODELS

PORTCHOICE

COMPILATION TIME   =   0.170 SECONDS   VERID MW2-25-085

GAMS 2.25.085 386/486 DOS   01/04/80 15:44:13 PAGE   5
General Algebraic Modeling System
Execution

----   18 PARAMETER EXPV   expected price of stock I

ESTOCK 19.667, MKT   1.083

----   22 PARAMETER COVM   covariance matrix showing variance and
                              covariance between stocks I and J

	ESTOCK	MKT
ESTOCK	2214.056	15.611
MKT	15.611	8.743

GAMS 2.25.085 386/486 DOS   01/04/80 15:44:13 PAGE   8
General Algebraic Modeling System
Model Statistics   SOLVE PORTCHOICE USING NLP FROM LINE 50

MODEL STATISTICS

BLOCKS OF EQUATIONS	4	SINGLE EQUATIONS	4
BLOCKS OF VARIABLES	5	SINGLE VARIABLES	6
NON ZERO ELEMENTS	13	NON LINEAR N-Z	2
DERIVATIVE POOL	7	CONSTANT POOL	11
CODE LENGTH	69		

GENERATION TIME   =   0.830 SECONDS

EXECUTION TIME   =   0.930 SECONDS   VERID MW2-25-085

GAMS 2.25.085 386/486 DOS   01/04/80 15:44:13 PAGE   9
General Algebraic Modeling System
Solution Report   SOLVE PORTCHOICE USING NLP FROM LINE 50

       S O L V E   S U M M A R Y

     MODEL   PORTCHOICE   OBJECTIVE   UTILITY
     TYPE   NLP   DIRECTION   MAXIMIZE
     SOLVER   MINOS5   FROM LINE   50

**** SOLVER STATUS   1 NORMAL COMPLETION
**** MODEL STATUS   2 LOCALLY OPTIMAL
**** OBJECTIVE VALUE   856229.9181

RESOURCE USAGE, LIMIT   0.330   1000.000
ITERATION COUNT, LIMIT   5   1000
EVALUATION ERRORS   0   0

       LOWER   LEVEL   UPPER   MARGINAL

---- EQU OBJECTIVE   .   .   .   -1.000
---- EQU DEFEXPP   -INF   .   .   1.000
---- EQU DEFVARP   .   .   +INF -5.000E-4
---- EQU ECSMCAP   -INF 8.5623E+5 8.5623E+5   1.000

       LOWER   LEVEL   UPPER   MARGINAL

---- VAR UTILITY   -INF 8.5623E+5   +INF   .
---- VAR CASH   .   8.5619E+5   +INF   .

     UTILITY   objective function to be maximized
     CASH   cash in the sector

GAMS 2.25.085 386/486 DOS   01/04/80 15:44:13 PAGE   10
General Algebraic Modeling System
Solution Report   SOLVE PORTCHOICE USING NLP FROM LINE 50

---- VAR Y   investment in stock I

       LOWER   LEVEL   UPPER   MARGINAL

```
ESTOCK        .    2.108   +INF    EPS
MKT           .      .     +INF   -5.950

              LOWER   LEVEL   UPPER   MARGINAL

---- VAR EXPP        .   41.452    +INF    .
---- VAR VARP        . 9836.148    +INF    .

   EXPP      mathematical expection of portfolio
   VARP      variance of portfolio


**** REPORT SUMMARY :     0       NONOPT
                          0       INFEASIBLE
                          0       UNBOUNDED
                          0       ERRORS
```

 GAMS 2.25.085 386/486 DOS   01/04/80 15:44:13 PAGE   13
General Algebraic Modeling System
Column Listing   SOLVE PORTCHOICE USING NLP FROM LINE 55

Model Statistics   SOLVE PORTCHOICE USING NLP FROM LINE 55

MODEL STATISTICS

```
BLOCKS OF EQUATIONS      4      SINGLE EQUATIONS      4
BLOCKS OF VARIABLES      5      SINGLE VARIABLES      6
NON ZERO ELEMENTS       13      NON LINEAR N-Z        2
DERIVATIVE POOL          7      CONSTANT POOL        11
CODE LENGTH             69
```

GENERATION TIME   =   1.040 SECONDS

EXECUTION TIME   =   1.260 SECONDS   VERID MW2-25-085

GAMS 2.25.085 386/486 DOS   01/04/80 15:44:13 PAGE   15
General Algebraic Modeling System
Solution Report   SOLVE PORTCHOICE USING NLP FROM LINE 55

        S O L V E   S U M M A R Y

    MODEL   PORTCHOICE   OBJECTIVE UTILITY
    TYPE   NLP   DIRECTION MAXIMIZE
    SOLVER MINOS5   FROM LINE 55

**** SOLVER STATUS   1 NORMAL COMPLETION
**** MODEL STATUS   2 LOCALLY OPTIMAL
**** OBJECTIVE VALUE   856229.0984

```
RESOURCE USAGE, LIMIT      0.330        1000.000
ITERATION COUNT, LIMIT     3            1000
EVALUATION ERRORS          0            0
```

```
        LOWER   LEVEL   UPPER   MARGINAL

---- EQU OBJECTIVE          .      .      .    -1.000
---- EQU DEFEXPP          -INF     .      .     1.000
---- EQU DEFVARP            .      .    +INF  -6.000E-4
---- EQU ECSMCAP          -INF 8.5623E+5 8.5623E+5  1.000

        LOWER   LEVEL   UPPER   MARGINAL

---- VAR UTILITY      -INF 8.5623E+5  +INF     .
---- VAR CASH           .  8.5620E+5  +INF     .

    UTILITY   objective function to be maximized
    CASH      cash in the sector
```

GAMS 2.25.085 386/486 DOS   01/04/80 15:44:13 PAGE   16
General Algebraic Modeling System
Solution Report   SOLVE PORTCHOICE USING NLP FROM LINE 55

```
---- VAR Y       investment in stock I

        LOWER   LEVEL   UPPER   MARGINAL

ESTOCK      .   1.756   +INF   EPS
MKT         .     .     +INF  -5.950

        LOWER   LEVEL   UPPER   MARGINAL

---- VAR EXPP     .   34.544   +INF    .
---- VAR VARP     .  6830.661  +INF    .

    EXPP   mathematical expection of portfolio
    VARP   variance of portfolio
```

Model Statistics   SOLVE PORTCHOICE USING NLP FROM LINE 58

MODEL STATISTICS

```
BLOCKS OF EQUATIONS       4    SINGLE EQUATIONS      4
BLOCKS OF VARIABLES       5    SINGLE VARIABLES      6
NON ZERO ELEMENTS        13    NON LINEAR N-Z        2
DERIVATIVE POOL           7    CONSTANT POOL        11
CODE LENGTH              69
```

GENERATION TIME   =   1.100 SECONDS

EXECUTION TIME   =   1.320 SECONDS   VERID MW2-25-085

Solution Report   SOLVE PORTCHOICE USING NLP FROM LINE 58

S O L V E   S U M M A R Y

MODEL PORTCHOICE	OBJECTIVE UTILITY
TYPE NLP	DIRECTION MAXIMIZE
SOLVER MINOS5	FROM LINE 58

**** SOLVER STATUS	1 NORMAL COMPLETION
**** MODEL STATUS	2 LOCALLY OPTIMAL
**** OBJECTIVE VALUE	856228.5129

RESOURCE USAGE, LIMIT	0.280	1000.000
ITERATION COUNT, LIMIT	4	1000
EVALUATION ERRORS	0	0

LOWER   LEVEL   UPPER   MARGINAL

---- EQU OBJECTIVE	.	.	.	-1.000
---- EQU DEFEXPP	-INF	.	.	1.000
---- EQU DEFVARP	.	.	+INF	-7.000E-4
---- EQU ECSMCAP	-INF	8.5623E+5	8.5623E+5	1.000

LOWER   LEVEL   UPPER   MARGINAL

| ---- VAR UTILITY | -INF | 8.5623E+5 | +INF | . |
| ---- VAR CASH | . | 8.5620E+5 | +INF | . |

| UTILITY | objective function to be maximized |
| CASH | cash in the sector |

Solution Report   SOLVE PORTCHOICE USING NLP FROM LINE 58

---- VAR Y   investment in stock I

LOWER   LEVEL   UPPER   MARGINAL

| ESTOCK | . | 1.506 | +INF | EPS |
| MKT | . | . | +INF | -5.950 |

LOWER   LEVEL   UPPER   MARGINAL

| ---- VAR EXPP | . | 29.609 | +INF | . |
| ---- VAR VARP | . | 5018.442 | +INF | . |

| EXPP | mathematical expection of portfolio |
| VARP | variance of portfolio |

**** REPORT SUMMARY :	0	NONOPT
	0	INFEASIBLE
	0	UNBOUNDED
	0	ERRORS

Model Statistics   SOLVE PORTCHOICE USING NLP FROM LINE 61

MODEL STATISTICS

BLOCKS OF EQUATIONS	4	SINGLE EQUATIONS	4
BLOCKS OF VARIABLES	5	SINGLE VARIABLES	6
NON ZERO ELEMENTS	13	NON LINEAR N-Z	2
DERIVATIVE POOL	7	CONSTANT POOL	11
CODE LENGTH	69		

GENERATION TIME   =   1.040 SECONDS

EXECUTION TIME   =   1.210 SECONDS   VERID MW2-25-085

        S O L V E   S U M M A R Y

MODEL PORTCHOICE	OBJECTIVE UTILITY	
TYPE NLP	DIRECTION MAXIMIZE	
SOLVER MINOS5	FROM LINE 61	

**** SOLVER STATUS   1 NORMAL COMPLETION
**** MODEL STATUS   2 LOCALLY OPTIMAL
**** OBJECTIVE VALUE   856228.0738

RESOURCE USAGE, LIMIT	0.330	1000.000
ITERATION COUNT, LIMIT	3	1000
EVALUATION ERRORS	0	0

           LOWER   LEVEL   UPPER   MARGINAL

	LOWER	LEVEL	UPPER	MARGINAL
---- EQU OBJECTIVE	.	.	.	-1.000
---- EQU DEFEXPP	-INF	.	.	1.000
---- EQU DEFVARP	.	.	+INF	-8.000E-4
---- EQU ECSMCAP	-INF	8.5623E+5	8.5623E+5	1.000

           LOWER   LEVEL   UPPER   MARGINAL

	LOWER	LEVEL	UPPER	MARGINAL
---- VAR UTILITY	-INF	8.5623E+5	+INF	.
---- VAR CASH	.	8.5621E+5	+INF	.

UTILITY	objective function to be maximized
CASH	cash in the sector

Solution Report   SOLVE PORTCHOICE USING NLP FROM LINE 61

---- VAR Y   investment in stock I

        LOWER   LEVEL   UPPER   MARGINAL

	LOWER	LEVEL	UPPER	MARGINAL
ESTOCK	.	1.317	+INF	EPS
MKT	.	.	+INF	-5.950

```
            LOWER   LEVEL   UPPER   MARGINAL

---- VAR EXPP      .     25.908   +INF    .
---- VAR VARP      .   3842.246   +INF    .
```

EXPP   mathematical expection of portfolio
VARP   variance of portfolio

```
**** REPORT SUMMARY :       0       NONOPT
                            0       INFEASIBLE
                            0       UNBOUNDED
                            0       ERRORS
```

GAMS 2.25.085 386/486 DOS   01/04/80 15:44:13 PAGE   29
G e n e r a l A l g e b r a i c M o d e l i n g S y s t e m
Model Statistics   SOLVE PORTCHOICE USING NLP FROM LINE 64

MODEL STATISTICS

BLOCKS OF EQUATIONS	4	SINGLE EQUATIONS	4
BLOCKS OF VARIABLES	5	SINGLE VARIABLES	6
NON ZERO ELEMENTS	13	NON LINEAR N-Z	2
DERIVATIVE POOL	7	CONSTANT POOL	11
CODE LENGTH	69		

GENERATION TIME   =   0.990 SECONDS

EXECUTION TIME   =   1.210 SECONDS   VERID MW2-25-085

GAMS 2.25.085 386/486 DOS   01/04/80 15:44:13 PAGE   30
G e n e r a l A l g e b r a i c M o d e l i n g S y s t e m
Solution Report   SOLVE PORTCHOICE USING NLP FROM LINE 64

          S O L V E   S U M M A R Y

    MODEL PORTCHOICE   OBJECTIVE UTILITY
    TYPE NLP   DIRECTION MAXIMIZE
    SOLVER MINOS5   FROM LINE 64

**** SOLVER STATUS   1 NORMAL COMPLETION
**** MODEL STATUS   2 LOCALLY OPTIMAL
**** OBJECTIVE VALUE   856227.7323

RESOURCE USAGE, LIMIT   0.330   1000.000
ITERATION COUNT, LIMIT   4   1000
EVALUATION ERRORS   0   0
```
```

Work space allocated   --   0.04 Mb

EXIT -- OPTIMAL SOLUTION FOUND
MAJOR ITNS, LIMIT   . 5   200
FUNOBJ, FUNCON CALLS   0   25
SUPERBASICS   1
INTERPRETER USAGE   0.05
NORM RG / NORM PI   5.938E-08

              LOWER   LEVEL   UPPER   MARGINAL

---- EQU OBJECTIVE   .   .   .   -1.000
---- EQU DEFEXPP   -INF   .   1.000
---- EQU DEFVARP   .   .   +INF -9.000E-4
---- EQU ECSMCAP   -INF 8.5623E+5 8.5623E+5   1.000

              LOWER   LEVEL   UPPER   MARGINAL

---- VAR UTILITY   -INF 8.5623E+5 +INF   .
---- VAR CASH   . 8.5621E+5 +INF   .

UTILITY   objective function to be maximized
CASH   cash in the sector

GAMS 2.25.085 386/486 DOS   01/04/80 15:44:13 PAGE   31
General Algebraic Modeling System
Solution Report   SOLVE PORTCHOICE USING NLP FROM LINE 64

---- VAR Y   investment in stock I

            LOWER   LEVEL   UPPER   MARGINAL

ESTOCK   .   1.171   +INF   EPS
MKT   .   .   +INF   -5.950

              LOWER   LEVEL   UPPER   MARGINAL

---- VAR EXPP   .   23.029   +INF   .
---- VAR VARP   . 3035.848 +INF   .

EXPP   mathematical expection of portfolio
VARP   variance of portfolio

**** REPORT SUMMARY :   0   NONOPT
                             0   INFEASIBLE
                             0   UNBOUNDED
                             0   ERRORS

GAMS 2.25.085 386/486 DOS   01/04/80 15:44:13 PAGE   32
General Algebraic Modeling System

GAMS 2.25.085 386/486 DOS   01/04/80 15:44:13 PAGE   34
General Algebraic Modeling System
Model Statistics   SOLVE PORTCHOICE USING NLP FROM LINE 67

MODEL STATISTICS

BLOCKS OF EQUATIONS	4	SINGLE EQUATIONS	4
BLOCKS OF VARIABLES	5	SINGLE VARIABLES	6
NON ZERO ELEMENTS	13	NON LINEAR N-Z	2
DERIVATIVE POOL	7	CONSTANT POOL	11
CODE LENGTH	69		

GENERATION TIME   =   1.100 SECONDS

EXECUTION TIME   =   1.270 SECONDS   VERID MW2-25-085

GAMS 2.25.085 386/486 DOS   01/04/80 15:44:13 PAGE   35
General Algebraic Modeling System
Solution Report   SOLVE PORTCHOICE USING NLP FROM LINE 67

SOLVE   SUMMARY

MODEL   PORTCHOICE   OBJECTIVE UTILITY
TYPE   NLP   DIRECTION MAXIMIZE
SOLVER   MINOS5   FROM LINE 67

**** SOLVER STATUS   1 NORMAL COMPLETION
**** MODEL STATUS   2 LOCALLY OPTIMAL
**** OBJECTIVE VALUE   856227.4590

RESOURCE USAGE, LIMIT   0.330   1000.000
ITERATION COUNT, LIMIT   4   1000
EVALUATION ERRORS   0   0

EXIT -- OPTIMAL SOLUTION FOUND
MAJOR ITNS, LIMIT   5   200
FUNOBJ, FUNCON CALLS   0   25
SUPERBASICS   1
INTERPRETER USAGE   0.00
NORM RG / NORM PI   4.941E-08

LOWER   LEVEL   UPPER   MARGINAL

---- EQU OBJECTIVE   .   .   .   -1.000
---- EQU DEFEXPP   -INF   .   .   1.000
---- EQU DEFVARP   .   .   +INF   -0.001
---- EQU ECSMCAP   -INF 8.5623E+5 8.5623E+5   1.000

LOWER   LEVEL   UPPER   MARGINAL

---- VAR UTILITY   -INF 8.5623E+5   +INF   .
---- VAR CASH   .   8.5621E+5   +INF   .

UTILITY   objective function to be maximized
CASH   cash in the sector

GAMS 2.25.085 386/486 DOS   01/04/80 15:44:13 PAGE   36
General Algebraic Modeling System
Solution Report   SOLVE PORTCHOICE USING NLP FROM LINE 67

---- VAR Y   investment in stock I

       LOWER   LEVEL   UPPER   MARGINAL

ESTOCK   .   1.054   +INF   EPS
MKT   .   .   +INF   -5.950

              LOWER   LEVEL   UPPER   MARGINAL

---- VAR EXPP   .   20.726   +INF   .
---- VAR VARP   .   2459.037   +INF   .

   EXPP   mathematical expection of portfolio
   VARP   variance of portfolio

**** REPORT SUMMARY :   0   NONOPT
                           0   INFEASIBLE
                           0   UNBOUNDED
                           0   ERRORS

GAMS 2.25.085 386/486 DOS   01/04/80 15:44:13 PAGE   39
General Algebraic Modeling System
Model Statistics   SOLVE PORTCHOICE USING NLP FROM LINE 70

MODEL STATISTICS

BLOCKS OF EQUATIONS   4   SINGLE EQUATIONS   4
BLOCKS OF VARIABLES   5   SINGLE VARIABLES   6
NON ZERO ELEMENTS   13   NON LINEAR N-Z   2
DERIVATIVE POOL   7   CONSTANT POOL   11
CODE LENGTH   69

GENERATION TIME   =   1.100 SECONDS

EXECUTION TIME   =   1.260 SECONDS   VERID MW2-25-085

GAMS 2.25.085 386/486 DOS   01/04/80 15:44:13 PAGE   40
General Algebraic Modeling System
Solution Report   SOLVE PORTCHOICE USING NLP FROM LINE 70

SOLVE SUMMARY

MODEL   PORTCHOICE   OBJECTIVE UTILITY
TYPE   NLP   DIRECTION MAXIMIZE
SOLVER MINOS5   FROM LINE 70

**** SOLVER STATUS   1 NORMAL COMPLETION
**** MODEL STATUS   2 LOCALLY OPTIMAL
**** OBJECTIVE VALUE   856226.6394

RESOURCE USAGE, LIMIT   0.220   1000.000
ITERATION COUNT, LIMIT   4   1000
EVALUATION ERRORS   0   0

EXIT -- OPTIMAL SOLUTION FOUND
MAJOR ITNS, LIMIT   5   200
FUNOBJ, FUNCON CALLS   0   24
SUPERBASICS   1
INTERPRETER USAGE   0.00
NORM RG / NORM PI   1.496E-07

LOWER   LEVEL   UPPER   MARGINAL

---- EQU OBJECTIVE   .   .   .   -1.000
---- EQU DEFEXPP   -INF   .   .   1.000
---- EQU DEFVARP   .   .   +INF   -0.001
---- EQU ECSMCAP   -INF 8.5623E+5 8.5623E+5   1.000

LOWER   LEVEL   UPPER   MARGINAL

---- VAR UTILITY   -INF 8.5623E+5   +INF   .
---- VAR CASH   . 8.5621E+5   +INF   .

UTILITY   objective function to be maximized
CASH   cash in the sector

GAMS 2.25.085 386/486 DOS   01/04/80 15:44:13 PAGE   41
General Algebraic Modeling System
Solution Report   SOLVE PORTCHOICE USING NLP FROM LINE 70

---- VAR Y   investment in stock I

LOWER   LEVEL   UPPER   MARGINAL

ESTOCK   .   0.703   +INF   EPS
MKT   .   .   +INF   -5.950

LOWER   LEVEL   UPPER   MARGINAL

---- VAR EXPP   .   13.817   +INF   .
---- VAR VARP   .   1092.905 +INF   .

EXPP   mathematical expection of portfolio

VARP   variance of portfolio

**** REPORT SUMMARY :   0   NONOPT
                          0   INFEASIBLE
                          0   UNBOUNDED
                          0   ERRORS

 GAMS 2.25.085 386/486 DOS   01/04/80 15:44:13 PAGE   44
General Algebraic Modeling System
Model Statistics   SOLVE PORTCHOICE USING NLP FROM LINE 73

MODEL STATISTICS

BLOCKS OF EQUATIONS   4   SINGLE EQUATIONS   4
BLOCKS OF VARIABLES   5   SINGLE VARIABLES   6
NON ZERO ELEMENTS   13   NON LINEAR N-Z   2
DERIVATIVE POOL   7   CONSTANT POOL   11
CODE LENGTH   69

GENERATION TIME   =   1.050 SECONDS

EXECUTION TIME   =   1.210 SECONDS   VERID MW2-25-085

GAMS 2.25.085 386/486 DOS   01/04/80 15:44:13 PAGE   45
General Algebraic Modeling System
Solution Report   SOLVE PORTCHOICE USING NLP FROM LINE 73

        SOLVE   SUMMARY

    MODEL   PORTCHOICE   OBJECTIVE UTILITY
    TYPE   NLP   DIRECTION MAXIMIZE
    SOLVER MINOS5   FROM LINE 73

**** SOLVER STATUS   1 NORMAL COMPLETION
**** MODEL STATUS   2 LOCALLY OPTIMAL
**** OBJECTIVE VALUE   856226.2295

RESOURCE USAGE, LIMIT   0.330   1000.000
ITERATION COUNT, LIMIT   4   1000
EVALUATION ERRORS   0   0

EXIT -- OPTIMAL SOLUTION FOUND
MAJOR ITNS, LIMIT   5   200
FUNOBJ, FUNCON CALLS   0   24
SUPERBASICS   1
INTERPRETER USAGE   0.00
NORM RG / NORM PI   3.697E-08

        LOWER   LEVEL   UPPER   MARGINAL

```
---- EQU OBJECTIVE              .      .      .   -1.000
---- EQU DEFEXPP          -INF      .      .    1.000
---- EQU DEFVARP              .      .   +INF   -0.002
---- EQU ECSMCAP          -INF 8.5623E+5 8.5623E+5   1.000
```

```
                 LOWER    LEVEL    UPPER   MARGINAL

---- VAR UTILITY      -INF 8.5623E+5   +INF      .
---- VAR CASH            . 8.5622E+5   +INF      .
```

UTILITY   objective function to be maximized
CASH   cash in the sector

GAMS 2.25.085 386/486 DOS   01/04/80 15:44:13 PAGE   46
G e n e r a l   A l g e b r a i c   M o d e l i n g   S y s t e m
Solution Report   SOLVE PORTCHOICE USING NLP FROM LINE 73

```
---- VAR Y        investment in stock I

         LOWER    LEVEL    UPPER   MARGINAL

ESTOCK       .    0.527    +INF    EPS
MKT          .      .      +INF   -5.950

                 LOWER    LEVEL    UPPER   MARGINAL

---- VAR EXPP         .    10.363   +INF      .
---- VAR VARP         .   614.759   +INF      .
```

EXPP   mathematical expection of portfolio
VARP   variance of portfolio

```
**** REPORT SUMMARY :       0      NONOPT
                            0      INFEASIBLE
                            0      UNBOUNDED
                            0      ERRORS
```

EXECUTION TIME   =   0.160 SECONDS   VERID MW2-25-085

USER: Dr. S.M.N. Islam   G950901:1341AR-MW2
   Centre for Strategic Economics Studies, Victoria University

**** FILE SUMMARY

```
INPUT        C:\GAMS386\PORTCHO.GMS
OUTPUT       C:\GAMS386\PORTCHO.LST
```

References

Agenor, P-R., Montiel, P.J., 1996, *Development Macroeconomics*, Princeton University Press, New Jersey.

Ahmed, Ehsan, Koppl, R., Rosser, B. and White, M. 1997, 'Complex Bubble Persistence in Closed-end Funds', *Journal of Economic Behaviour and Organisation*, no. 32, pp. 19-37.

Amihud, Y., Christensen, B. and Mandelson 1992, 'Further Evidence on the Risk- Return Relationship', working paper, New York University, New York.

Amir, E. and Lev, B. 1996, 'Value-Relevance of Non-Financial Information: The Wireless Communications Industry', *Journal of Accounting & Economics*, vol. 22, nos. 1-3, Aug.-Dec., pp. 3-30.

Anderson, J. R. and Leonardi, A. C. 1982, 'A Note of the the Effects of Efficiency Criteria and Portfolio Size on Characteristics of Efficient Portfolios', *Accounting and Finance*, (May).

Amram, M. and Kulatilaka, N. 1999, 'Disciplined Decisions: Aligning Strategy With The Financial Markets', *Harvard Business Review*, January-February.

Appleyard, A. R., Strong, N. and Walker, M. 1982, 'Mutual Fund Performance in the Context of Models of Equilibrium Capital Asset Pricing', *Journal of Business Finance and Accounting*, Autumn, pp. 289–295.

Arrow, K. J. 1996, 'The Economics of Information: An Exposition', *Empirica*, vol. 23, pp. 119-128.

Arthur, W. B. 1996, 'Increasing Returns and the New World of Business', *Harvard Business Review*, July-August.

Avramov, D. circa 2000, 'Stock Return Predictability and Model Uncertainty', The Rodney White Centre for Financial Research, The Wharton School, University of Pennylvania.

Baks, K. and Kramer, C. 1999, 'Global Liquidity and Asset Prices: Measurement, Implications and Spillovers', IMF Working Paper 99/168, International Monetary Fund, Washington DC.

Ball, R. 1978, 'Anomalies in Relationships between Securities' Yields and Yield-Surrogates', *Journal of Financial Economics*, vol. 6, pp. 103-126.

Ball, R., Brown, P. and Officer, R. 1976, 'Asset Pricing in the Australian Industrial Equity Market', *Australian Journal of Management*, April, pp.1-32.

Banerjee, A., Dolado, J., Galbraith, J. W. and Hendry, D. F. 1993, *Co-Integration, Error-Correction, and the Econometric Analysis of Non-Stationary Data*, Oxford University Press, Oxford.

Banz, R. 1981, 'The Relation between Return and Market Value of Common Stocks', *Journal of Financial Economics*, vol. 9, pp. 3-18.

Barro, R. 1990, 'The Stock Market and Investment', *Review of Financial Studies*, vol. 3, pp. 115-32.

Barro, R. 1993, *Macroeconomics*, John Wiley and Sons, New York.

Barsky, R. B. and De Long, J. B. 1993, 'Why Does Stock Market Fluctuate?', *Quarterly Journal of Economics*, vol. 108, no. 2, pp. 291-312.

Basu, S. 1977, 'The Investment Performance of Common Stocks in Relation to Their Price to Earnings ratios: A Test of the Efficient Market Hypothesis', *Journal of Finance,* vol. 32, pp. 663-682.

Benninga, S. 2000, *Financial Modelling,* The MIT Press, Massachusetts Institute of Technology, Cambridge, Massachusetts.

Berry, M., Burmeister, E. and McElroy, M. 1988, 'Sorting Out Risks Using Known APT Factors', *Financial Analysts Journal,* March/April, pp. 29-42.

Black, F. 1972, 'Capital Market Equilibrium with Restricted Borrowing', *Journal of Business,* vol. 45, no. 3, pp. 444-454.

Black, F. 1976, 'Studies of Stock Price Volatility Changes', in *Proceedings of the 1976 Meetings of the Business and Economics Statistics Section,* American Statistical Association, pp. 171-181.

Black, F. 1986, 'Noise', *The Journal of Finance,* vol. XLI, no. 3, July, pp. 529-543.

Black, F., Jensen, M. and Scholes, M. 1972, 'The Capital Pricing Asset Model: Some Empirical Tests', in M. Jensen (ed.) *Studies in the Theory of Capital Markets,* Praeger, New York, pp.79-121.

Blanchard, O. 1993, 'Movements in Equity Premium', *Brooking Papers on Economic Activity,* no. 2, pp. 75-138.

Blanchard, O. and Fisher, S. 1989, *Lectures on Macroeconomics,* MIT Press, Cambridge, Massachusetts.

Blume, M. and Friend, I. 1973, "A New Look at the Capital Pricing Asset," *Journal of Finance,* March, pp. 19-33.

Bollerslev, T., Engle, R. F. and Wooldridge, J. M. 1988, 'A Capital Asset Pricing Model with Time varying Covariances', *Journal of Political Economy,* vol. 96, pp. 116-131.

Bontis, N. 1996, 'There's a Price on Your Head: Managing Intellectual Capital Strategically', *Ivey Business Quarterly,* Summer.

Bontis, N. and Mills, J. 2000, 'Web-Based Metrics and Internet Stock Prices', DeGroote School of Business, McMaster University, Hamilton.

Borland, J. and Garvey, G. 1994, 'Recent Developments in the Theory of the Firm', *The Australian Economic Review,* 1st Quarter.

Brainard, W. and Tobin, J. 1963, 'Financial Intermediaries and the Effectiveness of Monetary Control', *American Economic Review,* vol. 43.

Brealey, R. A., Myers, S. C. and Marcus, A. J. 1999, 'Fundamentals of Corporate Finance', 2nd ed, Irwin McGraw-Hill.

Brealey R., Myers, S., Partington, G. and Robinson, D. 2000, *Principles of Corporate Finance,* McGraw-Hill, Sydney.

Breeden, D. 1979, 'An Inter-temporal Asset Pricing Model with Stochastic Consumption and Investment Opportunities', *Journal of Financial Economics,* vol. 7, pp. 265-296.

Brennan, M. J. 1989, 'Capital Asset Pricing Model', in J. Eatwell, M. Milgate and P. Nuemann (eds), *The New Palgrave Dictionary of Finance.* MacMillan Press, London.

Brigham, E., Gapenski, L. and Daves, P. 1999, *Intermediate Financial Management,* The Dryden Press, Harcourt Brace College Publishers, Orlando.

Brigham, E. and Houston, J. 2000, *Fundamentals of Financial Management,* 9th ed., The Dryden Press, Harcourt Brace College Publishers, Orlando.

Brock, W. 1982, 'Asset Prices in a Production Economy'. in J. J. McCall (ed.), *The Economics of Uncertainty,* University of Chicago Press, Chicago.

Brooke, A., Kendrick, D., Meeraus, A., Raman, R., 1997. *GAMS: A Users Guide*, GAMS Home Page, http://www.gams.com.

Campbell, J. Y., Lettau, M., Malkiel, B. G. and Xu, Y. 2001, 'Have Individual Stocks Become More Volatile? An Empirical Exploration of Idiosyncratic Risk', *Journal of Finance*, vol. 56, no. 1, pp. 1-43.

Campbell, J. Y., Lo, A. W. and MacKinlay, A. C. 1997, *The Econometrics of Financial Markets*, Princeton University Press, Princeton, New Jersey.

Chan, L. and Lakonishok, J. 1992, 'Are the Reports of Beta's Death Premature?', working paper, University of Illinois.

Chen, N. F. 1983, 'Some Empirical Tests of the Theory of Arbitrage Pricing', *Journal of Finance*, December, pp. 1393-1414.

Chen, Nai-Fu 1991, 'Financial Investment Opportunities and the Macroeconomy', *Journal of Finance*, vol. 46, pp. 529-54.

Chen, N. F., Roll, R. and Ross, S. 1986, 'Economic Forces and the Stock Market', *Journal of Business*, July, pp. 383-403.

Cheung, J. K. 1993, 'Management Flexibility in Capital Investment Decisions Literature', *Journal of Accounting Literature*, no. 12, pp. 29-66.

Chew, D. H. 1997, 'Introduction: Financial Innovation in the 1980s and 1990s', *The New Corporate Finance*, McGraw-Hill Irwin.

Chirinko, R. 1993, 'Business Fixed Investment Spending: A Critical Survey of Modelling Strategies, Empirical Results and Policy Implications', *Journal of Economic Literature*, vol. 31, pp. 1875-911.

Christie, A. A. 1982, 'The Stochastic Behaviour of Common Stock Variances: Value, Leverage and Interest Rate Effects', *Journal of Financial Economics*, vol. 10, pp. 407-432.

Chung, S. K. and Tai, S. S. 1997, 'Cointegration and Causality Between Macroeconomic Variables and Stock Market Returns', *Global Finance Journal*, vol. 10, no. 1, pp. 71-81.

Coase, R. H. 1937, 'The Nature of the Firm', *Econometrica*, no. 4, pp. 386-405, repr. in G.J. Stigler, and K.E. Boulding, (eds.), 1952, *Readings in Price Theory*, Homewood, Ill.

Cohen, S., DeLong, B. and Zysman, J. 2000, 'Tools for Thought: What Is New and Important About the 'E-conomy', BRIE Working Paper # 138, E_conomy@uclink4.berkerly.edu

Cohen, W. and Levin, R. 1989, 'Empirical Studies of Innovation and Market Structure', in R. Schmalensee and R. Willig (eds), *Handbook of Industrial Organisation*, Schmalensee, R. and Willig, R., Vol. II, Elsevier Science BV, Amsterdam.

Connor, G. and Korajczyk, R. 1988, 'Risk and Return in an Equilibrium APT: Application of a New Test Methodology', *Journal of Financial Economics*, vol. 21, pp. 255 –290.

Copeland, T., Koller, T. and Murrin, J. 1999, *Valuation: Measuring and Managing the Value of Companies*, 2nd edn, John Wiley and Sons, Inc., New York.

Coppel, J. 2000, 'E-Commerce: Impact and Policy Challenges', OECD Working Paper Eco/Wkp(2000)25, Economic Department, OECD, Paris.

Cox, J., Ingersoll, J. and Ross, S. 1985, An Intertemporal General Equilibrium Model of Asset Prices', *Econometrica*, vol. 53, pp. 363-384.

Cuthbertson, K. 1997, *Quantitative Financial Economics, Stocks, Bonds and Foreign Exchange*, John Wiley and Sons Ltd., West Sussex.

Dabek, R. A. 1999, 'Valuation of a Technology', paper presented at the Intellectual Property Licensing Seminar, University of Dayton, February, www.udayton.edu/~lawtech/cle99lic-dabek.html

Damodaran, A. 1994, Damodaran on Valuation: Security Analysis for Investment and Corporate Finance, John Wiley and Sons Inc., New York.

Daniel, K. and Titman, S. 1997, 'Evidence on the Characteristics of Cross Sectional Variation in Stock Returns', *Journal of Finance*, vol. 52, pp. 1-33.

Davidson, R. and MacKinnon, J. G. 1993, *Estimation and Inference in Econometrics*, Oxford University Press, New York.

De Long, J. B., Shleifer, A., Summers, L. H. and Waldmann, R. J. 1990, 'Noise Trader Risk in Financial Markets', *Journal of Political Economy*, vol. 98, no. 4, pp. 703-738.

De Long, J. B. 1996, 'Is the Stock Market Too High?', *Slate,* 20 December 1996, www.slate.com/gist/96-12-21/gist.asp

DeBondt, W. F. M. and Thaler, R. H. 1985, 'Does Stock Market Overreact?', *Journal of Finance*, vol. 40, no. 3, pp. 793-805.

Demers, E. and Lev, B. 2000, 'A Rude Awakening: Internet Value-Drivers in 2000', University of Rochester, Rochester, New York.

Desmet, D., Francis T., Hu A., Koller T. M. and Riedel G. A. 2000, 'Valuing Dot-Coms', *The McKinsey Quarterly*, no. 1.

Dhakal, D., Kandil,, M. and Sharma, S. C. 1993, 'Causality between the Money Supply and Share Prices: A VAR Investigation', *Quarterly Journal of Business and Economics,* no. 32(3), pp.52-74.

Dhrymes, P., Friend, I. and Gultekin, B. 1984, 'A Critical Re-examination of the Empirical Evidence on the APT', *Journal of Finance*, June, pp. 323-46.

Dickey, D. A. and Fuller, W. A. 1979, 'Distribution of The Estimators for Autoregressive Time Series With a Unit Root', *Journal of the American Statistical Association,* vol. 75, pp. 427-431.

Dickey, D. A. and Fuller, W. A. 1981, 'The Likelihood Ratio Statistics for Autoregressive Time Series with a Unit-Root', *Econometrica,* vol. 49, pp. 1057-1072.

Dow, C. H. 1920, 'Scientific Stock Speculation', *The Magazine of Wall Street*, New York.

Drucker, P. 1993, *Post-Capitalist Society*, Harper Business, New York.

Drummen, Martin, Zimmermann and Heinz 1992, 'The Structure of European Stock Returns,' *Financial Analysts Journal*, Jul/Aug.

Edvinsson, L. and Malone M. 1997, *Intellectual Capital: The Proven Way to Establish your Company's Real Value by Measuring its Hidden Brainpower*, Judy Piatkus (Publishers) Ltd., London.

Eichberger, J. and Harper, I. R. 1997, *Financial Economics*, Oxford University Press, New York.

Economist Intelligence Unit (EIU) 2000, 'E-Commerce and the CFO', The Economist Intelligence Unit, www.eiu.com/best practice/375683.as

Elton, E., and Gruber, M. 1977, 'Risk Reduction and Portfolio Size: An Analytical Solution', *Journal of Business*, October, pp. 415-437.

Elton, E., and Gruber, M. 1987, *Modern Portfolio Theory and Investment Analysis*, 3rd edn, John Wiley and Sons, New York.

Elton, E. J., Gruber, M. J. and Mei, J. 1994, 'Cost of Capital Using Arbitrage Pricing Theory: A Case Study of Nine New York Utilities', *Financial Markets, Institutions and Instruments*, vol. 3, August, pp. 46-73.

Engle, R. F. and Granger, C.W. 1987, 'Co-integration and Error-correction: Representation, Estimation and Testing', *Econometrica*, vol. 55, pp. 251-276.

Engle, R. F. and Granger, C. W. J 1991, *'Long-Run Economic Relationship: Readings in Cointegration'*, Oxford University Press.

Evans, P. and Wurster, T. 1999, 'Getting Real about Virtual Commerce', *Harvard Business Review*, November-December, pp. 85-94.

Fama, E. F. 1965, 'The Behaviour of Stock Market Prices', *Journal of Business*, vol. 38, pp. 34-105.

Fama, E. F. 1968, 'Risk, Return and Equilibrium: Some Clarifying Comments', *Journal of Finance*, March, pp. 29-40.

Fama, E. F. 1970, 'Efficient Capital Markets: A Review of Theory and Empirical Work', *Journal of Finance*, vol. 25, no. 5, May, pp. 383-417.

Fama, E. F. 1981, 'Stock Returns, Real Activity, Inflation and Money', *American Economic Review*, vol. 71, pp. 545-65.

Fama, E. F. 1990, 'Stock Returns, Expected Returns, and Real Activity', *Journal of Finance*, vol. 45, pp. 1089-108.

Fama, E. F. 1991, 'Efficient Capital Markets: II', *Journal of Finance*, vol. 46, no. 5, December, pp. 1575-1621.

Fama, E. F. and French, K. R. 1988a, 'Permanent and Temporary Components of Stock Prices', *Journal of Political Economy*, vol. 96, pp. 246-273.

Fama, E. F. and French, K. R. 1988b, 'Dividend Yields and Expected Stock Returns', *Journal of Financial Economics*, vol. 22, pp. 3-25.

Fama, E. F. and French, K. R. 1989, 'Business Conditions and Expected Returns on Stocks and Bonds', *Journal of Financial Economics*, vol. 25, pp. 23-49.

Fama, E. F. and French, K. R. 1992, 'The Cross-Section of Expected Stock Returns', *Journal of Financial Economics*, vol. 47, pp. 427 - 465.

Fama, E. F. and French, K. R. 1993, 'Common Risk factors in the Return on Stocks and Bonds', *Journal of Financial Economics*, vol. 33, no. 1, pp. 3-56.

Fama, E. F. and French, K. R. 1995, 'Size and Book-to-Market Factors in Earnings and Returns', *Journal of Finance*, no. 50, pp. 131-155.

Fama, E. F. and French, K. R. 1996, 'Multifactor Explanations of Asset Pricing Anomalies', *Journal of Finance*, no. 51, pp. 55-84.

Fama, E. F. and MacBeth, J. 1973, 'Risk, Return and Equilibrium: Empirical Tests', *Journal of Political Economy*, vol. 81, pp. 607-636.

Ferguson, R. 1997, 'Making the Dividend Discount Model Relevant for Financial Analysts', *Journal of Investing*, Summer.

Ferson, W. E. and Harvey, C. R. 1991, 'The Variation of Economic Risk Premiums', Journal of Political Economy, vol. 99, no. 2, pp. 385-415.

Ferson, W. E. and Harvey, C. R. 1993, 'The Risk and Predictability of International Equity Returns', *Review of Financial Studies*, vol. 6, no. 3, pp. 527-566.

Ferson, W. E. and Harvey, C. R. 1999, 'Conditioning Variables and the Cross Section of Stock Returns', *Journal of Finance*, vol. 54, no. 4, August.

Fifield S., Power, D. and Sinclair, C. 2002, 'The Role of Economic and Fundamental Factors in Emerging Share Returns', Paper presented at the 12th International Conference on Asia: The Survival Strategies in the Global Economy, International Trade and Finance Association, Bangkok.

FitzHerbert, R. 1998, *Blueprint for Investment – A Long Term Contrarian Approach*, 2nd edn., Wrightbooks Pty. Ltd., Melbourne.

Fizzari, S. 1993, 'Monetary Policy, Financial Structure and Investment', in Gary Dymski, Gerald Epstien and Robert Pollin (eds.), *Transforming the US Financial System*, M.E. Sharpe, Armonk, pp. 35-63.

Flood, R., Hodrick, R. and Kaplan, P. 1986, 'An Evaluation of Recent Evidence on Stock Market Bubbles', NBER Working Paper No. 1971, Cambridge, Massachusetts.

Foster, G. 1978, 'Asset Pricing Models: Further Tests', *Journal of Financial and Quantitative Analysis* (March), pp. 39-53.

French, K. R. and Roll, R. 1986, 'Stock Return Variances: The Arrival of Information and the Reaction of Traders', *Journal of Financial Economics*, vol. 17, pp. 5-26.

French, K. R., Schwert, G. W. and Stambaugh, R. F. 1987, 'Expected Stock Returns and Volatility', *Journal of Financial Economics,* vol. 19, pp. 3-29.

Fry, M. 1988, *Money, Interest, and Banking in Economic Development*, Johns Hopkins University Press, Baltimore.

Fuller, R. J. and Hsia, C. 1984, 'A Simplified Common Stock Valuation Model', *Financial Analysts Journal*, vol. 40, no. 5, September/October, pp. 49-56.

Fuller, W. A. 1976, *'Introduction to Statistical Time Series'*, John Wiley, New York.

Garber, P. 1990, 'Famous First Bubble', *Journal of Economic Perspectives*, no. 4, pp. 35-54.

Geske, R. and Roll, R. 1983, 'The Fiscal and Monetary Linkage between Stock Returns and Inflation', *Journal of Finance*, no. 38, pp. 1-33.

Gibbons, M. 1982, 'Multivariate Tests of Financial Models: A New Approach', *Journal of Financial Economics,* vol. 10, pp. 3-27.

Gibbons, M., Ross, S. and Shanken, J. 1989, 'A Test of the Efficiency of a Given Portfolio', *Econometrica,* September, pp. 1121-1152.

Glassman, K. and Hassett, K. 1999, K., "Stock Prices Are Still Far Too Low", *The Wall Street Journal*, 17 March 1999.

Gordon, M. J. and Shapiro 1956, 'Capital Equipment Analysis: The Required Rate of Profit', *Management Science*, October, pp. 102-110.

Granger, C. 1986, 'Development in the Study of Cointegrated Variables', *Oxford Bulletin of Economics and Statistics,* vol. 43, pp. 213-228.

Granger, C. and Newbold, P. 1988, 'Some Recent Developments in a Concept of Causality', *Journal of Econometrics*, vol. 39, pp. 199-211.

Greenspan, A. 2000, 'Speech to the Economic Club of New York', *The Business Times*, Singapore.

Grossman, S. and Shiller, R. 1981, 'The Determinants of the Variability of the Stock Market Prices', *American Economic Review*, vol. 71, pp. 222-227.

Guatri, L. 1994, *The Valuation of Firms*, Blackwell Publishers, Cambridge, Massachusetts.

Gurley, J and Shaw, E. 1955, 'Financial Aspects of Economic Development', *American Economic Review*, vol. 45, September.

Gurley, J and Shaw, E. 1960, *Money in a Theory of Finance*, The Brooking Institution, Washington D.C.

Hagel, J. and Armstrong, A. 1997, *Net Gain: Expanding Markets Through Virtual Communities,* Harvard Business School Press, Boston, Mass.

Hakansson, N. 1987, 'Changes in the Financial Market: Welfare and Price Effects and the Basic Theorem of Value Conservation', *Journal of Finance*, vol. 37, no. 4, September, pp. 977-1005.

Hamilton, J. and Whiteman, C. 1985, 'The Observable Implications of Self-Fulfilling Expectations', *Journal of Monetary Economics*, no. 16, pp. 353-74.

Hand, J. 1999, 'Profits, Losses and the Stock Prices of Internet Firms', Working Paper, University of North Caroline, Chapel Hill.

Hanoch, G. and Levy, H. 1969, 'The Efficiency Analysis of Choices Involving Risk', *The Review of Economic Studies*, vol. 36, pp. 335-346.

Hardouvelis, G. A. 1987, 'Macroeconomic Information and Stock Prices', *Journal of Economic Business*, no. 39, pp. 131–140.

Harrington, D. 1987, *Modern Portfolio Theory, The Capital Pricing Asset Model and Arbitrage Pricing Theory: A User's Guide*, Prentice Hall, Inc., Englewood Cliffs, New Jersey.

Hicks, J. R. 1946, *Value and Capital*, 2nd edn, Oxford University Press, London.

Huang, R. D. and Kracaw, W. A. 1984, 'Stock Market returns and Real Activity: A Note', *Journal of Finance*, vol. 39, pp. 267-273.

Hyndes, M., Adams, M., Duffy, A. and Bray, D. 1999, *Creating a Clearway on the New Silk Road*, Department of Foreign Affairs and Trade, Commonwealth of Australia, Canberra.

International Monetary Fund (IMF) 2000, 'World Economic Outlook: Asset Prices and the Business Cycle', International Monetary Fund, Publications Services, Washington, D.C.

Islam, S. M. N., 2001a, *Optimal Growth Economics: An Investigation of the Contemporary Issues, and Sustainability Implications*, Contributions to Economic Analysis Series, North Holland Publishing Co., Amsterdam.

Islam, S. M. N., 2001b, *Applied Welfare Economics: Measurement and Analysis of Social Welfare by Econometric Consumption Models*, CSES Research Monograph 2001/1, Centre for Strategic Economic Studies, Victoria University, Melbourne.

Islam, S. M. N., Billington, N. and Oh, K. B. 2001, 'Trade, Finance and Global Economic Growth: An Optimal Growth Model and Global Growth Prospects', conference paper presented at the European Trade Study Group 2001 Conference, September 14-16, Brussels.

Islam, S. M. N. and Oh, K. B. 2002a, 'E-Commerce Finance in the Knowledge Economy: Issues, Macroeconomic Determinants and Public Policies', conference paper prepared for the Fourth Annual Conference on Money and Finance in the Indian Economy, 13-15 December 2001, IGIDR, India.

Islam, S. M. N. and Oh, K. B. 2002b, 'The Impact of International Factors in Determining the Characteristics of Financial Markets: Implications for the Emerging Markets in Asia', conference paper presented at the 12th International Conference of the International Trade and Finance Association on 'Asia: The Survival Strategies in the Global Economy', Bangkok (May).

Islam, S. M. N. and Oh, K. B. 2002c, forthcoming, 'Econometric Analyses of E-Commerce Stocks: Valuation, Volatility and Predictability', *Journal of Applied Economics*.

Jensen, M. and Meckling, W. 1990, 'Theory of the Firm: Managerial Behaviour, Agency Costs and Ownership Structure', in C. W. Smith Jr. (ed.), *The Modern Theory of Corporate Finance,* McGraw-Hill Inc., New York.

Jorgenson, D. 1971, 'Econometric Studies of Investment Behaviour: A Survey', *Journal of Economic Literature,* no. 3, pp. 1111-1147.

Jorion, P. and Goetzmann, W. 1999, 'Global Stock Markets in the Twentieth Century', *Journal of Finance*, vol. 54, no. 3, American Association of Finance, NY, pp. 953-980.

Kandel, S. and Stambaugh, R. F. 1996, 'On the Predictability of Stock Returns: An Asset-Allocation Perspective', *The Journal of Finance*, Vol. 51, Issue 2, pg. 385, 40 pgs

Keenan, M. 1970, 'Models of Equity Valuation', Papers and Proceedings of the Twenty-Eighth Annual Meeting of the American Finance Association New York, *Journal of Finance*, May, pp. 243-273.

Keim, D. B. 1985, 'Dividend Yields and Stock Returns: Implications of Abnormal January Returns', *Journal of Financial Economics*, vol. 14, pp. 473-489.

Keynes, J. M. 1937, 'The Ex-ante Theory of the Rate of Interest', *The Economic Journal*, vol. 47, pp. 663-9.

Kindleberger C. P. 1989, *Manias, Panics and Crashes: A History of Financial Crises*, rev. edn, Basic, New York.

King, R. and Levine, R. 1993, 'Finance and Growth: Schumpeter Might be Right', *Quarterly Journal of Economics*, no. 108: pp. 717-737.

Kwon, C. S. and Shin, T. S. 1999, 'Cointegration and Causality between Macroeconomic Variables and Stock Market returns', *Global Finance Journal*, vol. 10, no. 1, pp. 71-81.

Kydland, F. and Prescott, E. 1982, 'Time to Build and Aggregate Fluctuations', *Econometrica*, vol. 50, pp. 1345-1369.

Laffort, J. J. 1989, 'Economics of Information and Uncertainty', MIT Press, Massachussets.

Lakonishok, J., Shleifer, A. and Vishny, R. W. 1994, 'Contrarian Investment, Extrapolation, and Risk', *Journal of Finance*, vol. 49, pp. 1541-1578.

Lauterbach, B. 1989, 'Consumption Volatility, Production Volatility, Spot Rate Volatility and the Returns on Treasury Bills and Bonds', *Journal of Financial Economics.*

Lee, Bong-Soo 1992, 'Causal Returns Among Stock Returns, Interest Rates, Real Activity and Inflation', *Journal of Finance*, no. 47, pp. 1591-1603.

Lee, C. F., Lee, C. L. and Lee, A. C. 2000, *Statistics for Business and Financial Economics*, World Scientific Publishing Co. Pte. Ltd., Singapore.

Lehman, B. A. 1996, 'Intellectual Property: America's Competitive Advantage in the Twenty-first Century', *The Columbia Journal of World Business*, vol. 31, no. 1 Spring, pp. 6-61.

Lehmann, B. and Modest, D. 1988, 'The Empirical Foundation of the Arbitrage Pricing Theory', *Journal of Financial Economics,* vol. 21, pp. 213-254.

Leo, K., Radford, J. and Hogget, J. 1995, *Accounting for Indentifiable Intangibles and Goodwill*, CPA Australia, Melbourne.

Leroy, S. and Parke, W. 1992, 'Stock Market Volatility: Tests Based on the Geometric Random Walk', *American Economic Review*, vol. 82, no. 4 pp. 981-992.

Leroy, S. and Porter, R. 1981, 'The Present Value Relation: Test Based on Implied Variance Bounds', *Econometrica*, vol. 49, pp. 555-574 .

Lintner, J. 1965a, 'Security Prices, Risk and Maximal Gains from Diversification', *Journal of Finance*, vol. 20, pp. 587-615.

Lintner, J. 1965b, 'The Valuation of Risky Assets and the Selection of Risky Investments in Stock Portfolios and Capital Budgets', *Review of Economics and Statistics,*" vol. 47, pp.13-37.

Lucas, R. 1972, 'Expectations and the Neutrality of Money', *Journal of Economic Theory*, vol. 4, pp. 103-124.

Lucas, R. 1978, 'Asset Prices in an Exchange Economy', *Econometrica*, vol. 46, pp. 1426-1446.

Mandelbrot, B. 1963, 'The Variation of Certain Speculative Prices', *Journal of Business*, no. 36, pp. 394-419.

Mankiw, N. G. and Shapiro, M. D. 1986, 'Risk and Return: Consumption Beta Versus Market Beta', *Review of Economics and Statistics*, vol. 68, no. 3, pp. 452-459.

Markowitz, H. 1952, 'Portfolio Selection', *Journal of Finance*, vol. 7, no 1, pp. 77-91.

Markowitz, H. 1959, *Portfolio Selection: Efficient Diversification of Investments*, John Wiley and Sons New York.

Mascaro, A. and Meltzer, A. H. 1983, 'Long- and Short-Term Interest Rates in a Risky World', *Journal of Monetary Economics*, vol. 12, pp. 485-518.

Mayer, C. 1994, 'The Assessment: Money and Banking: Theory and Evidence', *Oxford Review of Economic Policy*, no. 10, pp. 1-13.

Merton, R. C. 1973, 'An Inter-temporal Capital Asset Pricing Model', *Econometrica*, vol. 41, pp. 867-887.

Merton, R. C. 1980, 'On Estimating the Expected Return on the Market: An Exploratory Investigation', *Journal of Financial Economics*, vol. 8, pp. 323-361.

Mills, T. C. 1999, *The Econometric Modelling of Financial Time Series*, 2nd edn., Cambridge University Press.

Miller, M. and Modigliani, F. 1961, 'Dividend Policy, Growth and the Valuation of Shares', *Journal of Business*, vol. 34, no. 4, October, pp. 411-433.

Miller, M. and Scholes, M. 1972, 'Rates of Return in Relation to Risk', in M. Jensen (ed.), *Studies in the Theory of Capital Markets*, Praeger, New York, pp. 47-78.

Modigliani, F. and Miller, M. 1958, 'The Cost of Capital, Corporate Finance and the Theory of Investment', *American Economic Review*, June, pp. 261-297.

Modigliani, F. and Miller, M. 1963, 'Corporate Income Taxes and the Cost of Capital: A Correction', *American Economic Review*, June, pp. 433-443.

Morck, R., Shleifer, A., and Vishy, R. 1990, 'The Stock Market and Investment: Is the Market a Sideshow?', *Brookings Papers on Economic Activity*, no. 1, pp. 157-202.

Mossin, J. 1966, 'Equilibrium in a Capital Asset Market', *Econometrica*, vol. 35, pp. 768-783.

Mossin, J. 1968, 'Optimal Multiperiod Portfolio Policies', *Journal of Business*, vol. 41, pp. 215-229.

Mossin, J. 1969, 'Security Pricing and Investment Criteria in Competitive Markets', *American Economic Review*, December, pp. 749-756.

Mullins Jr., D. W. 1982, 'Does the Capital Pricing Asset Model Work?', *Harvard Business Review*, January.

Nelson, C. R. and Plosser, C. I. 1982, 'Trends and Random Walks in Macroeconomic Time Series', *Journal of Monetary Economics*, vol. 10, pp. 139-162.

OECD 1996, *The Knowledge-Based Economy*, OECD, Paris.

OECD 2000, 'Is There a New Economy?', First Report on the OECD Growth Project, Paris.

OECD 2000a, *Economic Outlook*, June 2000, Organisation for Economic Co-operation and Development, Paris, www.oecd.org/eco/eco

Officer, R. R. 1973, 'The Variability of the Market Factor of New York Stock Exchange', *Journal of Business*, vol. 46, pp. 434-453.

Officer, R. R. 1989, 'Rates of Return to Shares, Bond Yields and Inflation rates: An Historical Perspective', in *Share Markets and Portfolio Theory*, in R. Ball, P. Brown, F. Finn & R. Officer (eds.), 2nd edn., University of Queensland Press, St. Lucia.

Oh, K. B. 2001, 'An Empirical Analysis of Financial Issues in the Australian Electronic Commerce Sector', Doctoral Thesis, Victoria Graduate School of Business, Victoria University, Melbourne.

Oh, K. B. and Islam, S. M. N. 2002, 'The Predictability of Stock Prices: Further Evidence and Implications for Asian Financial Markets', Conference Paper to be presented at the Asia Pacific Economic and Business Conference 2002 (October), Kuching.

Oh, K. B., Islam, S. M. N. and Bose, S. 2002, 'The Dynamics of Economic Variables in E-Commerce Equity Valuation: Implications for ASEAN', 6th Quality, Innovation and Knowledge Conference held in February 2002, at Kuala Lumpur, Malaysia.

Pagano, M. 1992, 'Financial Markets and Growth: An Overview', Financial Markets Group Discussion Paper, 153, London School of Economics, London.

Page, C. and Meyer, D. 2000, 'Applied Research Design for Business and Management', McGraw-Hill Companies, Sydney.

Panayi, S. and Trigeogis, L. 1998, 'Multi-stage Real Options: The Case of Information Technology Infrastructure and International Bank Expansion', *Quarterly Review of Economics and Finance*.

Pastor, L. and Stambaugh, R. 2000, 'Comparing Asset Pricing Models: An Investment Perspective', *Journal of Financial Economics*, vol. 56, pp. 335-381.

Patelis, A. 1997, 'Stock Return Predictability: The Role of Monetary Policy', *Journal of Finance*, vol. 52, pp. 1951-1972.

Pearce. D. K. and Roley, V. V. 1988, 'Firm Characteristics, Unanticipated Inflation and Stock Returns', *Journal of Finance*, vol. 43, pp. 965-981.

Peasnell, K. V., Skerratt, L .C. L. and Taylor, P. A. 1979, 'An Arbitrage Rationale for Tests of Mutual Funds Performance', *Journal of Business Finance and Accounting*, Autumn, pp. 373–400.

Peiro, A. 1996, 'Stock Prices, Production and Interest Rates: Comparison of Three European Countries with the USA', *Empirical Economics*, vol. 2, pp. 221-234.

Perman, R. 1991, 'Cointegration: An Introduction to the Literature', *Journal of Economic Studies*, vol. 18, no. 3, pp. 3-30.

Porter, M. 1980, *Competitive Strategy*, Free Press, New York.

Porter, M. 1985, 'Technology and Competitive Advantage', *Journal of Business Strategy*, Winter, pp. 60-78.

Poterba, J. M. and Summers, L. H. 1986, 'The Persistence of Volatility and Stock Market Fluctuations', *American Economic Review,* no. 76, pp. 1142-1151.

Poterba, J. M. and Summers, L. H. 1988, 'Mean Reversion in Stock Prices: Evidence and Implications', *Journal of Financial Economics*, vol. 22, pp. 26-59.

Praetz, P. 1969, 'Australian Share Prices and the Random Walk Hypothesis', *Australian Journal of Statistics*, vol. 2, pp. 123-139.

Ramanathan, R. 1998, *Introductory Econometrics with Applications*, 4th edn., The Dryden Press.

Rayport, J. F. and Sviokla, J. J. 1999 'Exploiting the Virtual Value Chain', in Don Tapscott (ed.), *Creating Value in the Network Economy*, HBR Press, p. 36.

Reilly, F. K. 1989, *Investment Analysis and Portfolio Management*, 3rd ed., The Dryden Press, Orlando.

Reinganum, M. R. 1982, 'A Direct Test of Roll's Conjecture on the Firm Size Effect', *Journal of Finance*, vol. 37, no. 1, pp. 27-35.

Reinganum, M. R. 1983, 'The Anomalous Stock Market Behaviour of Small Firms in January: Empirical Tests for Tax Loss Selling Effects', *Journal of Financial Economics*, vol. 12, no. 1, pp. 89-104.

Remenyi, D., Money, A. and Sherwood-Smith, M. 2000, *'The Effective Measurement and Management of IT Costs and Benefits'* 2nd ed., Butterworth Heinemann, Oxford.

Rivette, K. G. and Kline, D. 2000, 'Discovering New Value in Intellectual Property', *Harvard Business Review*, January-February, pp. 54-61.

Roll, R. 1977, 'A Critique of the Asset Pricing Theory Tests: Part 1', *Journal of Financial Economics*, vol. 4, pp. 129-176.

Roll, R. 1978, 'Ambiguity When Performance is Measured by the Securities Market Line', *Journal of Finance*, September, pp. 1051-1069.

Roll, R. and Ross, S. 1980, 'An Empirical Investigation of the Arbitrage Pricing Theory', *Journal of Finance*, December.

Roll, R. and Ross, S. 1984, 'The Arbitrage Pricing Theory Approach to Strategic Portfolio Planning', *Financial Analysts Journal*, May/June.

Roll, R. and Ross, S. 1994, 'On the Cross-Sectional Relation between Expected Returns and Betas,' *Journal of Finance*, vol. 49, pp. 101-122.

Romer, P. 1993, 'Two Strategies for Economic Development: Using Ideas and Producing Ideas', in *Proceedings of the World Bank Annual research Conference 1992*, Supplement to the World Bank Economic Review, March, pp. 63-91.

Ross, S. A. 1973, 'The Economic Theory of Agency: The Principal's Problem', *American Economic Review*, vol. 63, no. 2, pp. 134-139.

Ross, S. 1976, 'The Arbitrage Theory of Capital Asset Pricing', *Journal of Economic Theory,* vol. 13, pp. 341-360.

Ross, S. A. 1980, 'A Test of the Efficiency of a Given Portfolio', Paper presented to the World Econometric Meetings, Aix-en-Provence.

Rouwenhorst, K. G. 1995, 'Asset Pricing Implications of Equilibrium Business Models', in *Frontier of Business Cycle Research,* T. F. Cooley (ed), Princeton University Press, Princeton, New Jersey.

Roy, A. D. 1952, 'Safety First and the Holding of Assets', *Econometrica*, vol. 20, pp. 431-449.

Rozeff, M. 1984, 'Dividend Yields are Equity Risk Premiums', *Journal of Portfolio Management*, pp. 68-75.

Ryan, J. B. and Heazlewood, C. T. 1995, 'Australian Company Financial Reporting', Accounting Research Study No. 13, Australian Company Accounting Practices Inc., Melbourne.

Sahlman, W. A. 1999, 'The New Economy is Stronger than you Think', *Harvard Business Review*.

Salomon, E. 1963, *The Theory of Financial Management*, Columbia University Press, New York.

Samih, A. A. 2002, 'Predictability of Stock Returns: Is It rational?', *Applied financial Economics.*

Samuelson, P. 1965, 'Proof that Properly Anticipated Prices Fluctuates Randomly', *Industrial Management Review*, vol. 6, pp. 41-49.

Schmookler, J. 1966, *Invention and Economic Growth*, Cambridge, Harvard University Press.

Schreyer, P. 2000, 'The Contribution of ICT to Output Growth: A Study of the G7 Countries', STI Working Paper 2000/2, OECD, Paris. Schumpeter, J. 1934, *The Theory of Economic Development*, Cambridge, Harvard University Press, Cambridge.

Schwert, G. W. 1989, 'Why Does Stock Market Volatility Change Over Time?', *Journal of Finance*, vol. 44, no. 5.

Schwert, G. W. 1990, 'Stock Return and Real Activity: A Century of Evidence', *Journal of Finance*, vol. 45, pp. 1237-1257.

Shank, J. K. and Govindarajan V. 1992, 'Strategic Cost Analysis of Technological Investments', *Sloan Management Review*; Fall.

Shanken, J. 1985, 'Multivariate Tests of the Zero-Beta CAPM', *Journal of Financial Economics*," vol. 14, pp. 327-348.

Shapiro, M. 1988, 'The Stabilisation of the US Economy: Evidence from the Stock Market', *American Economic Review,* no. 78, pp. 1067-1079.

Sharpe, W. F. 1964, 'Capital Asset Prices: A Theory of Market Equilibrium Under Conditions of Risk', *Journal of Finance*, no. 19, pp. 425-42.

Sharpe, W. F. 1970, *Portfolio Theory and Capital Markets*, McGraw-Hill, New York, NY.

Sharpe, W. F., Alexander, G. and Bailey, J. 1995, *Investments*, 5th edn., Prentice-Hall, Englewood Cliffs, NJ.

Sheehan, P. and Houghton, J. 2000, 'A Primer on the Knowledge Economy', Centre for Strategic Economic Studies, Victoria University, Melbourne.

Sheehan, P. and Tegart, G. 1998, 'Working for the Future: Technology and Employment in the Global Knowledge Economy', Victoria University Press, Melbourne.

Shiller, R. 1979, 'The Volatility of Long-Term Interest Rates and Expectations Models of the Term Structure', *Journal of Political Economy*, vol. 87, no. 6, pp. 1190-1219.

Shiller, R. 1981a, 'Do Stock Prices Move too Much to be Justified by Subsequent Changes in Dividends?', *American Economic Review*, vol. 71, pp. 421-436.

Shiller, R. 1981b, 'The Use of Volatility Measures in Assessing Market Efficiency', *Journal of Finance*, vol. 36, pp. 291-304.

Shiller, R. 1984, 'Stock Prices and Social Dynamics', *Brookings Papers on Economic Activity* 2, pp. 457-498.

Shiller, R. 1989, *Market Volatility*, The MIT Press, Cambridge, Massachussetts.

Shleifer, A., and Summers, L. H. 1990, 'The Noise Trader Approach to Finance', *Journal of Economic Perspectives*, vol. 4, no. 2, pp. 19-33.

Siglienti, S., Tefertiller, T., Westrup, J. and Wood, J. 1999, 'Internet Valuations: Surveying the Landscape', GSB Technical Report, no. 82, January, Stanford Graduate School of Business.

Soete, L. 1997, 'Macroeconomic and Structural Policy in the Knowledge-based Economy', in OECD *Industrial Competitiveness in the Knowledge-based Economy: The New Role of Governments*, Paris, p. 19.

Sorenson, E. H. and Williamson, D. A. 1985, 'Some Evidence on the Value of the Dividend Discount Model', *Financial Analysts Journal*, vol. 41, no. 6, November/December, 1985, pp. 60-69.

Stambaugh, R. 1982, 'On the Exclusion of Assets from Tests of the Two-Parameter Models: A Sensitivity Analysis', *Journal of Financial Economics*, vol. 10, pp. 237-268.

Stiglitz, J. 1990, "Symposium on Bubbles," *Journal of Economic Perspectives*, no. 4, pp. 13-17.

Stiglitz, J., 1993, The Role of State in Financial Markets, in *Proceedings of the World Bank Annual Conference on Development Economics*, Washington DC.

Stokie, M., 1982, 'The Testing of Australian Stock Market for Mean Variance Efficiency', *Accounting and Finance*, November.

Strong, R. A. 2000, *Portfolio Construction, Management, and Protection*, South-Western College Publishing, Thomson Learning, Cincinnati, Ohio.

Tam, K. Y. 1998, 'The Impact of Information Technology Investments on Firm Performance and Evaluation: Evidence from Newly Industrialised Economies', *Information Systems Research*, March.

Tapiero, C. S. 1998, *Applied Stochastic Models and Control for Insurance and Finance*, Kluwer Academic, London.

Tapscott, D., Lowy, A. and Ticoll, D. 1998, *Blueprint to the Digital Economy: Creating Wealth in the Era of E-Buisness*, McGraw-Hill, New York.

Tapscott, D., Ticoll, D. and Lowy, A. 2000, *Digital Capital: Harnessing the Power of Business Web*, Harvard Business School Press, Boston.

Taylor, C. 1999, 'Do Internet Valuations Make Sense', *Business Review Weekly*, October 29.

Tegart, G., Johnston, R. and Sheehan, P. 1998, 'Academy Study-Interim Report: A Preliminary Analysis of the Issues', in P. Sheehan, and G. Tegart (eds.), *Working for the Future: Technology and Employment in the Knowledge Economy*, Victoria University Press, Melbourne.

Thompson, G. L. and Thore, S. 1992, *Computational Economics: Economic Modelling with Optimisation Software*, The Scientific Press Series, International Thomson Publishing, Inc., New York.

Tobin, J. 1958, 'Liquidity Preference as Behaviour Towards Risk', *Review of Economic Studies*, vol. 25, pp. 65-86.

Tobin, J. 1969, 'A General Equilibrium Approach to Monetary Theory', *Journal of Money, Credit and Banking*, February, pp. 15-29.

Trueman, B., Wong, F. and Zhang, X. 2000, 'Back To Basics: Forecasting The Revenues of Internet Firms', Haas School of Business, University of California, Berkerly, CA.

Von Nuemann, J. and Morgenstern, O. 1953, *Theory of Games and Economic Behaviour*, Princeton University Press, New Jersey.

Watsham, T. J. and Parramore, K. 1998, *Quantitative Methods in Finance*, International Thompson Business Press, London.

Wei, K. C. J. and Wong, K. M. 1992, 'Tests of Inflation and Industry Portfolio Stock Returns', *Journal of Economic Business*, vol. 44, pp. 77-94.

Wilner, N., Koch, B. and Klammer, T. 1992, 'Justification of High Technology Capital Investment – An Empirical Study', *The Engineering Economist*, vol. 37, no. 4, Summer, pp. 341-353.

Wilson, R. B. 1968, 'The Theory of Syndicates', *Econometrica*, vol. 36, no. 1, pp. 119-132.

Wongbangpo, P. and Sharma, S. C. 2002, 'Stock Market and Macroeconomic Fundamental Dynamic Interactions: ASEAN-5 Countries', *Journal of Asian Economics*, no.13, pp. 27-51.

292   *References*

Wood, J. 1991, 'A Cross-Sectional Regression Test of the Mean-Variance Efficiency of an Australian Value Weighted Market Portfolio', *Accounting and Finance* November, pp. 96-109.

Wooley, S. 1999, 'Internet Insanity', *Money*, vol. 28, no. 1, January Special Forecast Issue.

Wooldridge, J. M. 2000, *Introductory Econometrics: A Modern Approach*, South-Western College Publishing, Thomson Learning.

Woolridge, R. 1995, 'Do Stock Prices Reflect Fundamental Values?', *Journal of Applied Corporate Finance*, no. 8, pp. 64-69.

Wysocki, P. D. 1998, 'Cheap Talk on the Web: The Determinants of Postings on Stock Message Boards', Working Paper, University of Michigan Business School, Michigan.

Zeinos, S. A. 1993, *Financial Optimisation*, Cambridge University Press, Cambridge.

Ziemba, W. T. and Vickson, R. G. 1975, *Stochastic Optimisation Models in Finance*, Academic Press, New York.

Index